AF632724

The Concept of Upāsanā : Worship In Sanskrit Literature

Sri Garib Das Oriental Series No. 198

The Concept of Upāsanā : Worship in Sanskrit Literature

Dr. Rajani Patki

Sri Satguru Publications
A Division of
Indian Books Centre
Delhi - INDIA.

Published by:
Sri Satguru Publications
Indological and Oriental Publishers
A Division of
Indian Books Centre
40/5, Shakti Nagar,
Delhi-110007
(INDIA)

All Rights Reserved

First Edition: Delhi, 1996

ISBN 81-7030-483-0

No part of this book may be used or reproduced in any manner whatsoever without written permission except in the case of brief quotations embodied in critical articles and reviews.

Printed in India.

Published by Sunil Gupta for Sri Satguru Publications, a division of Indian Books Centre, 40/5, Shakti Nagar, Delhi and Printed at D.K.Fine Art Press, Delhi-110 052

To,

My Mother
Mrs. Kumud Sadanand Kale

Foreword

It gives me pleasure to write this foreword to the book 'The Concept of Upāsanā : worship in Sanskrit Literature' written by Dr. Mrs. Rajani S. Patki. I happened to be an evaluator of her Ph.D. thesis submitted to the Bombay University. In my report I had observed that "The outline of the structure of the thesis deserves compliments for thought and planning on the part of the candidate and the guide. The data collected by the candidate is of wide utility for the research field.... The conclusion part of the thesis should reflect and it does so the contribution of the candidate. The candidate has neatly arranged the topics as: Meaning of Upānsanā, Aspects of Upānsanā : Physical, Psychological and Intellectual, Forms of Upāsanā-practices: Nature Worship, Social Religion, Universal Religion and Methods of Upāsanā : Āsuri, Daivi etc. The other topics covered by the candidate are : Epistemology, Concept of God and Religon as implicit in Upāsanā, Mysticism in Upāsanā and Philosophy in Upāsanā. The arrangement and treatment of these topics by the candidate are adequate enough to adjudicate the thesis fit for Ph.D. Degree."

At that time I had made some suggestions for making the thesis fit for publication. Now after two years the press copy is shown to me by Dr. Mrs. Rajani Patki with a happy news that it is being published by prestigious publisher like Indian Books Centre, Delhi. During this short interval I find that Dr. Mrs. Paṭki has undertaken a strenuous job to convert the thesis into a welcome book form. I had also occasions to attend her series of lectures on Upāsanā and I have experience the impact it has laid on the august audience of Gitā Dharma Maṅḍal, Pune. In fact I was profusely thanked by the organisers as well as eminent members of the audience for introducing her as a speaker to Gita Dharma Maṅḍal, Pune. I feel proud to recommend this publication to the readers belonging to religio-spiritual as well as research field. I hope it will be widely received by the readers on the strength of its intrinsic merit.

Dr. Prabhakar P. Apte

M.A.Ph.D. LL.M.
Ex Editor, Sanskrit Dictionary &
I.C.H.R. fellow, Deccan College.
Pune.

Preface

It is my pleasure that the expected study discussed in the 'Introduction' of this book has been completed in Jan. 1993 and the University of Bombay has awarded me the Degree of Ph.D. for the said work in the same year. Now the thesis is being published in the book-form by the wellknown publishing house : "Indian Books Centre" Delhi. For the convenience of the publication the thesis is modified. I hope, this book will help the scholars in their research field and the devotees in their progress towards emancipation and the service to the mankind and the Nature as well.

I offer my humble regards to Dr. N.A. Deshpande, my guide for Ph.D. for his constant guidence and help throughout the entire work. I have completed my study of Ph.D. in Ananthacharya Indological Resesarch Institute, Colaba, Bombay. I am thnakful to Dr. K.K.A. Venkatachari, the then Director of the Institute for rendering me all kinds of help during my study. I am thankful to H.H. Swami Purushottamananda Sarasvati (Acharya of Chinmaya Mission) for certain suggestions made by Him and His blessings to this work. I am thankful to Dr. P.P. Apte for offering the 'Foreword' to this book. I am thankful to the officers and staff of 'Indian Books Centre' for their prompt response in publishing my book, 'The Concept of Upāsanā : Worship In Sanskrit Literature'.

May the Almighty Omniscient, Omnipotent and Omnipresent God Dattatreya confer happiness on the readers.

Dr. Rajani Patki

Pune
December, 1995

Contents

Introduction

The great heritage of Indian culture is a mix of much diversity, religion forming the strongest element. The next element of equal strength, wisdom and profundity is Sanskrit Literature. In this book a constructive survey of the available relevant Sanskrit Literature is proposed to throw light on this literature to understand the concept of *Upāsanā* : Worship and the salient features of this concept which given rise to the richness of *Bhakti* literature and the tradition of saints in India. The objective of this book is to study the diverse forms of *Upāsanā* as they are developed; unity among these forms and the continuity they present throughout the cultural history. An attempt has been made to study the following literary forms to understand the concept of *Upāsanā* : Worship as implicit in them which together give us rather than an adequate reference frame. For the sake of convenience the study follows the following classification.

Vedic — The Ṛgveda, Yajurveda, Sāmaveda, Atharvaveda,
Upaniṣadic — 10 Main Upaniṣads, Minor Upaniṣads.
Paurāṇic — 18Main Purāṇas, Minor Purāṇas.
Āgama — Śaivāgama, Śāktāgama, Vaiṣṇavāgama.
Smṛti — Manu Smṛti, other smrtis.
Itihāsa — Rāmāyaṇa, Mahābhārata.
Sūtra — Brahmasūtra, Kalpasūtra, Bhaktisūtra.
Special — Bhagavadgitā, Śrimadbhāgavatam.
Forms of literature — Drama, Prose, Poetry.

Much as the cultural life is diverse, there is a thread of unity which binds all other diverse elements or ways of worship. We may call it *Hindu Dharma* which itself means the great understanding of the *Vedic* religion or *Vedic Sanātana Dharma*. Corresponding to the diverse customs and languages, are the different ways of worship or *Upāsanā*. *Vedic* religion contains hundreds of *Upāsanās* which appearing differently are in essence the same, i.e. they aim at understanding the nature of self and the

'Universe' first per se and also as an inter-related phenomenon. The diversity of Upāsanā methods are therefore natural and are individually chosen for their suitability. Each individual is different by nature, his physical, psychological and intellectual capacity is also different. *Śrutis* state that the spheres of animate and inanimate are nothing but *Paramātaman,* though we do not understand this fact because of our ignorance. But each one is capable of unifying with Him and to have His knowledge, and one can advance to that unification according to one's own capacity and in one's own way. Therefore *Upāsanā* methods naturally vary according to individuals.

In the *Ṛgveda,* the *Ṛṣis* thought that Natural phenomena have some divine forces behind them. These forces are personified into many gods, and they also think that all these are the aspects of one and the same all pervading *Brahman* which manifests itself in various forms. The worshipper prays to these gods for his welfare by pouring oblation into fire i.e. *Yajña*. Man wants a vision of his ideal; therefore, he starts to worship idols, (personified Gods), in the name and form, with some virtues attached to them. According to choices of different persons gods vary in number and so their idols. The worship method takes different forms according to individual capacity and nature.

Efficacy of Upāsanā

In general the life span of a person is divided into four stages i.e. *Āśramas : Brahmacarya,* in which studentship is covered: *Gṛhasthāśrama,* in which household life is covered; *Vānaprasth-āśrama,* in which the renunciation is prescribed with meditation and worship and, *Sanyāsāśrama,* in which the throwing away of Worldly bondages and unity with God is expected. *Paramātman* is worshipped in different ways in each of the *Āśramas,* which is related to Āśramadharma.

There is another classification of human beings : The fourfold system of Castes-*Brāhmaṇa, Kṣatriya, Vaiśya* and *Śūdra*. The three qualities of primordial Nature (*Prakṛti*) are *Sattva, Raja* and *Tama*. Pure sattva quality is not present in human beings unless they reach Godhood. More quantity of *Sattva* and less of the other two is the nature of *Brāhmaṇa; Sattva* and *Raja* are normally equal in the nature of *Kṣatriya. Rajas* is more prominent than the other two in the nature of *Vaiśya* and *Tama* is greater than the other two in the nature of *Śūdra*. Each person acts according to his nature. These *Upāsanās* vary to the capacity and nature of a person in *Varṇāśramadharma*. This book discusses the diversity of *Upāsanā* : Worship and tries to trace out *the concept of Upāsanā : Worship in Sanskrit literature*.

Scope of enquiry

A number of western and eastern scholars have studied the *Vedic* religion, its philosophy, its aspects etc. The various sects like *Śaiva, Vaiṣṇava* and other are also studied by scholars; but an integral (*Samanvayātmaka*) approach to *Upāsanā* will clarify the concept and resolve any ambiguity for the followers of various cults. Therefore an attempt of surveying the concept of *Upāsanā* in the *Vedas*, the *Upāniṣads*, the *Brahmasūtras*, the *Kalpasūtras*, the *Smṛtis*, the *Epics*, the *Bhāgavata Purāṇa*, the *Bhaktisūtras*, *Bhagavadgītā* as well as in the *Tāntrika* works, the religions symbols like *Svastika* etc. and classical literature like *Drama, Prose* and *poetry* is made. This literature is forbiddingly vast; therefore some of the aspects connected with worship methods are selected for convenience.

Śaivāgamas, Śaktāgamas, Vaiṣṇavāgamas are consulted for the study of cults. The medieval literature with the *Āgama* books is also consulted. *Śrimat Ādiśankarācārya* has written a commentary on *Prasthānatrayi* i.e. the *Upaniṣads* the *Bhagavadgītā*, and the *Brahmasūtras*, and various stotras of *Śiva, Viṣṇu, Devi, Gaṇapati* and other gods. These also are consulted to discuss the nature of god in *Upāsanā*. *Madhvācārya, Vallabhācārya* and other revered persons whose comments on the subject, have been referred to. This will help the study of the development of the concept of *Upāsanā*.

The research of the Oriental treatises is done by the western scholars like Maxmüllar, Keith, Wilson, Bloomsfield, Winternitz and other honourable scholars of European countries. These scholars have helped the object of the book. In India, scholars like Dr. Bhāṇḍārkar, Dr. Kāne, Dr. Radhākṛiṣṇan, Dr. Ghate, Yogi Arbindo and other honourable scholars studied Vedic religion and its various aspects, and they too have been consulted.

The saints like Kabira, Ekanātha, Jñaneśvara and others have their impact on *Upāsanā, Bhakti* element has been given importance and *Caitanya* Mahāprabhu and other saints reveal *Parābhakti*. The discipline of saints is important in *Upāsāna*; the saints have their literature too. The scope of enquiry for this study is limited to Sanskrit literature primarily, though the views of the modern scholars of the twentieth century on the literature of *Upāsanā* have been consulted for an integrated study of *Upāsanā*.

The study of the six systems of Indian philosophy (*Darśanas*) namely, *Sānkhya, Yoga, Nyāya, Vaiśeṣika, Pūrva* and *Uttara Mimāmsā*, is not aimed at. The philosophical study is referred to only where necessary; the views of *Uttara Mimāṁsā* are expressed in the context of *Upaniṣad Vidyās*. The reference to the *Sānkhya*, the *Yoga*, the *Karmakānd* of *Pūrva Mimāṁsā* is made in the relevant analysis of *Bhagavadgītā* and the *Kalpasūtras* as per necessity. *Nyāya* and *vaiśeṣika* have their separate views about the world, and they are mentioned where required.

The word *Upāsanā* is used with reference to the fine arts like painting, music, dancing, singing, carving etc. because these arts need devotion of many years and practice (*Tapasyā*), in order to become successful and renowned. This book does not deal with the type of *Upāsanās* which practised for personal fame and glory but only those that lead to self Realisation. The great value of these arts in human life is not ignored but very few use these arts as a way of self Realisation; therefore they are mentioned in connection with the study of *Nāṭyaśāstra* and *Mudras* only glancingly.

The study of sacrificial ceremonies : *Yajña*, in detail is not expected here but the topic is dealt with because for a period *Yajña* culture was present as a routine part of life. Bhagavadgitā states the symbolic meaning of *Yajñ* as *Upāsanā* and this aspect of *Yajña* is dealt with.

Vatsyāyana's Kāmasūtras does not find a place in this book, though the aim of experiencing the ecstasy of *Brahmānanda* is associated with sexual satisfaction. This type of life may lead the society to menace, and the saints do not prescribe this type of *Upāsanā* as means to an end.

The study of *Upāsanās* which leads a man to self realisation and teaches him to work for the welfare of society with real perception of the world is undertaken. *Śrutis* do not teach the renunciation of Action at the very beginning of *Upāsanā* as *Upāsanā* itself is an Action to be performed. Indian religion accepts the concept of life after death. This human life is more important than that of the other species on the Earth, because human brain alone is capable of understanding the phenomenal world. It should be the aim of human life that one must obtain the knowledge of reality and help others to do so. *Upāsanā* is a specific way of acquiring this knowledge according to the view of great sagas of India, after the realisation of self a person can work as a lighthouse for others. India has a great tradition of such saints. The way of worship, the philosophic and conceptual foundation of the same, its aspects, forms, nature, stages, aim etc. deserve a careful and detailed study.

1

Definition of Upāsanā

(i) What is Upāsanā?

The human species is comparatively physically weaker than many other species in this world. He has not claws, no horns, no powerful teeth and no physical strength like rhinoceros. But he possesses a fantastic brain which supercedes all these fighting equipments. By the sheer power of brain he has surpassed all animals of this world. he knows how to obtain the food and other necessities of life. But many a times he experiences that there are several physical and mental phenomenal occurrences. He can not understand the cause and effect of those incidents, as well as the causal relationship. He tries to understand the cause and the effect by studying the events scientifically, intellectually and rationally. He has often failed to comprehend the whole law and logic behind these natural incidences. Therefore he believes that there must be a superhuman power beyond the comprehension of mental capacities of human beings which is called the Almighty, Omniscient and Omnipotent. Therefore, he respects that power, bows before it and requests it to confer on him the blessings of wellbeing. Upāsanā consists in prayers, in offerings, in obeisance, in a way of respecting this power.

Mankind has a natural urge for Light, Bliss, Freedom, Immortality, Knowledge; this urge shows him the way to reach his goal which is called Upāsanā. The continuous and repeated thoughts about God make man pure like God this type of recitation is called Upāsanā. To sit near God and think about Him again and again is Upāsanā : Worship.

The word Upāsanā is derived from the root Ās of the second conjugation with the prefix Upa, i.e. Upāste. It is modified as per Panini's sutra of *Uttarakṛdantiya*, "*Ṇyāsaśrantho yuca*"[1].

Another sutra, "*Yuvornākau*"[2] modified Uca in An. these changes make the word neuter but because of `tāp' pratyaya it converts into feminine gender "*Striyāktin*"[3]. So, finally the word reads as `Upāsanā'. The Amarakośa gives us several words such as Pujā, Namasyā, Apaciti, Saparyā, Arcanā, Varivasyā, Sūśruṣa, Paricaryā which have the same meaning as Upāsanā[4]. Upāste means to sit near the deity and pray to it for desired objects like well-being, prosperity, knowledge and even the ultimate unification with the deity, which is called Sāyujyatā or Mokṣa.

Different authoritative writers have defined the term Upāsanā in different ways in their writings[5]. Dr. Kāne says, "Upāṣanā is proper worship." A worship of the deity which gives you your destination. It may be in the form of prayer, Yajña or meditation. Dr. Rādhākṛiṣṇan says,[6] "The higher kind of knowledge is called Upāsanā. It has the characteristic of devout meditation and consists in direct intuition of Brahman. Brahman is the ultimate truth, which is the knower of the known. Further he states the opinion of Śri Śaṅkarāchāry[7] that, Upāsanā and dhyāna mean the same thing, concentrating on a single object with a fixed look and without any movement of the limbs. To know the ultimate cause of all the effects and to go to the root of consciousness and experience the sheer happiness is the main aim of Upāsanā. Dr. E. Roar says,[8] `there is a way between the Karma and Jñāna called `Upāsanā. `It is said that every spiritual literature has three aspects; Karma, Upāsanā and Jñāna. Dr. Ghāte says that, Brāhmaṇa, Āraṇyaka and Upaniṣads make the three distinct paths of `niśreyas' i.e. Karma, Upāsanā and Jñāna[9]. In Upāsanā Pāda of Brahmasūtra, Upāsanā means `contemplation of Brahman'. To meditate upon the image of the Supreme Brahman in the antaḥkaraṇa (mind) is also Upāsanā[10].

The verse in Śivamahimna Stotra tells us, "*Ruciṇām vaicitryāt rujukuṭila nānā patha juṣam. Nṛnam eko gamys...*"; means every individual has different tastes or likings, therefore different modes of worship are prescribed for them. Every one has to undertake the way appropriate to his temperament. The way of getting knowledge by studying śāstras is called Jñāna Mārga, Yoga Mārga requires study of Aṣṭāṅga Yoga. Yoga Mārga includes Rāja Yoga, Haṭha Yoga, Mantra yoga, Laya Yoga etc.[11] The way of discharging one's duties skillfully is Karma Mārga. And to love God intensely is called Bhakti Mārga. These four ways are called

Sādhanā. Prayers, Pujā, Yajña, and other like them also form different ways of worship which are called Upāsanā. There are different types of personalities who want to perform Upāsanā.

1. Those who experience that they are chained to this 'Saṁsāracakra' and wish to get out of it, want to be free from the cycle of birth and death and from rebirth these people are called Baddha.
2. Those who feel to seek the way out of this 'Samsāra' are called Mumukṣu.
3. Those who actually begin to walk through the way they find are called Sādhaka.
4. Those who have reached the state of ultimate knowledge, unified with the deity are called Siddha.

There are four types of Upāsanā[12] :

Satyavati—This Upāsanā is done by intellect and mind. God is every where, so the devotee performs a mental worship and always tries to unite himself with God. In Nyāya Śastra this type of Upāsanā is called Yunjāna i.e. Yogic Upāsanā. Bhagavadgitā describes this Yoga as Buddhi Yoga. The Brahmavidyās come under Satyavati Upāsanā.

Aṅgavati—Aṅga means the limb or a part of a thing, for example, the six aṅgas of Vaiśvānara are Dyau, Āditya, Vāyu, Ākaśa, Āpa, Pṛithivi. Arādhanā, pūjā of one of these aṅgas is called Aṅgavati or Pratikavati Upāsanā. The religious symbols like cakra, svastika etc. come under this type.

Anyavati—In the Brāhmaṇas (Brāhmaṇa treatises) Yajñā is Puruśa and Puruśa is Yajñā. They are the same. In this Upāsanā the deity and the idol are identical 'Yajña as Upāsanā' is followed here.

Nidānavat—Nirguṇa, Nirākāra Brahman can not be identified with the idol. the knowledge of the Nirguṇa is the only way to understand Him. However, a certain idol is assumed to denote the Nirguṇa God. As black colour denotes sadness, red colour denotes anger, white denotes kirti (fame), elephant denotes Lakṣmi, flag denotes victory; the idol denotes the Nirguṇa Brahman. The svarūpa of Upāsanā itself is to "retract the mind from other worldly objects and try to unite with Brahman through the idol", means mind enters in Brahaman with the help of Nidāna Upāsanā by retracting other vṛtties. So sending away all other thoughts mind can think the idol as God, concentrate on it, and understand it; it is an Upāsanā. This is Paurāṇic type of Upāsanā : Worship.

In the Ṛgveda Indra, Agni, Varuṇa are various names given to one and the same Impersonal Absolute God, Brahman[13]. So whichever god you worship is the worship of Paramātman. The clear svarūpa of Upāsanā is given in Bhagavadgitā, in the discussion of yajña *"Brahmārpaṇam brahma havirbrahmāgnau brahmaṇa hutam. Bhramaiva ten gantavyam brahmakarma-samādhinā."*[14]. The same thing is said in the Ṛgveda *"Yajñena yajñamayajnata devāstāni dharmāṇi prathāmanyāsan,"*[15], i.e. learned men worship Yajñā by performing yajña. This is their first dharma-duty. By doing this they become yajña i.e Pure, then they can worship the purest Paramātman to become the same.

In Gopatha Brāhmaṇa the main sentence is *"Yad devāh akrurvan tat karavāṇi"* means what gods have done, I must do the same (one must follow Gods). In this way to perceive the virtues of God is the aim of Upāsanā. At samāvartana saṅskāra Ācārya says, *"Yāni asmakam sucaritāni, tāni tvayā upāsitāni no itarāṇi"*[16] i.e. our best virtues are to be imitated and not vices or despicable thoughts. By Upāsanā one can remember again and again the virtues of God, can meditate upon them and become one with God, because as you think so you become : *"Yanmanasā dhyāyati tat vāchā vadati, Yat vāchā vadati tat karmaṇā karoti, yat karma karoti tat abhisampadyate."*

God is doner of both powers, physical and spiritual. All the world performs Upāsanā of Paramātman, as the Ṛgveda says, *"Viśva upāsate"*[17]. God is the creator of this world so every atom sings the greatness of God. To unite with God is difficult. What one does for the unification with God is Upāsanā. The nature of Upāsanā as Śri Śaṅkarācārya says, "The deity one worships i.e. Upāsya, becomes the subject of his intellect, he goes near to it and as oily drops spread over the water without disturbance, he transfers his vṛtti to God and stays there forever.[18] In the Chāndogya Upaniṣad the verse, *"Sarvam Khalvidam brahman tajjalāniti śāntamupāsīta"*[19], asks us to become calm and quiet and worship Paramātmā by kratu i.e. sankalpa decision & positive thinking and Upāsanā. We perform the Upāsanā whom Himālaya praises who protects all of us[20].

Yajña i.e. sacrifice of havirdāna is the type of mūrta upāsanā and when it is performed with knowledge it gives Mokṣa and when it is performed without knowledge it leads to Samsāra. God is the ultimate knowledge to whom we worship by sacrifice. Puruṣa is *'kratumayaḥ'*, his nature is *'sankalpamayaḥ'*. Lower grade of thoughts; and sankalpa leads to lower category of existence, and higher sankalpa leads to higher consciousness. Therefore, one's sankalpa must be higher, that is 'to get the knowledge of Paramātmā.' One's aim must be to go very close to God and to experience the Truth and Knowledge. The same thing is said in Srimadbhāgavat.' As Gangā flows continuously towards sea to merge into it, similarly one should continuously think of Him and His virtues deep inside one's mind and try to stay near Him without stopping in the way[21]. *"Ā no bhadraḥ kratavo yantu viśvataḥ"*[22]. May our thoughts be pure. May the pure thoughts come to us from all over the world. When impure thoughts appear continuously the mind becomes perturbed and vexed and one does not find happiness any where. Man thinks that the world is useless, unhappy, hasty, imperfect etc.; but the fault is not in the surrounding world but it exists in his own mind. he makes his mind pure by performing Upāsanā. God is pure, so only a pure mind can understand Him.

In Upāsanā, one may accept the deity either Nirguṇa Nirākāra or Saguṇa Sākāra. In Upaniṣads, several disciplines, such as Dahara Vidyā, Śāṇḍilya Vidyā, Vaiśvānara Vidyā etc.; are described for Upāsanā. Upāsanā can be performed by conceiving God in any form as the devotee chooses. The devotee can worship Him as Hiraṇyagarbha, Iśvara, Virāṭ, Śiva, Viśṇu etc. The devotee may choose any forms of God or any of the type of the discipline suitable to his temperament or as per guidance of his Guru.

From a single atom to the universe, all through the unlimited space there is the existence of God only, in one or other form. Therefore, Upāsanā of any form or power is actually the Upāsanā of Paramātman or God. If one limits his consciousness to the *'sākara'* form of one's *'upāsyā'* only and doesn't understand all pervasiveness i.e. *'sarvātmaka bhāva'* of one's deity, one is unable to raise one's vision beyond a certain notion and one is unable to reach to the state of *'viśvātmaka bhāva.'* It is told in Bhagavadgitā that such people rise only to the state of consciousness of which they think that their deity is and after death they go to that 'loka' only; *'devān devayajo yānti, madbhakto yānti māmapi"*[24]. It is necessary in Upāsanā that one should start from the deity one loves and adores but progressively one should learn to rise beyond the gross form of that deity and should reach the all pervading one and merge in to *'Ānandaghana Supreme Ātmā.'* By this at the end one will loose one's name and form i.e. 'nāma rūpa' and become one with the Brahman Himself. *"Brahmavid brahmaiva bhavati."* He is called *'Jīvanmukta.'*

Upāsanā can have two different aspects; one is *'Sakāma'* other is *'Niṣkāma'*. In *'Sakāma Upāsanā'* the upāsaka worships the deities for worldly gain such as well being, wealth, sons, victory, or even life after death in the 'Svarga'. The Yajña is such a type of *'Sakāma Upāsanā.'* In the Yajña the devotee offers the deity different things as havirdāna, and many other available things. In Śrimat Bhāgavat the verse, *"Ye mayayā te hatamedhasastvat ..."*[25]; shows us that Paramātmā fulfills all the desires of the upāsaka; therefore, God confers on the devotee what he wishes (preyas) in *'Sakāma Upāsanā*. In *'Niṣkāma Upāsanā'* there exists no need of worldly or after death wellbeings. It only aims at the possession of ultimate knowledge and unification in Brahman. (*Niśśreyas*.)

The world Upāsanā has other alternatives 'archanā, ārādhanā, pūjā, paricharyā, varivasyā, sevā, yajana, vandana, dhyāna, cintana, japa, upasthāna, śravaṇa, kirtana, samaraṇa, bhajana, yoga and samāśrayaṇa.'; in the Vedas, Upaniṣads and Brāhmaṇas. For example

1. *"Yo devamuttaravantamupāṣate sanātanam."*[26] One who serves the God who is external.
2. *"Vandāmahe tvā"* [27] I prostate myself before you.
3. *"Marutvanta sakhyāya havāmahe."*[28] We offer oblations to Marut and his friends.
4. *"Bhargo devasya dhimahi."* [29] We meditate on the Supreme God.
5. *"Tryambakam yajāmahe.*[30] we do yajana of Trymbaka.
6. *"Yasyadeve parābhakti."*[31] One a who has devotion (deep faith) to God.

The underlined words are representatives of the word Upāsanā. The first important part of Upāsanā is to bow before the deity who is greater than any other power of this world. Upāsanā starts form 'Namana' and progresses gradually towards Bliss, Ānanda, and Love.

Dr. Henry Lindlahar says in his book entitled "Practice of Natural Therapeutics"; that, we can improve our mental and physical health if we achieve unification with an angel or `*Sarvavyāpi*' that is all-pervading energy. `*Viśvātmaka Ātmā*' is known by various names, as Iśvara, God, Brahman, paramātmā etc. When upāsaka meditates on Him who is the Omniscient and Omnipotent of Conscious energy and thereby gets himself uplifted. Human mind is always engaged in the duality of good and bad thoughts. It disturbs the mental and physical balance of human mind and body. Therefore it is necessary to align or tune up the mind with the undualistic `*Sat svarūpa Brahman*. Thereby it harmonises with the unoscillating nature of Brahman and becomes happy. Upāsanā is necessary to obtain this unification and unfading happiness. Gitā teaches that Jiva is `anśa': element of Iśvara[32] and Iśvara is Saccidānanda and immortal. So Jiva must be like Iśvara. Upāsanā of Iśvara makes man `*Saccidānanda Svarūpa*.'

Upāsanā is the path leading to ultimate salvation i.e. Mokṣa. In Bhagavadgitā Śri Kriṣṇa says; "*Manmanā bhava madbhakto madyāji mām namaskuru. Māmeveṣyasi....*"[33]; that is, unification with God is achieved by giving one's mind fully to Him only. One has to work with pure mind and try to surrender to God. After the state of complete surrender the real Upāsanā begins. Upāsanā is a voyage to discover Ātma and Paramātmā. To discover and to experience the `secret' of life is the very nature of Upāsanā. Uplifting of human being towards God is impossible without Upāsanā. By Upāsanā the vices of human nature like greed, anger, hate, convetuousness, etc. (Āsuri sampati) get slowly vanished and these are replaced by virtues like forbearance, forgiveness, calmness, friendliness, love, pity, humbleness etc. (Daivi sampati). These virtues are divine characters and with their acquisition, one is automatically led to God and gets `Sāyujyatā'.

Another definition of Upāsanā is given in Kulārṇava Tantra, i.e. "*Karmaṇā manasā vācā sarvāvasthāsu sarvadā; samipasevā vidhinā upāsitiriti kathyate.*"[34] It means when one worships God with mind, speech, in every bodily state and with humble service one qualifies for the practice of Upāsanā. One of the verses of Śrimadbhāgavat, "*upāsito yat puruṣaḥ purāṇaḥ.*"[35], tells that please serve the ever old: Purāna Person.

In Upāsanā the devotee (upāsaka) can have the direct vision of God. The verse "*Yam vinidrā jitaśvāsaḥ santuṣṭā saṅyatendriyaḥ jyatiḥi paṣyanti yunjānastsmai yogātmane namaḥ. Yogināstām prepāṣyanti bhagavati sanātanam."*[36], categorically proclaims that during Upāsanā or meditation devotee experiences vision of Iśvara.

In the Brahmasūtra the author says"; *Nanu samrādhya-samrādhakabhāvābhyupagamātparetarātmanornytvamasyāditi..."*[37]. It means the unity of upāska and upāsya is achieved. We find the same idea of unification in the Muṇḍakopaniṣad, *"Sa yo ha vaitatparamabrahmavid brahmaiva bhavati.*[38] and in *"Brahmaiva sasn bhrahmāpyeti.*[39]; and in the Manu smṛit, *"Dhyānayogen sampaṣyed gatimasyāntarātmanḥ. Samyagdarśnasamāpannaḥ dhyānayogen brahmābhyeti sanātanam."*[40] It is said in the Muktikopaniṣad that upāsaka gets salvation by Upāsanā, *"Caturvidhātu yā muktirma-dupāsanayā bhavet.*[41] Once this is achieved; the upāsaka is not detracted afterwards by worldly sorrows and happiness. Bhagavdgitā repeats the same effect, *"Yasminsthitonanadukkhena gurūṇāpi vicālyate.*[42]

When the unification of the devotee and God is achieved in Upāsanā, Upāsaka enters into the *'Viśvātmaka bhāva'* i.e. all pervading consciousness. Thereby his life views are changed and he works for the welfare of other human beings like his Master. (spiritual preceptor). He obtains the honour of Sadgurū. Śaṇkarācārya describes the behaviour of the *'Sākṣatkāri or Siddha'* devotee as follow *"Śānto mahānto nivasnti santo vasantavallokahitam carantiha. Tirṇā svayi bhimabhāvarṇavam janā na hetuanānyāpi tārayantaḥ.*[43]

In ancient India a man's life had four distinct stages properly called Aśramas, namely, *Brahmacarya,Gṛhastha, Vānaprastha,* and *Sanyāsa*. As these periods show different stages of life and different responsibilities, proper to them, the type of Upāsana prescribed for each state is different. The brhmacarya is the period of youth period, career building and strive for knowledge which can give him livelihood. Therefore only *'Sandhyāvandana'*, a part of Sun worship, is prescribed in this stage. In the Gṛhastha period *'Yajñā (pañca mahā yajñās), and Naimittika Karmas'* are told. Vānvaprasthi has to study the śāstras, has to retract his mind from life and Sanyāsi has to practise renunciation and he has to follow only Upāsanā.[44]

Thus, development of Upāsanā step by step throughout the entire life is spelt out. The main or only aim of human life is viewed as the ultimate unification with the Universal being. Not only that but the devotee achieving the ultimate unification i.e. '*Jīvanmukti*'; is supposed to guide the other people in their efforts in the same direction, then he is called Guru, precepter and he is very important in this path, and he gets the honour of God.

(ii) Upāsanā, Sādhanā and Bhakti

The three words, Upāsanā, Sādhanā and Bhakti are generally used as synonymous to mean the efforts on the way chosen to reach Godhead. But this general use of the synonymous meaning is not correct. These three words have different grammatical origins and indicate precisely different actions.

The word Upāsanā is derived from the root Up plus Ās of second conjugation and its meaning is to sit by higher or a divine personality. The word Sādhanā is derived from the root Sidha of fourth conjugation and the meaning of the word Sādhanā is the intense efforts made to achieve higher goal. The word Bhakti is derived from the root Bhaja of first conjugation and its meaning is to remember, to love, to sing the name and fame of God. The past passive participle of Bhaja is Bhakta which means one who is devoted to and adjuncted to God; and the love which he feels about God is Bhakti.

Upāsanā envisages Upāsya deity, its adoration, chanting of the magical letter or sentence i.e. Mantra, the meditation on the formless or the physical posture of the deity with fixed time and period of worship. Upāsanā can be of God or of saints; similarly, it can be performed either individually or by coming together of many people. The individual Upāsanā is performed daily whereas common (group) Upāsanās are carried out on certain occasions. The celebration of birth days of Śri Rāma, Śri Kṛṣṇa, of various saints, the Samādhi days of saints etc. come under common Upāsanā. Generally, the followers of the same deity or the saints gather together and worship their deity commonly. The cults (sampradāya) of Upāsanā systems of each deity or the saints are set. All the tradition (Sampradāya) are classified into four major groups namely, *Svarūpa, Ānanda, Caitanya,* and *Prakāśa Sampradāya*. Each Upāsaka falls under one of these categories. For example, the great poet saint of Maharāṣhtra, Samratha Rāmadāsa declares in one couplet, that, his Sampradāya is Svarūpa Sampradāya, the verse is *"Svarūpa Sampradāya ayodhyā maṭha. Jānaki devi śri Raghunātha daivata. Māruti Upāsanā nemasta. Vāḍhavilā paramārtha Rāmadāsi."*

Upāsanā can be a *mūrta* (concrete) or *Amūrta* (abstract). In the Mūrta Upāsanā, a physical form is taken for the worship and in the Amūrta Upāsanā a subtle symbol like Fire (vaiśvānara), a word like Omkāra etc. is taken for worship. The Upāsanā of various deities is Mūrta Upāsanā and the Upāsanā which includes subtle forms like Vaiśvānar etc. which are in Brahmavidyās of different Upaniṣads is Amūrta Upāsanā.

Upāsanā has five aspects namely, Sampradāya, deity, Guide (guru), Mantra, Vidhi (process). The Upāsya may be Brahman; a deity like Śiva, Viśnu etc; an incarnation like Rāma, Kṛṣṇa, etc. or saints like Kabir, Caitanya Mahāprabhu, Rāmkṛṣṇa Paramahansa, Jñaneśvara, Ekanāth, Samartha Ramādāsa etc. who are worshipped in the form of Guru, (Preceptor).

Sādhanā is the next stage or a further development of Upāsanā. Upāsanā itself becomes Sādhanā when the Upāsaka continues his daily Upāsanā for whole life as means to reach the Ultimate aim and spends his life by following one of the Sādhanā Paths (mārga), namely, Karma Mārga or Kramayoga, Jñāna Mārga, Yoga Mārga and Bhakti Mārga. These efforts are called Sādhanā and the person who follows this path is called Sādhaka. A Sādhaka owes his life to the Supreme Being. Further discussion of these three paths of Sādhanā follows in brief:

Karma Mārga or Krama Yoga — We shall see in the next Chapter on Upāsanā in Sūtra and Smṛti Literature, how the four Āśramas or the stages of life are the four steps to reach the state of Mokṣa, as well as the daily Upāsanā like twilight worship and the performance of Panchamahāyajñas. This is a Karma Mārga or Krama Yoga or Karmayoga. We shall discuss it broadly in the later chapter where the Upāsanā in Bhagavadgitā will be discussed. It also occurs in the Karmakāṇḍa of Pūrva Mimāmsā.

Jñāna Mārga or Jñāna Yoga — This way envisages experiencing the Knowledge of *Prakṛiti* and *Puruṣa* and then to live life as witness to worldly happenings but without getting involved in it. In this state of knowledge a person can work in society or he can remain a hermit. Meditation, contemplation and study of scriptures (*Savādhyāya*) is said to be the Upāsanā under Jñāna Mārga or Jñāna Yoga. The *Sānkhya* Philosophy is in evidence here.

Yoga mārga — The four types of yogas, *Pāntajala* or *Aṣṭāṅga Yoga, Haṭha Yoga, Laya Yoga* and *Mantra Yoga* come under Yoga Mārga. A sādhaka in this Marga follows one of these four types according to his likings. In *Pātanjala* or *Aṣṭāṅga Yoga,* there are eight successive stages to pass, these are *Yama, Niyama, Āsana, Prāṇāyāma, Pratyāhāra, Dhāraṇa, Dhyāna* and *Samādhi*. A Sādhaka slowly passes one step after another and reaches to the ultimate aim of the Supreme Bliss. *Omkāra Upāsanā* is proper for this Yoga. The yoga Darśana is followed here.

Haṭha Yoga—It is mainly followed by the Sādhakas of Nātha Cult. There are four components of this path viz. Mudrā, Baṅdha, Prāṇāyāṃa and Samādhi. A sādhaka gets hold of them one by one and awakens Kuṇḍalini (serpent power) which travels upwards and unites with Śiva who stays in Sahaśrara cakra. This unification is vital and the ultimate aim of this Sādhana. The Upāsanā prescribed in this Sādhanā is the recitation of *SO'HAM* mantra.

Mantra Yoga — The unification with the deity or the unification of Kuṇḍalini Śakti and Śiva by the mere recitation of magical spell bound words i.e. *bīja mantra* comes under this Yoga. The Upāsanā prescribed for this Yoga is to complete a course of certain circles of recitation of Mantra again and again (*Anuṣthāna*). By this process the inherent power (*Antaḥsakti*) of a man, which is a part of the Supreme power awakes and it merges in Śiva Tattva and he comes to know his real nature which is Śiva and *Sat, Cid* and *Ānanda. Tāntrika Upāsanā* of *Sridevi* is the example of this Yoga which we are going to discuss later.

Laya Yoga — The uplifting of the mind towards Paramātman through meditation and blending with the mind in Supreme Being, is the process of Laya Yoga. Meditation is the Upāsanā in this Yoga.

All the four types of Yoga are more or less similar, but there is difference in them, and according to their process the different names are given.

When a person performs Sādhanā with Upāsanā proper to it, he gets the real knowledge of the deity or Paramātman with purified mind and that knowledge creates the intimate love in him towards Brahman which is called Bhakti and he is now called Bhakta. The knowledge and experience of Supreme Bliss creates ecstasy in him and he sings his name and fame, form and glory now and then during the entire remaining part of his life. he virtually becomes unaware of his worldly existence. This is the state of Parā Bhakti which is the vital state of Bhakti and he never returns again in this world after leaving this body. the Upāsakas follow the Upāsanā according to their Sampradāya even in this last stage of *Parā Bhakti* to show the way of like to others, who want to follow them. Bhakti is nine fold: *Navavidhā* : and a Bhakta relates to God with one of these folds, which we will discuss later in the discussion of *Bhakti Sūtra*.

(iii) Yajña as Upāsanā

Puruṣa Sūkta says that the first duty of a human being is to perform the daily Yajña which is said to be the first Dharma. But what is the implicit meaning of *Yajña*? *Yajña* is '*Yajana*' i.e. worship with recitation of the Veda Mantras of *Sarveśvara Paramātman*; the all pervading Brahman. The Paramātman is not a person but the Omniscient and Omnipotent spirit, all embracing consciousness, power, existence and energy which creates and upholds the whole Universe. One has to do *Yajana* of this Paramātman with one's daily '*karma*' without selfishness, lust, greed. It should be 'Vāsana rahita' i.e. Unegoistic. This Karma should be done only for the sake of duty, without attachment. Because it is the Cosmic Energy by which we can work and enjoy the life, so the Karma should be done for that *Viśvātmaka* Energy.

In the introduction of the book on Śatapatha Brāhmaṇa Keith says,[1] that the idea of sacrifice ceremony of Brāhmaṇa is taken from *Puruṣa Sukta*, he says, "In the so-called Puruṣa hymn (Ṛgveda x-90) in which the supreme spirit is conceived of as `the Person of Man-Puruṣa, born in the beginning and consisting of `whatsoever hath been and whatsoever shall be' the creation of visible and invisible universe represented as originating from an `all offered sacrifice' (Yajña) in which the Puruṣa himself forms the offering material (Havis) or as one might say, victim. In this primeval or rather timeless, because ever proceeding sacrifice. Time itself, in the shape of its unit, the year is made to take its part, in as much as three seasons, spring, summer and autumn, of which it consists, constitute the ghee, the offering fuel, and the oblation respectively. These speculations may be said to have formed the foundation on which the theory of the sacrifice as propounded in the Brāhmaṇas, has been reared Prajāpati, who here takes the place of Puruṣa, the World Man or all embracing personality is offered up a new in every sacrifice and in as much as the very dismemberment of the Lord of creatures which took place at that archetypal sacrifice, was in itself the creation of that universe. So every sacrifice is also a repetition of that first creative act. Thus the periodical sacrifice is nothing else but a micro cosmic representation of the ever proceeding destruction and renewal of all Cosmic Life and Matter. The theologians of the Brāhmaṇas, however, gone an important step further by indicating the performer, or patron, of the sacrifice the sacrificer-with Prajāpati."

The view of Keith finds accord in Bhagvadgitā in the following verse, "*Brahmārpaṇam brahmanhavirbrahmāgnau bahamaṇā hutam Brahmaiva ten gantavyam brahmakarmasamādhinā*".[2] It means, every thing which is included in Yajña ceremony is Brahman. The liquid poured in Brahman, the havis is Brahman, the priest is Brahman, the Agni is Brahman and the whole process is Brahman. the aim of the Yajña is Brahman which is the state of pure and ultimate knowledge. This state of Knowledge is the same which is the state of pure and ultimate knowledge. This state of knowledge is the same which is perceived in the state of *Samādhi*. Only he who knows this meaning of the *Yajña*, can perform real *Yajña*.

Sri Candraśekharendra Sarasvati gives the definition of Yajña in his book 'The Vedas', like this "*Yajña* involves the performance of the prescribed rituals with the aid of Fire or Agni to the accompaniment of Veda mantras. *Yajña* is derived from the root 'Yaj' which means to worship, to sacrifice. To perform a rite or ritual whole heartedly with a feeling of devotion to the Paramātman or Supreme self and the devatas is *Yajña*".

The word *'Medha'* is used for the *Yajña*; as *Aśvamedha, Puruṣamedha, Gomedha, Avimedha* etc. Sāyaṇācārya gives the meaning of the word Medha as Yajña and Havi, in his commentary of the ṚK "*Indrasya nu sukrutam daivyam saho' gnigṛhe jarita medhiraḥ kaviḥ. Yajñasya bhudvidadhe cārurantama a sarvata-timaditim vṛṇimahe*".[3] Purity is also the other meaning of *'Medhya'* which is seen in the first chapter of Śatapatha Brāhmana where the *Yajamāna* becomes *'medhya'* by touching the *medhya* water standing in between *Ahavaniya* and *Gārhapatya* Agni,[4] when he takes the oath of Vrata. Havis is to be given in *Yajña Vidhi* for the purification of individual and social mind. The animal-like actions and thoughts of a man make him impure. So one has to give havis of these impure thoughts and actions, this is called the animal sacrifice or Paśu medha. We must remove a misconception here. Animal sacrifice does not mean the slaughtering of the animals. It means that we must look after them, feed them, make them healthy and then take service from them. We understand this meaning of animal sacrifice in Bhagavadgitā. The verse is *"Sahayajañā prajā sṛṣvā purvovarca prajāpati. Anena prasaviṣya-dhvameṣavostvistakāmadhuk. Devā bhāvayatānenea te devāh bhāvayantu vaḥ. Parasparam bhāvayanataḥ, śreyah paramavāpsyatha.*[5] it means Prajāpati has created the world along with the Yajña. He says that with this *Yajña* you satisfy the deities i.e. a particular form of energy : nature agents and then they will satisfy you. You get your success by this mutual service.(English authors opinion about *Paśumedha* etc.; is the actual killing : Oblation of animals in the sacrifice). (For a period people use to kill actual animals before a deity or in the Yajña, ignoring the real meaning of Yajña).

The *Puruṣa* has spread Himself among the Universe-according to *Puruṣa Sūkta*- so each part of this Universe is actually a part of that *Puruṣa,* who is called Paramātman. By performing this type of *Yajña* one can attain the state of *Mokṣa* by merging his so called separate 'Jiva bhāva' into all pervading Puruṣa, and one can become *Puruṣa* himself. This is a kind of Upāsanā by which one can elevate oneself and become God.

Most of the sacrifices are to be done for gaining worldly objects like children, wealth, cattle etc., in the Brāhmaṇa literature. But in the view of Upāsanā these type of *Yajñas* are not important because they do not lead a person to Mokṣa. The *Yajña* made for the sake of Iśvara is important and it destroys the selfishness of a person and then he proceeds to the way of *Niśśreyas*.

(iv) What is a Prayer?

A prayer is an address to a *Devatā* (deity), a paean and a song of devotion, seeking blessings. The world *'Deva'* is derived from the root *'Div'*, which means to shine, In the Vedas *'Deva'* means a Deity which is a bright, shining, radiant being. *Devatas* are different forms assigned to various supernatural powers; various prayers are offered to them in the Mantra portion of the Ṛgveda. The prayers are in the form of hymns which are called Sūktas. These are addressed and dedicated to *Agni, Indra, Marut, Vivśvadevās, Varuṇa, Mātriśvā, Āditya* and others. All these deities are representatives of the various aspects of one and the same Paramātman, the Almighty Power. Ṛgveda gives this explanation in this verse, (I) "*Indram, mitram, varuṇamagnimāhuratho divyaḥ sa suparṇa garutmān. Ekam sadvipra bahudhā vadanti agnim, yamam, mātriśvānamāhu*".[1] It means the Paramātman is one, but learned men call Him by different names as *Indra, Mitra, Varuṇa, Agni, Suparṇa, Yama, Garutman, Mātariśvāna* etc. It shows that the worship of any deity becomes the Upāsanā of one and the same God. The devotee worships this all pervading God and merges into that consciousness by singing the Vedic hymns.

In prayers one remembers one's deity, Praises Him or Her, offers Him something like milk, fruits etc., and asks Him for the goodness or well-being or for the Knowledge of Brahman. In chanting of the prayers one remembers the divinity of God again and again and gradually one uplifts oneself towards the Divinity. In the vedic times the prayers and worship take place in the dwelling of the worshipper. H.H. Wilson says "There is no mention of any temple, or any reference to a public place of worship, and it is clear that the worship was entirely domestic,"[2]. He further says, "The blessings prayed for are, for the most part, of a temporal and personal description-Wealth, food, life, prosperity, cattle, cows and horses, protection against enemies, victory over them, and sometimes their destruction... few indication of a hope of immortality and of future happiness."[3]

Each *Sūkta* is ascribed to a *Ṛṣi*, the inspired author. These are also called 'mantras'. Ṛgveda has a thousand and seventeen Suktas, more than ten thousand stanzas, eight *Kāndas* or *Aṣtakas*, each divides into eight Adhyāyas or Lectures. The other method contains Ten maṅḍalas subdivided into more than hundred *Anuvākas*. There is a subdivision of Sūktas into *Vargas*. A hymn is addressed to a single deity or some times to two or greater number of deities. The *Ṛṣis* of the hymns are *Gotama, Kaṇva, Bhāradvāj, Vasiṣtha, Viśvāmitra* and others. The worship comprehends offerings, prayers, and praise. Generally the offering is of clarified butter poured on a fire. Men preserved fire constantly kindled in their dwelling.[4] The habitual offerings are clarified butter and the juice of the Soma plant.

Every deity is identified with a separate power. For example, The Sun is identified as a divinity, the soul of all movable and immovable beings. He has different names like *Āditya, Viṣṇu, Mitra, Puṣāns, Bhaga, Tvaṣṭṛ*, etc. *Indra* is described as the god of battles and the giver of victory. *Uṣā* is the deity of the Dawn. *Maruts* are the deities of power. *Agni* is a symbol of the light of the Sun and the Brahman. *Rudra* is a terrible agni.[5] Agni is worshiped for gaining the food, great wealth, cattle, sons, grandsons etc.[6] Dr. Ghate says, "As a rule, the first group of hymns in each `maṅḍala' is addressed to *Agni*, the second to *Indra* and the rest to miscellaneous deities".[7] About *Agni* he further says, "*Agni* is spoken of under three forms, the fire on Earth, the lightning in the Atmosphere and the Sun in the Heaven".[8]

The priests occupy a very important position in the rituals, and in sacrifices for the purpose of God's favour. In one verse Vasiṣṭha says, "*Agni*, bestow upon our chiefs and nobles that favour power, that wealth which feeds many".[9] In the following verse the *Ṛsi* asks, "With precious things O Indra, thus content us; may we attain to your exalted favour. Send our chiefs plenteous food with heroic children. Preserve us evermore, you Gods with blessing".[10]

In the Ṛgveda the prayers are offered to live and to enjoy the healthy life of hundred years. "A hundred autumns may we see that bright eye, beneficent to Gods, arise, hundred autumns may we live".[11] The life must be healthy, wealthy and peaceful. The worshipper asks *Mitra, Varuṇa, Urukrama* to bestow the goodness to them in this verse, "*Śaṁ varuṇaḥ, śanno bhavatvaryamā. Śaṁ no Indro Bṛhaspati, Śaṁ no Viṣṇururukramaḥ*".[12]

The friendly communion with God is necessary for real happiness. This verse asks for friendliness with the divinity, "*Devo devānāmasi agne, sakhya ma riśam vayam tava*". [13] The relation between Varuṇa and his worshipper is also described as very friendly and intimate. The hymn describes *Varuṇa* as the guardian of moral orders also.[14]

In the hymns the life after death, in the world of Gods is assumed to be eternal or rather longest than life on the earth.[15]

That life is called *Amṛtattva* or immortality and it is asked as a favour of God to the worshipper.

The prayer is offered to the sole lord of beings, supporting heaven and earth is described in the hymn, *"Hiraṇyagarbhaḥ samavartātagre, bhutasyajātaḥ patirekāsit. Sa dhātāra Pṛthivi dyamuteman kasmai devāya haviṣā vidhema"*.[16] In the hymn known as *Puruṣa Sūkta*.[17] We find the idea that the whole world is one being, the *Virāṭpuruṣa*, who having pervaded the world from all sides, still remained over and above it. The idea of one or *Viśvātmaka Deva* is repeated in the *Eleventh Adhyāya* of Bhagvadgitā also.

Vedic sūktas are chanted in Yajña ceremony which is seen in Brāhmaṇa literature and later on there is a practice of chanting these sūktas at the time of the worship of deities, Gaṇapati, Śiva and others; for example Brahmaṇaspati Sūkta is chanted in the worship of *Gaṇapati, Puruṣa Sūkta* is chanted in *ṣodaṣopacāra pūjā* of all deities etc.

References

Section I -Definition of Upāsanā

1. Panini's Sutra—3-3-107
2. *Ibid*—7-1-1.
3. *Ibid*—3-3-94.
4. Amarkośa—2-7-34, 35.
5. History of Dharmaśāstra, Vol. IV—Page-316 Dr. P.V. Kane.
6. The Brahmasūtra—The Philosophy of spiritual Life—Page-281. Dr. Radhakrishanan
7. *Ibid*—page-528.
8. The Twelve Principal Upniṣads, Vol. I—Preface, Page VI. E. Roer
9. Ghate's Lectures on Ṛgveda—Page-38.
10. The Brahmasutra and Their Principal Commentaries, Vol-3, 12 Introduction Page-203.
11. See the 'Upāsanā, Sādhanā and Bhakti'—Part II
    There are four kinds of Upāsanā : Satyavati, Aṅgavati, Anyavati, and Nidānavati.
12. Vaidic Upāsanā aur usake cāra Bheda—by—Ācārya Aniruddhācārya Venkatācārya—Kalyāna Upāsanā Aṅka.
13. Ṛgveda—"Ekam sad Viprā Bahudhā vadanti"—1-164-46.
14. Bhagavadgiā—4-24.
15. Ṛgveda—1-164-50.—10th Maṅḍala.
16. Taitiriya Upāniṣad—1-11-2.
17. Ṛgveda 10 10-121-2.
18. Gitā—Śānkarabhāṣya—12-3.
19. Chāndogya Upaniṣad—2-14-1.
20. Sukla Yajus—25-12.

21. Srimadbhāgavat—3-29-11.
22. Ṛgveda—1-89-1.
24. Bhagavadgitā—7-23.
25. Srimadbhāgavat—3-21-14.
26. Atharvaveda—10-8-22.
27. Ṛgveda—3-8-9.
28. Ṛgveda—1-101-6.
29. *Ibid* 3.5.9.10
30. *Ibid* 5.4.30.12
31. Śvetāśvatara Upaniṣad—6-23.
32. Bhagavadgitā—15-7.
33. *Ibid*—18-65.
34. Kulārṇava Tantra—17-36.
35. Śrimad Bhāgavat—7-7-38.
36. Mahābhārat—Śāntiparva—47-54.
37. Brahmasūtra—3-2-25.
38. Muṇḍakopaniṣad—3-2-9.
39. Bṛhaḍārṇyakopanisad—4-4-6.
40. Manusmṛti—6-73, 74, 79.
41. Muktikopaniṣad—1-25.
42. Bhagavadgitā—6-22.
43. Vivekachudāmaṇi—39.
44. See in the chapter "Upāsanā in Kalpasūtra, Smṛiti and Epic Literature".

Section III-Yajña as Upāsanā

1. The Sacred Books of the East—vol 26. Śatapatha Brāhmaṇa, Part IV Introduction- Page—XIV.
2. Bhagavadgitā—4-24.
3. Ṛgveda—10-100-6.
4. Śatapatha Brāhmaṇa—1-1-1-1.
5. Bhagavadgitā—3-10, 11.

Section IV-What is a Prayer?

1. Ṛgveda—164-46.
2. Ṛgveda—Translation and Notes-Vol. 1-page xxi. H.H. Wilson
3. Ṛgveda—Translation and Notes-Vol. 1-page-xxiii.
4. Ṛgveda—1-12-9-4.
5. Ṛgveda—1-6-4-10
6. Ṛgveda—III-1-1-23, 24
7. Ghate's Lectures on Ṛgveda by Dr. V.S. Sukhathankar-page 61
8. Ghate's Lectures on Ṛgveda by Dr. V.S. Sukhathankar-page 1333
9. Ṛgveda—7
10. *Ibid*—7.24.6, 7-5-9
11. Ṛgveda—7-67-16
12. Ṛgveda-1.90.9
13. *Ibid*—1.94.13
14. *Ibid*—7.86
15. *Ibid*—5.55.4
16. *Ibid*—10.121.1.
17. *Ibid*—10.9.

2

Upaniṣadic Upāsanā : Brahmavidyās

Upaniṣạd, Brahmasūtra or Vedāntasūtra and Bhagavadgitā are together called the Prasthānatrayi of the Sanskrit Literature. Upaniṣads prescribe various Upāsanās by the process of meditation on the symbols (Pratika), or digits of Parabrahman which are called the *vidyās. Brahmasūtra* discusses these vidyās which are also called *Brahmavidyās*. This chapter deals with some of the popularly known *vidyās* as a form of upāsanā. A man always feels unsatisfied with what he has. He may be having abundant wealth, power and health; still he tries for more. Such longings of a Jiva bind him in the samsāra cakra (deluded perception of passing phenomena) and for the fulfilment of these longings he returns again and again into the world, and thereby is subjected to the temporal sorrows and joys. Actually this unhappiness of a human being comes out of his *ajnāna* (ignorance) of himself and the working of the world. This ajñāna or ignorance is called avidyā in scriptures. Dr. Rādhākṛṣṇan says, "... *avidyā* is the cause of bondage. Knowledge, enlightenment, *vidyā, jñāna* lead to release. *Avidyā* is not intellectual ignorance but spiritual blindness".[1]. the lessons and disciplines which destroy this *avidyā* are called *Brahmvidyās*.

Several *Brahmavidyās* are told in different Upaniṣads. Almost all of them find place in *Brahmasūtras*. The names of these vidyās are 1-*Udgītha*, 2-*Saṁvarga*, 3-*Paryaṅka*, 4-*Madhu*, 5-*Pancāgni*, 6-*Upakosala*, 7-*Vaiśvānara*, 8-*Dahara*, 9-*Śandilya*, 10-*Bhumā*, 11-*Mantha*, 12-*Bhārgavi Vāruṇi Vidyā*.

All these *vidyās* were more or less in practice in Vedic period. But very few have trickled down to the present age. the important and well-known *Brahmavidyā* in the present period is *Udgītha Vidyā* which is now known as *Praṇava* Upāsanā. *Praṇava* is *Omkāra*. *Praṇava* Upāsanā is also known by the names

Nādānusandhāna and *Surata Śabda Yoga*. *Śāndilya vidyā* is famous by *Śāndilyas* bhakti Sutras, in the form of Bhakti at preset. Some of the important *Brahma-Vidyās* are described below

1. Udgitha Vidyā

"Omityetadakṣramudgīthsmupāsīta. Omiti hyudgāyati. Tasyopavyākhyānam. Sa eṣa rasānanrasatamaḥ paramaḥ parārdhy'ṣtamo ya Udgīthaḥ".[2] it means the letter *OM* should be worshipped by considering it as the form of Supreme God. The divine *Sāmagāna* starts with *OM*. *Sāmagāna* is sung by *Udgāta* (*Udgāta* is one of the four *Ṛtvijas* of *Yajña* ceremony), therefore *OM* is called *Udgītha*. It is defined here that the *Kāvya rasa* of *Omkāra* is more beautiful and joyous than any or all of the nine *Kāvyarasas*.

Omkāra is *parnava*. *Praṇava* is described as *"Prakarṣeṇa stuyate nuyate anena iti Praṇavaḥ"*.; that which praises intensly. In *Pātanjali's Yoga Sūtra* Praṇava is described as the name of Iśvara. *"Tasya vācakaḥ Parṇavaḥ. Tad japaḥ tadartha bhāvanam"*.[3] It explains that if Onkāra is recited with conviction that it is the form of Iśvara it gives the ultimate happiness and unification with Supreme reality.

The importance of *'OM'* is also narrated in Kaṭhopaniṣad which runs like this, *"Sarve vedā yatpadamānananti tapāṅsi sarvāṇi ca yad vadanti. Yadicchanto brahmacaryam caranti tatte padam sangraheṇa bravimi. Omityetat"*.[4] It means 'I will tell you in short about Om which is the abode about which all the Vedas think deeply and which is discussed by Tapasvis and with the longing of which, they observe Brahmacarya etc." *Yamadharma* is endorsing the same as the secret of immortality to *Naciketa*. Again Yamadharma describes the greatness of the Upāsanā of OM in this verse *"Etadālambanam śresṭhmetadālabanam param. Etadālambanam Jñatvā brahmaloke mahiyat"*.[5] It means he who wants to understand and reach Brahman has no strong helper than *Om*. It is the highest significant symbol of Brahman. One who performs the Upāsanā of *OM* is highly respected in the abode of Brahman. The detailed description is also met with in Māṇḍukya Upaniṣad. Here it is said that *"Omityetadkṣaramidam sarvam tasyopavyākhyanam bhutam bhavadbhaviṣyaditi sarvamonkāra eva. Yaccanyattrikālātitam tadapyonkāra eva"*.[6], which means whatever is the existence here and there is *OM*. All the modes of time : present, past and future find place in *OM* only. It is that all which is transcendent of this time entity is also *OM*. This is the definition of *OM*. This Upaniṣad further says, *"So' yamātmādhyakṣaramonkāro' dhimātra pāda matrāśca pāda akāra ukāra makāra iti"*.[7] It means, if Ātamā is to be perceived through the letter of speech, then it is the letter *OM* which signifies it. The letter *OM* is formed of three syllables A,U,M. How these syllables relate to the three stages of consciousness namely, waking state (*Jāgṛti*), dream state (*Svapna*), sleep (*Suṣupti*), is explained in the next verses Nos. nine, ten and eleven. *"Jāgaritashāno Vaiśvānaro'karah prathama matrāpteradimattvadvāpnoti ha vai sarvakāmanādisca bhavati yaevam veda"*.[8] which means the wakefulness is the domain of *Vaiśvānara* which is represented by the first syllable `A'. The word *Vaiśvānara* in this verse is for the ego of the self in the wakeful consciousness. The ego in the dream state is called `*Tejas*'. Mind is its dwelling place. It is represented by the syllable `U'. It relates to the ego of Ātman in the state of dreams. The verse is *"Svapnasthānastaijasa ukāro dvitiyā mātrotkarsadubhayatvādvotkarṣati ha vai jñānasantatim samānasca bhavati nāsyābrahma vitkule bhavati ya evam veda"*.[9] The next verse calls *"Prajña"* to the consciousness in the sleeping state. *"Suṣuptasthānaḥ prājño makārastrtiyā mātrā miterapitervā minoti ha va idam sarvamapitiṣca bhavati ya evam veda"*.[10] One who understands this meaning of *OM*, he understands the reality of all creatures; animate and inanimate, material and immaterial world. He experiences all the world within himself. This Upaniṣad tells us about the nature and Upāsanā of *OM*. The Upāsaka gets the *Amātra* (soundless) state of Brahman with meditating on the three mātras of *OM*.

Muṇḍaka Upaniṣad describes a parable as the arrow of soul is to be mounted on the bow of Om and to be boomed on the target of Brahman where the arrow itself will become the target of Brahman, after reaching it. The verse goes, *"Praṇavo dhanuḥ śaro hyātmā brahma talkṣya uchyate. Aprarmatten vedhavyam śaravatnmayo bhavet"*.[11]

Taittiriya Upaniṣad says, that *OM* is Brahman. Om is all that is. *"Omiti brahma. Omiti idam sarvam"*.[12]

In Praśnopaniṣad Satyakāmā questions Pippalāda *Ṛsi*. *'Sa yo ha vai tadabhagavanmanuṣyeṣu prāṇāyāntamonkaramabhidhyāyita kataman vāva sa tena lokam jayatiti"*.[13] It means, O, holy Master to which abode does he go who has meditated on OM. The Sage replies, *'Etad vai Satyakāmaparam cāparam ca Brahma yadonkāraḥ,*

Tasmādvidvānetenaiva'yatanenaikataramanveti".[14] It means, *OM* signifies lower and higher, divided and undivided, limited and limitless all the modes of Brahman. Therefore, he who knows this way, definitely goes to either of abodes of Brahman. In the same Upaniṣad it is mentioned in questions No-three, four, five and six that *Omkāra* is formed of three syllables, A, U, M. The answer to question tells that the meditation on 'A' leads to birth on Earth (*Mṛtyuloka*), where he asserts superiority as he possesses penance and celibacy and faith (*śraddhā*), *"Sah tenaiva samveditasturṇameva jagatyāma-bhisampadyate..."*[15] Next answer to the question says, if one meditates on *OM* in which A and U are important syllables, he gets birth in *Candra Loka* and after enjoying prosperity there, returns to Earth, *"Sa Somaloke vibhutimanubhuya punarāvarate"*.[16] Next answer to the question says that he who meditates on Om dominant of all three syllables he goes to *Sūrya Maṅḍala*, becomes free of all vices and further goes to *Brahmaloka*.[17] The meditation of separate syllables (AUM) brings; limited virtues; therefore, meditation of the entire form of OM is recommended. This Upāsanā leads to steadfastness of enlightened soul, *"Samyakpra-yukteṣu na kampate jñaḥ"*.[18] Next answer to the question says, by the meditation of OM, the enlightened soul becomes calm, unperishable, immortal and carefree and reaches the highest abode of Brahmapada. see the verse, *"Tamonkāreṇaiva 'Yatane-nanveti vidvān. Yattaccāntanajaramamṛta mabhayam param ceti"*.[19]

Nearly all Upaniṣads tell about the importance of *Praṇava* i.e. *Omkāra* Upāsanā. Each and every mantra in Sanskrit Literature starts with *OM*. *OM* itself is a separate mantra and its meditation can bring the state of ultimate happiness.

2. Saṁvarga Vidyā

Saṁvarga means to accept and assimilate. The knowledge of technique of such an act is called *Saṁvarga*. Brahman absorbs everything into it and still remains as it is (unchanged), such a knowledge and capacity to act on the part of Brahman is called the *Saṁvarga Vidyā*. There is a story in Chāndogya Upaniṣad describing the meaning of *Saṁvarg*. Once upon a time *Śaunaka* and *Kākṣaseni* were taking meals when a *Brahmacāri* came there and requested them to give him a little food which they denied. *Brahmacāri* said to them "O Brāhmaṇa, you are not sparing me food because you don't know who is the eater, who is the food, who is the assimilator of all this and still who protects all this at the same time. If you could have His knowledge you might not have denied me the food." The *Ṛsis* could understood the meaning of his statement and happily accepted to spare him some food. They understood that he was talking about Brahman, who alone eats each and everything but cannot be eaten by anybody or anything, who absorbs everything in to Him but whom nobody can absorb. Brahman is the greatest entity and Supreme Power that creates and protects everything. The text is, "*Ātmā devānām janitā prajānām hirṇyadanṣtro babhaso' nasurirmahāntamasya mahimānamāhuranadyamāno yadanannamattīti*".[20]

There is one more story regarding this subject in Chāndogya Upaniṣad. King Jānuśruti learned this *Saṁvarga Vidyā* from *Raiqva*. King *Jānusruti* came to *Raiqva* to learn this particular *Vidyā*, about which king knew from the conversation of two swans. *Raiqva* gave the king this *Vidyā* which he divided into two separate parts; '*Adhidaivata Saṁvarga*, and *Adhyātma Saṁvarga*.' He said to the king that the *vāyu* (wind) is *Saṁvarga*, because when the fire disappears it is absorbed into the Wind. When the Sun disappears He is absorbed into Wind and so the Moon also gets absorbed into Wind. When water evaporates it is absorbed into Wind. This knowledge is *Adhidivata saṁvarga*. The text is, "*Vayurvāva Saṁvargo yadā vā agnirudvayatvāyumevāpyeti. Yada suryo'stameti vāyumevāpyeti. Yadā candro'stameti vāyumevāpyeti. Yadā āpa ucchyṣyanti vāyumevāpyeti. Vāyu hyaivaitān sarvān samvruṇkte, ityadhidaivatam*".[21] *Raiqva* further explained that prāṇa is Saṁvarga because when a man sleeps, all the senses i.e. speech, taste, touch, smell, sight get absorbed into Prāṇa. The text is, "*Adhyātma prāṇo vāva saṁvargaḥ sa yadā svapiti prāṇameva vāgapyeti. Prāṇam caksuḥu prāṇam śrotram prāṇam manaḥ prāṇo hyevaitan sarvan samvṛuktā iti. Tau vā etau dvau vāyureva deveśu prāṇah prāṇeṣu*." Śankarācārya explains this in his commentary of Chāndogya Upaniṣad.

Every thing gets absorbed into Brahman at the end but still It remains unaltered and therefore Brahman possesses the most superior *Saṁvarga Vidyā*.

3. Paryaṅka Vidyā

This is an Upāsanā of Brahman represented by the person who occupies the Āsana for the time being. Thus whoever sits on the *Āsana* becomes Brahman. This description of *Vidyā* appears in first chapter of *Kauṣitaki Brāhmaṇopaniṣad* of the Ṛgveda. The Upāsya of this *Vidyā* is the Throne of Brahman. This throne is termed *'Paryaṅka'*. The meaning of this vidyā in short is like this. The Upāsaka (devotee) during performance of this Upāsanā of Brahman automatically thinks about Brahman and step by step he comes nearer to this throne of Brahman with the progress of Upāsanā and ultimately unites with Brahman who is sitting on the throne. This is one of the cults of Upāsanā of Brahman. This cult accepts the name *'Paryaṅka Upāsanā'* as its speciality.

We find a detailed description of the route and stages of progress of the Upāsaka from *Mṛtyuloka* to *Brahmaloka*. The devotee of this vidyā who is the regular and ardent practitioner of *prāṇāyāma* leaves his body at the end of the life through *Suṣumnā Nādi*. It is held that when *Jīvātmā* leaves the body through *Suṣumnā*, he goes upwards by *Devayāna Marga* and does not return to Earth to take rebirth. But when a *Jīvātmā* leaves the body through any other outlet he has to return to take birth on the Earth again and again thus the Upāsaka of this *Vidyā* travels along the *Devayāna Mārga* after death. First he crosses *Agniloka*, then successively *Vāyuloka*, *Āditya loka*, *Varuṇaloka*, *Indraloka*, and *Prajāpatiloka*. At last he reaches *Brahmaloka*. But still he has to pass through so many examinations before he could reach the throne of Brahman. The text explains the various tests in a metaphoric manner. First he comes to the bank of a lake named Āra. The lake is full of sexual passions, anger, greeds, etc; he has to cross the lake without entangling in these passions. Then he comes across a big tree "Iyam" which stands for the temptations of Earthly life. But he has to neglect it and to go forward. Then only he is able to see the fantastic and richly decorated world of Brahman. At the centre of this world there is the dwelling house of Brahman called *`Aparājit'* where the ever unconquered Brahman lives. Indra and Prajāpati are the sentries of this house. There is a throne in the central part of this house. The throne is not physical but is a metaphor for sharpened intellect which is also called *Mahatattatva* and *Prāṇa*. This is the *`Paryaṅka'*. The text calls it as *`Amitaujasam Paryaṅkam'*. The verse is, *"Sa āgacchatyamitaujasam paryaṅkam sa praṇāḥ, ityuttaratra. Tasmin brahma āste, tamitthamvit pādenaivāgre ārohati iti"*.[22] When the Upāsaka comes in the vicinity of *Paryaṅka* he has been sufficiently purified and has overcome all the difficulties and tests. Then in a fraction of moment he steps on the *Paryaṅka* and unites with the Brahman.

The description of this *Paryaṅka* is very beautiful. It is in short like this. It has four legs of four *Sāmas* (a particular style of chanting a Vedic mantra) namely, *Bṛhad Sāma, Rathantra Sāma, Śyena Sāma* and *Naudhasa Sāma*. Its back means *Vairupa sāma, Vairāja Sāma, Sakvara Samā* and *Raivata Sāma*. The seat is woven with *Ṛk* and *Yajus Sāma*. The cushion is the rays of the Moon. The cushion cover is 'Udgith'. The pillow is *Lakṣmi*. The flowers spread on it are four types of creative beings, namely, *Udbhija, Svedaja, Aṇḍaja* and *Jaraja*. *Paryaṅka* represents *Prāṇa*, the Life Force. As soon as the Upāṣaka steps up to this seat he becomes one with the Brahman and thereby becomes Omniconscious, Omnipotent and Omnipresent.

The *Vidyā* teaches to conquer the human passions, to control breath, to control the habits of the body thus to control himself on the plains of the body, mind and brain. Then to reach Brahman and to unite with It, to merge into It.

4. Madhu Vidyā

This *Vidyā* occurs in first six sections of the third chapter of *Chāndogya Upaniṣad*. *Madhu* means honey. The idea is that the good deeds or *Puṇya* (virtues) secured by the devotees by performing various sacrifices as per directives enshrined in the *Ṛgveda* and *Yajur Veda* are the sweet flowers. The rays of the Sun are honey bees which extract honey from these flowers and convey it to the Sun. The Sun is the honey of Gods. *"Asau vā Ādityo dava madhu..."*.[23] with the collected honey the sun looks like a beehive. Gods extract and taste the honey of this Sun. The sky is the cross beam on which this honey-comb hangs.[24] The gods drink this honey from the beehive of the Sun and become pleased, then they send the gift of *Mokṣa* to the performer of sacrifices who have created this honey. One who knows this process, that the sacrifices and good deeds performed by him are conveyed to Gods through the Sun, he does good deeds and meditates on the Sun due to which he achieves *Mokṣa* and is set free from the bondages of the world.

5. Pañcāgni Vidyā

This *Vidyā* has its origin in Chāndogya Upaniṣad.[25]

Pravāhaṇa, the king of *Pāñcāla* narrated this *pañcāgni Vidyā* to *Śvetaketu* and *Gautma*. In this *Vidyā,* the activities of the Universe and the life in action are sub-divided into five successive parts and each of them is identified with a special type of Fire : *Agni*. It means the Creative activity travels through five successive stages called *Agins*.

First *Agni* is the entire world.[26] *"Asau vāva loka Gautama Agni..."* It sustains itself on the base provided by the energy of the Sun. Therefore the Sun is the fuel of this *Agni*. It gives rise to the second *Agni* which is the Rain : *Parjanya"*.[27] *"Parjanyo vāva Gautama Agni..."* Rain creates food. The food is consumed by the *Pursuṣa,* so the *puruṣa* (male) is the third *Agni*.[28] By consumption of the food the semen is created in the *puruṣa,* which he oblates in the fire of the womb of a women (female) by which the generation takes place, that is a further creation.[29] At the end the *puruṣa* and the woman both take refuge in the cremation fire which is the last fire of the creation cycle. In this way a man goes to the place from where he comes.[30]

Thus this world, the rain, the puruṣa, the woman, and the last cremation or extinction are the five fires.

The Paramātmā is the very essence and substance of all this creation cycle and he is immanent in all these five *Agnis*. All this happens because of Him and in Him only. Therefore he who knows these five fires, that the secret of life cycle, can only know and understand the Paramātman and can unite himself with him.

6. Upakosala Vidyā

This *vidyā* is met with in the Chāndogya Upaniṣad. It is in the subchapters ten to fifteen of the fourth section of the said Upaniṣad.[31] This *vidyā* is named after *Ṛsi Upakosala* who is a disciple of Satyakāma Jābāla. Upakosala during his education period was looking after the management of three holy fires namely, *Gārhapatya, Dākṣiṇātya,* and *Āhavaniya,* in the *Āṣrama* (hermit) of *Satyakāma Jābāla*. He was studying there along with other disciples. After completion of twelve years education period *Satyakāma Jābāla* addressed all the students except *Upakosala* and sent them back to their homes. *Upakosala* became very nervous as he was not addressed and favoured by his holy teacher.

Looking to his depressed condition the three holy fires to whom *Upakosala* had served all along stood before him and themselves started addressing him. They told him "*Prāṇo Brahma, kam Brahma, kham Brahma*".[32] *Upakosala* replied he knew *Prāṇa* is Brahma but was unaware how *kam* and *kham* were Brahman. The holy fires explained, it is the *knam* which is *kam*, and it is the *kam* which is *kham*." *Te hocuryadvāva kam tadeva kham yadeva kham tadeva kamiti prāṇam ca hāsmai tadākāśam cocuh*".[33] The holy fires said, '*Ka*' means pleasure, and '*Kha*' means space (*Ākāśa*). The pleasure is transitory, the space is materialistic (*jaḍa*). Brahman is limitless and all pervading like space but it is not temporary as pleasure. Pleasure is transitory but not materialistic like space. Brahman is pleasure and dynamic (*Cetana*), lively. Thereafter each Holy Fire advised Upakosala as follows

Gārhapatya Agni said,[34] that Earth, Fire, food and Sun are his body. He is the deity of *Āditya Maṅḍala*. He dwells in *Āditya Maṅḍala*. He possesses the quality of enjoyment (*Bhoktṛtva*). He eats food, the Sun and (*Gārhapaty agni*) Himself both are the same. Earth and food are his consumable goods. He who knows the indivisibility of the Sun and *Gārhapatya* and he, who knows, Earth, food, Sun and *Agni* collectively and thereby worships *Agni*, becomes worthy to dwell in *Agneya Loka*. He gets riches, attains longevity and he is protected by *Agni* or the holy fire, his lineage never extinguishes.[35]

The second holy fire *Dākṣinagni* said, "Water, Directions (*Diśā*), Stars (*Nakṣtra*) and the Moon these four form my body. I stand divided among them. I am the personality identified with the Moon. I dwell in *Candra Manḍala*. I enjoy the water and stars as Consumable materials. The Moon and I are unified."

The third holy Fire, *Āhavanīya Agni* said,[36] "the Vital Force, (*Prāṇa*). The space (*Ākāśa*), the Heaven (*Dyuloka*), and the lightening (*Vidyut*) all these four form my body. I am the personality identified with lightening. I dwell in it. The space is asylum of lightening. The space and heaven are my consumables." The lightening and *Āhavaniya Agni* are the same.

The Fires concluded with saying that if all these three fires were visualised together, it is seen that Earth, Fire, Food, Sun, Water, Directions, Stars, Moon, Vital Force, Space, Heaven and Lightening are all connected with each other by some or other way and essentially they are expositions of the same unified entity, which is the characteristic feature of Brahman. Therefore that Omniscient Brahman can be apprehended by the knowledge of the *Agni Vidyā*. The holy Fires taught both the *Agni Vidyā* and the Brahma *Vidyā* to *Upakosala* and told him that what happens to the knower of Brahman will be explained by his master (Gurū).

When the master returned to the hermitage (*Āśrama*) he saw the sparkling brightness on the face of *Upakosāla* and understood that he had acquired *Brahmavidyā : Ātmavidyā*. Then he said to *Upakosala*, "Now I will confer on you the knowledge by knowing which one gets free from effects of sins (*pāpakarma*) just as water does not stick to the leaves of lotus.[37] He explained that the viewer behind the eyes or he who looks through the eyes is *Ātmā*. *Ātmā* is deathless, Immortal, fearless and Brahman Himself. He is the eye of the eyes. This *Ātmā* is called *Netrāntarvarti Puruṣa*. All the happiness in the world follows towards Him.[38] He is called `*Vāmani*' because he delivers fruits of the good deeds on the doer.[39] He is reflected in all beings and therefore called `*Bhāmani*', "*Eṣa ua eva bhāmanieṣa hi sarveṣu lokeṣu bhāti sarveṣu lokeṣu bhati ya evam veda*".[40] He who understands this, proceeds gradually through the `*arcirādi*' path and reaches "*vidyut*" abode where a superhuman person leads him to Brahman. This is the devamārga, divine path, the path of Barhman. The knower of this path does not return to the Earth again. "*Nāvartante nāvarante*" says the text.[41]

In this way by having the knowledge of Brahman and its path ('*gati*') *Upakosala* became the knower of Barhman. Therefore this *Vidyā* is called the *Upakosala Vidyā*'.

7. Vaiśvānara Vidyā

The worship of the *Vaiśvānara* is found in parts eleven to eighteen of fifth chapter of Chāndogya Upaniṣad. The *Vaiśvānara* is Brahman. In the *Vaiśvānara* Upāsanā it is explained how to understand Brahman as the *Vaiśvānara* and how to worship Brahman in the garb of *Vaiśvānara*.

The son of *Upamanyu, Prācinaśāla*; the son of *Puluṣa Satyayajña*; the son of *Bhāllavi, Indradyumna*; the son of *Śārkrākṣa Jana*; the son of *Aśvatarāśva, Budila*, -all these were good householders and well-learned in the Vedas. Once they gathered together and started discussing questions like who is our *Ātmā*? Who is Brahma? etc. They thought that it would be better if such matter were discussed under the guidance of a person who knew something about it. Therefore they went to *Uddālaka*, the son of *Aruṇa*, for his guidance. They believed that he knew *'Vaiśvānara'* was the *Ātmā*. But *Uddālaka* said "king *Aśvapati* who is the son of *Kekaya* knows better about this and therefore all of them should go to him for the guidance." All of them went to king *Aśvapati*. The king welcomed them warmly and invited them next day to explain to them about *'Vaiśvānara Vidyā'*.

The next day the king asked each of them as to whom they worship as *Ātmā*. *Upamanyu's son Prācinśāla replied* " I worship Heaven as Ātmā.[42] Thereon *Aśvapati* replied "He whom you worship as *Ātmā* is *Vaiśvānara*. He is bright. Heaven is his head. He who knows Him this way eats the good food, sees the good things and understands Barhman".

Aśvapati asked *Satyayajaña* whom he worshipped as *Ātmā*. *Satyayajaña* replied that he worshipped the Sun as *Ātmā*.[43] *Aśvapati* replied "whom you worship, is the worldwide form (*Viśvarupa*) of the *Vaiśvānara*. The Sun is the eye of this *Vaiśvānara*. He who knows this eats, drinks and sees the good things and rides in the good chariots."

Aśvapati asked *Indradyumna* about his deity as *Ātmā*.[44] *Indradyumna* said that he worshipped *Vāyu* (Air) as *Ātmā*. Thereon *Aśvapati* commented "he, whom you worship is *Vaiśvānara* who blows in the different directions. It is the vital force behind the life. He who knows this understands Brahman and becomes happy".

Thereafter *Aśvapati* enquired of *Jana*, about his deity as *Ātmā*. *Jana* said that he worshipped space (*Ākāśa*) as *Ātmā*.[45] Thereon *Aśvapati* explained. "He whom you worship is the central part of the body of the *Vaiśvānara*. He who knows this eats and drinks good things and knowers of Brahman take birth in his lineage".

Aśvapati, thereafter asked *Buḍila* about his deity, *Buḍila* said he worshipped 'Water' (*Jala*) as *Ātmā*".[46] *Aśvapati* explained, "You, too, worship *Vaiśvānar*. Water is the wealth of *Vaiśvānara*. He who knows this becomes glorious, also the water is bladder of the *Vāiśvānara*. He who knows it becomes happy and all the members of his family become the knowers of Brahman.

At last in the end *Aśvapati* turned towards *Uddālaka* and questioned him about the same thing. *Uddālaka* replied: he worshipped the Earth as *Ātmā*".[47] Thereon *Aśvapati* explained,

"The Earth means two legs of *Vāiśvānara*. He who knows this becomes happy".

Aśvapati, in conclusion explained to all of them that what they understood about various entities as *Ātmā* were actually different parts of the same almighty power *'Vaiśvānara'*. But he must be understood as and all-compassing power with the Heavens as the head the Sun as an eye, the Air (*prāṇa*) as the vital force of life, Space as the central part of the body, the Water as bladder, the Earth as two legs, the Sacrificial altar as the chest, Kuśa grass as the hair, *Gārhapatya* fire as the heart. *Anavāhārya*, digestive fire as the mind, *Āhavanīya* fire as His mouth.[48] By understanding him in this way they will get the knowledge of Brahman and will eat good food through the form of all creatures.

This is called the *'Vaiśvānara vidyā'* explained by *Aśvapati* in which the *Vaiśvānara* is seen and understood as the *Ātmā*, Brahman or the all-mighty power of the world.

8. Dahara Vidyā

Dahara Vidyā is discussed in the eighth chapter of the Chāndogya Upaniṣad. It is narrated through discussion between the master and the disciple. This *vidyā* is a *Saguṇa* Upāsanā. *Dahara* means lotus like small space in the body, which is the heart; the central part of the body in which the Almighty Brahman exists. It is the dwelling place of Brahman, in the city of the body. One must know that Brahman within himself is his real self and it is immortal and does not decay, it has no disease. So it should be the aim of a person to realise Brahman in the *Dahara* to become ever happy. the verse is *"Om atha Yadidamasminbrahmapure daharam puṅḍarikam veṣma daharosminntarākāśa-stasminyadantastad-anveṣtavym tadvāvavijajñasitavyamiti"*.[49] The next verses say that Brahman is like the space (*Ākāśa*). The *Ākāśa* is all-pervading so is Brahman too. A question is raised by a disciple that the *Ākāśa* is very vast and so the Brahman should be, then how such a vast Brahman can live in the small space of lotus-like heart? And how a devotee should reach him? The teacher says[50] the space in the heart is as vast as the outer space.

It includes within it both Heaven and Earth, Fire and Air, the Sun and the Moon, the lightening and the Stars. All things exist in it. To reach Him one should observe some disciplines like celibacy and detachment from the external objects of sense organs. One should think of one's inner real self by closing one's eyes and to go to *Dahara* where Brahman exists as one's own soul.

The teacher, teaches the disciple that Brahman lives in his own heart. By telling the disciple further about the omni-virtuousness of Brahman, curiosity is aroused in the mind of the disciple. Then teaching step by step, the teacher leads the disciple from the *saguṇa* status of Brahman to its nirguṇa status.

9. Bhumā Vidyā

The seventh Chapter of Chāndogya Upaniṣad is conversation between *Santkumāra* and *Nārada. Nārada,* the holy seer had acquired many *vidyās* of worldly knowledge. Still he felt unfulfilled and felt something lacking in him. So he came to *Sanatkumāra* in the guise of a common man and asked him about that unique knowledge which gives one real satisfaction. *Nārada* asks him about the self because he has conviction that by this knowledge only one goes beyond sorrow.[51]

Sanatkumāra explains to him that one who meditated on one name and form of Brahman gains the knowledge and freedom to the limits of the scope of that name and form.[52] Though every name and form is a part of Brahman, it has its own limits of conception, comprehension. Continuing his exposition *Sanatkumāra* further said that the Speech, the mind, the will, the intellect, the meditation, the understanding *(vijñana)*, the strength, the food, water, fire, the space, memory, hope, the vital force limited to that apprehension, so it can't give the fullest or ultimate joy. It can only give the happiness to a certain extent. If one wants to get the infinite joy, one has to seek after the entire, infinite Brahman, which itself is the infinite joy. Sanatkumāra used the word '*Bhumā*' for the 'Infinite' state of Brahman. He said "*Yo vai bhumā tatsukhamasti bhumaiva sukhm bhumatveva vijiñasasva iti*".[53] It means Infinite alone is the only real joy. The infinite is that where one doesn't wish for anything more. Infinite is immortal.

A man always tries to get some thing which is not infinite, so he becomes unhappy. But when he acquires the infinite, he enjoys real happiness and satisfaction. So, please, know that the self is every where-below, above, behind, in front of us. Self is all that which we ever see and perceive. The world springs from, sustains itself and vanishes in the self.

Sanatkumāra delivered this knowledge of infinite Brahman by the name of *Bhumā* to *Nārada*. So this vidyā is called *'Bhumā Vidyā'*. With this knowledge *Nārada* became satisfied and experienced inner fulfillment.

10. Śāṅdilya Vidyā

The vedic seer *Śāṇḍilya* is very famous for his book *Sāṇḍilya Bhakti Sūtra*. *Śāṇḍilya* inquires into the question of Nature and so on. His thoughts are incorporated after his name in Śatapatha Brāhmaṇa.[54] And it is known as *Śāṇḍilya Vidyā*. The same ideology is also seen in the Chāndogya Upaniṣad.[55]

This *vidyā* states that the *Jīva (puruṣa)* is the master of his own creation or future. What he understands and holds his conviction about the ideals of the world and aspires for them, so he becomes in the next birth, *"Kratumayaḥ puruṣo yathākraturasmiṅloke puruṣo bhavati tathetah pretya bhavati sa kratum kurvīta"*.[56] Therefore, if one understands that every thing in the world is the form of Brahman, every thing originates, sustains and vanishes into the Brahman and that Brahman is omnipotent, omniconscious and omnipresent and full of ever joy then this conviction will lead him to the status of Brahman after departing this world.

11. Mantha Vidyā

This *vidyā* comments on the nature of rebirth and transmigration of self-*Jiva*, after death. This description is found in the fourth chapter of the *Bṛhadāraṇyaka Upaniṣad*.[57]

Here it is clarified that the self is attached to the deeds and its fruits-desires. The self gets rebirth according to results of these deeds. If one doesn't perform the deeds or has no desires for the results of his deeds (*Karma*) then there should not be any rebirth, transmigration of his self into any living thing. This can be achieved only if fulfilment of all desires and deeds is seen in Brhaman which is actually his self and therefore he should not seek any wandering outside the calm and quiet and pleasant self. If such a pattern of life is observed there will be no rebirth or transmigration but only unification with the ever happy Brhaman after the end of this life.

The word *Mantha* means *Karma* (like *yajña*) that is all the deeds being done during one's life. One can-not do any physical or mental act without any desire, but these desires bind the self with the fruits of the deeds. To avoid this one must act all along with the desire to reach Brahman. The verse is, "*Yo'kāmo niṣkāmo āptakāma na tasya prāṇā utkrāmanti, brahmaiva sanbrahmāpyeti*".[11]

12. Bhārgavi Vāruṇi Vidyā

The ultimate goal of human life and the topmost stage of human evolution is to understand and experience the Brahman which is the Truth, the Existence, the knowledge and the Limitlessness. Man has slipped down form his glorious true nature of pure Existence (*Satya tattva*), therefore is humiliated, but he can ascend with the same sequence as he has descended down. The five great elements: *pancamahābhuta*: are produced from Parabrahma. The Earth is in grosser form than the other four elements i.e. the sky, the fire, the wind and the water. The Earth produces food and from that food the bodies of creatures including mankind are born. The real existence of human life is beyond the five sheaths (*panca kośas*) which are created from food etc. But human being forgets it and identifies himself with the gross body. To understand his real nature again he has to practise some or other form of Upāsanā. Then only his further humiliation can be stopped. By experiencing *Ātmatattva* or Parabrahman only can one's fall be stopped. The process of knowing the self step by step is taught in this *Bhārgavi Vāruṇi Vidyā*. The *Vidyā* explains how to uncover the layers of physical nature accumulated over the self and to reach the *Ātmatattva* by analysis and meditation under the guidance for master i.e. *Gurū*. This *Vidyā* occurs in *Bṛguvalli* section of the *Taittiriya Upaniṣad*. Teenager *Bhṛgu* approaches his father *Ṛsi Varuṇa* who is his *Ācārya* too, to ask him about the knowledge of Supreme Brahman which is well known by the name '*Bhārgavi Vāruṇi Vidyā*'.

Bhṛgu's first question to his father is, "*Adhihi Bhagavo brahmeti,*" it means `O master please tell me about Brahman." His father tells him about the great five elements, the Life Force (breath), Ears, Eyes, Mind, and Speech and Brahman. And he from whom these elements are born, by whom they are sustained and in whom they dissolve is the Brahman. Try to understand Him now.[59]

Bhṛgu thoughts very deeply over this clarification about Brahman. He first came to the conclusion that food is Brahman because food possesses all the qualities of Brahman, i.e. all creatures are born from food, they are sustained by food and when they die, they merge into food. He explains his thoughts to his father who asks him to meditate further on this issue. He tells him to perform the penance: *Tapas*, because in his opinion *Tapas* is Brahman, only by *Tapas* Brahman can be achieved. He says *"Tapasā brahma Vijiñāsasvā"*.

Bhṛgu obeys his father and further thinks over the matter. Then he comes to understand that the Prāṇa: the Breath is Brahman. He sees his father and tells him his observation, but the father again sends him to meditate further. After some period *Bhṛgu* feels that the *Vijñāna*: the Intellect is Brahman. *"Vijñānam brahma iti vyajānāt."*[60]. He explains his finding to his father but he is not satisfied. He again sends him back to perform further penance. After a sizable period Bhṛgu returns to his father with the knowledge that the *Ānanda*: the Bliss is Brahman, *"Ānandam brahmeti vyajānat"*.[61] *Varuṇa Ṛsi*, his father agrees with him.

In this way *Bhṛgu* achieves step by step the knowledge of Blissful state of the supreme self, by the meditation, contemplation, self analysis and discrimination. This *Vidyā* is taught by *Ṛṣi Varuna* to *Bhṛgu*, therefore, it is famous by the name *'Bhārgavi vāruṇi Vidyā.'* The text further says that this *Vidyā* exists all the time in the space of universe, the verse is *"Parame vyoman pratiṣṭhitam"*.[62]

Bhārgavi Vāruṇi Vidyā teaches that human being experiences sorrows because he identifies himself with the gross body and the mind, if he transends this materialistic status and recognises his identity with the all-pervading Brahman, he will ever experience the ecstasy and the Bliss.

References

1. Udgitha Vidyā

1. The Brahmasūtras, The Philosophy of Spiritual Life-page-21. Dr Radhkrishnan
2. Chāndogya Upaniṣad—1-1-1,3.
3. Yogasūtras of Pātanjali—1-27-28.
4. Kaṭhopaniṣad—1-2-15.

5. *Ibid*—1-2-17.
6. Māṇḍukyopaniṣad—1-1.
7. *Ibid*—1-8.
8. *Ibid*—1-9.
9. *Ibid*—1-10.
10. *Ibid*—1-11.
11. Muṇḍakopaniṣad—2-4.
12. Taittiriya Upaniṣad—1-8-1.
13. Praśnopaniṣad—5-1.
14. *Ibid*—5-2.
15. *Ibid*—5-3.
16. Praśnopaniṣad—5-4.
17. *Ibid*—5-5.
18. *Ibid*—5-6.
19. *Ibid*—5-7.

2. Saṁvarga Vidyā

20. Chāndogya Upaniṣad—3-4-3-7.
21. *Ibid*—4-3-1-2.

3. Paryaṅka Vidyā

22. Kauṣitaki Brāhmaṇopaniṣad—1-3-5.

4. Madhu Vidyā

23. Chāndogya Upaniṣad—3-1-1.
24. Principal Upaniṣads-By Dr. Rādhākṛṣṇan—page-319.

5. Pañcāgni Vidyā

25. Chāndogya Upaniṣad—5-3-1 to 5-10-10. Muṇḍakopaniṣad—2-1-5.
26. *Ibid*—5-4-1.
27. *Ibid*—5-4-2.
28. *Ibid*—5-6-1.
29. *Ibid*—5-8-1.
30. *Ibid*—5-9-2.

6. Upakosala Vidyā

31. Chāndogya Upaniṣad—4-10-1 to 4-15-5.
32. *Ibid*—4-10-4.
33. *Ibid*—4-10-5.
34. *Ibid*—4-13-1.
35. Chāndogya Upaniṣad—4-12-1.
36. *Ibid*—4-13-1.
37. Chāndogya Upaniṣad—4.3.14.
38. *Ibid*—4.15.2.
39. *Ibid*—4.15.3.
40. *Ibid*—4.15.4.
41. *Ibid*—4.15.5.

7. Vaiśvānara Vidyā

42. Chāndogya Upaniṣad—5.12.1.
43. *Ibid*—5.13.1.
44. Chāndogya Upaniṣad—5.14.1.
45. *Ibid*—5.15.1.
46. *Ibid*—5.16.1.
47. *Ibid*—5.17.1.
48. Chāndogya Upaniṣad—5.18.1.

8. Dhara Vidyā

49. *Ibid*—8.1.1.
50. *Ibid*—8.1.3.

9. Bhūmā Vidyā

51. Chāndogya Upaniṣad—7.1.3.
52. *Ibid*—4.1.5.
53. Chāndogya Upaniṣad—7.23.1.

10. Śāṅdilya Vidyā

54. Śatapatha Brāhmaṇa—10.6.3.1.
55. Chāndogya Upaniṣad—3.14.1.
56. Chāndogya Upaniṣad—3.14.1.

11. Mantha Vidyā

57. Bṛhadāraṇyaka Upaniṣad—4.4.6.
    II. *Ibid*—4-4-6.

12. Bhārgavi Vāruṇi Vidyā

58. Taittiriya Upaniṣad-Bhṛgu valli-Anuvak—1,2.
59. *Ibid*—Anuvak—2.
60. Taittriya Upaniṣad—Bhṛgu Valli Anuvak—5.
61. *Ibid*—Anuvak—6.
62. *Ibid*—*Ibid*—5.

3

Upāsanā of Pañcamahādevatā

1. Gaṇapati Upāsanā

Vedic

Brahmaṇaspati Sūkta—the deity which later on came to be popularly known as *Gaṇapati* traces its source in *Brahmaṇaspati*, the deity praised in the Ṛgveda. *Brahmaṇaspati* is the God of Prowess and success. He is effulgent. He is compared to Indra in the qualities which he possesses. Both the Gods are supposed to be the same. The qualities of *Gaṇapati* are also seen in the *Brahmaṇaspati* sūkta. He is the God of culture. Therefore *Brahmaṇaspati Sūktas* of Ṛgveda are recited in *Gaṇapati Pujā*. Various names like *'Gaṇānām Pati'*, *'Jyeṣtha rāja'*, *'Vrātapati'*, *'Mahāhasti'* are given to *Gaṇapati* in this Sūkta. The significance of *Gaṇapati Pujā* with the conviction that not a single work can get completed without His blessings is clearly seen at two places in the Ṛgveda. (1) *"Yasmādṛte na sidhyati yajñovipaścitaścana sa dhimān yogaminvati."*[19] It means our *yajña* can never be completed without His blessings. Intelligent *Gaṇapati* may initiate our wisdom. (2) *'Ni ṣu sīda gaṇapati gaṇesu tvamāhurvipratamam kavinām. Na ṛte tvatkriyte kim canaremahamarkam maghavāncitramarca."*[20] It means, 'O *Gaṇapati*, please sit by our followers, you are omniscient, no big or small work completes without you. O *Indra*, please worship this self-illuminating and most powerful *Gaṇapati*.'

The Ṛgveda called *Brahmaṇaspati* as the first deity which came into existence prior to any other deity. The Ṛgveda also points out that He is born in the *Āditya Loka* of the space. He destroyed the darkness of ignorance and then He created different deities of various levels just like a blacksmith fashions various articles from raw iron. the verse is *"Brahmaṇaspatiretāsām karmāra ivādhamat. Devanām purvageyuge asataḥ sadajāyata"*.[31]

The origin of *Gaṇapati's* elephant head is also seen in this sūkta in these words; *"Mahāhasti dakṣiṇene ā no bhara dakṣiṇena abhi savyen"*. This verse probably has led us to believe that the Gaṇapati whose proboscis is turned right side is called *Siddhivināyaka.*[22] The idea that *Gaṇapati* is a master of *Riddhi*-deity of wealth, and *Siddhi*—the deity of power achievement, is also seen in this Sūkta. *Gaṇapati's* red colour is also mentioned here.[23] All the qualities of *Gaṇapati* which we assume to day are described in this Sūkta.

The *Brahmaṇaspati* Sūkta has eleven *adhyāyas*-chapters and number of *Ṛcs* in each chapter varies from one to nineteen. These sūktas come in different Maṅḍalas of the Ṛgveda, namely the first, the second, the sixth, the seventh, and the tenth. The Ṛsis are *Medhātithi, Kaṇva, Kānva Ghaur, Gṛtsmada Śaunaka, Vasiṣṭha Maitrāvaruṇi, Śirimbiṭha Bhārdvāja, Sanaka, Sanandana, Sasnātana, Pāyu Bhārdvāja, Pracetasa Aṅgirasa.*

The first *Adhyāya* of the *Brahmaṇaspati* Sūkta is taken from the first Maṅḍala.[24] The Ṛṣi is *Medhātithi Kaṇva*. The first three maṅtras of this *adhyāya* praise *Brahmaṇaspati*, the fourth maṅtra praises Indra, Indra and Brahmaṇaspati both are equal in valour, power, brightness etc. and Soma with Him and the fifth praises *Dakṣiṇā* with Him. the second *Ṛc* of this *adhyāya* describes that He is the deity of food and wealth.

The second *Adhyāya* is also taken from the first maṅḍala.[25] The Ṛṣi of these ṛcas is *Kāṇva Ghaur*.

The third *Adhyāya* is taken from the second maṅḍala of the Ṛgveda.[26] The Ṛṣi is *Gṛtsmada Śaunaka*. The first, the fifth, the ninth, the eleventh, the seventeenth and the nineteenth maṅtras of this *adhyāya* praise *Brahmaṇaspati* and the other maṅtras praise *Bṛhaspati*.

The forth *Adhyāya* also from the second maṅḍala, has the same Ṛṣi *Gṛtsmada Śaunaka*. The eighth *ṛc* describes the power of maṅtra of *Brahmaṇaspati* metaphorically. The second and the third *ṛcā* describes His victorious nature. The *ṛcā* mentions that because of Him only the Sun shines and the rain drops showers.

The fifth *adhyāya* is also taken from the second maṅḍala.[27] and the Ṛṣi is the same as in the fourth. This Sūkta repeats the line, *"Yam yam yujam kṛṇute Brahmaṇaspati"*. This sūkta says that the devotee wins the enemies by *Brahmaṇaspati's* blessings. The Upāsanā of *Brahmaṇaspati* confers the wealth, the progeny, the cattle, knowledge, victory, dignity on the devotee. Not only this but by His Upāsanā the rivers, the deities and the happiness itself become pleased with the devotees.

The sixth *adhyāya* is similarly taken from the second maṅḍala,[28] the Ṛṣi is the same. The first maṅtra says that Upāsaka conquers the enemies, achieves victory in battle, gets wealth and progeny. The fourth maṅtra says that the Upāsanā of *Brahmaṇaspati* with distribution of food-annadāna-confers on Upāsaka the freedom from sins and sorrows.

The seventh *adhyāya* is taken fron the seventh maṅḍala,[29] the Ṛṣi is *Vasiṣṭha Maitrāvaruṇi*. There are only two maṅtras in this *adhyāya* and these two maṅtras are selected from Indra *Brahmaṇaspati* Sūkta of the seventh maṅḍala.

The eighth *adhyāya* is taken from the tenth maṅḍala,[30] the Ṛṣi is *Śrimbiṭha Bhārdvāja*. The two maṅtras of this adhyāya request *Brahmaṇaspati* to destroy poverty and confer happiṇess.

The ninth *adhyāya* is taken from *Pariśiṣṭa,*[31] the Ṛṣis are *Sanaka, Sanandana* and *Sanatana*. A single ṛc praises *Brahmaṇaspati*.

The tenth *adhyāya* is taken from the sixth maṅḍala,[32] the Ṛṣi is *Pāyu Bhārdvāja*.

The eleventh *adhyāya* is taken from the tenth maṅḍala,[33] the Ṛṣi is *Pracetasa Aṅgirasa*. This maṅtra prays the deity to protect the devotee on the battle-field and to give him victory and happiness.

Later Gaṇapati Upāsanā

Indian people pray to *Gaṇapati* at the beginning of any religious or auspicious ceremony irrespective of their cult. He is the first God to call, first to praise, first to offer havis. The other deities of the ceremony are invoked after Him. *Gaṇapati* means the leader of *Gaṇas* (followers of Lord *Śiva*). *Gaṇapati* has other familiar names like *Vināyakja, Vighnahartā, Laṁbodara, Vakratuṇḍa, Gajānana, Bhālacandra*. It is believed that *Gaṇapati* removes the obstacles from the path of the devotees and so He is adored very passionately.

Different scholars have different views about the period of the beginning of *Gaṇapati Upāsanā*. Western scholars say that *Gaṇapati's* Upāsanā started from the time of *Purāṇas,* but the tradition says that *Gaṇapati* is a Vedic God, because the first

Mantra in His name in the Vedic literature, "*Gaṇānam tvām Gaṇapatim havāmahe....*"[34], occurs in the Ṛgveda. This mantra is the first ṛc of *Brahmaṇaspati* Sūkta. In the vedic period *Gaṇapati* was not a separate deity, his name came as an adjective of *Brahmaṇaspati* deity. It is held that *Gaṇapati* means *Brahmaṇaspati* of the vedic literature. The *Ṛcās* in the vedas dedicated to *Brahmaṇaspati* are compiled together and the compilation is known as the *Brahmaṇaspati* Sūkta. It is a practice to recite these *Ṛcās* during the *Abhiśeka Pujā* of *Gaṇapati*. The description that aśva and other animals are the *Gaṇas* of *Rudra* and the rat is their havis occurs in *Taittiriya* and *Vājasaneyi Saṁhitās*.[35] At another place in the same saṁhitā we find group of deities bowing to *Gaṇapati*.[36]

Four names of *Gaṇapati* occur in *Mānavgṛhyasūtra* as *Vināyaka*, namely, (1) *Śālakatankata* (2) *Kuṣmāṇḍarājaputra* (3) *Uṣmita* (4) *Devayajña*. According to this scripture, these devatas are evil spirits. The persons under influence of these deities suffer badly such as, the princess do not get their legitimate kingdom, matured girls do not get bridegrooms, women do not bear children, teachers do not get pupils, pupils can not concentrate on their studies etc. Those people under the influence of these evil spirits even see horrible dreams and get frightened. To get rid of these difficulties, a repentance process is prescribed in this Sūtra.[37]

It is said in the *Yājñavalkya Smṛti* that *Rudra* and *Brahmadeva* made *Vināyaka Gaṇapati* and was entrusted with the work of spreading obstacles in the endeavours of human beings. It is said that *Ambikā* is the mother of *Vināyaka*. There are other six names which are said to be forms of the first *Vināyaka*, namely. (1) *Mita*, (2) *Sanmita*, (3) *Śāla*, (4) *Katankata*, (5) *Kuṣmānda*, (6) *Rājaputra*.[38] With their description it is felt that *Gaṇapati* is like *Rudra*, a deity with destructive power, but like *Rudra*, if one performs His Upāsanā with great devotion *Gaṇapati* becomes a calm and quiet deity and blesses His Upāsakas.

The havis of sweet food named *Modaka* is always offered to Him to satisfy and please Him. the *Gaṇesa Purāṇa* gives four incarnations of *Gaṇapati* in four Yugas, as (1) For *Kṛtayuga* the son of *Kaṣyapa* named *Vināyaka* (2) *Tretā*-the son of *Śiva-Mayureśvara* (3) *Dvāpāra*—the son of *Śiva-Gājanana* 4] *Kali-dhumraketu*. *Brahmāṇḍa purāṇa* describes *Gaṇapati's* biography in detail by the name of *Nikumbha;* He is called *Vighnahartā* i.e. destroyer of obstacles.

Various names of *Gaṇapati* occur in *Baudhāyana Dharmasūtra* namely. 1. *Vighna* 2. *Vināyaka* 3. *Sthūla* 4. *Varada* 5. *Hastimukha* 6. *Vakratuṇḍa* 7. *Ekadanta* 8. *Lambodara*. *Gaṇapati* is also called *Gaṇeśa*.

Gaṇapati's form is very intriguing. The form is described in paurāṇic scriptures (*Gaṇeśa* and *Mudgala Purāṇas* include the praise and the nature of the *Gaṇapati* elaborately). His body below the neck is a human form but his head is like that of an elephant. His stomach is big, flappy, his colour is red. He likes red flowers, thin leaves of grass called *Harali, durvā,* He likes to eat *Modaka* (Sweet food made of coconut, sugar and rice). His riding vehicle is a rat.

There are different stories about *Gaṇeśā's* elephant head. In the *Śiva Purāṇa,* the story is[39] *Devi Pārvati* made a statue of a boy from the clay of her body and asked him to protect the door while she was bathing. She asked him not to allow anybody to enter the house. By chance Lord *Śiva* came during that period. The boy not knowing who was entering the house, obstructed Him. *Śiva* became angry, cut off his head and threw it away. When *Pārvati* came to know this, she requested *Śiva* to replant the head on the body of the boy, *Śiva* could not seek the original head of the boy. But in the mean time he found a head of a dead elephant. He put it on the body of the boy, and the boy became alive. Then *Śiva* conferred the blessings and the knowledge on Him and from that period *Gaṇeśa* became adorable as a god of knowledge and He is carved on the doors to keep off evils and as a mark of auspiciousness. The *Bhaviṣya Purāṇa* reads a different story—*Gaṇesa's* head is burnt by the sight of *Śani,* so other gods put *Gajmukha* on His head.[40] Some scholars say that because *Gaṇapati* is a god of knowledge, the big head of elephant is connected to him. The *Garga Bhāṣya* says that the *Gaja* is a symbol of *Omkāra,* and all the Vedas are born from *Omkāra,* so *Gaṇeśa* is a symbol of *Omkāra* so He is the first *God-Ādyadevatā*. The verse is, *"Gajaśabdena Omkāraḥ Kathyate, Vedaśāstro purāṇanyonkā-rorbhavāni, tadeva mukham yasyāsti ten gajamukhaḥ,"*[41]. Other stories of *Gaṇapati* take their origin in *Gaṇeśa* and *Mudgala Purāṇas*.

Gaṇapati has one tooth so he is called *Ekadanta*. Out of his two teeth one was cut down in a battle so He is *Ekadanta,* he holds in His hands that half tooth as a mark of victory. His description like this comes in *Gaṇapati Atharvaśiraṣa* as *'Radan ca varadam.' Gaṇapati* has four arms. He holds (noose) *pāśa,* (a hook, a goad) ankuśa, a lotus, a (sweet food) *modaka* in His hands.

The form of *Gaṇapati* looks like *Omkāra.* It is also held that the *Omkāra* is drawn as *Gaṇapati* for the visible form for the sake of Upāsanā. These connotations are seen in *Gaṇeśatāpini Upaniṣad, Gaṇeśa Purāṇa, Siva Purāṇa* and *Devi Bhāgavat.* People traditionally feel that the *Omkāra* Upāsanā and the *Gaṇeśa* Upāsanā are identical. So each and every Paurāṇika book starts from the words *"Śri Gaṇeśāya Namaḥ,"* means we bow to *Śri Gaṇapati.*

Japa, abhiṣeka, pujā, yajña, darśana are the main parts or *Gaṇeśa* Upāsanā. The *Brahmaṇaspati* Sukta and the *Gaṇeśa Atharvaśirṣa* are recited in the Gaṇeśa Upāsanā. The *Yajña* is performed with the havis of *Durvā* and *Modakas.* The *abhiṣeka* is performed with the recitation of the *Atharvaśirṣa.* The *japa* of the Mantras, *'Om gam gaṇapataye namaḥ'* and *'Śri Gaṇeśāya namaḥ'* is performed for either twenty one, one hundred and twenty one, two thousand and one hundred, twenty thousand times or so. The *durvāṣ* and modakas are also offered in these numbers. The leaves of *Śami* tree, the turmeric powder, the lotuses are used in the worship.

The day called *Caturthi* is important in the *Gaṇapati* Upāsanā. *Caturthi* is the fourth lunar day of each fortnight. Therefore the *Gaṣesa Caturthi Vrata* (vow) has special importance. It is the fourth lunar day of the month of *Bhādrapada* (September). People prepare fancy clay idols of *Gaṇapati* and establish them in the adoring place on the day with full sanctity and offer *pujā* to the idol, in the morning and evening time with twenty one *durvās,* leaves of *Śami* etc; this worship goes on for another five days, seven days or up to fourteenth lunar day upto *Anata caturdasi* as per tradition of each family. Then the idol is immersed in flowing water of a river with respect. The word *Caturthy* seems to have another meaning also. The *Gaṇesa* Upāsanā is mainly concerned with the three syllables of *Omkāra*; a,u,m, and the forth syllale is unaccented. It relates to the four stages of consciousness namely waking stage, sleeping stage, dreaming stage i.e. *Jāgṛti, Svapa,* and *Suṣupti,* as well as the fourth stage named *Turiyā* which is a stage witnessing all the developments with aloofness called *Sākṣisthiti.* Due to this fourth kind of consciousness only one comes to know that 'I am waking or dreaming or sleeping' etc. There are two such days of the *Caturthy* in a month and these are called the *Vināyaki Caturthy* and the *Sankaṣti Caturthy*. Devotees observe fast on the day, recite the *Gaṇesa Atharvaśirṣa* and pray to *Gaṇapati* very devotedly. The *Sankaṣti caturthy* falling on a Tuesday is named as *Angāraki caturthy*. According to the *Padmapurāṇa,* he who meditates on *Gaṇapati* on the *Angāraki Caturthy* gets health, wealth, children and blessings.[42]

The scriptures which prescribe the *Gaṇapati* Upāsanā are (1) *Varadatāpaniya* or *Gaṇśatāpaniya Upaniṣad* (2) *Gaṇesa* or *Gsaṇapati Upāniṣad* (3) *Gaṇesa Saṁhiā* (4) *Gaṇeśa Purāṇa* (5) *Gaṇeśa Khanda* of *Brahmavaivarta Purāṇa* (7) *Gaṇeśagitā* and *Gargācārya's Bhāṣya;* commentary on it (8) *Heramba Upaniṣad.*

Cults

Different *Gaṇapati Sampradāyas* or sects are found in India. The followers of these sects are called *Gāṇapatyās*. The *Gargabhāṣya* on the *Gaṇeśagitā* is the main scriptural book for these followers. These followers put on a mark of red sandal paste in the form of a sharp phase of the Moon (*Candrakalā*) on their forehead as their sect mark. *Ānandgiri,* in his book *'Śakaravijaya'*, and *Dhanapati* in his corresponding works of *Madhva* describe following six sects of *Gaṇapati* Upāsakas

(1) *Mahāgaṇapati Sampradāya—Ācārya Girijāsuta* is the founder of this sect. According to this sect, *Gaṇapati* is the creater of this world including *Brahmā* and the other deiteis. *Gaṇapati* alone remains at the end of dissolution of the Universe. He is meditated upon as His form having one tooth and embraced by *Śakti*. The Upāsakas hold that one who meditates upon this *Gaṇapati* attains *Mokṣa*-the Supreme Bliss.

(2) *Haridrā Gaṇapati Sampradāya-Ācārya Gaṇapati Kumāra* is the founder of this sect. He takes his opinion from the Ṛgveda.[43] Devotees of this sect worship *Gaṇapati* who wears yellow costumes, who has four hands, three eyes, red mouth and who holds the *pāśa* (noose) the *aṅkusa* (a hook) in his hands. These upāsakās hold that *Gaṇapati* is the leader of *Rudra, Viṣṇu, Brahmā, Indra* and the teacher of Ṛṣis like *Bhṛgu, Guru, Śeṣa*. The worshippers of this *Gaṇapati* bear on both their arms a mark of *Gaṇapati's* face and one tooth.

(3) *Ucciṣṭagaṇapati Sampradāya*—This sect is *Vāmamārgi* i.e. left handed sect. *Herambsuta* is the founder of this sect. The

idol of the God is obscene. These people act with no control on their behaviour. The Upāsakas wear a red mark on their forehead.

(4,5,6) *Navanīta, Svarṇa* and *Santāna Sampradāya*—The flowers of the sects mention that they worship *Gaṇapati* according to idol and form stated in the *Śruti*. As *Gaṇapati* is adored first than the other deities in all the ceremonies, the other deities are the forms of *Gaṇapati*. They hold that the entire world is *Gaṇesa* only and nothing else.[44]

All these sects are rarely seen now a days. But adoration of *Gaṇapati* is observed daily by Hindu people devotionally. The aim of the *Gaṇapati* Upāsanā is freedom from the bondage, though He is worshipped for the worldly belongings, as He is a God of knowledge, He sets the Upāsakas free from the cycle of births and deaths. The *Gaṇesa Purāṇa* says "*Dhyātena yenākhiladehabhājam, purṇā bhaviṣyanti mano bhilāṣā*"[45] It means who meditates upon *Gaṇapati* he gets all his desires fulfilled.

Popular Stotras

Gaṇesa Atharvaśirsa—This sukta of *Gaṇapati* is very popular even today because it is easy to recite and remember. It is recited in the daily worship by many Hindus. This sūkta is excerpted from the *Śirsa* part of the *Atharvaveda*. The *Nārāyaṇa Atharvaśirṣa*, the *Śiva Atharvaśirṣa*, the *Śūrya Atharvaśirṣa*, the *Devi Atharvaśirṣa* and the *Gaṇapati Atharvaśirṣa* are the five *Atharvaśirṣas* which are famous in the Upāsakas. These *Atharvaśirṣa* indicate the *'Bija Mantra'* of each deity, *'Om namo Nārāyaṇāya'* for God *Viṣṇu, 'Om ghruṇi Śūrya Ādityāya'* for *Āditya, 'Om gam Gaṇapataye namaḥ'* for *Gaṇapati* are famous among them.

The *Gaṇesa Atharvaśirṣa* is recited for *'kāmya upāsanā'* i.e. to achieve some physical targets. This sūkta sings the *Śānti* Mantra *'Sahanāvavatu saha nau bhunaktu saha viryam karavāvahai. Tejsvināvadhitamastu mā vidviśāvahai, Om śānti, śānti, śānti,'* from the Ṛgveda. According to this sūkta the physical form of *Gaṇapati* is like this *Gaṇapati* has one tooth, He is *vakratuṅḍa,* he has four arms, he holds four weapons namely, *pāśa* (noose), *aṅkuśa* (a hook), rada (a broken tooth) in His hands. One hand is in the post position of giving *vara* auspicious boon (*varada Mudrā*) His flag carries an emblem of a rat. His colour is red, the red sandal paste is besmeared on the body, He is adored with the red flowers. The Upāsaka has to meditate on this form.

The chanting of the *Bīja Mantra* is called *Gaṇesa Vidyā*. The method of pronouncing the Mantra is prescribed as follows, 'first speak G, then A, then *Omkāra*, the nasal sound, these syllables are to be spoken simultaneously.' The Ṛṣi of this *vidyā* is *Gaṇaka* and the metre is *Nicṛdgāyatri* and the deity is *Gaṇapati*.

This sūkta praises *Gaṇapati* as He is everything, *Paramātman*, the creator, the protector and the destroyer. The upāsaka prays *Gaṇapati* to protect him by praising the deity by various adjectives. He is called the knowledge, *Brahman, Viṣṇu, Rudra, Indra, Agni*.[46] Then the meditation is prescribed by the mantra *'Ekadantāya vidmahe, vakratuṇḍāya dhimahi, tanno danti pracodayāt'*.[47] (*Ganeśa Gāyatan*) The effect of this recitation is described in Mantras from sixty to eighty six. Then the details of process of physical adoration are described. It is held that one thousand repetitions of this sūkta fulfill all the desires of the devotee. The *abhiṣeka* with this sūkta gives oratory. The recitation of this sūkta on the fourth lunar day—caturthy—with observing fast gives all the knowledge. If the devotee performs the *Yajña* with the havis of durvās, one thousand *modakas*, clarified butter and sacred fuel-*samidhā*-becomes wealthy he gets the fame and the intellect, gets all his desires fulfilled, gets all the desired objects in accordance with the offering he has made, oblations must be given with the chanting of this sūkta.

The Upaniṣad says that one who knows the Atharvaśirṣa acquires all the knowledge of the world.

Sankaṭanśāna Gaṇesa Stotra—This stotra occurs in *Nārada Purāṇa*. The twelve names of *Gaṇapati* described in this stotra are—*Vakratunḍa, Ekadanta, Kṛṣṇapiṅgākṣa, Gajvaktra, Lambodara, Vikaṭa, Vighnarājendra, Dhumravarṇa, Bhālacandra, Vināyaka, Gaṇapati* and *Gajānana*. The first to the eighth stanzas of this stotra explain the fruits of recitation of this stotra. By reciting this stotra students get knowledge, wealth seekers get wealth, parents get son and even a mumukṣu gets *mokṣa*. It is held that if the Upāsaka continues the recitation of the japa for six months, his desires will be fulfilled.

In present times, this stotra is recited daily by the devotees of *Gaṇesa*:

2. Śiva Upāsanā

Vedic

Mṛtyuñjaya (Upāsanā) Mantra

The living creature is made up of a gross (*sthūla*) body, a subtle (*sukṣma*) body and consciousness (*cetanā*). The subtle body is the mind and the intellect. Consciousness is the power behind the subtle body and it illuminates and activates the gross and the subtle bodies. It is called the *Cetanā Śakti*. The level of consciousness is higher in mankind than in any other creature or animal. A Human being can observe and think about the surrounding world. When a person or an animal dies his or it gross body reduced to lifeless mass without sensation and soon the body becomes useless and putrefies. But it is not known as to what happens to its subtle body and consciousness. It is a riddle about which the seers have always been thinking since the dawn of civilization. It is generally held that if somebody dies at a very old age, he must have fulfilled all this desires, but if some one dies in early age his desires remain unsatiated. A premature death is severely mourned by the relatives of the dead. Premature death has to be averted. The Upāsanā of *Mṛtyunjaya* Mantra is one of the efforts to avert a premature death.

By *Mṛtyunajaya* Upāsanā Sādhaka may avoid premature death and enjoy a hundred years long life in which he would get his desire fulfilled. The Vedas hold that the full human life period is of hundred years and by observing correct discipline taught by scriptures he can get ultimate happiness at the end of his life. Therefore to utilise this human birth for the ultimate fulfilment of the soul he should live the life of hundred years. It is said in the *Atharva-Veda* that, *"paśyem Śaradḥ śatam. Jīvem Śaradah śatam"*.[47a] It means we may see hundred Autumns. We may live for hundred Autumns. The *Mṛtyuṅjaya* Upāsanā is prescribed for the purpose of increasing longevity of life, to enjoy the full span of life and to overcome the danger of early death.

The *Mṛtyuṅjaya Maṅtra* appears in the fifth *Aṣṭaka* of the Ṛgveda. The Maṅtra is *"Tryaṁbakam yajāmahe sugandhim puṣṭi-vardhanam. Urvārukamiva bandhanānmrutyormukṣiya māmrutāt."*[48] it is said that this maṅtra or *Ṛcā* is dedicated to *Mahāveda, Bhagavān Śiva* who is called *Tyambaka*. If one performs this

Upāsanā by giving oblations he will live happily for hundred years. Read the verse; *"samuddiṣya Māhaveda Tryambakam Tryambaketyaricā. Etat parvaśatam krutvā jivedvarṣaśatam sukhi"*.[49] It is also said in the *Ṛgvidhāna* that if one pours the rice fried in milk in *Agni* as offering to *Śiva* with accompanied by chanting of the mantra and with fasting for three days, he can live for a hundred years.[50]

Vasiṣṭha is the *Ṛṣi* of this mantra. The meaning of this mantra is "We worship (*yajana*) *Tryambaka,* to spread the fragrance of *Puṇya karma* and to create prosperity. He may relieve us from the bondage of death and decay like a ripe fruit which easily falls off the tree. But he should not keep us off from immortality.

This mantra is repeated in later works like *Vājasaneyi Samihiā* 3-6-; *Taittiriya Saṃhitā* 1-8-6-2; *Nirukta* 14-35.

This mantra is also called *Mahāmṛtyuñjaya* mantra. The *Baudhāyan Gṛuhyaśesa Sūtra* has given the six vedic mantras which are dedicated to *Śiva,* as *Mṛutyuñjaya* mantras; first of them is the said mantra under discussion. The other five mantras are like this—

2. *"Mā no mahāntamuta mā no arbhakam mā na vkhasantamuta mā na upkṣitam. Mā no vidhiḥi pitaram mota mātaram, mā naḥ priyās-tanvo Rudra ririśaḥ."*[51] It means O Rudra do not give diseases to we Upāsakas. Don't kill our younger or elder relatives, don't kill our fathers and mothers. This mantra comes in the *Rudra* Sūkta of the Ṛgveda. It also occurs in the *Vājasaneyi Saṃhitā* 16-15. The *Tattiriya saṃhitā* 4-5-10-2. The Ṛṣi of this Sūkta is *Kutsa Aṅgirasa.*

3. *"Mā nastoke tanaye mā no āyuyu mā no goṣu mā no aśveṣu ririśah. Virān mā no Rudra bhāmito vadhirhaviśmantaḥ sadamit tvā havāmahe.*[52] It means `O *Rudra* we pray to you with the oblation. Please don't kill through anger our valorous men, our grandsons, our servants and our cows and horses. This mantra comes in the same *Rudra* Sūkta of the Ṛgveda. The Ṛṣi is the same. This mantra is repeated in the *Vājasaneyi Saṃhitā* 16-16; *Tattiriya Saṃhitā* 3-4-11-2; 4-5-10-3.

4. *"Apaiti mṛtyuramṛtam na āgan.Vaivasvato no abhayam kruṇotu. Parṇam vanaspateriva. Abhinaḥ siyatamraihi. Sacatam naḥ śacipatiḥ."*[53] It means we may avoid early death and become immortal. The god of death i.e. *Yama* may leave us fearless. We may achieve the wealth as easily and abundantly like a blossom of the tree. May *Indra* bless us.

5. "*Param mṛtyoḥo anuparehipanthām. Yaste sva itaro devayānāt cakṣu-śmate śruṇvate te bravimi. Mānaḥ Prajām ririśo meta virām.*"[54] It means O blissful *Mrutyo*, (God of Death), I pray you that you go off our people and servants. This mantra comes in the Ṛgveda as well as in the *Tattiriya Brāhmaṇa* 3-7-14-5; in the Atharva veda 12-2-121; In the *Tattiriya Āraṇyaka* 3-15-2; 6-7-3; and in the *Nirukta* 11-8-6.

6. "*Ye te sahastramayutam pāśaha. Mṛutyo martyāya hantave. Tānyadanyasya māyayā. Savānavayajāmahe.*"[55] It means Oh *Mṛtyo*, by the grace of the God, we keep away your *pāśa* (hook) which takes the life of humans.

These six mantras together are called the *Mahamṛtyuṅjay* maṅtras. The first maṅtra is representative of other five mantras, and popular among devotees.

Tryambaka is one of the names of *Bhagavān Śankar*. When He is in destructive mood he is called *Rudra*. *Rudra* is *Mahādeva, Mahākala*. He is the controller of Time. The Time controls the life span of the mortals. *Rudra* is above Time and hence he is called *Mahākala*. He by the virtue of his command over mortality is called *Mṛtyuaṅjaya*. The verse prescribed for meditation of *Tryambaka* calls him Mṛutyuaṅjaya; "*Aruna Kamal kānti svardhunirājamanamkarak alitakapālamsvakṣmālām dadhānam. Kalaś amamaṛtapurṇam śulhastrinayanomabhivandemṛtyu mṛtyum maheśam*". It means I meditate upon the controller of Death who is named *Maheśa*. He has a pink skin like a lotus, who sits besides *Agni*, who holds a skull and *rudrākṣamālā*, a pot of nectar and a trident in his hand and also has three eyes.

There is also another description of Tryaṁbaka in the following verse, "*Svaccham svacchārvindasthitamubhayakare sansthitau purṇakumbhau dvābhyāmenakṣmāle nijakarakamale dvau ghaṭau nityapurṇau. Dvābhyām tvau ca śravantau śirasi śaśikalām cāmṛthaihi plāvayantam. Deham devo dadhānaḥ pradiṣatu viṣada kalpajalaḥ sriyam vaḥ*".[55a]. It means the body of *Tryambaka* is very clean. He is sitting on a beautiful lotus. He has eight hands. He holds two nectar pots in his two hands and he is dripping the nectar on the phase of the moon (*candrakalā*) which he holds on his head. He holds a *mṛgamudrā* and *rudrākṣmālā* and he is blessing his devotees with the other hand. The Upāsaka is asked to meditate upon one of these two postures of *Tryambaka* and then to recite the *Mṛtuṅjaya* maṅtra with *Praṇava* and *Vyāhruties*. It is like this,

"Om haum jyum saḥ, Ombhurbhuvaḥ svaḥ. Tryambakam yajāmahe, sugandhim puṣṭivardhanam, Uravārukamiva Bhandanānmṛtyromukṣiya māmrutāt. Haum jyum saḥ. Om bhurbhuvaḥ svaḥ".[55a]

Śri *Mārkandeya* Ṛṣi had performed this *Mṛtyuñjaya* Upāsanā for avoiding premature death. The following story appears in the *Padma Purāṇa* which shows the importance of *Mṛtyunjaya* Upāsanā, followed by Ṛṣi *Mārkanḍeya. Mahāmahima Mṛkunḍu,* the son of *Mahāmuni Mṛgśṛṇnga,* did not beget any child. Therefore, he worshipped Lord *Śaṅkara* very intensely. Lord *Śaṅkara,* pleased by his contemplation, appeared before him and knowing the intention of his worship asked *Mṛkuṅḍu* whether he would like to have a very virtuous son who would have life up to sixteen years only or he would be pleased with a foolish child with a longer life. *Mṛkuṅḍu* accepted the first alternative *Mṛkuṅḍu* gave birth to *Mārkanḍeya* who was very virtuous and religious. The period of sixteen years passed very quickly and *Mṛkuṅḍu* and his wife became very sad and nervous with the idea of impending premature death of *Mārkanḍeya. Mārkanḍeya* observed his parent's despair and asked his father the reason of their despair. *Mṛkuṅḍu* narrated the story of his birth and about his early death which was just to come. *Mārkanḍeya* was not frightened, but became resolute. He told his father that he would worship Lord *Śankar,* make him pleased and would try to avoid the death.

Then *Mārkanḍeya* went to the south sea shore. He established a *Śiva Liṅg* himself and contemplated on Lord *Śaṅkara* with *Mahāmṛtuṅjaya* maṅtra. His worship was so intense and the maṅtra was so effective that Lord *Śiva* presented himself before him and blessed him. *Mārkanḍeya* continued his worship unabated. On the day of death, *Mṛtyu Devatā Yama* came to take away his life. When *Mārkanḍeya* saw him, he embraced the *Śiva Liṅga* (phallus) and started reciting the *Mṛtyuṅjaya* maṅtra very intensely and passionately. It was not easy for *Yama* to snatch his life. But every death has to take place at a particular time and even *Yama* can not afford to miss it. Therefore, *Mṛtyu Deva* tried to pull his life forcibly when Lord *Śankar* appeared and pushed off *Mṛtyu* and protected the life of *Mārkanḍeya.*

Mārkanḍeya was very much astonished and happy with help of Lord *Śankar* and praised him with high adoration which is very famous as *"Mahādeva Stuti"* in the *Padma Purāna.*[56] Lord *Śankar* was very pleased with the devotee and conferred immortality on Him.

Mahāmṛtyunjaya Mantra which was recited and contemplated by *Mārkanḍeya* which gave him immortality by the grace of Lord *Śankar* is since then held in high esteem by the people and worshipped to avoid danger of premature death.

Later Upāsanā of Śiva

Śiva upāsanā is popular and in vogue all over India since time immemorial and it has become a part of daily routine for many people. The meaning of the word *Śiva* is 'auspicious'. It is interesting to observe that *Śiva* Upāsanā has its root in the *Rudra* Upāsanā of the Ṛgveda where *Rudra* is apprehended as a furious and destructive God. He is praised in the Ṛgveda that he should not destroy the devotees, their relatives and their property. People believe that though *Rudra* is destructive by nature he becomes benevolent, benignant and auspicious by adulation and offerings and arcanā as well as devotional prayers. We observe him in the Ṛgveda as He is an angry personality and attacks the lives of children, and the animals like cows etc., by diseases and other means. Generally the prayers say, "O *Rudra,* do not, out of your anger, injure our children and descendants, our people, our cattle, houses and men. We praise thee always by offerings".[57] Similar prayers are seen in the first *Mandal* where he is described as with possessing weapons, in various hymns. He is praised to protect the two-legged and four legged beings, belonging to them.[58] In the seventh *Mandala* he is even prayed with a request not to afflict their children with disease.[59] He is with his angry nature in many of the hymns spoken of as possessing remedies[60] and as being the best physician,[61] as well as the possessor of a thousand medicines.[62]

The destructive character of *Rudra* developed into the benign from in *Taittiriya Saṁhitā*.[63] He is called *Giriśa,* staying on mountain. He is called the heavenly physician and also the lord of cattle — '*Paśunām Patiḥi*. He becomes *Śambhu* or Benignant, *Śankara* or beneficent and *Śiva* or auspicious. Though *Rudra* is worshipped as an auspicious god, the fear about his furious nature is remembered even today.

In later times God *Rudra-Śiva* is worshipped as the Supreme God. In the third chapter of the *Śvetāśvatar Upaniṣad* we have this idea of *Śiva* as Supreme God. He is said to be the cause of the evolution, the growth and he who knows Him becomes immortal, He is the ruler of the world.[64] There is a description that He has eyes every where, his face everywhere, which is similar to the Ṛgveda.[65] In the fourth verse he is said to be the creator of *Hiraṇyagarbha. Maheśvara* is a name of *Śiva,* he is the boon-giver, *Iśāna.*[66]

The name *Umā,* wife of *Rudra-Śiva,* first occurs in *Kenopaniṣad.* She is called *Haimavati,* the daughter of *Himvat.* Later on she is known as the wife of *Śiva.*

In the *Atharvaśirsa Upaniśad* the worship of *Śiva* is mentioned along with his family members *Umā, Skand, Vināyaka* etc. *Śaṅkaranand* described some stanzas in the said Upaniṣad as follows, "For the knowledge of Rudra one should use moderate food, devote himself to reading (*Śravaṇa*) thinking (*Manan*) etc., become a Paramhaṅsa, or a single minded devotee, and spend his time thus. One should undertake *Pāśupata* vow (*Vrata*), and follow these rules:— Greed and anger should be given up. Forgiveness should be practised. The muttering of `*OM*' should be concentrated and meditation resulting in *Pragati* or perception should be restored to".[67]

The *Śiva* worship (Upāsanā) is met with abundantly in the *Mahābhārata*. At the beginning of *Bhiṣmaparva Arjuna* praises *Durgā* with hymn containing the name of *Umā,* Mother of *Skanda, Kātyāyani* etc. In the *Vanaparva Arjuna* performs the Upāsanā of *Śiva* for gaining *Pāśupatāstra.*[68] In the *Droṇaparva.*[69] *Arjuna* and *Kṛṣṇa* went to *Śankara* and sing a hymn and got an *astra*—a weapon.

Śiva is the greatest *Yogi* among all the other yogis. The story of *Śiva* as the *Yogi* is seen in the *Vāyurpurāṇa* chapter ten. *Brahmadeva* told *Mahādeva-Nilalohita*-to create. He created thousand of beings exactly like himself, who were immortal. He then found himself incapable of procreation. He resorted to all those processes of the yoga which in the *Purāṇa* are called the *Pāśupat Yoga.*

Śiva is a powerful, fiery and ardent god but generous and boon-giver too. He gives anything that his devotee desires or that he wishes, even Lord *Kṛṣṇa* with his wife *Jāmbavati* also perform the Long course of austerities of *Śiva* worship and *Mahādeva* with his wife *Umā* conferred twenty four boons on them including begetting a son.[70]

Mahādeva dwells in the *Himālayas* with his wife *Umā* called *Pārvati* or *Durgā* and He is attended by a number of *Gaṇas*. His vehicle is an ox. When He ceases to be creative he performs the process of *Yoga* (remains in *Samādhi*).

The idol of the worship in *Śaivism* is the *Liṅg* or phallus. The first trace of this kind of worship we find in the *Anuśāsana prava* of the *Mahābhārata*. *Patañjali* mentioned *Śaiva* sect, the members of it were known as *Śaivabhāgavatas*. A *Śaivabhāgavata* carried in his hand a long pointed weapon of iron as a emblem of the deity. *Bāṇa* in his *Kādambari* describes *pāśupatas* with red clothings. *Bhavabhuti* in *Mālatimādhava* act III has written that *Mālati* with her mother had gone to the temple of *Śankara* on the fourteenth day of the dark half of the month. This fourteenth day still continues as a sacred day—i.e. *Śivarātri*.[70a]

Cults

The *Pāśupat System*—It is a type of Upāsanā of Lord *Śiva*. All the older *Śiva* Sects were identified with the name *Pāsupat*. *Śankarācārya* has classified this *Pāśupat* systems in five major topics. These are *Kārya, Kāraṇa, Yoga, Vidhi* and *Dukḥānt*. The *Kārya* is itself the *Mahat Kārṇa*—The cause, Iśvar or *Maheśvar* and *Pradhāna*. Yoga—meditation, chanting of *Om* and contemplation. *Vidhi*—Daily routine i.e. three time bathing etc. *Dukhānt*—It is final deliverance.[71]

(A chart showing different sub topics and sub groups of these topics is shown on next page.)

(1) Vidyāpāda—*Pati* is *Śiva*. He is omniscient. He has a Body made of Five Powers.[72] These powers are imagined to be the different parts of his body. By these powers he does five actions, namely the creation, existence or protection, destruction, benevolence. He is *Mantreśvara*. These powers refer to the five faces of *Śiva* (1) *Sadyojāta* (2) *Vāmdeva* (3) *Aghora,* (4) *Tatpuruṣa,* (5) *Iśāna*.

Paśu—*Paśu* is the individual soul who is atomic and knows as *Kṣetrajña*. It is eternal. When the sins of *Paśu* come to end he becomes *Śiva*. *Paśu* is of three kinds (1) *Vijñānkala*—One who overcomes and disconnects himself from organs, by means of knowledge or austerities. (2) *Pralayakala*—Who is with karma and mala, sins, (3) *Sakala*—Who has all three pāśas i.e. *karma,*

1 Kārya

Condition — Organs — Individual soul

(Vidyā) — (Kāla) — (Paśu)

External Internal — Effects Causes — Pure Impure

Distinct Indistinct — 10 kinds 13 kinds

2 — Kāraṇa — The cause — Creation, Prosperity Destruction
2 — Yoga — connected with Citta : Secession from action

Action mere feeling, (Samvid)

Low Chanting Meditation

4 — Vidhi or Process — 1 — Primary — 2 — Secondary

Conduct-Caryā

Vows — Means or doors

Krāthana Spandana Maṅḍana Śṛṅgāraṇa Avitakarana Avitabhāṣa

5 — Dukhāṅta — Final Deliverance

Total — Power of Knowing and acting

Darśana Śarvaṇa Manana Vijñāna Sarvajñatva Manojavitva-Kāmarupitva Vikramāṅadharmitva

The *Śaiva System* — There are three principles in *Śaiva System*.
(1) *Pati,* The Lord (2) *Paśu,* Individual soul (3) *Pāśa,* Fetters.

There are four parts in Śaiva system —
(1) *Vidyā,* knowledge (2) *Kriyā,* Action (3) *Yoga* (4) *Caryā,* discipline or conduct.

Mala, and *Māya*. When all these sins and bondages of karman end, the Paśu becomes Śiva.

PĀŚA—*Pāśa* is four kinds. (1) *Mala* means impurity of soul (2) *Karman* means deeds, (3) *Māya* means ignorance, (4) *Rodhāśakti* means obstructive power.

(2) Kriyāpāda— It contains the mantra section, the adoration of *Śiva* in the evening, recitation of *Japa* and *Yajña* or oblations given to god. There is also description of occasional ceremonies for attainment of eternal bliss. This is a part of Upāsanā.

(3) Yoga—There is a description of the power i.e. *Śakti, Māya, Mahāmāya* which is said to be the cause of the world, the attainment of miraculous powers, (the *aṣṭamahāsiddhi*) *Praṇāyāma, Samādhi,* the position of the circles i.e. *Mulādhāra* etc., in the body.

(4) Caryā—The fourth part treats penance—*Pavitropana,* the foundations and natures of *Śivaling,* of *Skanda, Nandi* etc. and the funeral *śrādhas*. *Pāśupata* system and *Śaiva* system both are the ways of performing *Śiva* Upāsanā. When the sādhaka or devotee goes through the prescribed way he attains the final abode of the god that is *Śivatva*.

The Kāpāl and Kalāmukha Sects—These two sects are extremist and horrible. *Kāpāla* means six marks (*Mudrika*) (1) a necklace (2) an ear ornament (4) a crest Jewel (5) ashes (6) a sacred thread (*Yajñopavita*). The behaviour of *Kalāmukhas* is (1) eating food from a skull (2) besmearing the body with the ashes of a dead body (3) eating the ashes (4) holding a club (5) keeping a pot of wine (6) worshipping the god as seated there in.

Kāśmira Śaivism—It has two branches, one is *Spandśāṣtra* and other *Pratyabhijñasastra. Vasugupta* and *Kallaṭa* are the authors of *Spandaśāstra*. The two main scriptures of this branch are the *Śivasutram* or *Śivasutrāṇi* and the *Spandkārikās* which has fifty one verses. According to this school God created the world by the force of His will. He makes the world appear in himself. The individual soul is identical with the supreme soul. But individual soul is impure. This impurity is of three kinds, (1) Because of ignorance the soul supposes itself distinct from the Supreme soul and with less power. This impurity is called *Āṇava,* (2) This impurity is because of *Māya* known as the *Māyiya*. (3) The consciousness of the soul about having done good and evil deeds, this impurity is called *Karma*.[73] These impurities are brought into action by *Nāda*, which is the female power (*Śakti*) of *Śiva* and from which rises speech. This impurity vanishes when by means of intense contemplation, by Upāsanā the devotee understands his real nature and identifies himself with *Śiva*.

Somānanda is the founder of *Pratyabhijñā* school of *Kāśmira Śaivism*. His book is *Śivadṛṣti*. His pupil *Udayākara* wrote the principal treatise of the school which is called sturas. *Abhinavagupt* has given detailed explanation of these sutras. The doctrines of the creation and the relation of the individual and the supreme soul are similar to *Spandaśātra*. But they follow the Upaniṣadic text for the knowing of the self identified with the supreme soul. This school supposes that the recognition of oneself as God is the way of obtaining bliss.

The *Viraśaiva* or *Liṅgāyat* Sect—*Basava* is said to be the founder person of this sect. He used his political position to popularise the sect. The other person *Rāmayyā* is also claimed to be the founder of this sect. The doctrine of this school in short is—The highest Brahman which has the characters like *Sat* i.e. existence, *cit* i.e. knowledge /intelligence and *Ānand* i.e. joy (Bliss) is the essence of *Śiva*, and that is called *Sthala*. The devotee on following the discipline of this sect attains *sthala*, the place of highest happiness and this is the aim of a *Liṅgāyat* Devotee. *Sthala* divides himself into parts by his power *Śakti*. These two sections are called *Liṅgasthala* and *Aṅgasthala*. The *Lingasthala* is *Śiva* or *Rudra* who is worshipped by a devotee and the *Aṅgasthala* is the individual soul of a devotee. *Śakti* also divides herself into two halves, one part is the *Kalā* and other is the *Bhakti* or devotion placed in the individual soul. The former part of *Śiva* exists in *Śakti* or *Liṅga* and the later part exists in *Aṅga*. By the *Bhakti* the Union of soul and *Śakti* is possible.

The *Liṅga* is *Śiva* himself. The *Liṅgasthala* has three divisions. (1) *Bhāvalinga*, (2) *Prāṇaliṅga*, and (3) *Iṣṭaliṅga*. the *Bhāviliṅga* is without *Kalā*, it is highest and absolute existence. it is the highest principle. the *Prāṇa* linga is to be understood by the mind, It can be conceived of having parts and also without parts. It is the intelligence or *Cit* of the supreme soul. It is the subtle form. *Iṣṭaliṅga* is to be seen by the eye. This confers all the desires, *iṣṭa*, and removes sorrows. It is the gross form. These three liṅgas are connected to the soul, the life and the gross body and they have characteristics like *Prayoga, Mantra* and *Kriyā* form and are called *Kalā, Nāda* and *Bindu*. Each of these three has further divisions like *Mahāliṅga* and *Prasāda Liṅga; Caraliṅga* and *Śivalinba; Gurūliṅga* and *Ācāraliṅga*. Six kinds of *Śakti* operate on these six divisions and give rise to six more forms.

(1) Attributes of *Mahāliṅga* are absence of birth and death and the final release, perfection and *caitanyarūpa*. It is operated by the power of Cit. (2) *Parāśakti* operates on this form and produces a principle called *Sadākhya*. *Sadākhya* is the state which is the light, this is also called *Prasādliṅga, Sadākyas* are five (1) *Śiva sadākhya*, it develops into *Sadāśiva* (2) *Murta*. It becomes *Iśa*. (3) *Samurta*. It becomes *Brahmeśa*. (4) *Kartṛ*. It becomes *Iśvara*. (5) *Karman*. It develops into *Iśāna*. (3) Primeval Power or *Ādiśakti* operates this form called *Caraliṅga*. It is the infinite. It is the *Puruṣa* and the higher than the *Pradhāna* or *Prkṛti*. Its contemplation is possible by the mind alone. (4) The will Power or *Icchā-Śakti* operates this form called *Śivaliṅga*. It possesses the knowledge and the power, kalā. It is the finite principle. It has a sense of Egoism (5) Jñāna śakti operates this form called *Gurūliṅga*. It is full of the light. It dwells in the human intelligence. (6) *Kriyāśakti* operates this form. It is called *Ācāralinga*. It serves as the support for the existence of all things. It is imagined by the mind and it leads to a life of renunciation.

There are three divisions of *Aṅgasthala* corresponding to the three stages on the progress of *Bhakti* and tendency towards God. First stage is called *Yogāṅga*, it is a stage like a sound sleep. It has two subdivisions, one is *Aikya*, in this stage one reveals the truth that the world is unreal and experiences the blissful stage of *Śiva*. Second is *Śaraṇa*, it is called *Śaraṇa Bhakti*, in this stage one sees *Liṅga* in himself and in the whole world. It has two kinds[74] (1) *Prāṇalinga* and (2) *Prasādin*. The first envisages to concentrate the whole mind upon *Liṅga* and the second to attain the realised stage *Prasāda*. The second way is called *Bhogaṅga;* means the devotee enjoys with *Śiva*. The third stage is *Tyāgānga;* in this method the devotee realises the true nature of the world.

There are two classes of *Liṅgāyats*. One is *Liṅgi Brāhmins* and the other class is their followers, they wear the *Liṅga*. There are further two main classes in *Liṅgi Brāhmins*. One is *Ācāryas* and other *Pañcamas*. The *Acāryas* are of five types which are understood to have sprung form five faces of *Śiva* namely

Sadyojāta, Vāmadeva, Aghora, Tatpuruṣa and *Iśāna*.[75] The *Pañcamas* also spring from the five faces of *Śiva*. Their names are *Makhāri, Purāri, Smrāri, Vedāri* and *Kālāri*. From these the *Upapañcamas* arose. The *Pañcamas* connect with one of the five *Ācāryas* as *Guru*. *Jangamas, Śilvants, Bañjijs* and *Pañcamasālis* are the four classes of *Liṅgāyats*. Out of these categories *Jaṅgamas* are famous. *"Jānatyatiśāya ye tu śivam visvaprakāśakam. Svasvarūpatayā te tu Jaṅgamaiti Kirtitah."* It means those priests who comprehend the Almighty, all illuminating Divine *Śiva* in their own incarnation are called *Jaṅgamas*.

There is a practice of *Upanayana Saṅskāra* or thread ceremony in *Virśaiva*. Instead of *Gāyatri* mantra they have the Mantra *'Om namah Śivāya'* and have to wear *Liṅga*. Women also wear a *Liṅga*. *Virśaviva* besmear the body at fiften locations with ash. They wear *Rudrākṣa* on their body. Rūdrākṣa is a seed of a particular tree. It is said in *Siddhānta Śiromaṇi* that *"Rudrākṣadhāranādeva sa Rudro nātra samśayah. Sarvapāpāvinirmuktaḥ prayāti paramām gatim."* It means the person wearing *Rudrākṣa* becomes himself *Rudra* and attains the highest abode.

The philosophy of *Śaivism* is described so far. The other aspects of Upāsanā as nature of Upāsanā way and principles of worship and the final goal pertaining to *Śaivism* are as follows

The devotee of *Śaivism* is first required to go through the scriptures to understand the true nature of the Upāsanā. *Śivalinga* is the only external *Pratika* or symbol of *Śiva* but not His real form or nature. The devotee has to worship *Prakṛti, Śakti* and *Puruṣa, Śiva* through this *prtikopāsanā*. *Śvetsvatar Unaniṣad* says *"Māyām tu prakṛtim viddhi, Māyinam tu Maheśvaram. Tasyāvayavabhutaistu vyāpyam sarvamindam jagat"*.[76] It means *Māyā* is *prakṛti* i.e. Primeaval Nature and the master of the *Māyā* is *Śiva, Śaṅkar*. The entire universe dwells in this dual body. They together form the essence of the Existence. So *Śiva* is worshipped in the form of `*Ardhanāriśvara*'. This Upāsanā is the external part. The devotee surrenders himself to *Śiva* and says *"Ātmā tvam girijā matiḥ sahacaraḥ prāṇaḥ śariram gṛham, pujā te viśayopabhogaracaṇā nidrā samādhisthitiḥ. Samcāraḥ padayoḥ pradkṣinavidhiḥi stotrāṇi sarva giro, yadyatkarma karomi tatadakhilam Śambho tavārādhanam"*.[77] It means O Lord; You are my soul, my intelligence is *Girijā* (your wife), my breath is your attendant, my body is your home, my enjoyment is your worship, my wandering is your *Pradakṣinā* (circumambulation), my speech is your stotras (eulogy) my whole work is your worship, *Ārādhanā*.

The next step is internal upāsanā. The worship is performed in the mind *'Mānaspujā'*. The devotee says *"Ratnaiḥi kalpitamāsanam himajalaiḥi snānam ca divyāmbaram. Nānaratnavibhuṣitam mṛgamadamodāṅkitam puśpam ca dhupam tathā. Dipam deva dayānidhe paśupate hṛtkalpitam gṛhyatām"*.[78] It means O Lord, Magnanimous *Paśupati*, I imagine that I have spread the seat, studded with jewellery, for you, please sit on it. Get bathed with the holy water of the *Gaṅgā*, wear heavenly clothes. I apply you perfumes and the sandal paste. I shower on thee the sweet smelling flowers and the leaves of Bilva tree. I adore you with the incense and the holy lanterns. This is my mental worship, *Pujā* and please accept it and oblige. The devotee perceives mentally the *jyotirliṅga* of *Śiva*. He holds that Śiva is the everybody's heart in the form of flame which is shining gloriously and by which only the world is shining.

In this second stage the obstruction in the path of ultimate goal comes from within the devotee's egoism. His self ego obstructs him again and again with suspicious questions due to which devotee stops at midway or goes astray. So he prays again and again and says that what he does, may if be right or wrong, he is doing the work only for his Lord and oblates it to him *"Kāmato Kāmato vāpi yatkaromi śubhāśubham. Tatsarvam tvayi sanyastam tvatprayuktaḥ karomyaham."*

In the third stage the devotee, the *Jīva*, becomes *Śiva* and unifies with him. *Puṣpadanta* in the *Śivamahimna stotra* says *"tvam arkastvam somastvamasi pavanstvam hutavahastvamāpastvam vyoma tvamudharaṇirātmā tvamiti ca. Paricchinnāmevam tvayi pariṇata bibhratugiraḥ. Na vidmastatvam vayamih tu yatvam na bhavasi"*.[79] It means, O God, you are the Sun, the Moon, the Wind, the fire, the Water, the Sky, the Earth, and the *Ātma*. My speech mingle in thee. I do not see anything but thou everywhere.

Jīva is the *aṅśa* of *Śiva*, therefore finally he experiences *Ekatva* (unity) with him and says *"Śivo'hm, Śivo'hm, Śivo'hm"*. In the fourth stage the devotee experiences the transcendental state. Upāsaka, Upāsanā and Upāsya becomes one. This is the state of *Samādhi*.

There is a description of *Sākara* and *Nirākāra* form of *Śiva* in the 16th chapter of *Mādhyaṅdin* part of *Yajurveda*. *"Namaḥ śambhavāya ca mayobhavāya ca namaḥ śankarāya ca mayasakarāya ca namaḥ Śivāya ca, Śivatarāya, ca."* *Śiva* is adored with the names as *Śambhu, Mayobhāva, Mayaskara, Śankar, Śiva, Śivatara* etc. *Kaivalyopaniṣad* also described *Śiva* as *"Tamādimadhyānt vihināmakam, Vibhum cidānadamarupamadbhutam. Umāsahāyam parameśvaram Prabhum. Trilocanam nilakanṭham praśāntam."* It means, He is the pre original, present and endless personality. He is the formless, the master, the self-joyous, and fascinating, He lives with *Umā*. He has three eyes, blue neck and he is calm and quiet.

Śvetāśvatara Upaniṣad says that *Śiva* is god of gods i.e. *Maheśvara*, the master of masters, adorable and owner of the world. See the verse; *"Tvamiśvarāṇām paraman Maheśvasram, Tvam devatānām ca param ca daivatam. Patim patinām paramam parastātvidām devam bhuvaneśamiḍyam"*.[80]

In the *Jñāna adhyāya* of *Śivapurāṇa* He is called Brahman *"Tadeva prathamam proktam Brahmaiva Śivasanjñitam"*.[81] It also says that *Rudra* is *Śiva* and he takes a form for the requirement of his devotee. *"Rudra nāma sa vijñāto lokānugrahakārakaḥ."*[82]

According to manifesting modes of *Śiva* (*Rudra*), his several worship forms are formulated. Four worship forms out of these many are described below with their meditative symbols and Mantras. The rules and procedures of these worships are to be followed strictly. However, the general mantra *"Om namah Śivāya"* can be chanted freely without requiring any strict conditions of reciting.

Bālārkayutatejasam dhrutajatājutendukhanojjwalam nāgendraiḥi krutaśekhara japavaṭim śulam kapālam karaihi. Khatvāṅgam dadhātam trinetravilasatpancānanam sundarm, vyaghratvak paridhānama-bhanilayam śrinilakantham bhaje. "This meditative form is called *"Nilkanṭha Rūpa"*. *Śiva* in this form has thousand hands. He is as bright as the rising Sun. He has done his hair like a mound, knotted at the top. He wears a crescent moon and crown of serpent cobra on his head. In the hands there are rosary, the trident and the skull. The posture is `*Khaṭvāṅga mudrā*." He has three eyes and five faces. He wears the skin of tiger. He is seated on a lotus. We meditate or adore this *Śiva*. The mantra of this form is—*Proum rhim ṭhaha.*[82a]

"Nilapravālaruciram vilasattrinetram pāśārunotpala-kapālakaśulahasta. Ardhāmbikeśamaniśam pravibhaktbhuśam

bālendubadha mukytam praṇamāmi rūpam."[82a] This meditative form is bluish red in appearance. The body of God *Śiva* is as beautiful as *Nilamaṇi* (blue diamond) and *pravāla* (coral). He has three eyes, He holds a red lotus, the skull and the trident in the hands. Half part of body appears like a male God and half of a female Goddess (*Mahādevi*). Both the bodies wear different clothes and costumes. The crescent moon is worn on the forehead and the crown is on the head. We salute this exposition. The maṅtra of this form is—*Ram śam mam yam aum umm.*

"*Svaccham svccāravindasthitamubhayakara sansthiotou puraṇakumbhau dvābhyāmenākṣṃāle nijakarakamale dvau ghaṭau nityapurṇau. Dvābhyām tau ca stravantau śirasi śasikalām cāmrutaiḥi plāvayantam deham devo dadhānaha pradiśatu viṣadākalpajālaḥ śiryam vaḥ*"[82a]) "This form is "*Tryambaka bhagavāna*". The body is absolutely pure. He has taken a seat of beautiful lotus flower. Two hands hold nectar pots. Tow hands hold *Mṛgamudrā* (deer posture) and *Akṣamālā,* a rosary of *Rudrākṣa* seeds. Two hands are sprinkling nectar on the crescent moon positioned on the fore head. This pure and generous *Bhagavana* may bestow blessings on you. The maṅtra of this form is—`*Om haum jum saḥa. Om bhurbhuvaḥ Svaḥ. Tryambakam yajāmahe sugandhim puṣṭivardhanam. Urvārukamiva bandhanānmṛtyormukṣiya māmrutāt. Haum om jum om bhurbhuvaḥ svaḥ.*'

"*Vaṭavṛkṣam ṃahocchāyam padmarāgaphalojjvalam. Gārunmatamayaiḥi patrairvicitrairupaśobhitam: Navarachamhākalpairlambamāṇairalaṁkrutam Vicintya vaṭamulastham cintayellkanāyak. Sphatikarajatavarṇam muktikimākṣamālāmamṛtakalaśvijñanamudrāḥa karābjaiḥhi. Dadhatamuragak-akṣam candracuḍam trinetram vidrutavividhabhuśam dakṣiṇāmūrtimide.*"[82a] This form is called `*Dakṣiṇāmūrti*". There is a very big banyan tree. There are fruits of `*Padmarāga*' jewel on it. It's leaves are made of the Marakata jewels. The tree is adorned and decorated with the unlimited twinkling jewels of all nine types. God *Śiva* is resting beneath this three. The colour of his body is as white as a crystal. He is wearing the garlands of the pearls and the *Rudrākṣa*. He is holding nectar pot and the book of knowledge in the hands and exhibiting *jñānamudrā* by the hands. There is a sacred thread of the Cobra on the chest, a crescent moon on his hair. He has three eyes. There are various innumerable ornaments on the body. We salute this `*Dakṣināmuriti*'. The maṅtra for this form is "*Om namo bhagavate dakṣiṇamurtaye mahyam medhām prayaccha svāhā.*"

In addition to these four former forms there are a lot of other meditative forms and mantras. There is also one famous form named *Āśutoṣa* form. There are also a famous mantra called *Śiva Gāyatri—"Om tatpuruṣāya vidmahe mahādevaya dhimahi tanno Rudraḥ pracodayāt"*.

Rudra Worship is described in *Śiva Gītā* in *Padma Purāṇa*. Also there are many instances of *Śiva* Worship mentioned in *Devi Bhāgavat, Mahābhārata, Rāmāyaṇa* etc. Rudra Upāsanā is given importance in even *Śrimat Bhāgavat,* the verse for example is *"Tvamekaḥ sarvajagat iśvaro bandhamokṣyoḥ. Tam tvamarcanti kuṅsalaḥ prapannārtiharam gurūm"*.[83] Here śri *Śaṅkara* is adored as the supreme god who releases the devotee from the world bondage, who relieves the downtrodden from their greed and who is the Master (*Gurū*) of all. The *Brahma Vaivarta Purāṇa* expresses—*"Mahādeva Mahādeva Mahādevetivādiṇaḥ. Paścādyāmi bhayatrasto nāma śravaṇalobhataḥ."*[84] Here *Bhagavān Śri Kṛṣṇa* says, "I follow him who recites the name of *Mahādeva* (*Śiva*). In *Padma-purāṇa Śri Rāma* says to *Śatrughna* that he does not discriminate between *Śiva, Viṣṇu* and *Brahmā*. *Rāma* acknowledged the greatness of the Great power of *Śiva* by performing the act of touching with his forehead the feet of those who follow *Śiva*.[85] In *Śiva Purāṇa* it is mentioned that *Brahmadeva* meditates and adores *Śiva*.

Mahāśivarātri vrata is important in the *Śiva* Upāsanā. The various puraṇas, *Garuḍa* 1.124, *Skanda, Maheśvara* 1.33, *Padma,* —*Uatter* 240, and *Agni* 193 describe this varta at length. If *Śivaratri* falls on Tuesday, it has more importance. On this day, *Śaivas* observe the fast, worship *Śiva* with the bilva leaves and recite the Śiva mantra over-night. Oblations are also given to Śiva. Śivasahastranāma, Śivagitā, Śivastuti, Śivamahima, Laṅgarcan mahimā are some of the important short scriptures for Śiva Upāsakas.

Popular Stotras

Śivasahastranāma :— In the *Mahābhārata Śivashastranāma* appears in *Anuśāsana Parva*.[86] Here *Tandi* first explains them to *Upamanyu* and then *Upamanyu* relates it further to *Kṛṣṇa*. Later on in *Śānti Parva*.[87] *Dakṣa* praises *Śiva* by *Śivasahastranāma*. The names of *Śiva* incorporated in these two *Sahastranāmas* are more or less similar. In addition to these, there are different sets of *Śivasahastranāmas* in *Liṅga Purāṇa*[89] and *Śiva Purāṇa*.[88]

Śivagītā:—It is described in Padma Purāṇa, under Gauḍiya Print. (It is not mentioned in the *Ānadāśrama* print.) *Śivagītā* is expounded by *Śiva* to *Rāma* who is in agony by *Sitā's* kidnapping by *Rāvaṇa*. *Agasti Ṛṣi* asked *Rāma* to worship (Upāsanā) *Śiva*, *Rāma* obeyed and *Śiva* became happy with him, stood before him and preached him the *Śivagīta*.

There is another *Śivagītā* which is called *Iśvaragītā*. It finds its place in *Kūrma Purāṇa* (published by Indological Book House, Vārāṇasi 1968). *Pāśupata* Yoga is preached in this *gītā*.

Śivastuti:—It is seen at various places in the *Mahābhārata*. These are stories (ākhyānas) In *Upamnyupākhyāna*.[90] (2) *Kṛṣṇa*.[91] (3) by *Kṛṣṇa* and *Arjuna*,[92], (4) by *Tandin*,[93] (5) by *Dakṣa*[94] and (6) by *Marutta*[95] (7) By *Aśvatthāman*.[95]

Śiva Mahimnastotra—*Puṣpadanta* of *Gandharva* lineage sang this Praise to please *Śiva* and it is recited daily by the devotees.

Liṅgārcanamahimā—This myth story (*ākhyāna*) is also seen in the *Mahābhārata, Anuśāsan Parva* (247 (para-1, 15) and in ch. 146-16).

Ṛudrānuṣṭhāna—It has a very important and a vital place in the *Śiva* Upāsanā. In this Upāsanā, the *Rudrādhyāya* is recited again and again. The Rudrādhyāya is made of two *Prapāṭhakas*, one is the fifth *Prapāṭhaka* of the *ekādaśa anuvāka* in the fourth *kānda* and the other is the seventh *Prapāṭhaka* of the *ekādaśa anuvāka* in the same *kānda* of the *Taittiriya Saṃhitā* of Black Yajurved. One recitation of this adhyāya is called *Āvartana*. One set of eleven *Āvartanas* is called *Edkādaṣini*, eleven *Ekādaṣinies* form *Laghurudra* and eleven *Laghurudras* are called *Mahārurdra*, eleven *Maharudras* are called *Atrirudra*.

The reading of the *Rudrādhyāya* is called *Rudra Paṭhaṇa*. There are three traditions of *Rudrapaṭhaṇa*. (1) *Japa*—The recitation of the *Rudrādhyaya* with understanding its meaning is called *Japa*. It is generally practised in the *Śiva* temple near the *Śivaliṅga*. By this recitation the devotee becomes pure, generous, benevolent and immortal.

(2) Abhiṣeka : Dripping or pouring water continuously accompanied with the recitation of the *Rudrādhyāya* is called the *Rudrābhiṣeka*. It is described fully in the *Baudhāyana Gṛhyasūtra*.[96]

(3) Homa (Yajña) (a) : The pouring of oblation in the holy

fire with the recitation of the *Rudrādhyāya* is called *Home.* The *Kaivalyopaniṣad* praises the importance of *Rudra Japa* as— "*Yaḥ Śatarudriyamadhite so Surāpānāt puto bhavati Brahmahatyāt puto bhavati, Kṛtyākrityātputo bhavati, tasmādevimuktamāśrito.*"[97] It means one who recites daily the *Śatarudriya* mantra he becomes free from the various sins and becomes *Śiva.*

Twelve Jyotirilingas—Twelve very important places of *Śiva* temples located in different parts of India, as mentioned below are famous by the name '*Jyotirilingas.*

(1) Ghṛṣṇeśvar (Mahārāshtra)
(2) Tryambakeśvar (Mahārāshtra).
(3) Mallikārjun (Andhra Pradesh).
(4) Mahānkāleṣvar (M.P.)
(5) Vishweṣvar (U.P.)
(6) Rameshvar (Tāmilnādu)
(7) Somanāth (Gujrātha).
(8) Onkāra (M.P.).
(9) Kedāra (U.P.).
(10) Nāgesh
(11) Bhimāśankar (Mahārāshtra).
(12) Vaijyanāth (Mahārāshtra).

These twelve *Lingas* are said to be the twelve different modes of expression of the supreme power of *Śiva.* The *Śiva* devotees scrupulously do the pilgrimage of all these *Jyotirilingas* at least once in a life time.

In this way the devotee by meditating on *Śiva* in the different forms at the different stages of spiritual advancement and different spiritual levels, ultimately reaches and unites with the Supreme consciousness of Śiva and gets freed from all the bondages of *Sansāra* (a deluded perception of passing phenomena).

Rudrākṣa

Worshippers of *Śiva* wear and worship *Rudrāksa. Rudrāksa* is as valuable as *Śiva* Himself. The importance of *Rudrākṣa* is described in minor Upaniṣads, its brief description follows.

The *Rudrākṣas* are generated from the eye of the fire of *Rudra* hence they hold the qualities of *Rudra*. In the *Kālāgnirudra* Upaniṣad, *Śiva* in the form of *Kālāgnirudra* answers the question of *Santkumāra* about the importance of the *Rudrākṣa*. He says that the *rudrākṣas* are very important that even if a man speaks about it he gets the merit of making a gift of ten cows, by wearing it, he gets the merit of the gift and thousand cows. The wearer attains the state of eleven rudras. The *rudrākṣa* is to be worn in the hand, around the neck, in the ears, on the head, on the chaste, on the arms. *Kālāgnirudra* mention that a devotee should wear forty *rudrākṣas* over his head, three or one on the tuft of hair, twelve each in the ear, thirty two around the neck, sixteen each around the two arms, twelve each over the two wrists, six each round the two thumbs. the devotee should worship them during twilight (*sandhyā*) with muttering the mantra, "*Agni jyotir, jyotriagnih svāhā, suryo jytoir, jyotiḥ suryo svāhā.*[1]

Different stories are given about the origin of *rudrākṣa* in the *Śiva Purāṇa*; in the *Vājaseaneyi Saṃhitā*; chapter twentyfifth; *Devi Bhāgavata*. It is well known that the *rudrākṣa* tree sprung from the drops of water fallen on the ground of the eyes of *Śiva* therefore the fruits of the tree are called *rudrāksa*. *Śiva* is fond of wearing them. The *rudrākṣa* at the size of *Āmalaka* (myrobalan) is the best, at the size of beri fruit is medium and too much small is inferior. *Rudrākṣa* imparts happiness to devotee. For the recitation of *japa* smaller *rudrākṣas* are best. The equal size of *Rudrākṣas* which shine are strong, round and with rough surface are useful for the string of *japa*.

Rudrākṣa has many facets known as mukha. One faced (Ekamukhi) rudrākṣa is *Śiva* himself, *dvimukhi rudrākṣa* is *Śiva* and *Śakti*, *trimukhi* symbolises *Agni* and fulfills all the desires. The four-faced *rudrākṣa* symbolises Lord *Brahmā* who fulfils *dharmārthakāmumokṣa*; the four aims of life (*puruṣārtha*), *pancamukhi rudrākṣa* is *kālāgnirudra*, six faced is *Kārtikeya* or *Gaṇeśa*, the seven faced in *Kāmadeva*, *Aṣtamukhi* symbolises *Bhairava*, nine faced symbolises *Kapila* with *Bhairava*, *Durgā* lives in this *rudrākṣa*. Ten faced is *Viṣṇu*, eleven faced is Rudra, who gives victory. Twelve faced is as good as twelve *Ādityas*, thirteen faced is *Vāsudeva*, fourteen faced symbolises *Paramaśiva*,.[2]

The japamālā is prescribed for the counting of the repetition of mantras, stotras etc. This *mālā* (string) is made of coral, crystal, pearl, lotus seeds, conch-beads, Tulsi beads and *Rudrākṣa* beads. *Rudrākṣamālā* is more common and popular than other beads. The foremost of all the strings has hundred and eight *rudrākṣas*, the medium has one hundred, the lowest has fifty *rudrākṣas*. The use of little finger and thumb is more useful than use of other fingers for *japa*. If *japa* is done in the cow-shed, on river banks, in the temple, in front of Śiva and other deities it gives hundred times better success. The *Śiva Purāṇa* says that at the time of japa hair should be tied, body should be pure, one should not get angry; spitting, yawning, sneezing is prohibited.[3]

The Śiva Purāṇa gives the examination of Rudrākṣa which shows its quality in the verse "Nikaśe hemarekhābhā yusya rekhā pradṛśyate tadakṣam uttamam vidyāt tad-dhārayāṇi Śivapujakaiḥ."[4] It means when the rudrākṣa leaves the streak just like a streak of gold, after rubbing it on the testing stone of gold, then that rudrākṣa is best, that should be worn by the devotee.

The Akṣamālikopaniṣad, the Rudrākṣajābālopaniṣad, the Kālāgnirudropaniṣad provide us the details about the Rudrākṣa.

Śri Hanumān Upāsanā

Hanumān is the deity of power. His birth is said to be in the class of mammals designated as monkeys. His father's name is *Kesari* and mother's name is *Anjani*, so he is called *Ānjaneya*. *Māruti* is his popular name and he is better known by this name. It is said that as soon as he was born he leaped to catch the rising Sun thinking that it is some fruit, and he should eat it. But looking to the danger that he may really swallow the Sun and the world would be destroyed, *Indra* threw *vajra*, his powerful weapon to obstruct him. The God of Wind protected Māruti suffering from the heat of the weapon directly but the weapon dashed against Māruti's chin and his chin became flat. Therefore Māruti is called Hanumān. He is said to be the incarnation of Rudra who took birth to help *Śri Rāma*, the incarnation of *Viṣṇu*, in destroying *Rākṣasa* (demons race). He is said to be the best and foremost devotee and the most obedient follower of Rāma. He is called *Rāmbhakta Hanumān*. He loved and adored Rāma by considering himself as a servant of Rāma. That is why his devotion is famous by the name of *Dāsyabhakti*. In every temple of Rāma the idol of Māruti is always seen in a sitting or standing posture with both hands joined together in regard to bow to Rāma. He is in such a stance as if he is ever ready to accept Rāma's order.

It is said that *Kesari* and *Anjani* were going through a penance for the son. One day she found a *prasāda* (food offered to idols or its remnant) in her hands dropped from a flying bird's beak, she ate it earnestly as divine food. Then she had a son who is Māruti. He was exceptionally brilliant, strong and powerful from childhood. His body is described as strong as the vajra of Indra. he is deathless and counted amongst the seven such persons who are called *chirañjīva* (long lived), the traditional verse is, *"Aśvatthāmā balirvyāso hanumānsca bibhiṣaṇaḥ kṛpaḥ parśurāmaśca saptaite chrajīvanā."* It is believed that Hanumān is performing tapas even at present on the *Gandhamādana* mountain and he becomes pleased by his Upāsanā and blesses his devotees by fulfilling their longings.

In *Vālmikis's Rāmāyaṇa*[1] Hanumān's heroic deeds are described in numerous episodes and people love to read and hear them again and again. Māruti has done the greatest job of searching *Devi Sītā* and also in fighting heroically against Rāvaṇa. Māruti is worshipped by the people as symbol of strength and intelligence. He confers health, wealth, dignity on the devotees. He destroys weakness and timidity. He assures *Abhaya* (Protection) against the enemies, and thieves. A man can gather qualities of strength and intelligence by worshipping Māruti.

There are some mantras and the process of performing the worship of Māruti prescribed by the *Ṛṣi Sanatkumāra*. The mantras to be used during the meditation of Māruti are also given in the *Nārada Purāṇa*. The mantras prescribed by *Sanatkumāra* have twelve words *"Haum hasfrem hakphrem hastraum haskhprem hansaum hannumate namaḥ."*[2] The Ṛśi of this mantra is *Śrirāmachandra*, metre is *Jagati* and the deity is *Hanumān*. The first six words of this mantra are seeds i.e. *bijas*, by which the anganyāsa is done i.e. the limbs become ready to accept the power of the deity. After the completion of twelve thousand recitations i.e. *japa*, the devotee is to offer oblation of grains mixed with curd and milk into the holy fire. Then he is to worship Māruti by invoking his eight names—*Rāmbhakta, Mahāteja, Kapirāja, Mahābala, Droṇādridhāraka, Merupiṭhārcanakāraka, Dakṣināśābhāskara* and *Sarvavighnanāśaka*. Then he is to adore Sugriva, Aṅgada, Nila, Jāmbuvan, Suṣeṇa, Divida and Mainda. After that he is to greet the guardians of the directions-*Dikpāla* and their weapons like the *vajra* etc. This is the process of Māruti's mantra worship. Then only the mantra becomes potent. The japa of nine thousand recitation is to be performed in ten days at the rate of nine hundred repetitions per day. This japa is to be performed at night only, to destroy the difficulties occurring from the enemies and the kings. The water charged by hundred and eight times of recitation of the mantra, cures poisoning, dysentery and other diseases.

The other method of the ritual worship is that the devotee worships Hanumān's idol made from flour of *Udida* mixed with oil, on certain specific days viz fourteenth lunar day, Tuesday or Sunday. The devotee lights a lamp consuming oil, he requests Māruti to enter into that idol by '*Āvāhana* mantras' (calling) adores him with water, milk, red sandal, red flowers, sindūra, lantern, offers him the rice, sweets and various different types of food. He recites the japa for a thousand times which follows the recitations of prayers. At the end of the worship the idol is immersed into water and he is requested to come again when required or called. The devotee has to observe strict discipline and austerity during the day of worship.

Some devotees draw a picture of Māruti on the floor, write the mantra near it for hundred and eight times, light holy fire and pour oblations of milk, curd, durvās etc.; for the cure of different types of diseases, different oblations are offered into the holy fire. Another maātra of Māruti has eleven words, "*Om aim srim hram hrim hum haspharm hakphrem hastraum haskhaprem hasaum*,".[2] This mantra gives all mundane objects." "*Namo bhagavate Ānjaneyāya mahābalāya svāha*.", is the mantra with eighteen syllables. The Ṛṣi of this mantra is *Iśvara, ham* is the *bija, svāhā* is the *śakti* and the deity is *Hanumān*.

Nārada Purvātāpaniya upaniṣad gives some verses for the meditation and the japa of Māruti. Some of these are as follows:—
(1) "*Mahāśailam samutpātya dhāvantam rāvaṇam prati. Lākṣārasāruṇam raudram kālāntakāyamopamam. Jvālāgni samam jaitram suryakotisamaprabham. Angadādayairmahāvirairveṣtitam rudrarupiṇam. Tiṣṭha tiṣṭha raṇe duṣta srujantam ghoranihsvanam. Śaivarupiṇamabhyarcya dhāyatvā lakṣam japenmanum.*[3] The meditation of Māruti in the following form of expected followed by the ten million times recitation in this verse as: Hanumān is flying in the sky toward Rāvaṇa with a huge uprooted mountain held in his hand. His colour is bright red dyed in lac, he is looking fearful and furious like the destructive God *Yama*, as bright as the red flamed fire and victorious and effulgent as hundreds of Suns and surrounded by *Angada* and other victorious

war heroes. He is like *Rudra*. He ordered *Rāvaṇa* to stand still and stop aggression. After meditation the devotee pours oblations of milk, curd, rice mixed with butter in the fire.

This type of worship confers *Puṅya* (virtues), good results, destroys sins, fulfills expectations and grants victory. (2) *"Dhayāyedraṇe Hanumanatam suryakoṭi samprabham. Dhāvantam Rāvaṇam jetum dṛṣtvā sattvaramutthitam. Lakṣmaṇam ca mahāviram patitam raṇabhutale Gurun ca krodhamutpādya grahitum guruparvatam. hāhākaraiḥi sadrapaisca kampayantam jagattrayam. Ābrahmāṇḍam samvyāpya kṛtvā bhimam kalevaram."*[4] The meaning is—Hanumān suddenly stands up when he sees that lakṣmaṇa is lying down and angrily picks up a nearby mountain and runs to Rāvaṇa. He is effulgent like many Suns and reforms his body as large as the universe. His voice is so loud that the world trembles with it. After meditating on this image the upāsanā is performed with the recitation of maṅtra, the japa and the oblations.

(3) *"Vāme śailam varibhidam viśuddham ṭankamanyataḥ. Dadhānam svarṇavarṇam ca dhyāyet kundalinam harim"*.[5] It means, we meditate on Hanumān who is holding a mountain in the right hand and another weapon in the left hand who is shining like gold and wear earrings. After the recitation of maṅtra for one lakh times, oblations of leaves of mango tree are prescribed. By this Upāsanā *Māruti* confers wealth, food, sons, grandsons, good fortune, success, intellect, dignity and victory.

The recitation of some stanzas of the *Vālmiki Rāmāyaṇa* is prescribed for the Upāsanā, these stanzas are chosen from the *Suṅdarakāṅḍa*, the *sarga* thirty six and two. It is held that daily recitation of these stanzas is very important in the Māruti Upāsanā.

Apart from all these methods of the Upāsanā of Māruti, He is positively worshiped before Śri Rāma's worship.

3 Śakti Upāsanā

Vedic

(i) Rātri Sūkta

This Sūkta finds its place in the tenth maṅḍala of the Ṛgveda. It contains eight stanzas. The idea is : the *Rātridevi* i.e. Goddess of Night holds the roots of the universe. She bears the creation; see the first verse, *"Rātri vyakhyadāyati purutrā devyā kṣabhiḥ visvā adhi śriyo'dhitā*." It means the goddess Night holds the universe and displays the objects and the results of their works. The second ṛcā says that the goddess Night governs the deities in the heaven and the beings on the Earth, and of course, she will spread the light after some time. The third ṛcā says that the goddess Night is the cause of the dawn who spreads happiness. The next ṛcā says : O Night, we sleep soundly by your arrival and the birds also sleep in their nests. The fifth ṛcā describes how the people, animals birds and travellers sleep in the night. The sixth ṛcā is a prayer which requests the goddess to remove the ignorance and vices like anger, greed etc. The seventh ṛcā addresses Uṣā to quit the darkness of ignorance. The eighth ṛcā praises the goddess Night. It says that the *Rātri* is like a cow who gives milk, She is the daughter of the sky; by Her grace the singer of the Sūkta conquers the enemies, and she is requested to accept the offerings of havis.

This Sūkta asks to throw away the ignorance, egoistic nature and the vices and to become purified, after which a worshipper can see the real light of knowledge, i.e. *Uṣā*; therefore this Sūkta has become popular.

It is a tradition to recite this Śūkta before the reading of *Durgā Saptaśati*, in *Devi* Upāsanā.

(ii) Śri Sūkta

Śri is ṭhe name of *Ādyāśakti* of *Iśvara*. *Ādyaśakti* is the immanant power of *Iśvara* which cannot be separaṭed from Him and from whom all the creatures get their power. Śri Sukta iṣ the prayer to this *Ādyāśakti* of *Iśvara*. All the sects viz; *Vaiṣṇava, Śaiva, Gāṇapatya, Saura, Śākta* have accepted *Śri Sūkta* as a part of daily worship in their disciplines. All the forms of *Devi* are included in the name *Śri*. *Devi Purāṇa* says, "*Lalitā Śāradā, Lakṣmirekaiva Bhagavatyumā*." People belonging to all sects recite this Sūkta, it is famous as Lakṣmi Sūkta, because it confers the wealth, the happiness, the health, the food, the victory which are necessary for prestige, name and fame in the world. *Devi Purāṇa* gives this definition of *Lakṣmi* in the verse. "*Jnānaisvaryasukhārogyadhana-dhānyajayādikam lakṣma yasyāḥ samuddiṣtam Lakṣmiti nigadyate.*"

Śri Sūkta finds its place in the annexure-*Khila*-section of the Ṛgveda. It occurs in the first sixteen mantras of the sixth khila of the second *adhyāya*. The good results of the recitation of this Sūkta i.e. '*phalaśruti*' follows in the next thirteen Ṛcās.

The Ṛṣis of this Sūkta are *Ānanda, Kardama, Ciklita* and *Indirā-suta*. Four metres are used for this Sūkta namely, *Anuṣṭubha, Bṛhati, Triṣṭubha* and *Prastārapaṅkti*. The deities are *Śri* and *Agni*. *Agni* is mentioned here by the name of *Jātaveda*. *Yāskācārya* mentioned three names of Agni in *Nirkuta* viz; *Agni, Jātaveda* and *Vaiśvānara*.[1]

In the Vedic period, it was a procedure to adore *Agni* first and to invoke other deities afterwards through Him, because *Agni* is said to be the mouth of gods. Accordingly, this Sūkta follows the tradition of asking Agni to call *Lakṣmi*, in the first *Ṛcā*, the verse is, "*... Lakṣmim Jātavedo mamāvaha*." This Sūkta compares *Lakṣmi's* colour with gold. It further says that *Lakṣmi* wears golden and sliver ornaments, and she looks pleasant like the Moon.[2] In the second Ṛcā the devotee calls *Lakṣmi* to confer on him the cattle, the wealth, the friends, the servants, the sons and the grandsons, and praises *Lakṣmi* who comes in the chariot followed by horses and elephants. She is beyond description, has a smiling face, kind nature and she makes gods, like Indra, happy. So the devotee surrenders to her. He humbly requests her because she is able to give him the fruit of *Bilva* tree which destroys ignorance and poverty, as this tree is the outcome of *Lakṣmi's* penance.[3] In the next seven to fifteen mantras he requests her to confer on him wealth and to dispel poverty. He asks the Ṛṣis *Kardama* and *Ciklita* to come and stay with him, because they are sons of *Lakṣmi*. If they stay at his home, *Lakṣmi* will naturally come to meet her sons. The sixteenth ṛcā asks the devotee to recite this Sūkta every now and then with purified body and mind. "*Yaḥ śuci prayato bhutvā juhuyādāj yamanvaham. Sūktam pañcadaśarcāñca śrikāmaḥ satatam japet.*"

Each ṛcā of this Sūkta is treated as a separate mantra and number of cycles of recitations of each mantra has been fixed according to the desired goal of the devotee. The details are given in the *Mantrakalpārṇava* and the *Lakṣmiyāmala*. The brief description follows: The number of japa of first *ṛcā* is one lakh at the rate of three thousands a day. Each letter of the second *ṛcā* is to be recited for eleven thousand times. Third *ṛcā* is to be recited one thousand times daily for twelve years. Fourth ṛcā is to be chanted for eight lakhs times. The break-up and the procedure is like this : one hundred recitation each day, but on Friday you must do three thousand recitations. On the full Moon day it is recited for five hundred times. The fifth *ṛcā* is to be chanted by sitting near a cow in a cow shed for one thousand times per day, the japa of each letter of the *Ṛcā* is prescribed to be chanted three thousand times. The sixth *ṛcā* is to chanted for eleven lakh times. The food made with fruits of *Bilva* tree is prescribed to be eaten during that period. The process of Upāsanā with the seventh ṛcā is seen in *Śri Ratnakośa*. Here the devotee has to take mild *Sātvika* food and he has to tell the rosary of coral for *japa*. The number of *japa* is thirty two lakh. This *japa* is to be done at night after worshipping *Śri Yantra* with offerings like flowers, fruits etc. The Upāsanā with eighth *ṛcā* is prescribed in the *Vaikhānasa Vidyā*. The *japa* is to be done for six thousand times. The Upāsanā of the tenth and the eleventh *ṛcās* is given in *Mantrakalpārṇava*. The tenth *ṛcā* is to be chanted for eight lakhs times and eleventh ṛcā is to be recited by sitting near cows in a cow shed for one lakh times per letter. The Upāsanā with twelfth mantra is prescribed in *Suktārthasaṅgraha*. This *japa* is to be done for the sixtyfour thousand times. The Upāsanā of the thirteenth *ṛcā* is given in the *Mantrakalpārṇava*. The *japa* of this mantra is to be chanted for thirty six thousand times at the rate of three thousands per day sitting on the banks of a river or a lake. The upāsanā with the fourteenth *ṛcā* is given in the *Śritatva*. This *japa* is commenced in the night of the fifth lunar day and to be recited for one thousand times per night for ten days. The Upāsanā of the fifteenth and the sixteenth *ṛcās* is prescribed in the *Mantrakalpārṇava*. The *Ṛṣi* of the fifteenth *ṛcā* is *Kuber*. The sixteenth ṛcā is to be recited for three thousand and eight times per day sitting on conglomeration of the grains. If a devotee recites this *ṛcā* for five lakh times—with a rosary of Sapphires, he conquers enemies. If a devotee recites this mantra for nine lakhs times, sitting on a woollen or grass mat, he knows *Vidyās*. This mantra bestows all mundane objects including a kingdom.

After completion of the prescribed number of recitation of each mantra, the oblations of butter, curd, milk, *samidhā* (sacred fuel) white *Tila*, the leaves of *Bilva* tree etc. are to be offered and the *pujā* of a married *Brāhmin* woman is to be undertaken for getting the desired results of this Upāsanā.

Later Devi Upāsanā

The worship or Upāsanā of Divine *Śakti* is famous and is faithfully practised all over India. It is the Divine power worshiped in the form of the Mother Goddess with various names. The power or the Energy of all pervading Omniscient and Omnipotent Parabrahma Pramātman is called Divine Mother. She is called *Mātā, Ambicā, Pārvati, Devi, Mahālaksmi, Mahāsarasvat, Mahākāli, Durgā, Maheśini, Cāmauṅdā. Reṇukā, Kumāri, Brahmāṇi, Viṅdhyāvāsini, Bagalāmukhi* and by so many different names. Mostly she is known as *Śakti* and *Devi*.

The word śakti is derived form the root 'Śak', meaning "to be able" and the suffix 'ktin'. The volatile dynamic impulsive character part of any object, which is immanent in itself is called "śakti" i.e. the Power or the Energy of the said object. For example take Fire (*Agni*) and its character of burning. Both are inseparable from each other. That is the *śakti* for *Agni*. With the same analogy, the creation of the universe, its preservation, its maintenance and its destruction is an inseparable or immanent power of Brahman, which is called *Śakti* in Sanskrit Literature.

In India the worship of *Devi* is as ancient as the Sanskrit literature itself. In the Ṛgveda this *Śakti* is identified by various names as *Uṣā, Sarasvati, Aditi, Ilā, Rātri* etc., and the sūktas for them are abundantly available in the script. In the Yajurveda there is a reference to an oblation to *Sarasvati*. There is a *Devi* sūkta and a *Śri* sūkta in the veda. The Tantra, the technique of the worship of *Śakti*, or *Devi*, is seen in the *Saubhāgya kānd* of the Atharvaveda. We find in Upaniṣad the famous similie of the *Puruṣa* and the *Prakṛti* for *Paramātman* and His Divine Power. In the Mahābhārata *Devi* is mentioned by the name of '*Durgā*'.

The five great natural-entities called paṅcāmbahābhutas are various forms of energies. The existence of life and the progress of it are due to various forces of one Divine energy called *Śakti*. The power ascribed to Indra, Varuṇa, Sūrya, Maruta, Puṣan, Tvaṣtru, etc., in the vedas for a particular action is the power of *Paramātman*, and these Devatas are different manifestation of the same Energy or *Śakti*.

The important concept of *Śakti* or *Devi* in various scripture is as follows—*Śakti* is called *Devi*, goddess "*Namo devyai Mahādevyai śivāyai satatam namaḥ. Namaḥ prakṛityai bhadrāyai, niyataḥ praṇatāsmatām*." means I bow to Śivā, Devi, Prakṛiti who secures our welfare. Devi Atharvaśirsa says "*Sai śaṣṭo vasvaḥ śaiśekādaśā rudraḥ, saiśā dvadaśādityāḥa jñānānām cinmayānandā*."[3a] It means *Devi* herself is the eight *Vasus*, she is the elevan *Rudras*, she is the twelve *Ādityas*. She is the embodiment of Happiness.

In *Śvetāśvatar* Upaniṣad we read, "*Parasya saktirvividhā sruyate svābhāviki jnāna bal kriyā ca.*" It means *Śakti* is natural and reveals itself in many forms. She is Jñāna, Omniscient, power and Action i.e. Kriyā. In *Viṣṇu* Purāṇa there is a verse, "*Ekadeśasthitasyagner-jyotsnā vistāriṇi yathā. Parasya Brahmaṇaḥ śaktistatheda-makhilam jagat.*"[3a] it means as the light of the fire spreads afar but the fire stays unmoved, Parama Brahman stays unaltered and unmoved and the *Śakti* spreads throughout in the form of the Jagat.

Ahirbudhanya Saṃhitā says the same with some difference, "*Sarvabhāvanugā śaktirjyotsneve himadditeh. Candrasya candrikeveyam śivasys sahajā śivā.*"[3a] It means as the moon light spreads from the Moon the *Śakti* derives and spreads from *Śiva*.

Brahma Vaivarta Purāṇa says, "*Parabraham svarupā tvam satyā nityā sanātani. Sarvasvarupā sarveśā sarvādhārā Parātparā.*"[3a] It means *Śakti* is the Nature of Parabrahman. She is the Truth everlasting (Sanātan), she is without beginning and end, she is the essence of every thing, she is the master, she holds the world and she is omniscient. Nāradiya Purāṇa calls her, "*Sarvādyā tu bhavechaktirānandaghana gocarā Brahmarupā cidānandā parabrahmaiva kevalam.*"[3a] It means *Śakti* is the foremost entity of the Universe. She is full of joy, she is Brahmarupā, and Brahman itself. Śiva Purāna says, "*Śakti svābhāvikotasya vidyā viśvalaksaṇā. Ekānekasvarupeṇa bhāti manoriva prabhā.*"[3a] It means Śakti is naturally His knowledge. Śakti is the manifestation of the almighty with its essential nature of the creation and preservation of the universe. She is the only Power in the universe unfolding elegantly with the quality of reigning the universe. Mahopaniṣad Sūtasaṃhitā says, "*Svātmi svaparispandeḥi sphuratyacaiscidārṇavā, tanmayaiva sphuratyachatrevormirivārṇave.*"[3a] It means Śakti is the spontaneous manifestation of Paramātman himself. She evolves out of Him as the tides spring out of the ocean. *Śrimad Śankarācārya* says in his Bhavānibhujangam Stotra, "*Vinodāya caitanyamekam vibhājya dvidhā devi jivaḥ śivasceti nāmḥā,*" It means there is only self existing entity known as *Caitany*—Consciousness—*Śiva*. It bisects itself to become Devi-Śakti as one part of it. In his Brahmasutra Bhāṣya, *Śankarācārya* says, "*Na hi tvayā vinā parameśvarasya śruṣtatvam sambhavati. Śaktirahitasya tasya pravrutyunupapatteḥe.*"[4] It means "O Devi, without your help God cannot create the universe. You are absolutely essential for the creation of the universe."

Brahman i.e. paramātman transcends the universe. He produces the universe from his Power : *Śakti,* and enjoys his creation. He divides Himself into two. One is he himself and other is his concert Devi. We find this idea in Bṛhadāraṇyaka Upaniṣad as, "*...sa dvitiyamaichat sa imamevātmānam dvidhāpātayat tatah patiśca patnisca abhavat.*"[5]

It is said in the Ṛgveda that *Vāk śakti* is a mantra mother and gives birth to the *Ṛk,* the *Sāman* and the *Yajus.*[6] She is called as *Sarasvati* who is an active power of Brahman proceeding from Him.

Māya and Brahman, Lakṣmi and Nārāyaṇa, Pārvati and Śiva are the two appearances of the Brahman as the two faces of the same coin. Therefore Parabrahman Paramātmān is worshipped in the form of *Ardhanāriśvara* i.e. half body of a male and half of a female. *Devi Bhāgavat* is a text book for *Devi* upāsakas. It says, "*Sarvam khalvidamevāham nānyadasti sanātanam.*"[7] *Devi* says, that everything which is animate and inanimate is she herself. Nobody was before her and she is everlasting.

In short *Devi* is a name of an inherent Power of the Lord himself without which he can do nothing. We experience this Śakti in various ways i.e. Producing, Maintaining and destroying power. See the verse, "*Ekeva śaktihi parameśvarasya. Vividhā vadanti vyavahārakāle. Bhoge bhavāni, puruṣeśu lakṣmi, kope tu durgā. Pralaye tu kāli.*" It means the single Power of God is described by various names in different situations. When she maintains the world she is called *Bhavāni.* When she is in action (*kartṛtva*) she is called Lakṣmi. In her angry appearance she is called Durgā. In destructive stance she is called Kāli. There is the third form in which we obtain together both Śiva and Śakti (the form *Tripursundari*). Śakti is worshipped by the *Śaiva,* the *Vaiśṇava* and the other sects of Upāsakas. *Devi Bhāgavat, Durgā, Saptaśati, Devi Purāṇa, Devi Mahātmya* are main scriptures of Devi worshippers.

Devi worshippers are called Śāktas. Śāktas have Āgamas for the guidance in their Upāsanā. There are different ways of Devi worship which are called the Śākta Mārga. Tantra mārga is one of them. There are lot of books on the Tantra mārga, these are about sixtyfour or so. these books have their origin in the Ṛgveda, in the hymns addressed to a particular goddess. Some of the books found their origin in the Purāṇas. The Tantra books contain treaties on the theology, the *Yoga,* the construction of temples, the images etc. The occult side of the Yoga also-plays an important part in Śaktism. the superhuman powers are attained by the use of the *Bijas*, the *Mantras*, the Yantras, the Kavacas, the Nyāsa and the Mudrās. (particular type of formation of fingers of hands).

In the vedic times the meaning of the *Mantra* was "an inspired stanza", but according to *Śaktas* the meaning of the *Mantra* is not the same. It is a letter of the alphabet, which is instinct with the power of *Śakti*. It may also be a clustei of alphabet or words formed from these letters. These mantra words possess a power capable of doing good or evil to oneself and to one's enemies if properly recited according to prescribed formula. These mantras act like a spell or charm.

A *Bija* is only one letter to denote the particular powerful form of a deity or its characters. The *bijas* are related to the *Nāḍi*. *Nāḍi* means an occult channel which is in the human trunk. The main *Nāḍies* are three, *Iḍā, Piṅgalā*, and *Suṣumnā*. The *Suṣumnā* is important from the *Tantra* point of view, because by the utterance of bija mantra the *Kuṇḍalini Śakti* (the serpent power) awakes which is supposed to be asleep (dormant) in the lower side of the spinal cord. *Kuṇḍalini* goes upwards from this *Suṣumnā* channel which is connected with six great circles, called *Cakras*. There is a controversy over the number of these cakras but generally it is held that they are six. Each *cakra* possesses an occult power. *Kuṇḍalini* travels upward from the one *cākra* to the other and finally reaches to the *Sahasrāra Cakra* in which Brahman or *Śiva* stays. When *kuṇḍalini* meets with *Śiva*, the devotee who performs the Upāsanā by *Bīja mṅntra* is said to be successful in attaining his ultimate goal, i.e. unification with God.

Yantras are the diagrams inscribed on a metallic plate, often of copper, and these diagrams are supposed to possess an occult power. The different diagrams have different meanings. For example a triangle with its apex upwards represents *Mahādevā* who is fire personified.[8] The triangle with its apex downwards symbolises water or humidity and God *Viṣṇu*. Both the above triangles joined together Symbolises *Brahmadeva*. *Śri Cakra* is most important of these diagrams. This *Cakra* represents the orb of the earth. In the center of this *Cakra* there is a drawing of a woman's face to represent *Śakti*. *Śri Śaṅkācārya* is stated to have placed *Śri Cakras* in each of the four monasteries founded by him.

Kavaca means a sect mark consisting of lines, curves, circles spots and designs which are painted over the body of the

Upāsakas. The user of these marks comes under the protection of the particular deity. The *śākta* mark is generally the *tripuṇḍra* painted with charcoal dust pasted with charcoal butter. This *kavaca* protects against evil influences. There is also a practice of wearing a stone, a metal piece or a piece of paper charged with the mantras.

Touching various parts of the body mentally or physically by fingers while reciting the mantra is called *Nyāsa*.

The *Mudrās* are different formations of the fingers of hands. The particular posture of the fingers is supposed to possess some occult meaning and power.

Devi Bhāgvat is a main *Purāṇa* text of *Śaktism* and the *Sakti* Upāsakas. Devi Purāṇa and the Mārkaṅdeya Purāṇa consist the description of Śakti. The Upaniṣad which prescribe the *Tantra* are *Kaul, Tripurmahopaniṣad, Advait Bhāvanā, Kālika, Tāra, Aruṇopaniṣad* etc.

Cults

There are three main centres of Śaktism. One is in Kashmir, second is in Kāṅchi and the third is in Kāmākhyā (*Āsam*). Kashmir and Kānchi are the centres of *Śrividyā* discipline. Kāmākhya is the centre of *Kaul* discipline.

Srividyā— 'Datta Saṃhita' is the main scripture or the text book regarding this worship. This book written by 'Śri Dattātraya originally contained one hundred and eight thousand stanzas, compiled in fifty volumes. Afterwards Haitāyana Sumedhā further shortened the text and named it "Paraśurāma Kalpasūtra".

Śrividyā has three paths of Upāsanā. One is *Kālikrama* or *Kuṅḍalini krama* or *Kādi viyā*. Second is *Suṅdari krama* or *Haṅsa krama* or *Hādi vidyā*. Third is *Tārā karma* or *Samavarodhin krama* or *Sādi vidya. Kālikrama* is *satvaguṇa* dominant, *Suṅdarikrama* is *Rājoguṇa* dominant and *Tārakrama* is *Tamoguṇa* dominant. One who performs the Upāsanā by these paths becomes Devi and thereafter merges into Śiva, refer the verse, *"Sundari tāriṇi kāli kramadikṣābhigāmini. Kramapurano Maheśāni kramātśambhurbhaviśyati"*.[8a] This *Krama* upāsanā is performed five times in a day. The form of deity as Upāsya is different at each time. In *Kadi vidyā, Kāli* is in the form of '*Kāmakalākāli*' in morning time, at noon she is called `*Bhuvaneśvari*', in the evening she is in the form of `*chāmuṅḍa*' at night she is `*Samayakubjā*' and at midnight she is `*Kādi paṅcadaśi*'. *Mahātripurasuṅdari* is the deity in *Hādividyā*. She is worshipped in the form of `*Ādyākāli*' in the morning, at noon she is `*Tārā*', in the evening she is `*Chinnamastā*', at night she is `*Bagalā*' at midnight she is `*Hadipaṅcadaśi*'. Tārā is the deity in *Sādividyā*, she is called `*Anirudhā sarasvati dakshiṇākāli*' in the morning, at noon she is `*Tārā*', in the evening *Bālā*', at night `*Jnānasarasvati*' and at midnight `*Sādipancadasi*'.[8a]

Kashmir School : In Kashmir school of Śākta known as *Trikaśāsana*, (Trika : 'Triad') the Upāsanā of *Śakti* is done with motherly passion, i.e. *Mātṛ bhāva* or *Mātṛkā Śakti*. *Puṇyānanda*, a well know writer of the *Trika* school has quoted several references from the *Śvetāśvatara Upaniṣad* in his commentary on *Kāmakalāvilās* (9) "*Eko'varṇo Śaciyogat.....*" etc. *Abhiṇavagupta* the most famous writer quotes the *Bṛahadāraṇyaka Upaniṣad* II 5.29 in his '*Pratyabhiñāvimarśiṇi* 1-1-5, in support of *Trik* doctrine that the *Vimarśā Śakti* is the *Prakāsa* or the ever-illuminating principle of *Paripurṇāhantā* or what we may call "completeness consciousness of the self."[10] He quotes the *Kaṭhopanisad* II-2 in support of his theory of the *Śakti*. *Kṣemarāja* quotes the *Kaṭha* IV-1 in his commentary of *Pratyabhiñāhṛdaya*, sutra 18, to explain the Yogic process for the realisation of true self. The Kenopanisad has the story of Umā Haimavati in its third Kānd.

Trikaśāsana (triad) has three main principles.[1] Śiva—the Supreme called Prakāśa,[2] Śakti—a personal entity of the nature of perfect consciousness of the self.[3] *Aṇu*—the individual soul. *Mālinivijayottara Tantra* is an authoritative book of this school. This school has faith in the *Advaita siddhānta*, and call is *Iśvarādvait*. The school says that Śiva is *Prakāśarūpa* and Śakti is *Vimarśārūpa*. "*Yā devi sarva buteśu Śaktirupeṇa samsthitā ṇamastasyai, namastasyai, namastasyai, namo namaḥ*"[10a] It means I bow three times to Devi who is present in every atom as its own Power. This mantra is the main theme of this school.

Mālinivijayottarvārttika says, "*Śaktisca no śaktimato vibhinnā. Tenaitinobhedamiyam pṛthaktvam. Amātrutāyam na ca śaktirasti. Tena svarupam na hi śaktiyuktam.*"[11] It means Śakti, again, is not different from the *Śaktimat*. Hence this separation does not lead to its distinction. In the absence of the *Śaktimat* Śakti does not exist.

Mālinivijayottar Tantra gives the description of *Umā* with Parameśa. His divine consort i.e. *Maheśini*.[11] There are the details of the cosmic form of evolution of the Śakti.[12] There is the description of Yogic methods by which the devotee merges into Śakti.[13] There is also the theory of mantras .[14] And there is a description of *Dikṣā*.[15] All these are explained specially from the Śakti point of view.

Śakti plays in this world with the three modes namely. *Icchā, Jñānā, Kriyā*. It is a play of *Māyā* Śakti by which the physical and mental world appears before the self. Similar concepts are seen in Tantrasāra of Abhinava Gupta. It says (i) God's independence is *Ānanda Śakti* (ii). The feeling of "divine wonder' at His independence is *Icchā Śakti* (iii) The power of knowing without reference to feeling or emotion is *Jñāna Śakti* (iv) The power of shining or revealing his own self is *Cit-Śakti* (v) The power of creating any and every form is *Kriyā Śakti*[16] There are further sub classifications of these appearances of the *Śakti*. They are tabulised below for an easy onlook.

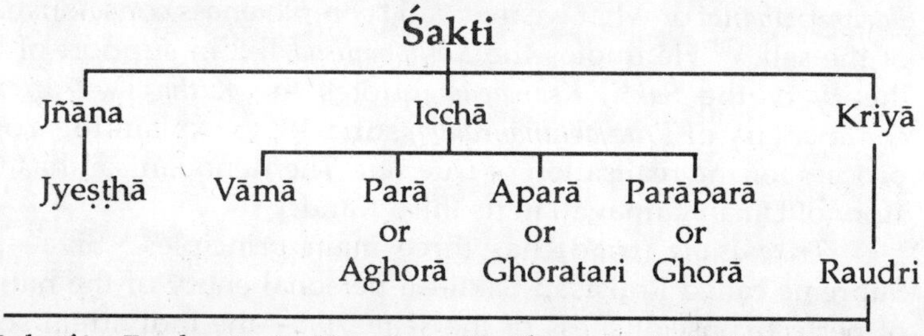

Maheśi, Brahmāṇi, Kumāri, Vaiśṇavi, Aeindri, Yāmyā, Chāmundā, Yogiśi

The word *Kriyā* has a special *Trik* (triad) sense as *'Spanda'*. *Spanda* means " a kind of spontaneous self-initiated vibration not stimulated by any thing" i.e. *Sphurattā*.[17] When one is ignorant of this *Kriyā Śakti*, one falls into the worldly bondage of ignorance (*ajñāna*), but if one comes to know it, one realises his true self. The ignorance is because of *Māyā Śakti* which is an external manifestation of *Vimarśā Śakti*.

Other *Trik* works are *'Svacchanda'* and *'Vijñānabhairava'* and some other books.

It is understood in Śakta Sect that there are three psychological moods in every person, namely (1) *Paśubhāva* i.e. animal—like passions (2) *Vira bhāva* i.e. to fight with the animal passions and conquer them (3) *Divya Bhāva* i.e. Divine Nature. These are looked upon as three progressive steps of a Upāsaka towards the Divine Life. According to these three moods the seven *Ācāras* are specified in Śakta namely, *Vedācāra, Vaiṣṇavācāra, Śaivācāra, Dakṣincāra, Vāmācāra, Siddhāntacāra,* and *Kaulācār*. Out of these *Dakṣiṇācāra* and *Vāmacāra* are relatively more well-known.

Dakṣiṇacāra—In *Dakṣinacāra* the people worship the deity mainly in the temples. The deities are the *Grāmdevatā,* the *Kula devatā,* and the *Iṣṭdevatā. Dakṣiṇācāra* devotee has two separate characteristic classes of the rituals—(1) One in which the worship is strictly according to the Vedic and the Purāṇic rites. (2) The other in which the worship is according to the Purāṇic rites but the devotees offer wine and flesh to the *Devi*. In the first practice the Bhakti element is predominant and the devotees follows *'Devi Bhāgavat'* faithfully. They worship *Mahālakṣmi* or *Śri, Pārvati Umā* or *Gauri* and *Durgā devi. Devi Durgā* has angry and heroic posture, but when she stands quietly she is called *Śāntā-Durgā*.

Vāmācāra—The chief deities of this discipline are the same with *Dakṣiṇacāra* i.e. *Devi* or *Śakti,* or *Durgā* or *Kāli*. But in this *Ācāra* the unfair postures of the *Śakti* in the form of fiendly goddess like *Nāyikās,* Yoginis, Dākinis, Śākinis are also prayed. The master God of *Śakti* is termed as Bhairava which is actually the form of *Śiva*.

Kaulācāra—The almighty Paramātman who is *Śiva* is without any tradition or origin and he is always described as *'Akul'*, whereas *Śakti* originated from *Śiva* therefore she is described a *'Kula'*. The worship rituals of *Śakti* or *Kula* means *Kaulācāra*. This worship presupposes that all the objects in this world are only the offshoots of the *Śakti* and all of them have equal value and importance. This thought is made clear in the verse *"Kardame candane; bhinne putre śatṛu tathā pryie. Smaśāne bhavane devi tathaiva kāncane truṇe. Na bhedo yasya deveśi sa kaulaḥ parikirtitaṇ.*[21]

Kāmākhyā is the main centre of this cult. This discipline has two sub categories namely, Purva Kaula and Uttar Kaul. The discipline gives importance to five factors called panca 'M' kāras.

These are Madya (wine), Māṅsa (meat), Matsya (fish) Mudrā (posture), Maithuna (copulation). The meaning of these words follows—

Madya — It is the nectar of *Sahasrār Cakra*.
Māṅsa — It is the meat of an animal of sin.
Matsya — Incoming and outgoing breath.
Mudra — Postures during yogic meditation.
Maithuna — It is the unification of Śiva and Śakti.

With this symbolic meaning of 'M' kar words, the acceptance of 'M' kar worship essentially means the worshiper has to kill the animal of sin with the sword of knowledge, has to train the inhaled and exhaled breaths to command the vital breath travelling in *Suṣumnā* duct, to fix himself in the yogic posture and by awakening the Kuṅḍalini to drink the nectar from the *Sahasrāra cakra*.

The worship of a circle is also prescribed in *Kaulācāra*. This circle represents the yogic symbol in the sky of heart. It is related with the unlimited flow of Time.

Forms of Devi—There are various forms of Devi according to her different moods. Mahālakṣmi, Mahāsaraswati and Mahākāli—these three forms represent the three modes of *Prakṛti Guṇās* namely *Satvaguṇa, Rjoguṇa* and *Tamoguṇa* respectively. The other well-known forms are Aṣṭbhujā, Aṣṭādaśbhujā, Tripursundari and Śābari. The brief description follows—

Mahālakṣmi—Mahālakṣmi is *Satvaguṇa pradhāna* Devi. In Maharashtra, Kolhapur is a centre of the Mahālakṣmi Upāsakas. The following image of Devi is described for meditation in Durgāsaptaśati, *"Akṣrakparaṣum gadeśukuliśam padmamdhanuśkuṅḍikām. Daṅdam śaktimasim ca carmajalajam ghantām sudhābhājanam. Pāśasūdārśane ca dadhatim hasṭaihi pravālaprobhām. Seve sairibhamardinimiḥ Mahālakṣmim sarjosthitām.*[18] It means we meditate upon *Mahiśāsurmardini Lakṣmi* who has a smiling face and who sits on a lotus, who holds akṣamāla, paraśu, gadā, an arrow, vajra, lotus, bow, danda, Śakti, sword, śankḥa (conch), bell, pot of nectar, śula (trident) and a pāśa (a noose) in her hands. Mahālakṣmi also possesses some other names viz. Kamalā, Śri, and Padmā. She is perceived with two hands when she is worshipped with Bhagavān Viṣṇu. In this posture she confers blessings and distributes wealth with her two hand. She is perceived as having four hands when she is worshipped as *Kamalāsanā* i.e. sitting on a lotus. In this posture she holds a lotus, a leaf of bilva tree, a nectar pot and a *śankḥa* (conch) in here hands and two elephants are shown besides her. Knowledge, Power, Valour, Wealth can be acquired by her Upāsanā. Mahāḷakṣmi is also perceived as concert of Lord Viṣṇu, serving Him who is reclining on the King serpent. The *Ahantā* of Bhagavān Viṣṇu is called *Mahālakṣmi* or *Nārāyani*. She is without any blemish i.e. stainless personality, She is munificent, she creates, sustains and destroys the world, does good to the devotees.

Mahāsarasvati—The Durgā Saptaśati gives the description of Mahāsarasvati as *"Ghantāśulahalāni śankhamusale cakram dhanussāyakam. Hastābha-irdadhatim ghanāntvitolasa ccitāṅśutulya prabhām. Gauridehasamudbhavām trijagatamādhārabhutam mahapurvamatra sarasvatimanubhaje śumbhādidaityārd-inim."*[19] It means we bow to *Devi* Mahāsarasvati who holds in her hands a bell, a trident, an anchor, *Śaṅkha, musala,* a whee, a *dhanuṣa* (bow), and an arrow, who is born of the body of *Gauri,* who shines like the Moon in the Autumn, who is the sustainer of three words and the destroyer of the demon Śumbha and other rākṣas.

Sarvasvati is goddess of speed and light. The word sarasvati is derived from the root *'Sru'* meaning to move at speed. All the knowledge springs from her. She is the goddess of *Vāk,* i.e. speech. The variations of the sound, wind and even of the atom originate from her *Kriyāśakti* only. It is said that Bhagavān *Aśvalāyan* has obtained *Brahmajñāna* by performing her Upāsanā with the recitation of her sotra, later became known as *'Sarasvati Daśaśloki'*. In the sixth śloka of the said stotra she is described as *Vagiśvari* i.e. the Goddess of speech.

Kāli or Mahākāli—Mahākāli is worshipped with the offerings of animal sacrifices and wine. She is shown with a gaping mouth, free fanned hair, four hands, garland of the skulls of demons around her neck, sword held in one hand and dead body in the other hand, she is black in colour and has terrible teeth. she is worshipped most in Bengāl. This posture is *Tamoguṇātmaka*. Kālipurāṇa says that *Kāli* is born from *Mahāmāyā*. Her main job is to destroy the evil souls. She is called *Ādirupiṇi*. Read this verse, *"Kālasaṅkalanāt kāli sarveśāmādirūpiṇi kālātvādedibhutatvādyākāliti giyate."*[7a]

It means, Devi controls the Time i.e. *Kāla* therefore she is called *Kāli*. She is the beginning of *kāla* and from her only Kāla has come into existence. And she is called *Ādyākāli*.

Often the deities are given a form to facilitate Upāsanā. In Kālikāpurāṇa her form for Upāsanā is described as "*Śavārudḥām, mahabhimām ghoradanṣtrāmhasanmukhim. Caturbhujām Khaḍaga-munḍavarābhayakarāmśivām Muṅdamālādharām Devim laljivhām digambaram*"[17a] It means *Devi* is pressing her leg on a dead victim, she is very furious, has terrible teeth, smiles gently, has four arms, holds a sword and a human skull but gives *abhaya* (assurance of protection) to her devotees. She wears a garland of skulls and lives in the cremation yard. The devotee has to meditate on this form of Devi.

Aṣtabhujā or Aṣtādaśabhujā Devi—Devi Bhāgavat describes, "*Sarvāngabhuṣaṇā devi sarvaratnopaśobhitā. Na mānuṣi nāsuri sā divyarupā manoharā. Simhārudhā ayudhādharā castādaśākarā varā. Sa nādam kurute devi laksyate madagarvitā.*"[20] It means Devi wears golden ornaments and jewellary. Her appearance is beautiful and attractive and yet mysterious. She has eighteen hands with many weapons, sat on a lion, has full command and she is roaring. Devi has two sets of hands eighteen: *Aṣṭādaśbhūjā*; as well as eight hands i.e. *Aṣtabhujā Devi*.

Tripurasuṅdari—The unity of *Śiva* and *Śakti bhāva* is the *Tripurabhāva*. *Śiva* and *Śakti* are in the form of *Kāmeśvara* and *Kāmeśvari*. Their equality (*sāmyāvasthā*) is a sundri i.e. a beautiful lady. Pure Brahman without any upādhi is kāmeśvara and the svātmā (own self) who is ever happy and with upādhi is *Kāmeśvari, Tripurasundari*. She is the root of creation, the Truth, the happiness and called *Lalitāmbikā*. Upāsaka worships her in the form of the moon. The moon has sixteen phases (*kalā*). The sixteenth phase is always the complete appearance. *Devi* is like the sixteenth phase, that is complete in her own exposition, so she is called *Śoḍaṣi*. She is the embodiment of beauty and happiness. To perceive *Lalitāmbikā* with advait concept is the main aim of Upāsakas. *Gaudapāda* says that *Idā, Piṅgalā* and *Suṣumnā* nadis are called *Tripurā*. *Vāmeśvara Tantra* says that *Jñāna Śakti, Kriyā Śakti* and *Icchā Śakti* are called *Tripurā*.

Śābari—The yogis of Nātha *Paṅth (Navanāthas)* evolved different maṅtras for different deities of *Śakti* and the names of the deities are compiled in the mantra itself. If the devotee recites and worships these mantras with strict discipline he gets the reward from the deity of the mantra. These mantras are verses which praise different deities and the praise is *Śabari Kavitva,* and the worship method is called *Śabari vidyā*. The main goddess is *Sakti Devi* who is riding on a Tiger and who is called *Śābari-devi*.

Śākta sect has different upāsanā practices. The masters of the *Śakta panth* however give a substantial importance to the Upāsanā with the help of different occult diagrams called yantras. Out of these *Yantras Śri Yantra* is important. This yantra shows unification of *Pinḍa* and *Brahmānd* (Micro and Macro Universe). *Ācārya Sānkara* had worshipped this *yantra*. The *Śākta* literature holds *Śri yantra* as the body of god and the mantras relating to the yantra as the soul of God. Tantrikas believe that after the intense meditation followed by the recitation of particular mantras the devotee perceives a definite figure of *Yantra* in the space. This yantra can be drawn and charged with occult power with mantras and it can be seen upon as the physical nature of the particular Godhead. This *yantra* is useful to concentrate the mind and to experience the unity with upāsya deity.

Śri Yantra—*Śri yantra* consists of two sets of triangles. In one set the apexes of all the triangles are directed upwards, whereas in the second set all the triangles point downwards. There is a central spot at the centre of the yantra. At the four sides of this centre point there are nine triangles out of them five triangles pointing upwards and four pointing downwards. The upward triangles are for seen as *Bhagavati Devi* or *Śiva Yuvati*. The downwards triangles are for *Śiva* which are also called *Śrikanṭh*. These five triangles symbolise the universal aspects like five tanmātrās, five sense organs, five *karmendriyas,* five types of breaths and also represent the physical side skin, flesh, bones, fat and blood. The downward four triangles represent *Cit*, Intellect, Ego, and the mind from universe point of view and from individual point of view they suggest nerves, semen, *Prāṇa* and *Jiva*. From the spiritual point of view these nine triangles are representatives of nine qualities of *Śiva*. The intermixing of these nine triangles produce forty three small internal triangles. There is lotus of eight petal around the inner circle and there is a sixteen petalled lotus outside the outer circle and there is *Bhupura* around the *Yantra*.

This Yantra shows development from all sides of the Universe and the devotee. There are also destructive and other types of *Yantras* which are used by different types of people for different purposes.

Popular Stotras—Maharṣi Agasti's *Mahālakṣmi Stotra* is popular and known as well as recited for destroying the poverty and the sorrows. This stotra has seventeen stanzas. A devotee surrenders himself to *Lakṣmi* and asks her to stay with him constantly. In the first nine stanza the devotee praises her eagerly. From the tenth stanzas onwards *Lakṣmi* stands before him and confers on him wealth and happiness and assures him protection from evils.

Saundaryalahari, Kanakadhārāstotra, Devyāparādhakṣmāpanstotra, Ambā aṣṭakam are popular stotras of *Devi* written by *Śri Śankarācārya. Mahālakṣmi kavaca* from *Brahmapurāna, Bhagvati Aṣṭakam, Śristotra* from *Angipurāna, Lakṣmisahsranāma stotra* from *Skandpurāṇa* are recited by *Devi* worshippers.

4. Sūrya Upāsanā

Vedic

Gāyatri Upāsanā

In this world each and every person wants to lead a well established and happy life. There are some people who desire to have a blissful life even after death. There are others who don't wish for material goodness but want the vision of God's *Sākśātkāra'* under the guidance of *Guru*. Man can become fully happy only when all his desires get fulfilled. The desires born in the mind. It is told in the *Śāstra* (Scriptures) that the mind is both pure and impure. The impure mind is said to be fully occupied with all types of desires 'good or bad'. The pure mind is one that is without desires. The purity of the mind is achieved by performing Upāsanā. *"Mana evatu manuṣyāṇam kāraṇam bandha mokṣyoḥ, Bandhāya viṣayasangi muktainirviṣayam manaḥ."*[A] It means the mind itself is the root cause of all the worldly bondages and unhappiness. Due to the rise of sensuous-*vaiṣyika*-thoughts it becomes bound and with the absence of such thoughts it becomes free and therefore is bereft of any sorrow or repentance.

Gāyatri Upāsanā is a kind of worship which leads to the purity of mind. The meaning of the word *'Gāyatri'* itself implies that the recitation of this mantra protects one from impure sensuous thoughts. The various śāstras say that one who recites this mantra with devotion and with correct pronunciation, will be protected from all types of impurities of this world. For example-(1) *"Pratigrahānnadośācca pātakādupāpatakāt, Gāyatri procaiyate tasmād gāyantām trāyate yataḥ."*[1] One who sings this verse is protected from *'pratigrahodośa, annadośa,* any other kind of errors, so it is called *'Gāyatri'*. The same meaning is observed in the following verses as (2) *"Gāyantām trāyate yasmād gāyatritataḥ smurtā."*[2] (3) *Gāyantām trāyate yasmād gāyatriti smritā budhaihi*[3]. (4) *Gātāram trāyate yasmād gāyatri ten gīyate.*[4]

The word *'Gāyatri'*is derived from the root *'gai'* of first conjugation, it means 'to sing'. In the Nirukta the meaning of the word *'Gāyatri'* is given as, *"Gāyatri gāyate stuti karmaṇaḥ*[5]; it means the singing of praise is *'Gāyatri'*. The meaning of *'Gāyatri'* is given in *Śatapathā Brāhmaṇa* like this, *"Sā haiṣā gayānstatre Prāṇavai gayānstatprāṇānstatre tad gayānstatre tasmad gāyatri nāma."*[6] It means, *Gāyatri* has protected gayān i.e.*prāṇa; prāṇa* is called *'gaya'*. These gayan are protected by gāyatri, so the world is called *'Gāyatri'*. Bṛhadāraṇyaka Upaniṣad also gives the same meaning.[7]

The other names of *'Gāyatri'* are *Sāvitri, Brahmagāyatri, Gurumantra, Vedamātā,* etc. The meter of this mantra is *Gayatri* so this mantra is called *'Gāyatri Mantra'*. This mantra is addressed to the Sun i.e. *Savitṛ*, and hence it is also called *Sāvitri'*. This mantra gives the information about Brahman, and it is an Upāsanā of Brahman, so it is called *'Brahma Gāyatri'*. In the thread bestowing ceremony (Upanayan), the Guru confers the upāsanā of this mantra on the *'Batu'*, (pupil) and therefore it is called *Gurumantra*. And this mantra is accepted as the mother of the Vedas so it is called *'Vedamātā'*.

The verse of the *'Gāyatri mantra'* is *"Om bhurbhuvaḥ svaḥ tastaviturareṇyam bhargo devasya dhīmahi dhiyoyonaḥ pracodayāt."*[8] The meaning is *"Om"* signifies the one syllable Brahman, Bhuhu, Bhuvaḥ, Svaḥ are the vyāṛhuties denoting the earth, the space, and the heaven". (These words are generally recited before various mantras.) "we meditate on the sun who spreads 'Pure Light' who destroys the obstacles in getting self knowledge. May the almighty Sun flash the flame of knowledge in our minds and intellect."

Every Ṛcā has its deity and its Ṛṣi. The deity of the *'Gāyatri Mantra'* is the Sun and the Ṛṣi is *Viśvāmitra*. The devotee prays to the Sun for bestowing the 'Purified intellect' on him. The correct guessing of the situation is necessary for the success. One who can discern correctly between proper and improper behaviour is capable of getting happiness and calmness in the life.

There are various Upāsanā processes prescribed by the scriptures, out of them three types are wellknown, namely, *"Japātmaka, Pāṭhātatmaka,* and *Havanātmaka Upāsanā."* In the Japātmaka Upāsanā there is a mere recitation of the mantra. The Pāṭhātmaka Upāsanā envisages continuous recitation of the entire *Gāyatri Stotra* or the hymn. In the Havanātmaka Upāsanā the havis is offered in *yajña* with the chanting of the *Gāyatri mantra*.

The deity *Gāyatri* is apprehended in three different female forms corresponding to the three periods of the day. Maharṣi Vedavyāsa named the female forms for the morning worship as the *'Gāyatri'*, for the noon worship as the *'Sāvitri'* for the evening worship as *'Sarasvati.'* However she is called *'Sandhyā'* at any time. The verse reads as *"Gāyatri nāmapurvāhne, Sāvitri madhyame dine Sarasvati ca sāyāhne, saiva Sandhyā triṣu smṛtā."* The appearances or the personalities of the three female forms are described in the following verses: (1) *"Om Prātargāyatri ravimaṇḍala madhyasthā raktavarṇā dvibhujā akṣasūtrakamanḍaludharā hansāsamnamārudhā brahmāṇi brahmadaivatyā kumari Ṛgvedāhṛtā dhyeyā."* It means the morning form of Gāyatri is who dwells in the centre of the sun, whose colour is red, who has two arms, who wears Rudrākṣa, a sacred thread and holds a bowl, who sits on a swan, who is a virgin girl, who is, Brahmāni, mentioned in the Ṛgveda. (2) *"Om madhyāhne Sāvitri ravimaṅ-ḍalamadhyasthā Krisṇavaraṇā, caturbhujā, trinetrā, śankhacakr-agadūpadmahastā, garuḍārudha yuvati vaiṣṇavi viṣṇudaivatyā yajurvedohrutā dhyeyā."* The afternoon appearance of the *'Gāyatri'* is *'Sāvitri'*, who dwell in the centre of the Sun, whose colour is black, who has four arms, holding a conch, a cakra, a mace, and a lotus, who sits on an eagle, who is young.,Vaiṣṇavi, and who is prescribed by the Yajurveda. (3) *"Om sāyahne sarasva-tiravimaṅḍalmdhyasthā śuklavarṇā caturbhujā triṣulḍamarupātre karā vṛśabhāsansamārudhā vṛdhā Rudrāṇi rudradevatyā Sāmavedarhuta dhyeyā"*. It means the evening form of *'Gāyatri'* is *Sarasvati*, who dwells in the centre of the Sun whose colour is white, who has four arms holding triśula (trident), damaru (a type of drum), and pot, who is rested on a bull. She is *Rudrāṇi* old and prescribed by the Sāmveda. (Gāyatri Rahasya Up has the same description with a little change)

We find similar forms of *Gāyatri* in *Devibhāgavat* for meditation.[9] Generally the process of *Gāyatri* Upāsanā consists of five successive steps, as *Āvāhana, Aṅganyāsa, Dhyāna, Japa,* and *Visrajan* (immersion). The verse of *Āvahana* i.e. ask to come, is, *"Om tejosi śukramsyāmṛitamasi, dhāmanāmasi priyam devānāmanādhruṣtam devyajanamasi"*.[10] It means, O *Gāyatri,* you are the brightness i.e. Teja, of the Brahman, you are the aim of the devotee, you deserve to be worshipped and praised, all maṅtras end in you, you are the victorious, the gods love you, you are the maṅtra of the upāsanā and a source of the worship. In the step of *Aṇganyāsa,* every part of the body is to be charged by the power of the maṅtra. So that the body can resist the power of the deity. The devotee meditates on the particular form of *Gāyatri* according to the appropriate period of the day. (Appropriate forms are already described). This is called the *Dhyāna* (meditation) process followed by the Japa. The Japa is to be recited only after the full concentration of the mind is achieved. This recitation continues for some fixed time. *Visrjan* (immersion) is the last step of the process. The verse of Visarjana is to *"Maheśa vadanotpannā viṣṇorhṛdaya sambhavā, brahmaṇā samanudjñātā gacha devi yatechayā."* It means "Devi, who is originated from Maheśa's mouth, who is evolved from Viṣṇu and who has all permission from Brahmā, you can go as you wish, good bye."

The *Gāyatri* maṅtra is a vedic maṅtra. It is a custom that after the thread bestowing ceremony the *'Baṭu'* deserves to follow the Upāsanā of the Gāyatri maṅtra. The Upāsanā of the *Gāyatri* is ultimately the Upāsanā of Parbrahman, Pramātman. *Devibhāgavat* says *"Parbahmaswarupā ca nirvāṇapadādayini, brahmatejomayi śaktistadudhiṣṭhātṛdevatā."*[11] It means *Gāyatri* herself is Parabrhamasvarupā, is the giver of Mokṣa, has the brightness and the energy of Brahman and Brahman is the God of *Gāyatri* herself.

Gāyatri is the most important maṅtra in Sanskrit literature. It is said in the Chāndogya Upaniṣad that, *"Gāyatri, vā idam sarvam bhutam, Yadidam, kiṅc, vāg vai gāyatri, vāg vā idam sarvam bhutam, gāyati ca trāyate ca"*.[12] It means every thing in this world in *Gāyatri*. The speech is *Gāyatri,* the speech is every thing, because the speech sings this maṅtra and protects the devotee by singing the *Gāyatri* mantra. Similar thought is expressed in the *Padmapurāṇa* as "*Gāyatri vedajanani, Gāyatri lokapāvani. Gāyatri na param jāpyam tad vijñāya mucyate.*"[13]. It means, *Gāyatri* is the mother of the Vedas. She purifies all the people. No other mantra is more excellent than *Gāyatri*. One who understands the meaning of this mantra becomes ultimately free form the *Sansāracakra*. (phenomenal occurrences). The same thing is repeated in the *Kurmapurāṇa* also.[14]

This mantra is not a hypnotization, nor only a simple prayer, but it is the meditative process in which the devotee becomes identified with the Deity.

Later Sun Worship or Sūryopāsanā

The sun worship is practised in India since the vedic period and it has become a part of daily routine of Indian people. The Ṛgveda calls the Sun as the soul of the world in this verse; "*Citram devānāmudagānikam caksurmitrasya varuṇasyāgneḥe. Aparā dyavā pṛithivi antarikṣam, Surya ātmā jagatasthuṣasca*".[15] It means the amazing sphere of the Sun is rising. It is the eye of Mitra, Varuṇa, and Agni. It engulfs the Earth, the Space and the Heaven. It is the essential part of the movable and the immovable world. the vedic seers thought that illumination, vital energy and dynamism are the essential requirements of life in the world and the Sun is the very origin of them and therefore he is the soul of the world. The sprouting and germination, and the showering of the rain are because of the Sun. Life is possible on the Earth only because of the Sun. He is the essential ingredient of our life.

In the Ṛgveda the Sun is called *Savitṛ*. *Yāskācāry* gives the meaning of *Savitṛ* as "*Sarvasya prasavitā*"[16] the originator of every thing. the Ṛgveda refers to the Sun by the following names (1) *Puṣan*—The word Puṣan is derived from the root `*Puṣa*' to feed. Puṣan is intelligent and good-looking. He travels in the chariot driven by lambs. He has thick hair. he holds golden weapons in his hands. He is the owner of the material and the immaterial world. (2) *Bhaga-Bhaga* is the giver of wealth. He is the supporter of the universe. He is victorious. He is the son of Aditi. *Yāskācārya* says that *Bhaga* is the name of the rising, tender appearance of the Sun.[17] (3) *Varuṇa*—*Sāyaṇācārya* says that "*Astam gacchan surya eva varuṇa ityucyate*. "The setting sun is called *Varuṇa*. The word varuṇa is derived from the root `vṛu', to cover, to engulf, to envelope. (4) *Uṣas*—It is the light on the eastern horizon which springs before the Sunrise. The Ṛgveda describes *Uṣā* with the fantastic and beautiful stanzas. *Uṣā* is the sister of *Bhaga* and the daughter of *Varuṇa*. *Uṣā* gives the light. She is wealthy and giver of abundant food. She is beloved of the Sun.[19] She is luminous, eternal and she initiates the people to work. The sūktas No. 75, 81 in the 7th Maṅḍal and 48,49,92,123,124 in the first Maṅḍala are dedicated to Uṣas and are known commonly as the Uṣā sūkta. (5) *Viṣṇu*—Viṣṇu is also one of the names of the Sun. Viṣṇu sūktas occur in the first Maṅḍala at No. 154 to 156 and in the seventh Maṅḍala at No. 100. The Ṛgveda describes him as "Triṇi padā vicakrame viṣṇur gopā adābhyaḥ". Viṣṇu pervades the world with three strides, is said in "*Tredhā nidadhe padam*." (Viṣṇusūkta). it is held that these three steps are the Earth, the space, and the Heaven. (6) *Sūrya*—There are several saura sūktas in the Ṛgveda.[20] There is a poetical simile for the rising sun in the Ṛgveda; see the verse; "*Udutya jātavedasam devam vahanti ketavaḥ. Dṛśe viśvāya Suryam*."[21] It means the all-knower and the self luminous majestic Sun is brought in the world by his rays by holding him on their heads to show him to the world. (7) *Mitra*—The name Mitra often comes in conjunction with *Varuṇa*. The 59th sukta of the third Maṅḍala is dedicated to Mitra. Mitra is the controller of the rising, growing and setting Sun. Mitra is a creative power of the *Sūrya*.

Puśan, Bhaga, Varuṇa, Uśas, Viṣṇu, Sūrya, Mitra etc. are the epithets of the Sun. They are also called Saura Deities.

In *Yajña* performance the Sun is invited to take the offerings. In the Hindu tradition sixteen *Samskāras* are bestowed on each person. The thread ceremony of a male child is very important among them and in this samskāra the child is initiated in the *Sūrya* Upāsanā with the *Gāyatri Mantra* and then it becomes a daily part of his life. The upāsanā of the *Gayatri maṅtra* has thus become a part of Indian life. The upāsaka improves his grasping capacity and alertness by the recitation of this maṅtra. He tries to brighten his intellect like the Sun.

Mānavgṛihyasutra and *kāṭhaka gṛihyasutra* has prescribed a *saṁskāra* on a new born baby called *Āditya Darśana* means showing the Sun for the first time to the baby. *Āditya* is one of the twelve names given to the Sun namely *Mitra, Ravi, Sūrya, Bhānu, Khaga,*

Puṣaṇa, Hiraṇyagarbha, Marici, Āditya, Savitṛ, Arka and *Bhaskara*. *Āditya sūkta* finds its place in the second Maṅḍala of the Ṛgveda. The Ṛṣi of this sukta is *Kurmagurṭsmada* and the deity is *Āditya*. This sukta praises *Āditya* as he is the protector of the universe, giver of happiness, shows people the vigorous way of living, protects them from enemies etc. There are six sūktas for *Āditya* in the Ṛgveda. In these sūktas the Sun is denoted with six different names as *Mitra, Aryaman, Bhaga, Varuṇa, Dakṣa*, and *Aṇśa*. These are separate deities with slight difference in them. They are together called *Āditya saṅgha*.

We see that *Sūryopāsanā* flourished in the period of the *Rāmāyaṇa* and the *Mahābhārata*. In the *Ayodhyā Kāṅda* of the *Rāmāyaṇa* there is mention of the *Sūryopāsanā* performed in the morning and evening by the father and mother of *Śrāvaṇa Kumāra*. In the same kānda there is also an incident in which *Rāma, Lakṣmaṇa* and *Sitā* with the other Ṛiṣis prayed to the Sun and gave him offerings.[22] There is also one full chapter on the adoration of the Sun (*Sūryastuti*) which is called *'Āditya Hṛdaya'*. In this chapter *Agasti Ṛisi* directed *Rāma* to perform the Upāsanā of the Sun with this *'Āditya Hṛdaya Stotra'* to conquer the enemies. It is held in the *Rāmāyaṇa* that *Rāma* was *Sūrya vaṅsi* i.e. born in legacy, dynasty of the *Sūrya* and he is said to be the incarnation of Viṣṇu which is one of the names of the Sun in the Ṛgveda.

In the *Āraṇyaka Parva* of *Mahābhārat* the Sun is described with hundred and eight names. He is said to be *Deveśvara*.[23] In the *Śāntiparva* the Sun is called *Ātmā*, the soul of the world. The Upāsanā of *Sūrya* in the *Mahābhārata* period was being performed by certain vedic maṅtras, with some prescribed methodology called tāntrik rituals such as giving oblations, offering the flower garland, fasting etc. *Kunti* prayed to the Sun and the Sun gave her a son who latter on became famous by the name of *Karṇa*.[24]

By the period of *Śunga*, the Upāsanā of the Sun developed into idol worship and some sort of tāntric rituals had come in practice. The idol of the Sun is portrayed like this—the Sun is travelling in the chariot driven by four horses. His two wives *Uṣā* and *Pratyūṣā* are besides him. The demon is crushed under his chariot. He is wearing iron jacket and holding weapons in his hands. *Cakra, svastika*, lotus, golden plate and eagle are supposed to be the symbols of the Sun.

The *Sūryopāsanā* was extremely popular during the *Gupta* and *Vardhana* dynasties (10th Cen). Actually the Sun worship started for the protection of the body from illness, for progeny, for the destruction of enemies, for physical welfare of mankind but afterwards it is turned towards the goal of *Mokṣa, Ātmaprāpti* etc. i.e. for the spiritual attainments. The method of worship changed with time and various methods came into practice. He is worshipped with the recitation of the Vedic mantras, all pray to him, his idols are worshipped with the flowers, the sandal paste, the incense, holy lantern, devotional songs, the dances etc. The Sun is always shown as wearing a sacred thread, crown and earings. Tāntrik rituals also became prevalent.

Ādya Śaṅkarācārya has tried to unify the worship of *Saura, Vaiṣṇava, Śaiva, Śākta,* and *Gāṇapatya* sects under the name of *Pancāyatana Pujā*. Nearly all Hindus follow this worship.

In the Ṛgveda *Uṣā, Prtyuṣā, Sandhyā, Chāya* are the names of the wives of the Sun. In *Mastyapurāṇa Rājñā, Savarṇā, Chāyā, Savarcasā* are the names give to the wives of the Sun. In Gujarāt state the worship of the wife of the Sun named *Ratnādevi* is popular. In Mahārāshtra the same goddess is worshipped by the name *Āditya Rāṇubai*. The Sun is said to have four sons named *Revent, Yama, Aśvin* and *Manu*.

The details of the technique of the Sun worship is described in the *Bṛhatsaṃhitā*, the *Śilparatna*, the *Visvakarmāvatar Śāstra*, the *Visvakarmā Śilpa*. *Varāha Mihir* bows to *Sūrya* and prays him as God of Gods the creator of the universe and Paramātman in the beginning of the *Bṛihat saṃhitā*. He also describes how the idol of the Sun should be. He says that the limbs of the Sun must be attractive, He must hold two lotuses in his hands. He must wear a garland of gold *Mauktik* (pearl), he must wear a crown with the earings. He must wear an iron jacket, and there must be a fresh smile on his face, and an illumined circle must be carved around his figure. *Viśvakarmā Śilp* gives the description of the idol of the Sun with a little difference i.e. the Sun is sitting on chariot which has only a wheel and seven horses. *Viśvakarmāvatār Śāstra* differs only with a driver of the chariot and the colour of the idol slightly red.

There is a lot of information traceable in the Purāṇas on the Sun worship. The Purāṇas like the Mārkaṅdeya 78-3, 14, the Agni 1-123-33, the Garuḍa, the Matsya 52-53, the Liṅga 54, the

Padma—Sṛṣṭi Khanda 76,23, the Brhma, the Skanda—Kāśi Khanda, the Viṣṇu Dharmottar, the Sāmba, provide the details of *Sūryopāsanā* and idol science. The Sāmba Purāṇa specifically describes *Sūryopāsanā* at length and in details. *Nārada* recommended *Sūropāsanā* to *Sāmba* for curing leprosy.

The *Sāmba Purāṇa* mentions the twelve principles of the saura power and these are said to be responsible for all the phenomenon of the physical world. These twelve principals are Indra, *Dhātā, Prajñā, Pujā, Tvaṣtā, Aryamān, Bhaga, Vivaśvān, Viṣṇu, Aṇśa, Varuṇa, Mitra*. These are called, the twelve *Ādityas* too. The first part of the *Sāmba Purāṇa* deals with the different types of the worships of the Sun, the diseases suffered by Sāmba and relief from them, the temple of the Sun built by him etc. The second part of the Purāṇa describes the Tāntrik procedure of *Sūryopāsaña* and undualism between *Śiva* and the *Sūrya*.[24a]

Cults

Saura Sampradāya—The Sun is the deity of this *Sampradāya*. This cult was spread in the north and the south India and it still holds ground there. There is a mention in the book written by *Ānandgiri*,[25] a meeting between *Ādi Śañkarācārya* and *Mahant Śri Divākara*, who was the chief or *Ācārya* of the *Saur Panth* at that time, and the place *'Subramaṇyam'* in Madras Province (Near Trivendram) was the centre of this Panth. It is said that there are six sub-sects of this sect and all of the followers apply a round mark of red sandal paste on the forehead and wear garlands of red flowers. They recite the eight lettered mantra of *Surya*. ("*Om ghṛṇi Sūrya Ādityāya*" This mañtra is given in the *Sūrya Atharvaśirṣa*). Some followers worship rising Sun as the creator of all the Universe, some worship him as a God of destruction in the form of *Maheśa*, some adore the mid-day sun, some worship the setting Sun in the form of Viṣṇu who is the creator, guardian and destroyer of the world and some devotees worship him in all the three stages o rising, mid-day and setting. One sect observes to salute the Sun every day and performing *pujā* on the sixteenth days. They oblate all their doings to the Sun. Followers of one set emboss impressions of the Sun on the various organs of the body by heated metal stamps and meditate on the Sun. They accept with reference to *Puruṣa Sūkta* that by wearing signs of *Sūrya* on the body, and by worshipping the Sun with the help of eight lettered mañtra of the Sun, one gets the eternal place of peace.

The celebration of the *Makara Sañkrānta* and *Ratha Saptami* is a part of *Sūryopāsanā* which is in practice all over India even today.

Popular Stotras

(1) *Āditya Hṛdaya Stotra* in *Vālmiki Rāmāyaṇa*[26].— It was preached by *Agasti Ṛṣi* to *Rāma* to conquer *Rāvaṇa* in the battle. *Rāma* was under tension and anxious about the victory. So *Agasti Ṛṣi* told him to recite this stotra. He expressed this stotra as the secret of the veda and knowing which *Rāma* could get victory. He further added that this stotra is the giver of *puṇya,* (virtues), it destroy enemies and it confer ultimate release from worldly bonds. It is auspicious, benevolent, destroyer of sins, diseases and gives long life. The verse is *"Āditya hṛdayam puṇyam sarvaśatruvināśanam. Jayāvaham japennityamakṣayam paramam śivam. Sarvamangalmāngalyam sarvapāpapraṇāśnam. Cintāśokapraś amanamāyurvardhanamuttamam"*.

The further stanzas of the stotra describe the importance of the Upāsanā of the rising Sun. He is called *Bhāskar* and *Vivaśvān* in the sixth stanza. In the eighth he is praised as *Brhmā, Viṣṇu, Śiva, Skanda, Mahendra, Kubera* the great Time *(Kāla)*, the Moon, the master of Waters. Further he is said to be the father of the world, Omniconscious, *Jñātā*. The following names of the Sun occur next : *Savitā, Sūrya, Khaga, Puṣan, Divākaraḥ* etc. His colour is golden. In the stanzas 14th to 21st, the Sun is adored by praising him by different elegant names. In the twentysixth stanza *Agasti* asked *Rāma* to worship the Sun, the master of world, with full concentration of mind and to recite this stotra three times a day to conquer the enemy. *Rāma* performed this Upāsanā three times with taking sips of water (*ācamana*). Then he felt clam and confident and was ready to battle with Rāvaṇa with great zeal and at last he won the combat.

(2) *Bhaviṣyapurāṇokta Ādityahṛdays Stotram*—Lord *Kṛṣṇa* had revealed this *stotra* to *Arjuna* after the *Mahābhārata* war. *Kṛṣṇa* on request of *Arjuna* taught this *Sūryastuti* with *nyāsa* to *Arjuna*. This worship of the Sun is to be performed in the morning time with the nyāsa at the beginning and end of the stotra. *Kṛṣṇa* expressed that this is the *Ādityahṛdaya stotra* which is auspicious, the destroyer of the sins, the destroyer of the disease, conferring long life, the

destroyer of the enemy, the giver of victory, the giver of health and progeny. The verses are *"Sarvamangala māngalyam sarvapāpapraṇāśanam. Sarvarogapraśamanamāyurverdhanamuttamam. Atridamanam Pārtha Sangrāme jayavardhanam. Vardhanam dhanaputrāṇāmādityahṛadayam śruṇu."*[27] The Ṛṣi of this *Ādityahṛdayastotra* is *Srikṛṣna,* the deity is *Sūryātmā,* meter is *Anuṣtubha, bija* is *Haritahayevratham. Śakti* is *"Om namo bhagavate jitvaiśvanār jātavedase," kilakam* is *"Om namo bhagavate Ādityāya namaḥ"* its *astram* is *`Om agnigarbha devatā,'* its mantra is *"Om namo bhagavate tubhyam ādityāya namo namaḥ."* With reciting the Ṛṣi etc. the devotee has to offer the water to the Sun with dedication. Then there is a recitation of the nyāsa, means to keep the different forms of the deity on the different parts of body, for example *"Om hrām añguṣtābhyam namaḥ."* etc.

Then there is a dhyāna of the Sun, the form on which the devotee has to meditate. In this stotra the meditative form of the Sun is : "The Sun wears the crown with the jewellery, he is bright, he has taken lotus in his hands, his colour is golden, he pervades the sky and the space, he has appeared on the east horizon, he gives happiness to all the people. Viṣṇu and Śiva are bowing to him. May this eye of the world, Bhagavān Sūrya protect me."

In this stotra it is prescribed to draw a diagram; on any background after *dhyāna*. This diagram is as follows—First draw a lotus with eight petals, inscribe *'OM'* and *'hrim'* on the petals, write eight names of the Sun i.e. *Āditya, Bhāskara, Bhānu, Ravi, Sūrya, Divākara, Mārtanḍa* and *Tapan,* with these names write *Diptā, Sukṣmā, Jayā, Bhadrā, Vibhuti, Vimalā, Amoghā, Vidyutā* respectively and in the middle *Śri,* the name of *Lakṣmi.*

Then there is a prayer and offering the respect to the Sun by various names. Then again the process of *nyāsa* is described. In this *nyāsa* different names of the Sun are chanted and He is asked to protect the different parts of the body. The *nyāsa* is very important in this stotra. It is said that one who recites this nyāsa three times a day i.e. at dawn, midday and evening, becomes holy as the Sun. The the Sun is praised with hundred names in the verses twentyfive to fiftyseven. He is called Puruṣottam in the verse sixtyfive. Again *Śrikṛṣna* asked *Arjuna* to worship the Sun for three times with these names given in this *stotra*. The recitation of the *stotra* on sunday has more importance.

The process of the *Pujā* (worship) is described after the nintyseventh verse. This worship is again a worship of a diagram of eight-petaled louts. The oblation is offered to the Sun, followed by an invocation and offering with mantras by surrendering to Him and at last the result of this stotra is told upto hundred and forty verses. Then the *maṇḍalāṣṭaka* is given. The *stotra* ends with *dhyāna ślokas*.

Navagraha Upāsanā

The adoration of the nine planets including the Sun occupies an important place in the ritualistic ceremonies, it was practised in ancient days and it is practised even to day. In the Indian scriptures and the Science of Astrology the Sun is also identified as a planet along with others. The methodical study of the nine planets is clearly seen in the treatises on the *Jotiṣa Śāstra* like the *Bṛhat Parāśara Saṃhitā*, the *Jemini Saṃhitā* etc. *Jyotiṣa* is a *Vedāṅga* which is related to daily life of mankind. It helps in preparing calendars, ascertaining the movements of the constellations and the planets, anticipating the seasons, counting the periods etc. which is used in daily life. A work named *Atharvaṇa Jyotiṣa* sets forth the divisions of time, the names of the *Nakṣtras* etc.; The Sun, the Moon, the Mars, the Mercury, the Jupiter, the Venus, the Saturn, the two nodes-Rāhu and Ketu are nine planets which are important according to the astrological point of view. It is held that these planets exerts effects on the life on the Earth. They cast effects on the physical and the mental life of man and also have effect on the major physical turnover in affairs of the World. In order to harness the wild effects of these planets some Upāsanā methods are prescribed in the scriptures. These are specially seen in the Purāṇa literature.

Each planet has its own characteristics and a separate field of jurisdiction. These are personified into deities. They are classified into the three guṇas according to characteristics. Gitā says that every phenomenon on the Earth, the Space and the Heaven is bound by three characteristics viz; *Sātvika*, *Rājasika*, and *Tāmasika*. The verse is, "*Na tadasti pṛthivyām vā divi devaṣu vā punaḥ. Satvam prakṛtijairmuktam ya debhihisyād tribhirguṇaiḥ.*[28] Planets Jupiter and Venus are *Sātvika*, the Mars and the Sun are

Rājasika, the Saturn, the Rāhu and the Ketu are *Tāmasika*, the mercury and the Moon change their nature, thus they are *Sātvika* with the *Sātvika* planets and *Rājasika* and the *Tāmaskia* with the *Rājasika* and the *Tāmasika* planets. The planets affect the human life so the person dominated by the *Sātvika* planets performs the Upāsanā of *Iśvara* and with the *Tāmasika* planets performs the *Tāmasika* Upāsanā of *Dākinis, Jārana Māraṇa mantra* etc. The details of each planet and its effects are described in the Astrological scriptures. Each planet is either malefic or benefic, so the Upāsanā differs according to the quality of the planets.

The Sun and the Moon are the masters of the constellations, Mars is the son of the Earth, Mercury is the son of the Moon, Jupiter is the spiritual preceptor : *Gurū* of gods, Venus is the Guru of *Rākṣasas*, Saturn is the son of the Sun and Rāhu and Kẹtu, the two nodes are described as the shadow sons of the Earth. All these personified planets are worshipped at the beginning of the religious ceremonies like Upanayan, marriage, *Yajña, Satyanārāyaṇa Pujā* etc. These planets complete their round through the twenty seven constellations and the twelve sings : *Rāśis*. These signs of zodiac are Aries, Taurus, Gemini, Cancer, Leo, Virgo, Libra, Scorpion, Sagittarius, Capricorn, Aquarius and Pisces. Each Zodiacal Sign has a Svāmi i.e. the Mars governs the Aries and Scorpion, the Venus governs Taurus and Libra, the Mercury governs Gemini and Virgo, the Sun governs Leo, the Moon governs Cancer, the Jupiter governs Sagittarius and Pisces, the Saturn governs Capricorn and Aquarius.

The human life span is held to be minimum a hundred and twenty years. Different planets dominate different periods of human life with certain definite cycle and logic. The period of all planets cover hundred and twenty years i.e. one human life. These periods are called *Mahādaśās*. Each planet has definite period of *Mahādaśā* as follows; the Sun has six years, the Moon has ten years, the Mars has seven years, Rāhu has eighteen years, Jupiter has sixteen years, the Saturn has nineteen years, the Mercury has seventeen years, Ketu has seven years and Venus has twenty years. These periods traverse the human life in pre-scheduled definite succession. Which planet would give happiness and which would cause sufferings depends upon its place in the horoscope of the person. Which planet would cause the hardships and sorrows can be ascertained by the readings of the horoscope.

Certain Upāsanās are prescribed to get rid of or to mitigate the ill effects. These Upāsanās contain recitation of the specific mantras, readings of the holy books, wearing a particular gem, distributing charitable offerings and the worship of that planet as per instructions given in authoritative books.

The specific mantras for recitations in this context are also taken from the *Ṛgveda*, the *Yajurveda*, the *Śivapurāṇa* etc. Certain such Upāsanā mantras are given below—

(1) The Sun— *"Om ā Kṛṣṇena rajasā varatmāno niveśayannamṛtam martyaca. Hiraṇyena savitā ratheṇādevo yāti bhuvanāni paśyan."*[29]

(2) The Moon—*"Om imam deva asapatnansu vadhvam mahate kṣatrāya mahate jyeṣṭhāya mahate jānarājyāyendrasyendriyāya. Imamamupya putramammusyai putramṣyai viśaeṣa vo'mi rajā somo' smākam brāhmaṇānamrājā."*[30]

(3) The Mars—*"Om agnirmurddhā divaḥ kakutpatihi pṛthivyā ayam. Apām retānsi jivanti."*[31]

(4) Mercury—*"Om udhudhyasvāgne prati jāgṛhi tvamiṣṭāpurte sansṛjethāmayam ca asminsandhasthe adhyautarsmin viśvedevā yajamānaśca śidata."*[32]

(5) Jupiter—*"Om bṛhaspate ati yadaryo arhād dyumad vibhāti kratumajjaneṣu. Yaddidayaccavasa ṛtaprajāta tadasmāsu draviṇam dhehi citram."*[33]

(6) Venus—*"Om annātparisṛṣto rasam brahmaṇā vyapibat kṣtram payaḥ somam prajāpatiḥi ṛtena satyamindriyam vipānan śukramandhasa indrayendriyamidam payo' mṛtam madhu."*[34]

(7) Saturn—*"Om śam no devirabhiṣtays āpo bhavantu pitaye. Śam yorabhi sravantu naḥ."*[35]

(8) Rāhu—*"Om kayā naścitra ā bhuvaduti sadāvṛdhaḥ sakhā. Kayāśaścaiṣṭḥāya vṛtā."*[36]

(9) Ketu—*"Om Ketu Kṛṇvannaketave peśo maryā apeaśase. Samuṣadbhirajayathaḥ."*[37]

The *bījamantras* of each planet are to be pronounced along with the above mantras. The number of the cycles of recitations of these mantras in case of each planet-worship is—The Sun—7000, The Moon—11000, Mars—10,000, Mercury—19,000, Jupiter—19,000, Venus—6000, Saturn—23000, Rāhu—18,000, Ketu—17,000.

The *Pūjā* of the picture representing these planets is done with milk, flowers, sandal paste, lighting of the lamps etc. The reading of the holy scriptures advised for each planet is as below—

The Sun—*Harivaṅśa Purāṇa*. The Moon—*Śivastuti*, Mars—*Śivastuti*, Mercury—the vow of *Amāvasyā*—dark night, for the Jupiter, the same as mercury, for Venus the worship of the cow, for Saturn *Mṛtyunjaya japa*, and for Ketu the same as Saturn.

To wear the precious stones, jewels is also beneficial for good favours of the planets. A particular gem is prescribed for a particular planet. These are as follows—The Sun—Ruby, The Moon—Pearl, Mars—Coral, Mercury—Emerald, Jupiter—Topaz, Venus—diamond, Saturn—Sapphire, Rāhu—Zircon, Ketu—Cat's eye. The things for charitable distribution are also specific for each planet.

Śri Vyāsa is said to have written *Navagraha Stotra* which is recited in the daily worship. This stotra has a value of maṅtra. The *Navagraha Kavaca* is important in the *Navagraha* Upāsanā. It is a practice to wear an amulet (a small metal box called *'Taita'*) which contains *Navagraha Kavaca* which is written on *Bhurjapatra*. This *stotra* (*kavaca*) occurs in the *Yāmala Tantra*.

The *Navagraha* Upāsanā in this way, plays a prominent role in all the ritualistic and special occasions in Hindu tradition.

In addition to this *Navagraha* Upāsanā, the particular constellation called *Puṣya* has great importance in Hindu scriptures. The day is said to be very auspicious when the constellation *Puṣya* appears on Thursday. This combination is called *"Gurupuṣyāmṛta Yoga'*. It is said to be very benificial if gold is purchased on this day of the yoga. *Śiva Purāṇa* says that *Puṣya* is the vibhuti-anśa-fraction of *Śiva*, the verse is, *"Kratunāmaśvamedho' si, Yugānam prathamo yugah. Puṣyastvam sarvadhiṣṇyānāmamāvasya tithiṣvasi."*[38]

5. Viṣṇu Upāsanā

Vedic

(1) Puruṣa Sūkta

Puruṣa Sūkta is included in all the four Vedas. In the Ṛgveda it comes in the 9th *sūkta* of the Tenth Maṅḍala, it has sixteen stanzas. It finds its place in the 31st adhyāya of the Yajurveda with additional six stanzas. It is placed in the sixth sūkta of 19th kanda of the Atharvaveda, it has sixteen stanzas similar to the Ṛgveda with some difference in the order of stanzas and with change in some words. In the Sāmaveda it appears with five stanzas. It is also seen in the Taitiriya Saṃhitā with eighteen stanzas.

In this sūkta the *Puruṣa* is described as Paramātmā in the Universe as well as Jīvātmā in the world. The ultimate aim of every Upāsaka is to know this *Puruṣa*. This sūkta is the key to know the crux of the Vedas. *Maharṣi Veda Vyāsa* says, "*Idam Puruṣa suktam hi sarva vedeṣu pārthiva. Ṛtam satyam ca vikhyātam ṛṣisinhen cintitam.*"[1] It means this *Puruṣa sūkta* is more important than all other *sūktas* of all the Vedas. It conveys the truth and it is experienced by the greatest ṛṣis. In the *Padmapurāṇa* it is said that *Puruṣa sūkta* is superior to all the *sūktas*. The verse is "*Vedeṣu pauruṣam sūktam Purāṇesu ca vaiṣṇavam bhārate bhagavadgītā dharmaśātreṣu mānavam.*" It means *Puruṣa sukta* is superior to all the sūktas, *Viṣṇu Purāṇa* in all purāṇas, Bhagavadgītā in the Mahābhārata and the Manusmṛti is superior in the *Dharmaśātras*. In the *Śvetāśvatar Upaniṣad* there are the three mantras which describe the svarūpa of *Iśvar*, taken from the *Puruṣa Sūkta*. These are `*Vedāhmetam puruṣam mahāntam..., Sahaśraśirṣā puruṣaḥ..., Puruṣa evedam sarvam....*"[2]

It is held that one gets his desires definitely fulfilled if he recites the *Puruṣa sūkta* correctly. *Viṣṇu Dharmottar Purāṇa* says "*Brahma yajñe japan sūktam puruṣam cintayan harim. Sa satvan jayate vedān sāngopāngvidhānataḥ,*" (3) It means if one recites *Puruṣa Sūkta* with the sacrifice, he gets the fruits of the study of the Vedas, *Bhaviṣya Purāṇa* also says the same thing.[4]

Different deities are referred to with this sūkta. The *Garuḍa* and the *Agni Purāṇa* say that the deity of this *sūkta* is *Viṣṇu* and the *Liṅg Purāṇa* says that the deity of this sūkta is *Śiva*.[5] This *sūkta* is recited in the different *Yajña* ceremonies, it is an important part of the *Yajña*.[6] Various stanzas of this *sūkta* are used in the different *vratas*, worships and *Yajña*. This *sūkta* is used in the *Ṣoḍaśopacāra Pujā* too.

The Meaning of the *Puruṣa Sūkta* is as follows : The word *Puruṣa* means *Mahāviṣṇu*.[7] This word can be split as "*Purṇatvād vai puruṣah*" means one who is complete in himself is *Puruṣa*. the meaning of Puruṣa can be taken as *Jivātma* with *Prakṛti* and

Puruṣa.[8] This *Puruṣa* has thousands of heads, eyes and legs. He pervades everything in this world and still remains beyond it. Everything in this world is He Himself. He is the root cause, he is all the creation, he is the owner and master of movable and immovable things. The *Hiraṇyagarbha* or *Virāt Brahman* is born of him. All the *ṛcas* and *chandas* are born out of the *Karmic Yajña* performed by the *Virāṭ Puruṣa*. All the oblations came from him. All the Ṛṣis and the Deities have understood this *Yajña* and thereby they have understood the *Puruṣa*. The tamed and wild animals born from this *Yājña*. The *Puruṣa* is embodied Himself in all the creatures. *Brāhmaṇas* are his mouth, *Kṣatriyas* are His hands, *Vaiśyas* are His stomach, *Śudras* are his legs. It is His Universal body. The Moon is born from His mind. The Sun is born from His eyes. The Agni and Indra are born from His mouth and the *Vāyu* from His breath. The space is born from His middle part and the Heaven is born from His head. The *chandas* like *Gāyatri, Triṣtubh, Anuṣtubh* etc; are born from the *Yajña* performed by Him. It has seven redii and twenty one samidhas. Seven worlds viz. *Bhuḥ, Bhuvaḥ, Svaḥ, Mahaḥ, Tapaḥ, Janaḥ, Satyam;* seven sages viz. *Marici, Atri, Aṅgirasa, Pulastya, Pulah, Kratu* and *Vasiṣṭha;* the seven constituents of the body viz. blood, chyle, flesh, fat, bone, marrow and semen. (The No.7 has importance in the marriage ceremony. The bride and bridegroom walk together seven steps —*Saptapadi.*) This great *Puruṣa* is the subject to be known. His colour is like the Sun and he is beyond the darkness. Every part of this world is created by Him so please bow to Him and try to become identical with Him. There is no other path of knowledge than this.

The deity of this *Sūkta* is *Puruṣa* i.e. Paramātman and the Ṛṣi is *Nārāyaṇa, Maharṣi Veda Vyāsa* says that *Nārāyaṇa* is the very name of Paramātman; the verse is *"Tatra yaḥ paramātmā hi saḥ nityam nirgunaḥ smṛtaḥ. Sa hi Nārāyaṇo jñeyād, sarvātmā Puruṣaḥ hi saḥ".*[9] The meters of this *Sūkta* are *Anuṣtubh* and *Triṣtubh*. The *svara* (accents) is important to know the exact meaning. In the vedic literature the pitch of voice can differ the whole meaning of the word. So the recitation must be done according to the chandas. This *Sūkta* is a *Mantra*. The meaning of all the *Mantras* are mysterious. By understanding the meaning of this *mantrasūkta* the meaning of all the Vedas is revealed. Therefore the learned men go deep to understand the implicit meaning of the *Puruṣa*

Sūkta. Śatapath Brāhmaṇa says *"Puruṣa vai sahasrasya pratimā."*[10] He is *Piṅda* (body-micro) and *Brahmāṅda* (universe-macro). The *Puruṣa* is reflected in all the particles of the world and therefore by understanding this *sūkta* the knowledge of the entire world is revealed. *"Puruṣa eva idam sarvam yat bhutam, yacca bhavyam."*[11]. The *Purāṇa Puruṣa* described by the *Padma Purāṇa* is this divine entity.[12] The *Padma Purāṇa* says that the eighteen *Purāṇas* are the eighteen limbs of this *Puruṣa*. In the *Bhagvadgītā Srikṛṣṇa* says *"Uttamaḥ puruṣastvanyaḥ paramātmetyudāhṛtā, yo lokatrayamāviṣya bibhartyavyaya iśvaraḥ."*[13] It means *Puruṣa* is the Paramātman who pervades the three worlds and upholds them.

In the Vedas the Upāsanā of the *Puruṣa* is prescribed at various places. *"Kasmi devāya haviṣā vidhem?"* is a question in which the answer is included, that no other deity than Paramātman is worth to worship, so we offer oblations to this *Puruṣa* only. By the Upāsanā with the *Puruṣa Sūkta* the devotee gets the prosperity and bliss in this life only. The *Puruṣa* is the very substance of all the existence. He is blissful and one can reach to him by the Upāsanā.

(2) Viṣṇu Sūkta

In the Sanskrit Literature we find Paramātman is described by various names according to virtues and expression of physical or spiritual powers. The Paramātman is one but learned men call Him by different names. It is said the Ṛgveda that *"Ekam sad viprā bahudhā vadanti"*.[14] The whole universe is the emancipation of Paramātman. The Ṛgveda says, *"Indro māyābhiḥi pururūpa īyate."*[15]

It is reiterated in the *Anuśāsan Parvam* of *Mahābhārat* in this verse, *"Ekadhā ca dvidhācaiva bāhudhā ca sa eva hi. Śatadhā caiva tathā śatasahrśah"*.[16]

Viṣṇu is one of the names given to the Paramātman. The Viṣṇu Upāsanā is popular and well known in India. The idol worship of Viṣṇu is not traceable in the Ṛgveda. It must have come into practice during later period probably inspired from this *Viṣṇu Sūkta*.

The *Viṣṇu Sūkta* is generally recited with the *Puruṣa Sūkta*. This *Sūkta* occurs in the first *Aṣṭaka* of the *Ṛgveda*. However some of its stanzas are repeated in the *Yajurveda* and the *Atharvaveda*. The word *'Viṣṇu'* is derived from the root *Viśa* of the sixth conjugation. It means 'To enter'. Paramatmān has created the universe from him at the same time He remains entered and pervaded in everything that He has created, and therefore He is called Viṣṇu.

The meaning of the *Viṣṇu Sūkta* in brief is "May God Viṣṇu protect us. He has seven dwellings including the Earth. He has three strides by which he has covered the universe. (Probably this verse may be the root of the *Vāmana Avatāra*). He is the guardian of the cows and He upholds and administrates all the laws and rules of nature (*Ṛtam*). He is a friend of Indra. All Gods always want to get parama pada (His abode). He sees at all directions at a time. By Upāsanā of God Viṣṇu man can reach that ultimate state of knowledge and become identical with Paramātman. By recitation of this *Sūkta* man gets quietness, happiness and health. These six stanzas of the *Viṣṇu sūkta* are written by *Medhātithi Ṛṣi,* its meter is *Gāyatri* and its Deity is *Viṣṇu*.

Viṣṇu is called by various names in the Ṛgveda. These names are given to Him according to qualities exhibited by Him at different times and in different situations. The *Mahābhārata* gives the following names of Viṣṇu *"Sa ca rudraḥ śivah, so'gnihi sarvah sa sarvajit."*[17] It means *Viṣṇu* is *Rudra, Śiva, Agni,* he is everything and also the owner of everything. The *Maitrāyaṇi Āraṇyaka* also gives various names, *"tvam brahmā tvam ca vai Viṣṇustvam rudrastvam prajāpatiḥi, tvamagnirvaruṇo vāyustvam indrastvam niśākaraḥ, tvamasy yamāh pṛthivi tvam visvamtvamathācyutaḥ Svārthe svābhavikerthe ca bahudhā samasthitastvayi."* It means you are *Viṣṇu, Rudra, Prajāpati, Yama, Indra, Pṛthvi,* and everything. The *Puruṣa* described in the *Puruṣa Sūkta* and *Viṣṇu* described in the *Viṣṇu sūkta* resemble each other, therefore *Viṣṇu* is also called *Virāt Puruṣa*. In the *Mahābhārata Viṣṇu* is called *Nārāyaṇa* and he is described as *Virāṭ Puruṣa, "Nārāyaṇāya viśvāya nirguṇāya guṇātmane. Tapo yajñya sca yasta ca purāṇaḥ puruṣo virāt"*[18]

Savitā and *Agni* are the names of Viṣṇu because he is the giver of the intellect and the light to know the real nature of Brahman. The Upāsanā of Viṣṇu illuminates the way of spiritual enlightenment. *Viṣṇu Sūkta* says, *"Tadviṣṇoho paramam padam sadā paśyanti surayaḥ. Diviva cakṣurātatam"*.[19] When Viṣṇu is worshipped as Light, he becomes *Savitā* whose second name is *Āditya*. Viṣṇu covers the world with only three steps. It is said in the *Viṣṇu Sūkta "Idam visṇurvicakrame tredhā nidadhe padam, samuḷahamasya pāṇsure"*.[20] Viṣṇu has all pervading nature. Similarly the other *Devatā* in Ṛgveda namely, *Varuṇa* has also the same characteristics and therefore in the *Taitiriya Saṃhitā, Varuṇa* is also described as Viṣṇu. The *Tatiriya Saṃhitā* says *"Varuṇā-nāmaka somadevo jagadiśvareṇābhinnaḥ."*[21] Therefore *Viṣṇu* is *Āditya* as well as *Varuṇa*. *Viṣṇu* is valourous and dwells on the mountain top. This description is given in the Ṛgveda where the verse says *"Prated Viṣṇuḥu stavate viryeṇa mṛgo nā bhimah kucari giriṣṭhaha."*[22]. He is strong and powerful. Viṣṇu maintains the world and loves It. Viṣṇu Sūkta says, *"Viṣṇoḥ karmāṇi paśyatayotao vratāni paspaśe. Indrasya yujyaḥ sakhā."*[23] Its meaning is : Viṣṇu works for His creation and carefully observes the work of all creatures, and He is a friend of Indra.

Viṣṇu Himself is *Yajñaḥa*. In *Bhagavadgiā Sri Kṛṣṇa* says. *"Aham Krturaham Yajñaḥ, svadhāhamahamauṣadham. Mantrohamahamevā-jyamahagiraham hutam."*[24] *Sri Kṛṣṇa* is the incarnation of the Viṣṇu, so he says that he is *yajña*, etc. Viṣṇu is the guardian of cows, says *Viṣṇu Sūkta* in *"Viṣṇurgopā adābhyām."*[25] It is also said in the Ṛgveda that the cows with sharp horns stay with Viṣṇu. The verse is *"Yatra bhurisṛing āyāsaḥ."*[26]

Nārāyaṇa is another name of *Viṣṇu*. *Nārāyaṇa* means *"Āpo nārā iti proktaha āpo vai narasunavaḥ. Ayanam tasyataha sarvam ten nārāyaṇaḥ smṛtā."* It means the body is *āpo* means nārā and who lives in each and every body is *Nārāyaṇa*.

The Paramātmā is without qualities and form but when He creates His world he himself incarnates in various shapes and qualities. In the *Taittiriya Āraṇyaka* it is seen that when a master gives the mantra of *Viṣṇu Gāyatri* to his disciple, he says, *"Nārāyaṇāy vidmahe, vaṣṇudevāya dhmahi tanno viṣṇuḥ pracodayāt."* It means "I try to understand this all pervading Viṣṇutatva. (the element which is all-pervading). I always thought about him in my mind and may He protect us."

The Upāsanā of Viṣṇu is important. The *Puruṣa sūkta* and *Viṣṇu sūkta* are recited in the Upāsanā of Viṣṇu. Later on Viṣṇu Upāsanā has taken different form and it has changed into *Vaiṣṇava Sampradāya*.

The idea is that Viṣṇu maintains and preserves the world. Therefore though He is formless Paramātmā, He incarnates in the various forms according to necessity. The Puraṇas describe

His different forms, among them the ten forms namely. *Matsya* (Fish), *Kurma* (tortoise) *Varāha* (Pig) *Nṛsiṅha* (a manlion), *Vāman* (a short man), *Parasūrāma, Śri Rāma, Śri Kṛṣṇa,* (or Kajula) *Buddha* and *Kalki* are famous and worshipped devotionally.

Later Upāsanā of Viṣṇu

Very few people worship the nirguṇa and formless Paramātman, because it is difficult to conceive the all-pervading Paramātman by sheer intellect. Man has always tried to worship some visible form with the understanding that this visible form is only a phase of His great existence. In the Vedas, He is worshipped in the various abstract forms namely *Vaiśvānara, Praṇava, Āditya, Viṣṇu, Varuṇa, Indra, Agni* etc. But later on the mode of Upāsanā turned into actual idol worship of specific forms identified by particular names given to that nameless and formless all-pervading *'Parmātma-tatva'*. In the *Viṣṇu sūkta* of the Ṛgveda Paramātman is praised as *Viṣṇu* and it is accepted that this *Sūkta* is the origin of *Vaiṣṇavism*.

The *Viṣṇu* Upāsanā follows the idol worship of *Viṣṇu* also called *"Nārāyaṇa."* We have already seen the meaning of the word Viṣṇu i.e. all pervading nature. *Viṣṇu* is always adjuncted with the word *`Bhagavān'*. *`Bhaga'* means `riches' and *Vān* means `with'. Who is with all the riches is called Bhagvān. there are six types of riches, namely, success, charity, wealth, valour, brightness, (*Yaśa, Śri, Audarya, Bala, Vīrya, Teja*). One who possesses all of them completely and in whom there is no single disposable vice is called *Bhagavān*. Because all these virtues are ascribed to Him, He has now become *`Saguṇa' Iśvar*.

Vaiṣṇava Sampradāya is identified with the *Saguṇa* worship of *Bhagavān Viṣṇu*. The Ṛgveda reads, *"Tanstotārāh purvyam yarthāvida ṛtasya garbham januśa privartan. Asya jānato nam cidviktam mahāste Viṣṇo sumatim bhajāmahe."*[27] It means Viṣṇu resides in the heart of every existence, we perceive Him like that and worship Him. In the Ṛgveda there is also a well know verse-that is *"Yasya tri purṇā madhunā kṣiyamāmaswadhāyā madayanti. Ya ua tridhātu pṛthivimuta dyāmeko dādhārā bhuvanāni viśva."*[28] It means *Viṣṇu* has three sweet feet full of nectar with which He protects Earth, Heaven and Space. This description of *Viṣṇu* might have later on popularised the idea that *Viṣṇu* is the guardian of all the three Lokas.[29]

In India people worship various types of idols of *Viṣṇu*. Some of them are as follow—

1. A little child lay on a leaf of *Pipple* (Banyan) tree sucking a thumb of his leg, floating on the Ocean.
2. God Viṣṇu lay leisurely in the Ocean of milk of the Great Serpent called *Śeṣa,* His wife *Lakṣmi* is serving Him affectionately, a lotus has sprung form his navel, Lord Brahmā is sitting on it.
3. *Śri Nārāyana* is standing with *Lakṣmi.*
4. Idols of ten incarnations of Lord *Viṣṇu;* namely, Matsya, Kurma, Varāha, Nṛsinha, Vāmana, Paraśurāma, Śri Rāma, Śri Kṛṣṇa, Bhagavān Buddha, and Kalki.

The idol of *Viṣṇu* has four arms holding four weapons namely *Śankha* (conch), *Cakra* (a disk), *Gadā* (mace) and the *Padma* (lotus). These weapons are symbolic. *Śankha* means Sound, *Cakra* suggests speed, *Gadā* is striking Power and Lotus is Knowledge. *Viṣṇu* wears a garland called *Vaijayanti Mālā.* He wears a necklace with a diamond called *Kaustubha Maṇi.* The *Mālā* and *Diamaond* are said to be like the *Savitā* i.e. the Sun. *Viṣṇu* and *Lakṣmi* are shown together to imply the unification of prosperity of spiritual and physical worlds respectively.

The upāsakas undertake the Upāsanā of *Viṣṇu* in the idol forms. There are different sects in Vaisnavism and each sect worships different types of idols. Also there are different types of Upāsanā methods. These methods follow the *Āgama* books which are *Pāñcarātrāgama, Sātvatāgama, Ekāyana,* and *Vaikhānas Āgama.* There are manuals (*saṃhitās*) for each of these methods. These are *Ahirbudhnya Saṃhitā, Iśvar Saṃhitā, Kapiñjal Saṃhitā* and other which are probably thirteen or so. *Sātvat, Pauṣkar* and the *Jāyākhya saṃhitās* are said to be originated from *Bhagavān Viṣṇu* himself, they are called *'Ratntrayi'.* Some say that there are hundred and eight total *Saṃhitās.* Any way the *Viṣṇu* Upāsanā is performed according to the prescription of these *Saṁhitās.*

In the *Sātvat Saṃhitā Viṣṇu* is worshipped by four names. viz. *Vāsudeo, Saṅkarṣaṇa, Pradyumna,* and *Anirūddha.* There is a separate *mantra* for each of these names. The *Saṁhitā* describes the types of the temples and the methods of the idol worship in detail. It is said that Lord *Kṛṣṇa* took birth in the family which was worshipped Lord Viṣṇu by *Sātvat Āgama.* He nourished and flourished this *Āgama.*

The *Pauṣkara Saṁhitā* envisages four theories or *Siddhānta*, namely, *Āgama siddhānt*, *Taṅtrasiddhānt*, *Maṅtrasiddhāṅt* and *Taṅtrātaṅtrasiddhānt*. *Āgama siddhānt* prescribes idol worship of Bhagavān Viṣṇu. Maṅtra siddhāṅt prescribes four-idol worship, namely *Vāsudeva, Saṅkarśaṇa, Pradyumna,* and *Aniruddhā* as *Sātvat* type. Taṅtra siddhāṅt accepts the worship of nine idols of nine incarnations of Lord Viṣṇu, namely *Matsya, Kurma, Varāha, Vāmana, Nṛsinha, Paraśurāma, Śri Rāma, Śri Kṛṣṇa* and *Kalki*. Pauṣkar Saṃhitā enumerates four stages of Upāsaka, namely, *Samayi, Putraka, Sādhaka,* and *Ācārya*. When a student enters in the *Pauṣkar Āgama* discipline he becomes *Samayi,* whom the Upāsanā of a circle which has a lotus in the middle is prescribed. When he completes this Upāsanā he becomes *'Putraka'*. This period of the upāsanā of a circle, which contains many lotuses is called *Cakrābijamaṅdalāntargata upāsanā*. After he completes this upāsanā he become *'Sādhaka'* and now the upāsanā of many different circles placed in one big circle is prescribed. After completion of these studies he becomes *Ācārya*.

The third book i.e. Saṁhitā, is Jāyākhya Saṁhitā. Formulation of maṅtras, mudrā, circles etc. are the subjects of this Saṃhitā which are technical (Tāntrika) in essence. This Saṃhitā states that there are sixteen types of Vaiṣṇavas namely, *ekānti, sātvat, sikḥi, yati, yogi, śāstrājana śāstradhāraka* etc. The individuals have different likings. According to their vṛtties they have to choose suitable type of upāsanā.

Nārāyaṇa, Vāsudeo and *Viṣṇu* are three major deities of *Vaiṣṇava* before the birth of Śrikṛṣṇa who is the founder of Bhāgavat Dharma and has also become the main deity of this sect. It is believed that these four deities have situated themselves in their original forms at four locations in Bhārat Varṣa. In West at *Nārāyaṇādri* He is in the form of *Nārāyaṇa,* in the South at Śrirangapaṭṭaṇam, as *Vāsudeo,* in the East at *Kānci* as *Viṣṇu*. In the North at *Tirupati* as *Srikṛṣṇa*. The worship rituals are different at all these places. At *Venkteśvar* of *Tirupati* the *pujāvidhi* is performed as per Vaikhānas Āgama. For other three deities though Paṅcarātra Āgma is prescribed. There is a separate process of Pujā for each deity. For *Nārāyaṇa, Sātvat Saṃhitā, Isvara Saṃhitā* and *Aṣṭākṣara Mantra* are followed. For *Vāsudeva Pauṣkar* and *Parameśvara ṣamhitā* and *dvāḍaśākṣara Mantra* is practised. For *Viṣṇu Jāyākhya* and *Padma Saṃhitā* and *Śaḍākṣara Mantra* is prescribed. The *Mantras* of four deities are—

1. "Om namo Venkaṭeśāya." It means I bow to *Venkaṭeśvara*.
2. "Om namo Nārāyaṇāya." It means I bow to *Nārāyaṇa*.
3. "Om namo bhagavate Vāsudevāya." It means I bow to *Bhagavān Vāsudeva*.
4. "Om namo Viṣṇave." It means I bow to *Viṣṇu*. (Nāradiya Saṃhitā 2nd Ch.)

Kṛṣṇa is called *Venkaṭeśvara* and *Bālaji* at *Tirupati*. *Nārāyaṇa* is called as *Śrinivāsa* and *Sampatkumāra at Nārāyaṇādri*. *Vāsudeva* is called *Ranganāth at Śrirangam*. *Viṣṇu* is called as *Varadarāja* and *Devarāja* at *Viṣṇukañchi*. We have a table for this description.

Place	*Direction*	*Deity*	*Idol*	*Saṃhitā (Pramāna)*	*Saṃhitā (Vyākhyān)*	*Mantra*
Venkatādri Tirumal Āndhra	North	Kriṣṇa	Tirupati Venkateśvar Bālāji	Marici		Om namo Venkateśāya
Narayanādri Yadavādri Mysura State	West	Nārāyaṇa	Śrinivāsa Sampatkumāra	Sātvat	Iśvar	Om namo Nārāyaṇāya
Srirangam	South	Vāsudeva	Ranganātha	Pauṣkara	Parameśvar	Om namo Bhagavate Vāsudevāya
Hastagiri Viṣnukāñci (Tāmilnādu)	East	Viṣṇu	Varadarāja Devarāja	Jāyākhya	Padma	Om namo Viṣṇave

All these types of pujā rituals from different Saṁhitā and Āgamas are generally followed in all the Vaiṣṇava Temples. But there are some temples in south India which follow a self styled Pūjā rituals which is independent of these types. It is called Paraśurāma method.

The *Pūjā* rituals described in the different Saṁhitās in the Vaikhānasa Āgama are ascribed to the four Ṛṣis, namely, *Marici, Atri, Bhṛgu* and *Kaśyapa*. These rituals are practised in different temples of Vaikhānasa Āgama, however the Pāncarātra Saṁhitās are numerous, some different Saṁhitās are used for convenience in different temples. The architecture of different Vaiṣṇava Temples is closely connected with the different types of Upāsanā symbols in various *Āgamas* and *Saṁhitās*.

Vaiṣṇava sampradāya flourished in the South India after the period of Gupta Dynasty. Learned Priests started studying and understanding the original roots of the dharma. *Ācārya Śankara* wrote expositions on the *Prasthāntrayi* i.e. the *Upaniṣads* the *Brahmasūtra* and the *Bhagavadgītā*. However some other *Ācāryas* did not agree with the opinions professed by *Ācārya Śankara* and they established different schools of thoughts. With this development different types of Vaiṣṇava disciplines took shape. However it should not forget that all these disciplines follow the original *Vaiṣṇava Dharma* principle. These disciplines then started forming definite dogmas, viz; *Advaita, Viśiṣtādvaita, Śuddhādvaita, Dvaitādvaita dvaita* etc. Also the *Ācāryas* who enthusiastically spread these dogmas are named after them.

Cults

The following disciplines in the *Vaiṣṇava Sampradāya* are famous and prevalent in different parts of the country.

Śri Sampradāya of Viśiṣtādvaita Sampradāya—*Śri Yamunācārya* founded this discipline or *Sampradāya*. He lived in the first quarter of the tenth century. He was fourth disciple in order from the first Ācarya of the *Vaiṣṇava Sampradāya, Śri Raghunāthācārya*. Taking the ideas from the Bhāgavat and the Pāncarātra Āgama he defined a new dogma of the *Viśiṣtādvaita* in which the devotee even after the identification of his unification with the deity remains aloof, (separate conscious state from the deity) as the devotee to worship the deity.

Śri Rāmānujācārya Sampradāya—*Śri Rāmānujācārya* lived in the first quarter of the 11th century. He was *Ācārya* in the tradition of *Śri Sampradāya*. He forwarded his relatively different idea. His prophesy was '*jiva* and *Iśvara* are different entities and they posses a mutual relationship of servant and master respectively.'

Sanaka Sampradāya—*Śri Nimbārkācārya* who lived in the first quarter of the twelfth century near Mathurā in North India, founded this discipline. He advocated the dogma of *Dvaitādvaita*. He holds that the *Jiva*, the *Jagat*, and the *Iśvar* are different. The existence and the relationship between the *Jiva* and the *Jagat* are dependent in *Iśvara*. The unselfish devotion is itself the service to God. It mainly emphasizes the devotion comparable to the relationship between *Rādhā* and *Kṛṣṇa*. This discipline is very popular in North India.

Brahma Sampradāya—This discipline is founded by *Śri Madhvācārya* who lived in the first quarter of the thirteenth century at Udipi in the South India. He holds that the *Jiva* and the *Iśvar* are different. *Iśvar* is self potent and the *Jiva* is dependent on Him. The *Jiva* can get *Mukti* either by the ardent devotion or by the *Dhyāna Yoga*.

There is also *Puṣti Sampradāya* led by *Sri Vallabhācārya*. It flourished in Āndhra Pradesh during the period of Vijayanagara dynasty. *Caitanya Sampradāya* took shape in Bengal in the fifteenth century. There is also *Viṣṇusvāmi Sampradāya* prevalent in some part of the South India.

Popular Stotras

Viṣṇu Sahasranāma is a popular stotra which finds it place in the *Mahābhārata*. One thousand names of *Viṣṇu* are praised by the devotee regularly.

Śāḷigrāma

Viṣṇu worshippers adore and honour *Śāḷigrāṃa* as the symbol of *Viṣṇu*. Its brief discussion follows—

Particular type of stones are found in the Gaṇḍaki river with black, brown, greenish, white colour at outer surface and golden in the inside, which are called *Śāḷigrāma*. Gaṇḍaki flows from the village *Śālagrāma*. The word *Śālagrāma* is used in the *Mahābhārata* as a name of the place where *Viṣṇu* is said to be always present.[1] *Śālagrāma* as a holy place in mentioned in the *Varāha Purāṇa*, the *Matsya Purāṇa*, the *Brahmāṇḍa Purāṇa*, the *Agni Purāṇa*, the *Vāmana Purāṇa* and the *Viṣṇupurāṇa*.[2] Each of this type of the *Śālagrāma* has a hole, and we can see the lines resembling *cakra* of *Viṣṇu* inside it.

The *Śāḷigrāma* is kept in the milk or rice to examine its reality; if the weight and size of the stone increases then it is taken as a real *Śāligrāma*.

Maddhva-cult devotees give more importance to *Śāḷigrāma* than the image of *Viṣṇu*.[3] It is said that a celibate should worship the *śāḷigrāma*, with five dots and having two unequal cakras.[4] There is a chapter in the *Padmapurāṇa* where the importance of *śāḷigrama* is narrated. It is said that *śāḷigrama* is very holy and this brings *Dharma* to the house. It is the icon of God.[5] The name of this chapter is *Śāḷigrāma Pujā Mahātmya*. Various *Purāṇas* mention varieties of *Śālgrāma*. In the fourteenth chapter of the *Garuḍa Purāṇa* more than twenty varieties are mentioned. These are (1) *Śāligrāma* with *cakras* near to each other. (2) Red *śāligrāma* with two *cakras* joining face to face. (3) *Śāligrama*, with a subtle *cakra* and yellow colour. (4) *Śāligrāma*, round and a long hole. (5) Black *śaligrāma* with three lines drawn on it. (6) *Śāligrāma* with mace sign in the middle and elevated navel circle. (7) *Śāligrāma* with three dots. (8) *Śāligrāma* with five dots, two unequal *cakras*, it is called *Varāhaśakti*. (9) *Śaligrāma* having three blue lines. (10) *Śaligrāma* with a whirl-pool and a dot. (11) *Śāligrāma* with five lines. (12) *Śāligrāma* with a mark of a mace. (13) Circular *Śāligrāma*. (14) With *cakra* on its left side. (15) Multicoloured *Śāligrāma*. (16) Gross *śāligrāma*. (17) Dark blue *śāligrāma*. (18) Red *śāligrāma* with one hole and long line. (19) With one *cakra* and lotus. (20) With broad hole and gross *cākra*. (21) With short stick and a dot. (22) With five lines and lustrous. (23) With *cakra* and one lotus, black in colour. (24) With a line and big lotus. (25) *Śāligrāma* belonging to *Dvārakā*. (26) With a line, black colour, (27) With one door, four *cakras*, with golden line and a foot-print of a cow, with the shape of *Kadamba* flower, these are three varieties which belong to *Lakṣmi Nārāyaṇa*.[6]

Śri Rāma Upāsanā

The personality of *Śri Rāma* is an indivisible part of the Hindu mind. It is held that He is the seventh incarnation of *Bhagavān Viṣṇu*. It is said in the *Gitā* that whenever social evils upsurge and the entire civilization comes under the threat of barbarous persecution, Paramātman incarnates Himself and destroys the enemies of humanity and restores the virtues. The verse is "*Yadā yadā hi dharmasya glānirbhavati Bhārata abhyutthānam adharmasya tadātmānam sṛjāmyaham. Paritrāṇāya sādhunām vināśāyaca duṣkṛtām dharma sansthāpanārthāya sambhavāmi yuge yuge.*"[1] God *Viṣṇu* is incarnated as *Rāma* to end the tyranny of King *Rāvaṇa* who held the entire human race on the Earth at ransom. *Rāma* took birth as the eldest son of King *Daśaratha*. The entire biography of *Rāma* is described in the book 'Rāmāyaṇa' written by Vālmiki. Atterwards many books like *Adhyātma*

Rāmāyaṇa, Adbhūta Rāmāyaṇa, Mahārāmāyaṇa etc. are written on Him which praise *Rāma* as God, not as a person and prescribe different methods of His worship. *Nārada Purva Tāpaniya upaniṣad* also describes various Upāsanās of *Śri Rāma* for gaining happiness etc. The personality of *Rāma* is known to every Indian and therefore detailing about it here is not warranted.

Some Upāsanā methods of worship of *Śri Rāma* are given below—The word *Śri Rāma* itself carries potential spiritual power and therefore even Lord *Śiva* recites it now and then. In *Ramarakṣā stotra,* it is mentioned that *Śiva* tells *Pārvati* to recite *'Rāmanāma'* as the single word *'Rāma'* carries the power of thousand names of God in its one letter. The verse is *"Rāmarāmeti rāmeti rame rāme manorame. Sahasranāmatattulyam rāmanāma varānane."*[2] *Mahārāmāyaṇa* gives the meaning of the word *Rāma* like this, *"Rakāro' nalabijam syād ye sarve vādavādayaḥ. Akāro bhānubijam syād vedaśāstraprakāśakaḥ. Makāraścandrabijam ca sadambuparipūraṇam."* It means 'R' is the original : root : word of Fire—the Fire which is in the Man's body (*Jaṭharāgni*), the Fire which is in the ocean (*Vaḍavānala*) and the fire which is in the forest (*Dāvāgni*)—all these three modes of Fire have their origin in the syllable 'R'. 'A' syllable destroys the ignorance. And 'M' syllable takes away the sorrows of worldly life. It is the root word of the Moon.

In the another verse the meaning of the word *Rāma* is : the syllable 'R' is the root of *vairāgya,* 'A' denotes knowledge and 'M' suggests devotion. The verse is, *"Rakārahaituvairāgyam paramam yacca kathyate, Akāro jñānahetuśca makāro bhakti haitukam."*

Śri Rāmāyaṇa explains the meaning of this word as 'R' means God with wealth, *saguṇa Rāma,* 'M' is individual ego : *Jiva*: who serves *Saguṇa Rāma,* between these two stands *Sītā : Prakṛti*: who joins Jiva and *Iśvara.* See the verse, *"Rakārārtho Rāmaḥ saguṇaparamaiśvaryajaladhirmakārārtho jīvah sakalavidhikaiñkayanipunaḥ. Tayormadhyākāro yugulamatha sambandhamanayoḥo"*[3]

Different mantras are formulated according to the meaning of the root word of *Rāmā,* few are given below—

(1) *"Ram Rāmāya namaḥ"*. It means I bow before *Rāma* whose root is *'Ram'*. This mantra has six letters.[4]

(2) *"Śri Rāmaḥ śaraṇam mama."* I surrender whole-heartedly to *Rāma.*

(3) *"Sri Rāma Jaya Rāma Jaya Jaya Rāma."* Victory to *Rāma.*

(4) *"Om hrim śrim śrim Dāśarathāya namaḥ."* I bow to the

son of *Daśaratha*. "This maṅtra has *bijas* which have mystical meaning according to *Tantra Śāstra*.

(5) *"Trilokanāthāya namaḥ."* I am humble to the Lord of the three worlds, viz. the Earth, Space and Heaven.

(6) *"Rāmacandrāya svāhā."* I oblate to *Rāmacandra*.

(7) *"Rāmabhadrāya svāhā."* These two maṅtras say that the devotee obliges to *Rāma* by giving every thing to Him. Next maṅtras also shows the same meaning with some mystical words extra.

(8) *"Om Rāmāya hum fat svāhā."*

(9) *"Dāśarathāya vidmahe, sītāvallabhāya dhimahi, tanno Rāmaḥ pracodayāt."*[4] This maṅtra is famous by the name *Rāmagāyatri*, it means I try to understand Rāma. I think continuously about *Rāma*, may *Rāma* protect me and confer happiness upon me.

All these maṅtras have their different methods of worship processes : Upāsanā vidhis : All these maṅtras are prescribed by various *Ṛṣis* like *Brahmā, Satya, Agasti, Śiva, Vasiṣtha, Viśvāmitra* etc. These maṅtras are in different metres namely, *Gāyatri, Svarāt, Dhṛti, Anuṣṭubha* etc.

Among all these maṅtras, *"Śri Rāma Jaya Rāma Jaya Jaya Rāma"* is very famous and popular in this age. Any body can recite this maṅtra even without *Gurū* and initiator. This maṅtra has thirteen letters. The *Ṛṣi* of this maṅtra is *Brahmā*, the metre is *Virāt* and the deity is *Śri Rāma*. Hanumān recites this maṅtra. *Samartha Rāmadāsa* of Mahārāstra got the title `*Samartha*' by Upāsanā of *Rāma* with this maṅtra. This is a very powerful maṅtra which confers knowledge as well as worldly powers on the upāsaka. See the verse *"Śriyam Rāmam jaya Rāmam dvirjayam Ramamīrayet, Trayodaśākṣaro mantraḥ sarvasiddhikarḥ sthitaḥ."*

The *Rāma* maṅtra includes *Sītā* and *Sītā* maṅtra includes *Rāma* is a faith among devotees. The *Rāma* Upāsanā is known as the *Sītā Rāma Upāsanā* i.e. the *Yugula Upāsanā*, though there are some maṅtras like, *"Śrim Sītāyai svāhā"* used for the *Sītā Upāsanā*. The process of the Upāsanā includes meditation, *dhyāna* prior to recitation of any maṅtra and actual worship with offering flowers etc. *Dhyāna* includes name of the deity, form, life story character of the deity. So when *Rāma's dhyāna* is described, his nature and character is illustrated. Some of the *dhyāna ślokas* are given here

"Ayodhyānagareratnacitrasauvarṇa maṇdape. Mandārapuṣpirābaddh vitāne toraṇānvite. Sinhāsanasmāṣinam puṣpakopari Rāghavam. Rakṣobhirhari-bhirdevaihi suvimanāgataḥiśubhaiḥi. Sanstuyamāna munibhiḥi prahvaiśca parisevitam. Śyāmam prasannavadanam sarvābharaṇabhuṣitam."[5] It means the following form of *Śri Rāma* is prescribed for meditation, *Rāma* is rested on the throne which is tied with *mandāra* flowers and on which the jewels are studded which is made of gold. *Rāma* is served by beautiful maids, who is praised by *Ṛsis*. His face is happy and he is ornamented completely.

There are other *dhyāna* maṅtras in which the form of *Rāma* is so accurately described that the picture of *Rāma* stands before the eyes which is helpful for concentration before the beginning of the recitation of the maṅtra. *Dhyāna* is followed by *Nyāsa*, this gives strength to body to resist the power of the deity. The head forehead between the eyebrows, neck, heart, navel, thighs are touched with the different name. Then follows Japa which is fixed is numbers, such as six thousands, thirteen crores, three lakhs etc. After this recitation the oblation of lotus flowers in prescribed.

There are various methods of worship in vogue. Though in these worships the meditation of God in the qualitative form of *Rāma (saguṇa sākāra)* is accepted, the aim behind it is to approach the formless and supra qualitative status of Brahman through the worship of the form. The following verses show that the personality of *Śri Rāma* is identified with Brahman. -O *Rāma*, you are Paramātman who is *Sāt, Cit, Ānanda* : existence, Consciousness and Bliss.

1. *"Rāma tvam Paramātmāsi saccidānandavigraḥ"*.[7]
2. *"Akṣaram Brahma satyam madhye cānte ca Rāghavah." Rāma* is in the middle and at the end (everywhere) in the *Akṣara* (imperishable) Brahman.
3. *"Parama puruṣo Rāma Dāśarathirbabhuva."*[7] The Greatest *Puruṣa* (*Virāt Puruṣa*) became the son of *Daśaratha*.

Sri Gurudatta Upāsanā

God *Datta* is famous by the names *Gurudatta* and *Dattātreya*. *'Datta'* means to be given. The story of His birth is : *Atri Ṛṣi* undertook a deep penance with his wife *Anasuyā* on the mountain named *Ṛkṣa* with the expectation of getting a son like Paramātman Himself. Pleased by his penance Gods *Brahmā, Viṣṇu* and *Maheśa* appeared before the couple and blessed the *Ṛṣi* and his wife and agreed to become their son. They said *'Datta'* means 'We have given ourselves to you'. They took birth combindly as the son of *Atri Ṛṣi;* therefore he is called *Datta,* and also, as He is the son of *Atri,* He is called *Dattātreya.* The verse in *Bhāgavata* gives the description about the origin of His name *'Datta Atreya'* as,

"Atrerapatyamabhikāṅkṣatāhatuṣto Datto mayāhamiti yad bhagavān sa Dattaḥ. Yadpādapaṅkajaparāgapavitradehā yogardhimā-purumayim yaduhaihayādyah."[1] The *purāṇa* further says that from *Brahmā's aṅśa Soma* is born, from *Viṣṇu's aṅśa Dattātreya* is born and from *Maheśa's aṅśa Ṛṣi Durvāsa* is born, the verse *"Somo' bhud Brahmaṇonśena Datto Viṣṇostu yogavit. Durvāsaḥ Śankarasyāṅśo nibodāvigiraḥ prajāḥ."*[2] The devotees see all the three gods in *Dattātreya* only. *Sati Anasuyā* who is the sister of *Kapial Muni* and the daughter of *Kardama Ṛṣi* is the mother of *Dattātreya.*

Sixteen different forms and names of *Datta* are accepted generally. These names are (1) *Śriyogirāja Datta,* (2) *Atrivarada Datta,* (3) *Dattātreya,* (4) *Kālāgnisamāna Datta,* (8) *Śrijñasāgara Datta,* (9) *Śri Viśvambhara Avadhūta Datta* (10) *Māyāmukta Avadhuta Datta,* (11) *Śrimāyāyukta Avadhuta Datta,* (12) *Śri Ādiguru Datta,* (13) *Śri Śivarupa Datta,* (14) *Śri Devadeva Datta,* (15) *Śri Digaṁbara Datta,* (16) *Śri Kṛṣṇa Śāmalanayana Datta.* We find the description about these names and forms in the *Mahābhārata,* the *Harivaṅśa,* the *Śrimadbhāgavat,* the *Viṣṇupurāṇa,* the *Vāyupurāṇa,* the *Brahmavaivartapurāṇa,* the *Mārkaṇḍeyapurāṇa,* the *Mastyapurāṇa,* the *Brahmāṇḍapurāṇa,* the *Agnipurāṇa,* the *Padmapurāṇa,* the *Kṛṣṇayāmalatantra,* the *Ahribudhnya Saṁhitā.*[3] etc. These forms are also called incarnations of *Śri Dattātreya. Dattātreya* is generally called by the name *Gurudev Datta.* He, all in his forms and incarnations, is regarded as the Master, *Gurū* spiritual preceptor, who has come to Earth to deliver the knowledge of Paramātman to mankind. The word *Gurū* can be split up in different ways like *"Gṛunāti upadiṣati brahmajñanam svabhaktebhyaḥ iti Gurū",* means one who gives the knowledge of Brahman is *Gurū* and, *"girati ajñanam iti guruḥ",* means one who dispels the followers ignorance by conferring real knowledge on them is *Gurū. Dattātreya* does this work of the *Gurū* so He is called *Gurū.* He is called *Deva* because He is effulgent and destroys the darkness of others by His luminous sight. Therefore combining all these virtues He is called *Gurudeva Datta*.

Śri Harṣa praised *Avadhuta Datta* as, "*Advayamaye' dhvanisarantam*" in *Naiṣadhīya Carītam*,[4] means, `who always proceeds on the advaita way.' The great poet Māgha also praised Him as `*Avināśi Vigraḥa*' or `*Siddhadeva*', in his creation `*Śiśupālavadha*.' *Śri Śankarācārya* described *Datta* in *Jivan-mukhtānanda Lahari* in the verse, "*Maune muni guṇini guṇavan paṇḍite paṇḍitaśca, dīne dīnaḥ sukhini sukhavān bhogini prāptobhogaḥ. Murkhe murkho yuvatiṣu yuvā vāgmini prauḍhāvāgmi. Dhanyaḥ Ko' pi tribhuvanajayi yo' vadhūte' vadhūtah.* "It means, the God is a blessed one-who is silent in the silent people, virtuous in the virtuous men, scholar among the scholars, the poor in the poor, happy in the happy people, ignorant in the innocent people, who is the orator among the great orators, mukta within the self-realised people.

The disciples of *Dattātreya* see three gods viz. *Brahmā, Viṣṇu, Mahśa* in *Gurudatta* because there is a story that, these gods once approached *Sati Anasuyā* to test her single devotion & deep love for her husband. At that time her husband was out of house. The gods said to her if she really worships and adores them as God she should serve them the dinner nakedly. She thought if she denied, the gods would be insulted and if she obeyed she would loose her '*Pātivratya*' by standing naked before any male person other than husband. But she found a novel idea. She took holy water from *Kamanḍalu* (wooden bowl) and sprinkled on them and converted them into children. The gods pleased with her devotion towards her husband, gave her one child which has combined features of all of them.[5] Also it is presumed that the child has three heads. So He is worshipped as a God with three faces of *Brahmā, Viṣṇu* and *Maheśa*. Therefore, the followers of *Datta* observe that these three Gods are one only.

Dattātreya is a *Yogi, Jñani* and a revealer of *Ātmavidyā*. He had undergone a deep penance of Lord *Śiva* in pursuance of the will of His father in the *Gautami* forest by following the yogic process and after completion of it became eligible of *Jñāna* and Salvation. Thereafter He delivers the *jñāna* to others. He was the teacher of the Upāsanā of *Śrividyā-Mantra* of *Bhagavati Tripura Sundari* to *Parśurāma*. It is described in *Paraśurāma Tantra*, that He held the position of an *Ācārya* in the religious ceremony of the last *sanskāra* : funeral of *Ṛṣi Jamadagni*, according to the request of *Reṇuka*, the mother of *Paraśurāma*. he has delivered the knowledge of *vairgāya* and Bliss to *Pralhāda*, the son of *Kayādhu*. He preached *Yadu* and conferred on him *Sparśa Dikṣā*. He has given the list of His twenty four masters to *Yadu*.[6] he advised King *Kārtavirya* in the *mantra, tantra* and *siddhies*. He taught the Upāsanā of *Yogamārga* to King *Alarka*, the son of *Madālasā*. He blessed king *Āyu* with a son named *Nahuṣa* and with the knowledge. He gave the knowledge of chemistry and metallurgy to *Nāgārjuna*. He conferred the knowledge of *caturanga yoga* viz. *Āsana, Prāṇāyama, Mudra* and *Samādhi (Haṭhayoga)* to *Gorakṣanātha*, the leader of *'Nātha Sampradāya'*.

There is a scriptural book for the disciples of *Gurudatta* named *Datta Saṁhitā* which contains eighteen thousand stanzas. *Paraśurāma* compressed it in six thousand stanzas. The book containing *Dattātreya's* advice is famous by thė name *'Avadhūta Gitā'*. The meaning of the word *'Avadhūta'* is given in *Avadhūtopaniṣad* as the syllable 'a' suggests imperishability, 'v' means acme of perfection, 'dh' means to shatter the trammels of *samsāra*, 'ta' suggests the *Mahāvākyas* like *'Tattvamasi'*. *Ācārya Sajani* wrote a book named *Kathābodha*. The other book of the same name is also present. These books are the basic books for *Datātreya* cult. There is a criticism called *Prakāśa* of this book by *Śri Nilakantha Caturdhara*. *Gangādhara Sarasvati* of Maharashtra wrote a book *'Gurucaritra'* for this cult and there is a biography of incarnation of *Dattātreya* included in this book. *Śri Vāsudevānanda Sarasvati* has written a book in Sanskrit named *'Datta Purāṇa'* and in Marāthi language named *'Datta Māhātmya'* in which he has discussed the greatness of *Bhagvān Śri Gurudatta*.

Datta is worshipped in the form *'Ekamukhi'* and *'Trimukhi'*. His idol is made in a *sanyasi* and a *rājasa Bhāva* : expressions. He has six hands, He holds a *damaru*, a *rudrākṣa mālā*, a trident, a *kamaṇḍalu* (wooden bowl), a conch, and a *cakra* in his hands. *Datta* Upāsanā is performed with *pūjā, stotra* recitations, *mantra-japa, Datta-kavaca, Dattavajrapanjara, Dattahṛdaya, Datta sahasranāma* and with *Śridatta siddhayantra*. *Datta yantra* consists of eight different mantras formed of different single letters, in addition to this a *Malāmantra* is also inscribed in the yantra. There are other several mantras too. Datta is said as *smaraṇagāmi* means He at once appears before the devotee when he remembers Him.

God *Dattātraya* is known and worshipped all over India. He has attracted attention every where and at all times. It is believed that He takes rest in *Mātāpura*, He lives on the peaks of the mount *Sahyādri*, He bathes in the holy *Gangā* at *Kāśi*, He performs daily routine religious activities like *Sandhyā* etc; in *Kuhvāda*, He gathers *'bhikṣa'* (begging for food) at *Kolhāpur*. He dines at *Pāncālapur*, He performs *Yogasādhana* at *Gāṇagāpur*. But he rushes at once when His devotee calls Him.

Avadhūta Cult—The philosophy of *Datta sampradāya : Avadhuta* cult : -In this cult it is held that the Supreme Self, beyond the qualities and forms, Paramātman, descends into Pure *Māyā* as *Hiraṇyagarbha*. Then He further descends into egoistic consciousness called *jīvabhāva* and gets himself engulfed into bondages of *Samsāra cakra* i.e. deluded perception of passing phenomena, created by Himself alone. Every individual self is a particle of the Supreme Self, Paramātman. Therefore knowledge of the self means the knowledge of Supreme self i.e. *Ātmavidyā*, and one can reach the Supreme Self by knowing the real Self only. Various gods represent the different parts, qualities and forms of the Supreme Self, therefore, one may worship any god but one must understand that the god whom he is worshipping is the Self, then only one can know *Ātmavidyā* by worshipping any of the gods. If one identifies One's god with only the qualities which the god manifests, then one will unify with him or with the abode of that god but will not get self knowledge: that is the knowledge of Supreme Self. By *Ātmavidyā* alone one can become free from bondages of *Saṇsāra cakra* and become an *Avadhūta*.

In this cult it is assumed that dissolution of the universe takes place exactly in the reverse direction of the evolution. The individual self ascends to the Pure *Māyā* and the Pure *Māyā* unifies with the Supreme Self. At last only the Supreme Self remains. This dissolution is called *Pralaya*. Five types of *pralaya* are mentioned in *Datta* cult—(1) daily sleep of individual's gross body, (2) sleep of *Brahmāṇḍa* : daily pralaya, (3) death of individual's gross body. (4) death of *Brahmāṇḍa* (5) greatest doom-*ātyaṅtik pralaya*.

From ancient to the modern times worship of *Dattātreya* or *Dattopāsanā* occupies a prominent place in the Upāsanā literature. This is because of the status of the deity as the *Gurū Avatāra*. The purpose of worshipping this deity is *Jñāna* and *Mokṣa*. *Dattātreya* signifies the role of preceptor who initiates the disciple into the path of liberation.

In the popular life *Datta* worship was mainly practised at His sacred places in different shrines for worldly gains. However *P.P. Śri Vāsudevānanda Sarasvati* in His different works purified the cult making the deity as the Divine expression of the Upaniṣadic Brahman, and bringing different Upāsanās under the central theme i.e. *Gurū Upāsanā*. The initiator — *Dikṣśa Gurū* is to be looked upon not as an embodied human being but God in the human form *'Śrigurustrimūrtiti'*; therefore the terms *Datta* and *Gurū* become identified.

This has led to positive unification in the Upāsanā practices and establishment of their relation with the main stream of the Indian way of philosophy. God *Dattātreya* in Indian thought represents unifying force of the *Vedic* Tradition (*Nigama*), *Tantra* Tradition (*Āgama*) and the *Bhakti* Tradition. *Varṇāśrama Dharma, Śaktipāt Kuṇdalini Yoga* and *Advaita* view of life are the main aspects of *Śrividyā* and *Dattātreya* representing as *Guruṇām Gurū, Yogināṁ Cakravarti* of this *Śrividyā*.

Similarly, in the nineteen-fifties *Nyāyaratna Dhuṇḍirāja Śāstri Vinod* has written a *Stotra* on *Śrividyā* and *Śrigurū* following the tradition of *Avadhūta Sampradāya*. The name of this *stotra* is *'Gurupādukodaya Stotra'*. The two sandles (*Pāduka*) of *Gurū* denote *Puruṣa* and *Prakṛti;* and their unification. This *stotra* praises *Advaita* of *Upāsaka* and *Upāsya*. It includes the application of *Śrividya* and it is useful for donation of *Śreyas* and *Preyas*, i.e. worldly gains and emancipation. *Śri Gurū* is called *Paramātmabija* and His Upāsanā is threefold : *Parā* (topmost), *Parāpara* (medium), *Aparā* (lower type). By this stotra the *Vimarśā Śakti* of the devotee awakes and the devotee can see *Ātmagurū*. The first step of this Upāsanā is the duality of Upāsya and Upāsaka (*Aparā*), in the second step (*Parāparā*) the duality remains but the knowledge of unity is awakened and the third step is non-dualism (*Advaita*) of *Upāsya* and *Upāsaka*. The awakening of *Vimarśā Śakti* is the awakening of *Kuṇḍalini*. Various deities disclose themselves before the Upāsaka because the Upāsanā of *Śri Gurū* includes the Upāsanā of all deities.

References

(1) Gaṇapati Upāsanā

19. Ṛgveda—1-18-7
20. *Ibid*—10-112-9
21. *Ibid*—10-72-2
22. *Ibid*8-81-1, 6
23. *Ibid*5-43-12
24. *Ibid*1-18-1 to 5
25. *Ibid*—1-40-1 to 8
26. *Ibid*—2-23-2 to 19
27. *Ibid*—2-25-1 to 5
28. *Ibid*—2-26-1 to 4
29. *Ibid*7-97-3, 9
30. *Ibid*—10-155-2, 3
31. Ṛgveda Pariśiṣta—27-11
32. Ṛgveda—6-75-17
33. *Ibid*—10-164-4
34. *Ibid*—2-31-1
35. Taittiriya Saṁhitā—4-1-2-2 Vājasaneyi Saṁhitā 3-57
36. Vajasaneyi Saṁhitā—16-25
37. Mānavagṛhyasūtra—2-14
38. Yājñavaikya Smṛti—1-271
39. Saiva Purāna-Rudra-Kumāra—16
40. Bhaviṣya Purāṇa—4-2 Brahmavaivarta Purāṇa—3-18
41. Gargabhāṣya—1-13
42. Padmpurāṇa—Adi-24
43. Ṛgveda—2-23-1
44. Vaiṣṇvism, Śaivism and Minor religious system. By Sir R.G. Bhandarkar
45. Gaṇesh Purāṇa—Upāsanākhanda—8
46. Gaṇapati Atharvasirsa—40
47. *Ibid*—51

(2) Śiva Upāsanā

47a. Atharva Veda—19th Kānd—8
48. Ṛgveda—5-4-30-12
49. Ṛgvidhān—2-15
50. *Ibid*—2-27
51. *Ibid*—1-114-7
52. *Ibid*—1-147-7
53. Taittiriya Brāhmaṇa—3-7-14-4
54. Ṛgveda—10-18-1
55. Taittiriya Brāhmaṇa—3-10-8-2
55a. Kalyāṇa Upāsanā Anka—Śivatattva aur Śaivopāsanā. Page 375-376.
56. Padmapurāna Ṣṛsti khanda—32
57. Ṛgveda—I-114-8
58. *Ibid*—I-114-1
59. *Ibid*—VII-46-2

60. *Ibid*—I-43-4
61. *Ibid*—II-33-4
62. *Ibid*—VII-46-3
63. Taittiriya Saṁhitā IV—5-1 Vājasaneyi Saṁhitā Chapter 16
64. Śvetāsvatar Upaniṣad—3-1
65. Śvetāśvatar Upaniṣad—3-3 Ṛgveda—X-81-3
66. Śvetāśvatar Upaniṣad—4-11
67. Vaiṣṇavism Śaivism and Minor Religious System—By Sir R.G. Bhandarkar.
68. Mahābhārat-Vanaparva-Chapter—39-21 to 23. B.O.R.I. Edition
69. Mahābhārat-Droṇaparva—Ch. 80-81 B.O.R.I. Edition.
70. Mahābhārat-Anuśāsana Parva—Ch.-14
70a. See the references in Ch. VII
71. Pancārthasya dipika—by Madhav
72. Taittiriya Āraṇyaka—X-43-47. Mahānārāyaṇiya Up.—17.
73. Śivasūtravimarśiṇi by Kṣemarāja under Sutras 1.2.3.
74. Anubhava Sūtras of Mayideva. Solapur 1909
75. Vaiṣṇvism Śaivism and Minor Religious Systems by Sir R.G. Bhandarkar Page—124-Notes.
76. Śvetāśvatar Upaniṣad 4-10
77. Śivamānasa pūjā-Śankarācārya.
78. Śivamānasa pūjā—1
79. Śivamahimna Stotra—26
80. Śvetāśvatar Upaniṣad—6-7.
81. Śivapurāṇa-Jñāna Adhyāya—76.
82. Śivapurāṇa Jñāna Adhyāya—77
82a. Kalyāṇa Upāsanā Aṅka-Śivatattva Śaivopāsanā.
83. Śrimat Bhagavata—8-7-22.
84. Brahma Vaivarta purāṇa-Janma khanda.
85. Padma Purāṇa—4-250.
86. Mahābhāratā Anu. Parva-Ch. 17-B.O.R.I. edition
87. *Ibid,* Śānti Parva Pari—1-28.
88. Śiva Purāṇa-Śiva Koti—35.
89. Liṅga Purāṇa—65-98.
90. Mahābhārat-Ch. 14. B.O.R.I. Edition.
91. Mahābhārat-Anu parva Ch. 14. Ch. 45, 46. B.O.R.I. edition and Sauptika Parva CH. 17, 18.
92. Mahabhārata-Droṇa parva-Ch. 57-Stanzas-38 to 44, 49 to 58 B.O.R.I. Edition.
93. Mahābhārata-Anu Parva—47.
94. Mahābhārata Shanti Parva—1-28.
95. Mahābhārata Aśva-B. 14. by Aśvathāman in Saupatika Parva-Ch. 7.
96. Baudhāyana Gṛyasutra 2.18.11-16.
97. Kaivalyopaniṣad 2.1.

Rudrākṣa

1. Bṛhajjābālopaniṣad—VII.
2. Śiva Rahasya.
3. Śiva Purāṇa. Vājasaneyi Saṃhitā, Uttara Kānda—Ch. 14.
4. Siva Purāṇa—13-16.

Śri Hanumān Upāsanā

1. Rāmāyaṇa-Kiṣkindhā kānda, Sundar Kānda, Yuddha kānda.
2. Kalyāṇa Upāsanā Aṅka-Śir Hanumānjiki Upāsanāke kuncha mantra aur Sansksipta Anuṣṭhāna Vidhi.
3. Nārad Purva Tāpaniya up—74-122-125.
4. *Ibid*—74-145, 147
5. *Ibid*—74-169, 170

(3) Śakti Upāsanā

1. Nirukta—7. 21. 1.
2. Śir Sūkta—1.
3. Śri Sūtka—5, 6.

3a. For all of these stanzas I owe to 'Prasāda' Aug. 71. Special issue on Devi.

4. Brahmasūtra Bhāṣya—1.4.3.
5. Bṛhadāraṇyaka Upaniṣad—1.4.3.
6. Ṛgveda—10.125.
7. Devi Bhāgavata—1.15.52.

7a. Kalyāṇa Upāsanā Anka. P. 386 (Śakti Upāsanāki Āvaśyakatā Aur Usakā Ādhyātmika Rahasya. Śri Svāmiji Divyānanda Sarasvati.)

8. Religious Sects in Ancient India. Page 79. D.A. Pai.

8a. Kalyāṇa-Upāsanā Aṅka Page 413-'Śricakraki Upāsanā'

9. Commentary on Sloka 5, 7 & 20
10. Sakti, A Divine Power-page 51, by Sudhendukumara Das.

10a. Durgā Saptaśati

11. Mālinivijayottara-Prathama Adhikāra. 51.8.13. (For these references I owe to Sudhendu Kumara Das.)
12. *Ibid*—3-4, 1.25.35.
13. *Ibid*—12, 13, 14, 15, 16, 17 Adhikars
14. *Ibid*—3-25-29-34.35.52, 18.37.39.
15. *Ibid*—9, 11 Adhikāra.
16. Śakit, A Divine Power-Page 94. By-Sudhendukumar Das.
17. *Ibid*—Page 118.

17a. Prasāda. Agu. 71. special issue on Devi.

18. Durgā Saptaśati. 2nd Adhyāya.
19. *Ibid*—5 Adhyāya.
20. Devi Bhāgavata—5th—9, 49, 50.
21. Prasāda-Aug. 71 Special issue on Devi.

(4) Sūrya Upāsanā

Gāyatri Upāsanā

(a) Brahmabindu Upaniṣad-2

1. Bṛhadyājñavalkyasmṛti-Kalyāṇa-Upāsanā Aṅka. P. 158
2. *Ibid*—4-35
3. Bhāradvāja Smṛti—6-146 (Kalyāṇa p. 158)
4. Skandapurāṇa Kāshikhānd—9-3 (Kalyāṇa-p. 158)
5. Nirukta—7-12-5 (Kalyāṇa. p. 158)
6. Śatapath Brāhmaṇa—14-8-15-7

7. Bṛhadāraṇyaka Upaniṣad—5.14.4
8. Ṛgveda—3-5-9-10
9. Devibhāgvat—12-6 and 12-3
10. Śukla Yajurveda—1-31
11. Devibhāgvat—9-1-42
12. Chāndogya Upaniṣad—3-12-1
13. Padma Purāṇa-Svargakhand 53-58.
14. Kurmapurāṇa—14-58.
15. Ṛgveda—1-115-1
16. Nirukta—10-31
17. *Ibid*—12, 13
18. Ṛgveda 7-76-1
20. *Ibid* 1-50, 115, 164, 191, 5-40, 44, 47. 10-39, 88, 139, 158, 170, 181, 189.
21. *Ibid* 1-50-1
22. Rāmayaṇa-Ayodhyā Kāṅḍa—87-18, 97-7
23. Mahābhārata-Āraṇyakaparva—3-18 to 33 B.O.R.I. Edition.
24. Mahābhārata-Ādiparva 104, 7 to 11
24a. Prasāda (Special issue on Sūrya).
25. Biography of Ādi Śankarācārya-by-Ānandagiri
26. Ādityahṛdays Stotra-4.5 Vālmiki Rāmāyana Edition-Baroda-Sarga 107 Yuddha Kāṅḍa Page 1082. Appendix (65)
27. Ādityahṛdaya—11, 12 (Bhaviṣya Purāṇa)
28. Bhagavdgitā—18-40
29. Ṛgveda 1-35-2 Yajurveda-33-43
30. Yajurveda 9-40.
31. Ṛgveda 8-4-16. Yajurveda 13-14.
32. Yajurveda 15-54.
33. Ṛgveda 2-23-15 Yajurveda 26-3
34. Yajurveda—19-75
35. Ṛgveda 10-9-4 Yajurveda 36-12
36. Ṛgveda 4-31-3 Yajurveda 27-39
37. Ṛgveda 1-6-34 Yajurveda 29-37
38. Śiva Purāṇa—2-5-2-46
39. Prasāda August 76 special issue on Sūrya Upāsanā.

(5) Viṣṇu Upāsanā

1. Māhabhārat Śantiparva-338-(Punah Sanskaran)
2. Śevtāśvatara Upaniṣad—3-8-14, 15.
3. Viṣṇu Dharmottar Purāṇa—12-31.
4. Bhaviṣya Purāṇa—2-2-19-181
5. Garuḍa Purāṇa-Purvkhanda-50-61, 62 Agni Purāṇa-58-27 Linga Purāṇa-Purvabhāga-27-43
6. Brahma Purāṇa-161-28
7. Puruṣa Sūkta Bhāṣyam-Page vi-By-Anantāchary Swami
8. *Ibid*-Page 7
9. Mahābhārat-Śantiparva-351-14
10. Śatapatha Brāhamṇa—7-5-2-17
11. Puruṣa Sūkta—2
12. padma Purāṇa—1-62-2-7

13. Bhagvadgitā—17-17
14. Ṛgveda—1-164-46
15. Ṛgveda—6-47-1
16. Mahābhārat Anuśāsana parvam—160-43
17. *Ibid*—160-36
18. Mahābhārat Śāniti Parvam—341-15
19. Ṛgveda—1-22-20 Yaurveda—6-5-Atharvaveda—7-26-7
20. Ṛgveda—1-22-17
21. Tattiriya Saṁhitā—1-2-81
22. Ṛgveda—1-154-2
23. Ṛgveda—1-22-19
24. Gitā—9-16
25. Ṛgveda—1-154-6
27. Ṛgveda—1-156-3
28. Ṛgveda—1-154-4
29. For later Viṣṇu Upāsanā-'Prsāda' special issue on the Viṣṇu worship. (August 82)

Sāḷigrāma

1. Mahābhārata-Āraṇyaka Parva—13-16.
2. Varāha Purāṇa—144. 3 Viṣṇu Purāṇa—2-13
3. Symbols of Art, Relgion and Philosophy-by-Dr. Padma Sudhi-Page 164. (I owe to Dr. Padmā Sudhi for the discussion of Sāḷigrama).
4. Garuḍa Purāṇa-Purva-19-18.
5. Padma Purāṇa—II. 3.4.7.
6. Symbols of Art, Religion and Philosophy-by-Dr. Padmā Sudi-Pge-167.

Śri Rāma Upāsanā

1. Bhagvdgitā—4-7-8
2. Rāmrakṣā Stotra-38
3. Kalyāṇa Upāsanā Aṅka- 'Śri Rāmopāsanā' by Śri Jaynārāyaṇa Lālaji-Advocate.
4. Rāmarahasya Upaniṣad—2-44 to 47.
6. Vālmiki Rāmāyana. 6.117.14 (from Index).
7. Kalyāṇa Upāsanā Aṅka—Śri Rāmopāsanā' by Śri Jaynarayana Lalaji-Advocate.

Śri Gurudatta Upāsanā

1. Śrimadbhāgavatam—2.7.4.
2. *Ibid*—4.1.33.
3. Skanda Purāna—1.2.46; 163-164. Śiva Purāṇa-3.19.26. Mārkanḍeya Purāna 15.25; 18. 16-41; 37.5; 7. Padma Purāṇa-Bhūmikā Khanḍa-103.101.
4. Naiṣadhiya Caritam—2.194-Epic Poem.
5. This story is not found in main Purānas.
6. Śrimadbhāgavatam—11.9.11.

4

Upāsanā in Kalpasūtra, Smṛti and Epic Literature

The *Vedāṅgas* are the auxiliary descriptive guide books specifically written to explain the intricacies of the Vedas. Separate books are written to explain the specific dimension of the Vedas. The study of these guide books is absolutely essential to read and understand the meaning of the Vedic language.

Muṇḍaka Upaniṣad mentions six *Vedāṅgas*[1], namely, *Śikṣā, Kalpa, Vyākaraṇa, Nirukta, Chanda,* and *Jyotiṣa*. The four Vedas, the Ṛgveda, the Yajurveda, the Samaveda, the Atharvaveda and the six Vedāṅgas constitute the lower level of knowledge (*Aparā Vidyā*) whereas the knowledge which takes you to the Supreme existence beyond words and human senses is called the higher knowledge (*Parā Vidyā*). The study of the *Aparā Vidyā* is the ladder provided to reach the field of the *Parā Vidyā*.

The *Vedāṅga Śikṣā* explains in detail phonetics and syntax of language in the Vedas. The origin and construction of words in the Vedas and their grammar is given in the *Vyākaraṇa* and the *Nirukta*. *Chand Vedāṅga* has undertaken the detail study of various meters in the Vedas. The *Jyotiṣa Vedāṅga* discusses the time schedule and the calendar of performing various *Yajñas*. The detail study of astronomy is seen in this *Vedāṅga*. How and when to perform public and domestic *Yajña* ceremonies (rituals) is explained in the *Kalpa Vedāṅga*. Out of these six *Vedāṅgas* only the *Kalpasūtra*, while detailing out the religious efficacies, prescribes certain Upāsanās for individuals. Hence only this *Kalpa* Vedāṅga is included in the discussion of Upāsanā.

The *Kalpa Vedāṅga* is a vast and exhaustive literature. It narrates about the procedures and importance of the *yajña* rituals in vogue during *Brāhmaṇa* period. This *Vedāṅga* incorporates three sub-sections, namely. The *Śrauta Sūtra*, the *Gṛhyasūtra* and the *Dharmasūtra*. Different *Kalpasūtras* are connected with the different branches of the Vedic schools. In general, in the *Śrautasūtra*, the large scale *Yajña* ceremonies which are performed by a number of people coming together are described. Such ceremonies are *Rājasūya, Aśvemedha* etc. The aim of these *yajñas* is to fulfill the worldly aspirations. There is no aim of achieving Supreme Existence in this *yajñas* and no description on this subject is seen in the *Śrautasūtra*. In the *Gṛhyasūtra* a worship of the *Agni* is told to a *Brahmacārin* and to a householder (*Gṛhastha*). It is felt that this *Agni Upāsanā* is prescribed with the view that the householder should study the Vedas, concentrate and meditate on them to obtain purification of mind and prepare himself for *Mokṣa*. Only the *Brahmcarya* and *Grahasthāśrama* are dealt with the *Gṛhyasūtras*. In the *Dharmasūtras* all the four *Āśramas* namely, the *Brahmacarya*, the *Gṛhastha*, the *Vānaprastha* and the *Sanyāsa* are dealt with. The religious rituals and worships in every *Āśrama* are prescribed and the sequence of worship is so maintained that the Supreme Bliss is reached in the *Sanyāsāśrama*. The concept of *Dharma* and the rules and regulations to uphold it are explained in the *Dharmasūtras*. In addition to these three sub-sections the *Kalpasūtra* includes *Śrāddha Kalpa, Pitṛmedha sūtra, Prayoga* and *Kārikā*.

All this literature is in aphorisms, but in prose. It seems that the expansion of the *Dharmaśāstras* or *Smṛties* are based on the *Dharmasūtras* because it is seen that the disciplines, rules and regulations in the *Āśrama* and the *Varṇa* and the rules of behaviour during entire life which are told in the *Dharmasūtras*, are further elaborated in the *Smṛti Saṁhitās*. The *Smṛties* are in couplets. These are not connected with any particular branch of the Vedic school. These prescribe the rules of individual behaviour, but they say that those rules are based on the principles of the Vedas. The four *Varṇas* and the four *Āśrmas* are also explained in the *Smṛties*, and the rules to be followed in the every *Āśrama* and by the person of a particular *Varṇa* are prescribed. The study of these rules reveals that the rules are prepared with a view that one should adopt noble behaviour (*Sadācāra*) and should worship Brahman daily in order to remember the real nature of the Supreme Self. For this purpose the different Upāsanās are prescribed for individuals. The Upāsanās mentioned in the *Dharmasūtra* and the *Smṛti* literature being more or less similar, are explained in one chapter. Though there are about thirty

Smṛties, the most important is the *Manu Smṛti*. The *Manu Smṛti* is the primal *Smṛti* told by *Prajāpati Brahmā* to *Svāyaṁbhuva Manu*[2], which is based on the principles of the Vedas. Other *Smṛties* are formed in due course as per requirements of the then prevailing time, but based on the *Manu Smṛti*. Therefore, in this chapter the *Manu Smṛti* has been mainly dealt with.

Like *Sūtra* and *Smṛti* Literature the two great epics viz. The *Rāmāyaṇa* and the *Mahābhārata* have great influence on Indian Religious systems *Mahābhārata* is also called *Smṛti* and *Itihāsa*, therefore the upāsanās mentioned in these two epics are included in this chapter. These two epics also prescribe the rules of behaviour : *Sadācāra*, which are accepted by noble persons.

I

Upāsanā in Kalpasūtras

(i) Upāsanā in the Śrauta Sūtras

The Vedic sacrifices prescribed in the *Kalpa Sūtras* are of two kinds, viz. *Śrauta* sacrifices and *Gṛhya* sacrifices. *Śrauta* sacrifices are based on the *Śruti*, the divine revelation and the *Gṛhya* sacrifices are based on the *Smṛtis* i.e. human tradition based on the Vedic scriptures. The *Śrauta* sacrifices were largely in practice during the *Brāhmaṇa* period. These sacrificial rituals were performed on a large scale and were primarily undertaken with the help of priests. Information about these *Śrauta* rites is seen in the *Śrauta Sūtras*. Main *Śrauta Sūtras* are the *Āśvalāyana*, the *Śānkhāyana*, the *Baudhāyaṇa*, the *Āpastamba*, the *Hiraṇyakeśi*, the *Kātyāyana*, the *Laṭyāyana*, the *Drāhyāyaṇa*, the *Jaiminiya*, the *Vaitāna* etc. The subject of these *Sūtras* is to explain the process and method of the Vedic *Haviryajñas* and *Somayajñas*. These *Sūtras* contain the description of fourteen Vedic sacrifices. The sacrificial objects are different in different types of *Yajñas*. The *Śrauta* rites can be divided in to three major groups according to these different objects, namely (1) The *Haviryajñas*, also called *Iṣtis*. Cakes, porridge, milk and butter are offered in these sacrifices. (2) The *Paśubandha*. It is an animal sacrifice. (3) The *Somayāgas*. In these sacrifices *soma* is offered and animals are sacrificed. There are no divisions stated in the *Haviryajñas* and the *Paśubandha*. But the *Some Yajñas* has divisions according to its duration.

Soma sacrifices are divided into *Ekāhas* or one day rites, *Āhinas* which is a two to twelve-day rite and *Sattras*, which are continued for some fixed days. *Jyotiṣṭoma* is important in these *Soma Yajñas*. *Agniṣtoma, Atyāgniṣtoma, Aptoryāma* are different sub-divisions of the *Jyotiṣṭoma*.

In all these *Śrauta* sacrifices, the priests play an important role. Main priests are four, viz *Brahmā, Udgātā, Adhvaryu* and *Hotā*. Each main priest has three assistants. Generally sixteen or seventeen priests perform the *Soma* sacrifice for the host and the priests get a good monetary reward for their job. The oblations are poured in the *Āhavaniya Agni*. The host and his wife take part in this ceremony.

The main object of these rites : which are *yajñas*, is the fulfilment of worldly wishes including heaven, children, cattle, food, kingdom etc. These objects are mainly mundane, so these are *Kāmya Upāsanās* and not the Upāsanās done for getting ultimate Bliss or salvation. These rites are not important in the way of common man's pursuit for imperishable Bliss and Happiness, and therefore these sacrifices are not made obligatory to the common man like the performance of the *Pañca Mahāyajñas* described in the *Gṛhyasūtras*. As the *Śrauta Yajñas* are relevant only to certain class of high society people and are mainly undertaken to achieve worldly desires, the detailed study of these *Sūtras* is not felt necessary in the context of the study of Upāsanās for *Mokṣa* or Salvation.

(ii) The Upāsanā in the Gṛhyasūtras

The *Gṛhyasūtras* contain the rules of daily and occasional sacred activities to be performed by a person in the stage of bachelorship (*Brahmacarya*) and householdership (*Gṛhastha*). These performances are sacred rites joined with certain mantras and instructions given in the Vedic literature. These Vedic mantras or stanzas are to be recited with each of the specific rites.

The important and vital rite prescribed for the *Brahmcarya* stage is the *Upanayana Saṁskāra*. A young boy at the age of eight or so is initiated by this ceremony to enter into *Brahmacaryāśrama*.

In this *Āśrama* an ardent discipline and hard life is to be led by the boy at the house of the *Gurū* to acquire knowledge of the Vedas and general education. The Vedic knowledge acquired by the student needs to be continuously kept in memory by the person throughout his whole life. The sacred mantras associated with various rites and ceremonies prescribed are probably with an intention to help to retain this knowledge of the Vedas without fail. The different types of the worships and sacrifices mentioned in the *Gṛhyasūtras* are generally of such a philosophy that one always remembers and acts with the conviction that the ultimate aim of human life is the achievement of Supreme Knowledge, the entire Universe and the joys in it are created by God and we have to live and consume them humbly by sacrifices and good wills.

A bride and bridegroom worship the *Agni* together at the time of marriage. They place the same *Agni* in their home and worship this *Agni* daily. This is a life long worship. This worship includes the *Pañcamahāyajñas*, new Moon and full Moon sacrifice, *Daśpurṇimās*, periodical sacrifices like *Śrāddha* i.e. ancestor worship, *Śrāvaṇa* ceremony i.e. worship of ṣnakes, daily *Agnihotra* i.e. morning and evening libation. These ceremonies can be performed with or without the assistance of a priest. These rites are to be performed with the recitation of the Vedic mantras. The mantras are taken mostly from one *śākhā* (branch) of the Veda. Generally each *Gṛhyasūtra* is connected with one *śākhā* of the Veda and the followers of particular *śākhā* follow the rules prescribed by that text.

The *Aśvalāyana*, the *Śāṅkhāyana* and the *Kauṣitaka Gṛhysūtras* belong to the Rigveda. The *Śāṅkhāyana Gṛhyasutras* are composed by *Suyajñą* and the *Kauṣitaka* by *Śāṁbhava*. The *Pāraskara Gṛhyasutra belongs* to the white Yajurveda. The *Hiraṇyakeśin* and the *Āpastamba Gṛhyasūtras* belong tot he Taittiriya school of Black Yajurveda. The *Āpastamba Gṛhyasūtra* gives only rules necessary for the *Gṛhya* rites without the *mantras*, but the *mantras* are given in a special collection named, *Mantrapāṭha;* which is connected to the *Sūtra* text. *Āpastamba's Yajñaparibhāṣa sutras* are also available. These contain the general rules of the sacrifice. The *Khādira Gṛhyasutra* belongs to *Drāhyāyaṇa* school of the Sāmaveda. The *Gobhila Gṛhyasutra* belongs to the Sāmaveda, but it has another collection of the *mantras, "the Mantra Brāhmaṇa"* is the name of this collection.

The *Baudhāyana Gṛhyasūtra* is the first *Gṛhyasūtra* text. It belongs to the Taittiriya Saṁhitā. It is a standard for the other *Gṛhyasūtras* according to the verse *"Svasūtre vidyamāne tu Parasūtreṇa vartate. Bodhāyana matamkṛtvā svasūtraphalabhāg bhavet"*.[1] The *Bodhāyana Gṛhyasūtra* has three sub sections namely the *Paribhāṣāsūtra*, the *Gṛhyaśesasūtra* and the *Pitṛmedhasūtra*. The *Bodhāyana Gṛhyasūtra* starts from the *Vivāha Saṁskāra*, i.e. Marriage ceremony. According to all the *Gṛhyasūtras*, the Upāsanā of *Agni* is important for a householder and the Upāsanā of *Savitṛ* (the Sun) is important for a student. These Upāsanās are a part of daily routine of life. The main aim of these Upāsanās is salvation, ultimate happiness. The *Bodhāyana Gṛhyasūtra* says, `One who performs the five great sacrifices i.e. `*Pañcamahāyajñas*', which is an important part of daily *Agni* Upāsanā, definitely attains Bliss State of Brahman. The verse is, *"Etāsām Sāmyatām* (or *Sātmatām*) *gatva devatānām śatam samḥ. Ānandam Brahma gaccanti ḍhruvam śāsvatamvyayam."*,[2] It is said in the same text that, one who avoids to perform this *Agni* Upāsanā, must take the `*Prāyascitta*' i.e. the vow of repentance; otherwise will not get the ultimate happiness. *Savitṛ* Upāsanā, *Pañcamahāyajñas* and *Agnihotra* are daily Upāsanās and the new Moon, the full Moon sacrifices, the *Daśapurṇimas*, the *Sarpabali* or *Śrāvana* sacrifice, the *Śulagava* or spit ox sacrifices are to be performed occasionally. The *Śulagava* sacrifice is performed to avoid the illness among cattle; (This is a sacrifice to *Rudra* and the different names of *Śiva* occurs in this ceremony. These names are *Hara, Mṛḍa, Śarva, Śiva, Bhava, Mahādeva, Ugra, Bhīma, Paśupati, Rudra, Śankara, Iśāna*. The oblations are given to *Rudra* with these names.)[3] *Śrāddha* or adoration to ancestors is also a part of occasional Upāsanā. The periodical sacrifices are also important in addition to the daily sacrifices, but these aim at certain earthly or physical acquirements or protection against difficulties unavoidable by human efforts. (There is a description of the Sun worship for getting love of husband).[4] The *Bodhāyana Gṛhyasūtra* gives the description of the Upāsanā of *Omkāra, Durgādevi, Śri, Sarsvati, Viṣṇu, Ravi, Vināyaka, Mṛtyuñjaya*, in the third *Praśna* with the process of *Āvāhana, Pujā, Visarjana* (immersion) etc., to fulfill all the worldly desires; for example in *Vināyakapujā*, the worshipper asks *Vināyaka*, the success in all his works, the verse is, *"Vināyaka mahābāho Vighneśa bhavadājñaya, Kāmā me sādhitāssarve idam badhnāmi kañkaṇam"* [5]. There are fortyeight vratas in Bau. Gṛ. Sū., one of these vratas is the *Aṣtami* Vrata. It is an evening worship acted on eighth day of two halfs of the month. One who worships on this *Aṣtami* to *Rudra, Viṣṇu* and *Brahmā*, gets the same loka of *Rudra, Viṣṇu* and *Brahmā*.[5a]

We shall discuss here the Sun worship prescribed for a student, which is famous by the name *'Sañdhyā'* because it is a twilight worship; and daily *Agni* worship of a householder, done with *Pañcamahāyajñas* which are observed by a Hindu family more or less even today.

The Sun Worship or 'Sandhyā Upāsanā' of a Student

'Sandhyā Upāsanā' is described in all *Gṛhyasūtras*. After the *Upanayana Saṁskāra* a boy becomes a student of the Veda, it is a vow of *Brahmacarya*, so he is called *Brahmacārin*. The year of *Upanayana saṁskāra* is the eighth year for a *Brāhmin* boy, eleventh for a *Kṣatriya*, twelfth for a *Vaiśya* boy.[6] The teacher initiates a *Brāhmin* student with *Sāvitri* or *Gāyatri Mantra* of the Ṛgveda, which is ascribed to *Viśvāmitra*[7], a *Kṣatriya* boy with the *Triṣtubha*, which is ascribed to *Hiraṇyastupa*,[8] and the *Jagati* to a *Vaiśya* boy, which is ascribed to *Vāmadeva* or *Hiraṇyastupa*.[9] The teacher starts his initiation with the syllable Om.[10] He teaches the *Gāyatri mantra* to the student, at first pāda by pāda, then hemistitch by hemistitch, then the whole verse in the following way, *"Bhuḥ, Tat Savitur - vareṇyam; Bhuvaḥ, Bhargo devasya dhimahi; suvaḥ, Dhiyo Yonaḥ pracodayāt. Bhurbhuvasvaḥ Tat savitur vareṇyam bhargo devasya dhimahi, dhiyo yonaḥ pracodāyat"*[11]

The teacher ties a girdle of *Munjā* grass to his waist, so this ceremony is also called *'Munja'*. The sacred thread called yajñopavita is also put around his neck and chest, and a *daṇḍa* or stick of a particular tree is given in his hands. This particular tree is different in the case of a *Brāhmin, Kṣatriya* and *Vaiśya* student. The daily kindling of a fire, to go for begging alms, sleeping on the ground, the obedience to the teacher and daily *Sandhyā* Upāsanā are the duties of a student in addition to his studies. The student lives with the teacher until his study is over.

Sandhyā is a worship of the Sun with recitation of the *Gāyatri*, performed in the early morning and evening. A student must observe this worship without fail. A student goes to the forest with the *Samidhā* in his hands and performs *Sandhyā* while sitting near the fire, murmuring the *Mahāvyāhṛties, Om, Bhuḥ, Bhuvaḥ, Svāḥ*. He puts the wet ash i.e. *Bhasma* on his forehead and does a *nyāsa* with the following words, he says *'Sarsvati'* on the head, *'Medhāvi'* on forehead, *Tejasvi* on the shoulders, *'Varcasi'* and *Brahmavarcasi'* on the right and left sides, *'Ayuṣmān'* on the neck, *'Bhuyāsām'* on the back and *'Svasti'* on the head. Then he keeps silence for a while and recites the *Gāyatri Mantra* with auspicious vedic hymns.[12] He worships thus in the morning from dawn till the Sun appears, and in the evening from Sunset till the stars come up. A student has to serve *Agni*, the Sun, and *Viśvadevas*.[13]

This worship makes the student healthy, intelligent and powerful.

The Agni Worship of a Householder-Pañcamahāyajñas

The *Samāvartana* ceremony, which is a sacred bath, is performed at the end of the study of the Vedas. This ceremony signifies the end of the studentship as well as of *Brahmacarya*. After this ceremony the student returns to his parents' house from his teacher's house. Now he can marry a girl of the same caste with the permission of his parents. Marriage is a *saṁskāra* in which the bride and bridegroom worship the *Agni* together which they place in their home after marriage. This *Agni* is called the Aupāsana *Agni*, with which the daily Upāsanā is performed, the oblations of all daily sacrifices are poured in this *Agni*. It is a sacred domestic fire.[14] The *Pañcamahāyajñas* are to be performed daily with this *Agni*. These *Yajñas* are described in all the *Gṛhyasūtras*. These are the *Manuṣya Yajña*, the *Deva Yajña*, the *Ṛṣi Yajña, Pitṛ yajña* and *Brahma yajña*. Some Gṛhyasūtras describe Bhūta yajña; according to those texts *Ṛṣi Yajña* and *Brahma Yajña* are the same. The *Kauṣitaka Gṛhyasūtras* describes these *Yajñas* in the following verse as *"Ete Pañcamahāyajñaḥ Atithipūjā Manuṣya Yajñaḥ Deva Yajñah Viśvadevena, Ṛṣi Yajñaḥ, Pitṛ Yajñaḥ, Brahma Yajñaḥ., Pancaite mahāyajñaḥ nityaso vartante sa muktaḥ sarvapāpebhyo nākapṛṣthe mahiyate"*.[15] It means manuṣya *yajña* is performed by welcoming and serving the guests. The *Devayajña* is performed by the worship of *Vaiśvadevas*, by giving oblations to them. The *Ṛṣi yajña* is performed by the study of scriptures written by the *Ṛṣis*. The *Pitṛyajña* is a worship and service to elders and ancestors. The *Brahma Yajña* is the study of the Vedas. This stanza further says that man becomes free from all sins and he stands superior to all beings. *Bodhāyan Gṛhyasutra* gives the *Bhūtayajña* along with *Brahmayajña, Devayajña, Pitṛ yajña* and *Manuṣya Yajña*. The verse is "*Yadadhite sa Brahmayajño Yajjuhoti sa deva yajña Yatpitṛbhya svadhā karoti sa pitṛ yajño, yadbhūtebhyo balim harati sa Bhutayajño yadbrāhmeṇebhyo' nnam dadāti sa manuṣya yajña iti.*"[16] This text further says "*Ete pañcamahāyajñassatatam suprayuktānayanti paramām gatim*"[17] It means these great *yajñas* lead him (who performs them) to the highest position i.e. *Brahmapada*. The text says that if one is unable to worship even any one of these *yajñas* one must take the vow of repentance, `*Prāyaścitta*'. The *Vāruṇi japa*, various oblations are suggested to wash away this sin.[18] The next verses give the favourable fruit of these *yajñas*. One who worships these *yajñas* daily will be united with the deity of the particular *yajña*. By the *devayajña* he becomes *deva*; he unites with forefathers with *Pitṛyajña*, with living creatures by *Bhūtayajña*, with *Brāhmins* by *Manuṣya Yajña* and with *Brahman* by *Brahmayajña*. It means that he unifies with everything which is Brahman because Brahman pervades all the things.[19]

Aśvalāyana Gṛhyasūtra describes the five great sacrifices in these words: "the sacrifice to the Gods, *Devayajña*, the sacrifice to Fathers, *Pitṛyajña*, the sacrifice to Brahman, *Brahmayajña*, the sacrifice to Beings, *Bhūtayajña*, the sacrifice to men, *Manuṣya yajña*".[20] The text explains these sacrifices as : if a person oblates over the sacred fire, he sacrifices to Gods, if he offers food to animals he sacrifices to beings, if he gives *Piñḍa* (a particular quantity of fried rice) to the Fathers, he sacrifices to Fathers, if he studies Vedic texts, he sacrifices to Brahman, and if he gives necessary things to men or serves mankind, he sacrifices to men; these five great sacrifices he must perform daily.[20] The *Pāraskara Gṛhyasūtra* also describes the five great yajñas in the same manner.[22]

All the *Gṛhyasūtras* state the rules to observe them daily or periodically with the intention that everyone may live happily. One should not forget Brahman in one's daily busy life. If one comes across any difficulties, one can even perform other *Kāmya* worships to overcome them.[23]

All these domestic rites give the picture of sacred life of each Hindu family.

Perhaps the great sages have fixed the pattern of life in such a way that a man becomes happy and free from worldly bondage if he observes these systems daily. *Bodhāyam Gṛhyaparibhāṣā sūtra* says that a man is born with three debts and he must repay the debts. These debts are *Ṛṣirṇa. Devarṇa* and *Piṭṛṛṇa*. The text also suggests how to be free from these three ṛṇas. See the verse *"Jāyamāno vai Brāhmaṇaḥ tribhirṛṇavā jāyate. Brahmacaryeṇa ṛṣibyo yajñena devebhyāh prajayā pitṛabhayḥ iti"*.[24] It means a man is born with the debt of the *Ṛṣis*, the Gods and the Fathers. As a student he can repay the debts of the *Ṛṣis* by studying the Vedas, and as a householder he can repay the debt of the Fathers by giving birth to a male child (for having the continuation of the generation) and the debt of Gods by performing daily sacrifices and other four subtle yajñas like *Svādhyāya yajña, Japayjña, Karmayajña* and *mānasayajña*. *Svādhyāya yajña* means regular study and teaching of the Vedas. *Japayajña* means the recitation of the *Mantras*, the *Karmayajña* is performing the duties for the sake of God and the *Mānasayajña* means to remember the presence of Brahman in the mind continuously, the *Japayajña* is ten times stronger than the *Svādhyāya yajña*, the *Karmayajña* is ten times stronger that the *Japayajña* and the *Mānasayjña* is ten times stronger than the *Karmayajña*.[25] According to the *Gṛhyasūtras*, the worship of *Agni* with all these various *yajñas* is the Upāsanā for the whole life.

(iii) Upāsanā in Dharmasūtras

The *Dharma sūtras* are included in the *Kalpaṣūtras*. Like the *Gṛhyasutras* the *Dharmasūtras* also give the highest authority to the Vedas. These *sūtras* are connected with the one *śākha* of the Vedas like the *Gṛhyasūtras*. Some *Dharmasūtras* are a part of the *Kalpasūtras* and some are separate works. The *Āpastamba Dh. Sūtra* is the part of *Āp. Kalpa Sūtra* and it belongs to the *Kṛṣṇa*, (black) Yajurveda. The *Bodhāyana Dh. Sūtra* is a part of the *Bodhāyana Kalpasūtra* which belongs to the Taittiriya Saṁhitā of the Black Yajus. The *Hiraṇyakeśin Kalpasūtra* which belongs to the Taittiriya saṁhitā of the Black Yajus. The separate works of Dh. Sūtras are the *Gautama Dh. Sūtra* which belongs to the *Rāṇāyaṇiya* School of the Sāmaveda, the *Hārita Dh. Sūtra* which belongs to the *Maitrāyaṇiya* School of the black yajus, the *Śaṅkhalikhita* which belongs to the *Vājasaneyi* Saṁhitā, the *Mānava Dh. Sūtra* which belongs to the *Maitrāyaṇiya* School, *Vasiṣṭha Dh. Su., Vaikhānas Dh. Sūtra*, the *Viṣṇu Dh. Sūtra* are the other well-known *Dh. Sūtras*.

Dh. Sūtras deal with some of the topics dealt with in the *Gṛhya-Sūtras* but in addition to that they deal with the civil life, the economic matters, customs and the ceremonial laws, the manner of worship, expiations, etc. They mostly concern with the conduct of people of the *Āryan* community. There is no description of any kind of rituals in the *Dh. Sūtras,* but there are religious laws, rules and regulations for the four castes, viz. *Brāhmaṇa, Kṣatriya, Vaiśya* and *Śudra,* and the stages of life i.e. four *Āśrams,* viz. *Brahmacarya, Gṛhastha, Vānaparastha* and *Sanyāsāśrama.*

The word *'Dharma'* signifies right, duty, law, religion, customs, usage etc. The *Bodhāyana Dh. sūtra* says that there are three main *Dharmas,* first is the *Śrauta Dharma,* which contains the duties prescribed by the *Śruits,* second is the *Smārta Dharma* which comes down to us by tradition based on the *Śruits,* which has five divisions, namely, (i) *Varṇa dharma,* (ii) *Āśrama Dharma,* (iii) *Guṇa Dharma,* (the burning capacity of *Agni*), (iv) *Nimitta Dharma,* (the hotness of water after heating is its *Nimitta Dharma* because after some time it becomes cold.) (1) third is *Śṣṭācāra,* it means the behaviour of the noble men. Then *sūtra* says that the word 'noble men' means the particular persons who have no ego, no envy, no lust, no pretension, who have mercy in their heart for each creature, so their manner (way) of behaviour is *Dharma.* (2) *Vasiṣṭha Dh. Sūtra* also supports this view that, *"Sruti smṛti vihito dharmaḥ. Tadalābhe śiṣṭācārch pramāṇam, śiṣṭaḥ punarakāmataḥ."*[3] It means *Dharma* is the manner of behaviour which is prescribed by *Śruti* and *Smṛti,* but if their trace is missed then *Śiṣṭācāra* is the guideline for dharma. *Bodhāyana Dh. Sūtra* further says that if previous three types of *Dharmas* are lost then there should be the committee of ten leading men, which is called *'Pariṣad',* : it includes four learned : persons who know at least the four (*vidyās*) lores, a *mimānsaka,* a *vaiyākaraṇi,* a *Dharma Pāṭhaka,* and three *Brahmaṇas* who live in *Vānaprasthāśrma.* This *Pariṣada* decides the *Dharma.*[4]

Haradatta Miśra, in his commentary on the *Āpastamba Dh. Sūtra,* says, that the *Ātmā* experiences the happiness and sorrows in this and the other life after death, as the results of his deed (*karma*) done in this life. So he should do such deeds in this life which definitely confer on him the happiness in this and other life. The description of such karmas is the description of *Dharma.* The line is *"Karmajanyobhyudayaniśreyasaheturvākhyā ātmaguṇo dharmaḥ, tadhetubhūtakarmavyākhyānameva dharmavyākhyānam."*[5] *Āp. Dh. sūtra* also gives importance to nobel men i.e. the *Āryas*, like the *Bodhāyana* and the *Vasiṣṭha*. The verse is, *"Yattvāryaḥ kriyamāṇam praśansanti Dharmo yadgarhante sodharmaḥ."*[6] It means that the manner of behaviour, which the *Āryas* praise is *Dharma* and which they dismiss is *Adharma*.

The definition of *Dharma*, daily routine and rules of conduct of people of four *Āśramas*, the causes and occasions of expiations (*Prāyasccitta*) like *Kṛcchra* and *Cāndrāyaṇ Vratas*, duties of a woman, the *Sandhyā* Upāsanā, the Upāsanā of *Pañcamahāyajñas*, the process of the *japa*, the tapas, the fasting, the homa etc. are the contents of all the *Dharma sūtras*. The *Sandhyopāsanā* and the *Pañcamahāyajñas* are already discussed in the *Gṛyasūtras* so *Dh. Sūtras* only mention them as the *Dharma* of a *Brahmacārin* and of a *Gṛhastha*, but these *Sūtras* describe expiations in the failure of observing them. The sixteen main saṁskāras which are prescribed by the *Gṛhyasūtras* have their importance in the *Dh. Sūtras* too. But the *Dh. Sūtras* add the possession of moral qualities with these *saṁskāras*. It is said in the *Gautama Dh. Sūtra* that a man who possesses *dayā*. (sympathy), *kṣamā* (forgiveness) and other moral qualities attains *Sāyujya* (company) and *Sālokya* (the same abode) with Brahman, even though he may not have undergone all the *saṁskāras*.[7] *Āp. Dh. Sūtra* also gives the importance to recognize Brahman and to unite with it, the verse is *"Atma lābhanna param vidyate."*[8] It means self realization is the real profit. *Viṣṇu Dh. Sūtra* also gives the importance to self restraint and worship of *Vāsudeva* for *Mukti*. It describes the process of worship of *Vāsudeva* with the flowers and the other sacred materials, offering of food to deities etc. Moral qualities as well as proper *karma* (work) are the means to reach the *Brahman* is the view of the *Dharmasūtras*.

Leading towards the aim of *Mokṣa* the *Dh. Sūtras* divided the life span of a man into the four *Āśramas*, namely the *Brahmacarya*, the *Gṛhastha*, the *Vānaprastha* and the *Sanyāsa*. These sūtras prescribe particular duties for particular *Āśrama* and hope that observing these duties, a man can fulfill all his worldly desires and at the end of his life he can obtain the real knowledge of the self by the study of the scriptures and by the self restraint as well as the meditation, and will be united with *Brahman*. We shall see in brief, how these *Āśramas* lead a man towards *Mokṣa*.[1]
(1) *Brahmacaryāśrama*-We have already seen in the *Gṛhyasūtras*

that a boy at the age of eight, eleven, and twelve (*Brāhmin, Kṣatriya* and *Vaiśya* respectively) enters in *Brahmacaryāśrama* with the *Upanayana saṁskāra*. The *Dh. Sūtras* prescribe duties for him with the *Sandhyopāsanā*. These sūtras say that a *Brahmacārin* should wear a *Kaupin* (briefs) and minimum required clothes, tie a girdle of a particular grass round the waist, as prescribed by the *Gurū*, hold a stick (*daṇḍa*) of a particular tree in his hands and should wear a *Yajñopavita*, a sacred thread. *Ācārya* or *Gurū Upāsanā* is important for him. He should attend to his master for twenty four hours. He should be *Aghāsanśāyai* i.e. to sleep on the grassmat.[9] He should not eat a meal at Śrāddha and sweets and meat, not sleep during day time, not embrace a women, not crop his hair completely, he can sleep after his *Gurū* has slept, and wake up early before his master wakes up. His bath should be with cold water. He must bring *Samidhā* i.e. woods of sacred tree, for his master and do all the work ordered by his master, in addition to his studies, he should observe the rules of hermit. *Svādhyāya* is important for him. Even in the recess he should revise in his mind which has been taught so far. The *sūtra* is, "*manasā ca anadhyāye.*"[10] His preceptor is as great as God for him, see the sutra, "*Devamivācāryamupāsitavikathayannavimanā vācam suśruśāmānosyāt.*"[11] By observing such a difficult *dharma* a brahmacārin pleases his master and the master also teaches him all the *vidyās*. A *brahmacārin* can stay at his master's hermit for a minimum of twelve year or maximum forty eight years, because minimum twelve years period is supposed to be necessary for study at least one of the four Vedas. and the period is decided by a brahmacārin according to his need of education. A *brahmacārin* leaves the hermit after the completion of his studies, he give *Gurudakṣinā* (a token of respect) before he returns to his parents.

Brahmacaryāśrama is the base of knowledge and the preparation for earning livelihood.

(2) *Gṛhasthāśrama* — The *Brahmacārin* youth returns home after his master's consent and then marries a girl and starts his *Gṛhasthāśrama*. There are eight kinds of marriage described in *Bodhāyana Dh. Sūtra*.[12]

1. *Brāhma Vivāha* — This type of marriage is to be performed with the prescriptions of *Śrutis*. This marriage is said to be the most important of all other types of

marriages, because it helps to lead a life towards *mokṣa* easily, following the way prescribed by the Vedas.

2. *Prājāpatya Vivāha*—If a father of a girl asks a youth to accept his ornamented daughter as his wife and if he accepts this offer, then the marriage that would take place is called the *Prājāpatya Vivāha*.
3. *Ārṣa Vivāha*—When a father of a bride presents a couple of cow and a bull to a bridegroom, and then the *Vivāha* that would take place is called *Ārṣa Vivāha*.
4. *Daiva Vivāha*—If a father performs a *Yajña* and at the end of *Yajña* he offers a *Dakṣiṇā* and his girl as wife to a youth and the latter accepts it and after that the marriage that would take place after some days on an auspicious day, is called the *Daiva Vivāha*.
5. *Gandharva Vivāha*—When a girl and a youth mutually accept each other as wife and husband and exchange garlands, that marriage is called the *Gandharva Vivāha*.
6. *Asura Vivāha*—The *Asura Vivāha* is clarified as the case of marriage when a person pays bride price to a father.
7. *Rākṣasa Vivāha*—When a person under wicked passions rapes a girl and then marries her when she is unconscious due to fear, then it is called the *Paiśāca* or *Rakṣasa Vivāha*.

In all these eight types of marriages the first four are accepted as good for a *Gṛhastha* and the remaining are dismissed as unprestigious. But the first one is more prestigious than the other three types because this marriage helps the couple to live life calmly. After this marriage the *gṛhasthāśram* starts with the worship of *Pañcamahāyajñas*. His other duties are : to perform *Sandhyā*, to serve father, mother and other elders of the family., to serve his master if he is staying in the same place, to look after his brothers and sisters, to worship Gods as per tradition of his noble descent. He should look at other women excepting his wife as his mother or sister, live with austerity, observing *satya* (truth), non violence, pity and other moral qualities, pay 1/6th part of his income to the king for the welfare of the society, distribute charitable things, serve food to a *sanyāsin* who asks for alms, etc.

If a *gṛhastha* fails to observe his *Dharma* he should undergo the *Prāyaśccitta* (the vow of repentance). The same is prescribed for a woman also if she commits the sin of *Adharma*. *Kṛcchra* and

Cāndrāyaṇa Vratas are the main *Prāyaścitta Vratas*. These expiations are very difficult to perform. These include strict fasting, *homa, tapas, japa* and staying away from the family. These vows run from three to six months according to the extent of the sin.

In this *Āśrama* the man is allowed to enjoy all material and worldly happiness like the wealth, the power etc. When he is satisfied with the worldly enjoyments, he may retire from *Gṛhasthāśrma* and enter into *Vānaprasthāśrama*. But the time frame for this transition is kept flexible according to one's will.

Gṛhasthāsrama is back bone of all the other three *Āśramas* and the entire society. *Ṛṣis* and *Ācāryas* run their hermitages with the help of *gṛhasthāśramies*. *Sanyāsins* can get food only from *Gṛhasthas*. All the productive work in the society and the protection of the society depend on this *Āśrama* only. It is said in the commentary of *Bodhāyana Dh. Sūtra, "Gṛhasthāsramyameva niśśreyasakaram. Uktam ca Gṛhasthopi vimucyate iti."*[12]. It means by observing duties of *gṛhasthadharma* faithfully a man can attain *mokṣa* like a Jñāni even without resorting to *vānaprasthāśrama* and *Sanyāsāśrama*.

(3) *Vānaprasthāśrama*—This is the third stage of life, When a person fulfills all duties and responsibilities of his family he retires from the busy life and enters in a hermit stage away from township. Here he passes his life calmly and quietly either with or without the company of his wife, but essentially it should be a celibated life. Either he prepares the food or eats or lives only on natural food like fruits, roots etc. In this stage of life he turns his mind from worldly attachment towards spiritual aspirations. He undertakes meditation, *japa* and *tapas*. However, he is required to perform *Pañcamahāyajñas* and *Agnihotra*.

(4) *Sanyāsāśrama*—When a person passes a sufficient time in *Vānaprasthāśrama* and becomes sure that he is out of all worldly desires and has come fully under spiritual state of mind he denounces the *Vānaprasthāśrama* and enters the life of a sanyāsi. Here he breaks all the relationships with belongings and family and becomes truly all alone and independent. In the *Gṛhasthāśrama* and the *Vānaprasthāśrama* the person has already relieved from the three debts namely *Pitṛ ṛṇa, Deva ṛṇa* and *Ṛṣi ṛṇa* which he had borne since birth, therefore, in *Sanyāsāśrama* he has no obligations towards anybody therefore, he is not required now even to undertake any religious duties like *Pañcamahāyajñas* etc.

like *Vānaprasthya*, this is called *"Vānaprasthya Samsārakarma virma"*:[14] "Renunciation of all Actions (*Karmas*).

In *Sanyāsāśrama* the person is required to undergo tonsure, use only wooden bowl, not to prepare or cook meal. He collects alms and lives only on that by eating once a day only. He observes strict discipline and remains unattached, recites *Sāvitri* and all the while engages himself into deep meditation and tries to surrender his self or *Ātman* to *Paramātman*.[15] At the end he becomes enlightened and leaves the gross body.

The aim of human life is to uplift the soul from human state to the state of God, lead himself to Bliss. This is to be achieved step by step. It is the worship which starts from human bondage and ends into the ultimate *Mokṣa*. All the four *Āśramas* are arranged for step by step evolution of human aspiration to the higher goal. The knowledge and education received during the *Brahmancaryāśrama* helps the person in discharging his duties in the *Gṛhasthasrāśma* with high ideals and sanctity. In the *Vānaprasthāśrama* and *Sayāsāśram* he renounces the world step by step and reaches the highest goal at the end. Thus all the *Āśramas* form a continuous thread of the Upāsanā of the Supreme Brahman from birth to death. Even if one wants only to pursue the Supreme Knowledge without accepting any worldly enjoyments he can continue the celibate life and accept *sanyāsa* : monism without entering into the *Gṛhastāśrama* and the *Vānaprasth āśrama*. He becomes an enlightened soul and can have the grace of *Gurū*.

II

Upāsanā in the Smṛti Literature

The *Śruti* and the *Smṛti* are two important factors of the Hindu religion. The *Śrutis* are divine teachings and the *Smṛtis* are traditional ways of life based on the teachings of the *Śrutis*. There are about thirty *Smṛtis*. The *Manu Smṛti*, the *Yajñavalkya Smṛti*, the *Nārada Smṛti* and the *Parāśara Smṛti* are said to be more important among them. The *Manu Samhitā* is most important of all these *Smṛtis*, because it is very near to the teachings of the Vedas. Different *Smṛties* are prescribed for the different great ages i.e. *Yuga*. It is said in the *Parāśara Samhitā* that the *Manu Smṛti* is an authoritative book of code of conduct in the *Satya Yuga*, the *Gautama Samhitā* is prescribed for the *Tretā Yuga*, the code of *Śaṅkha Likhita* is prescribed for the *Dvāpāra Yuga* and the *Parāśara Smṛti* is prescribed for the *Kali Yuga*.[1] The *Manu Smṛti* minutely explains many subjects related to manner of behaviour of the four *Varṇas*, the four *Āśramas*, the duties of a king, the duties of women, the *Adharma* and the expitations for *Adharma*. The *Manu Smṛti* is supposed to be as important as the Vedas because it describes the way of life by which a person can obtain well-being and *Mokṣa*, see the verse, "*Ya Kascitikasyacitdharmo manunā parikirtitaḥ. Sa sarvo'bhihito vede sarvajñānamayo hi saḥ*."[2] The *Yājñavalkya Smṛti* follows the *Manu Smṛti* in the various subjects. The *Nārada Smṛti* deals with the *Vyavahāra* (law points), the *Varṇa*, the *Āśrama*, the *Ācāra* (behaviour), the *Prāyaścitta* etc. Subject of the *Parāśara Smṛti* is limited to the sins of *Adharma*, the *Varṇa*, the *Aśrama*, the *Prāyaścitta* etc.

All the *Smṛties* talk about *Dharma* so they are called the *Dharmaśāstra*. The meaning of *Dharma* is the same as duties, manner of behaviour which is praised by noble men, religion, conduct, customs, which is explained by *Dharmasūtras*. The *Dharma Sūtras* described *Dharma* in aphorisms (pithy sentences) and *Smṛtis* describe *Dharma* minutely, Both have the base of the Vedas. The *Manu Smṛti* says that, "*Vedo'khilam dharmamulam Smṛtiśileca tadvidām*."[3] *Dharmaśāstra* is a science of *Ācāra* i.e. conduct. *Manu* says that the correct manner of behaviour with observation of rules prescribed by the *Śrutis* and the *Smṛtis* makes a man *Ātmavid*, the verse is, "*Ācāraḥ paramo dharmaḥ srutyuktah smārta eva ca. Tasmādasminsadā yuktao nityam syādātmavāndvijaḥ*."[4] Not only *Ācāra* but the possession of ten qualities of *Dharma* are also important. These qualities are : *Dhṛti* (fortitude, firmness), *Kṣamā* (forgiveness), *Dama* (self command), *Asteya* (non stealing), *Indriya nigraha* (command on sense organs), *Dhi* (intellect), *Vidyā* (learning), *Satyam* (truth), and *Akrodha* (Not to be angry),[5] and Anāyāsa (steadiness).

The *Smṛti* Literature prescribes the different rules to be followed for the different stages in life i.e. four *Āśramas*. The rules for the four castes are also different. The four castes are originated from the three qualities (*guṇas*) of Divine Nature (*prakṛti*), namely *Satva, Raja* and the *Tama*. These qualities are common in non-being (*jaḍa*) and being (*cetana*) worlds. Therefore, human beings are divided in these qualities. In the Universal division the *Satva* is the quality of Gods, the *Rajas* is the quality of the human beings and the *Tamas* is the quality of the animals. Though the human beings born with the *Rajoguṇa*, the other two qualities exist in them in a small quantity. Some people hold the *Satva* guṇa prominently with the *Rajoguṇa*. Some hold the *Rajoguṇa* more than the *Satva*, some hold the *Raja* plus *Tamaguṇa* and some hold only the *Tamoguṇa*. Therefore, there are four divisions in the human beings, and they follow different ways of life according to the quality they possess. A person who is born with prominent *Satva* quality seeks knowledge. One who is born with the *Raja* quality works heavily with love and envy. One who is born with the *Tamoguṇa* works with ignorance and violence.[6] A man gets the result of his work (*karma*) according to the nature of the work done. If a man understands his prominent quality he can work accordingly and can uplift himself towards the *Satva* quality which confers the knowledge and the happiness. Therefore, *Smṛtis* mention rules for behaviour for a particular quality and ways to uplift oneself to a higher quality.

According to *Dharmaśāstras Mokṣa* (salvation) is the highest achievement i.e. *Parama Puruṣārtha*, and this should be the aim of each person, so they form the rules of conduct by following which a man can attain Salvation. *Manu* says that softness, hardness, truth, untruth, *dharma, adharama* all are originated from Brahman.[7] A man starts acting as soon as he is born. There are two kinds of work which a man undertakes, namely, *Pravṛtta* i.e. the work done for the worldly achievements viz. money, power, prestige etc., and *Nivṛtta*, (see the verse, "*Sukhābhyudayikam caiva niśśreyasikamevaca. Pravṛttam ca nivṛttam ca dvividham karma vaidikam.*").[8] These two types of work give different results. The *Pravṛtta karma* leads to the cycle of birth and death and the *Nivṛtta karma* leads to *Mokṣa*. A man acts selfishly and unknowingly, harms somebody else when he follows *Pravṛtta karma* which gives him another birth as its reaction. *Manu Smṛti* describes the types of the birth as the result of such *adhārmic* deeds that is why the *Smṛtis* form the rules of conduct i.e. *dhārmic* deeds. In this way the whole life becomes a means (*Sādhanā*) to emancipation, because the deeds which are followed as *Dharma* i.e. duty, which is called *Niṣkāma karma*, leads to purification of the mind and the self knowledge.

The *Smṛtis* arrange the life of man in such a way that, inspite of *Varṇa* and *Āśrama*, he may not forget his real nature, i.e. *Ātmasvarūpa*. The *Smṛtis* give the Upāsanā of Paramātman for each *Varṇa* and *Āśrama*, these are similar to the *Dharmasūtras*. The *Smṛtis* do not give detailed description of these Upāsanā, but they say that these Upāsanās are obligatory for everybody. The Upāsanā for a *Brahmacārin* is to serve his *Gurū* and to perform the *Sandhyā* and the *Agni Upāsanā* which we have already explained in the chapter 'Upāsanā of Dharmasūtras'.[9] The *Manu Smṛti* adds the *Prāṇāyāma* (breathing exercise) with this Upāsanā. It prescribes the *Prāṇāyāma* with *Japa* of *Om* and recitation of the *Sāvitri* with *Vyāhṛties*.[10] This Upāsanā is called the *Japayajña* and it has been given more importance than the *Vidhiyajñas* like *Daśapurṇimās* etc.[11] *Smṛties* also give the importance to restrain the desires of the mind, which is mentioned in the *Dharmasūtras* also.

The *Smṛtis* agree with the *Dharmasūtras* about the Upāsanās of a *Gṛhastha*. The *Smṛtis* ask a *Gṛhastha* to perform *Pañcamahāyajñas* and daily *Agnihotra*.[12] The types of marriages are also the same in the *Smṛtis* and *Dharmasūtras* and both agree that the first four types of marriages are good to lead a life towards *Mokṣa*.

In the *Vānaprasthāśrama*, a man has to undertake *Svādhyāya* i.e. reading of holy literature and the meditation on the same, along with the *Agnihotra* and the *Pañcamahāyajñas*. The other details of the life style in the *Vānaprasthāśrama* are the same with the description of the *Dharmasūtras*.[13]

The *Manu Smṛti* prescribes *Prāṇopāsanā*, the practice of *Prāṇāyāma* for a *Sanyāsin*, to cleanse the sins committed inadvertently like harm to insects under feet while walking etc. The *Prāṇāyāma* washes the unclean body and the mind and then both become ready for meditation of *Brahman* with deep thinking about unity of *Ātman* and *Brahman* along with the recitation of the famous mantra *'So'ham'*, (I am Brahman and Brahman is I). *Kalluka Bhatta* explains *'Prāṇāyāma'* in his commentary on *Manusmṛti*. It is like this, *Prāṇāyāma* means *Pūraka, Kumbhaka,* and *Recaka; Pūraka* means to take breath inside the body in a fixed time, *Kumbhaka* means to hold the breath inside the body for a fixed time and *Recaka* means to breathe out in a fixed time. All this process should be done with recitation of *Sāvitri*.[14] The next verses say that after *Prāṇāyāma* a man can meditate on *Brahman* and slowly achieves its knowledge which makes him *Brahmavid*. This knowledge helps him to leave his gross body easily for not to return again in this world.

Mokṣa which is achieved in the *Sanyāsāśrama* and the release from bondages of *Karma* after death is a result of *Kramyoga*.[15] The *Brahmacarya*, the *Gṛhastha*, the *Vānaprastha* and the *Sanyāsa* are four steps leading to the state of *Mokṣa*. If a man follows the prescription of the *Smṛtis* and observes his *Dharma* he easily gets salvation by this *Kramayoga*.[16]

A king is more busy in his works than any other person but *Smṛties* do not forget to have (to compulse him) daily Upāsanā to perform. A king is aksed to perform the *Sandhyopāsanā* twice a day and to serve old *Brāhmins* who have self knowledge, as well as to bow before *Śrotriya Brāhmins* to take their blessings early in the morning.[17]

All the *Smṛtis* give importance to the *Niṣkāma Karma* i.e. a work done with detachment (*Āsakti rahita*), which purifies the mind and confers self knowledge after meditation. The *Niṣkāma karma* is the Upāsanā of *Ātman*. But this is a difficult task, therefore, *Manu* asks a man to see himself in the every creature and every creature in him, so he may not do injustice to others. When a man behaves like this, he is called Ātmayāji and he gets *Svārājya* i.e. *Brahmatva*. The verse is, "*Sarvabhuteṣucātmānam sarvabhutā-nicātmani. Samam Paśyannātmayāji svārājyamādhigacchati.*"[18] The four *Varṇas* have four types of characteristics, therefore, the *Niṣkāma karma* prescribed for each one is different. The qualities of Nature (*Prakṛti*) are, inevitable in each personality, but if a person follows his *Dharma* then he is able to win his qualities and obtains *Satva guṇa* by controlling other two qualities i.e. *Rājasa* and *Tāmasa*. It is said in the *Yājañvalkya Saṁhitā* that if a man performs his duties without attachment and without coming under the hold of natural qualities he will get ultimate freedom from all worldly bondages, after leaving his gross body. This is called *karmayoga*.[19]

If a man fails to attend his *Dharma*, the expiations like *Cāndrāyaṇa* etc., are prescribed to wash away this sin of *Adharma*. According to the *Smṛtis Dharma* is important because it protects a man from bondages of *Karma*, which is the cause of several births and deaths. The *Manu Saṁhitā* says," *Dharma eva hato hanti dharmo rakṣati rakṣitaḥ. Tasmādharmo mā hantavyo mā no dharmo hato'vadhit*."[20] The correct manner of behaviour is important in this point of view.

The Upāsanā described as part of duty in the different *Āśramas* is intended to uplift, purify cleanse the mind towards Brahman. In the concluding section of the *Manusmṛti*, sage *Manu* tells us the same thing, He says that each worship is the Upāsanā of *Ātman* e.g. a *gṛhastha* performs *Agni* Upāsanā with *Pañcamahāyajañas* and *Agnihotra* is the Upāsanā of *Paramātman* through *Agni*. when he observes *Dharma* which is proclaimed by *Prajāpati* to *Manu*, he performs the Upāsanā of *Parmātman* through *Prajāpati* and when he collects wealth in a gentle manner, he worships *Brahman* through *Indra*, when he practices *Prāṇopāsanā*, he worships *Brahman* through the Vital Force. These Upāsanās are subtle and gross i.e. *Mūrta* and *Amūrta*. The verse is, "*Etameke vadantyagnim manumanye prajāpatim. Indrameke pare prāṇamapare brahma śāśvatam.*[21]

The *Jīvātmā* is a fraction of Paramātman, therefore, the *Jivātmā* is able to uplift self to the state of Paramātman if he works with an unattached mind and by following the rules of the *Dharma*, But a conduct of *Adharma* degrades him to impure state. The *Smṛtis* ask people to follow the code of *Dharma* and they say that this is the Upāsanā of Paramātman.[22]

III

Upāsanā in the Epic Literature

Upāsanā in the Ramāyaṇa and the Mahābhārata

Upāsanā in the Rāmāyaṇa

The *Rāmāyaṇa* is called *Ādikāvya* i.e. first ever poetry. It is a narration of *Śri Rāma's* life, his exile from *Ayodhyā* and his victory over *Rāvaṇa*. It is written by *Vālmiki Ṛṣi*. According to the ancient division of great Ages, *Rāma* belongs to the *Tretā Yuga*. *Yajña* has more importance for gaining favour of deities than idol worship and other forms of Upāsanā. Even the birth of Rāma and his brothers is a fruit of *Yajña* performed by King *Daśaratha* for getting children.[1]

There are other references to *Yajña* by which gods confer happiness upon the performers. *Sītā* mentions the *Yajña* and its fruits when she mourns after observing the false head of *Rāma* shown to her by Rāvaṇa. She says, "*Agniṣṭomādibhiryajñairiṣṭa-vānāpta dakṣiṇaihi.*"[2]. etc. *Indrajit* performs *Nikumbhilām Yajña* with pouring oblations to *Devi* for getting victory in the battle with Rāma.[3] *Rāma* also had performed the *Aśvamedha Yajña*.

The Upāsanā of the *Sandhyā*, the *Agnihotra*, the *Japa* and the Meditation are mentioned in different places. *Rāma* performs *Sandhyā* twice a day as a part of routine life. The verses are, "*Upāsya paścimām sandhyāsaha bhrātā yathāvidhi.*"[4] "*Upāsya tu svāmsandhyām dṛṣtvā rātrimupasthitām. Rāmasya śayanam cakre sutah saumitriṇām saha,*"[5] The Upāsanā of *Sandhyā* and the *Agnihotra* was a routine of people, when *Rāma* is exalted to the forest by *Kaikeyi*; the people left the daily performance of *Agnihotra*; the verse is "*Nāgnihotraṇyāhuyanta suryaścāntaradhiyata...*"[6] *Śrāvana's* father mourned the death of his Son, saying, `who will perform *Sandhyā Upāsanā* and daily oblations for me?'.[7]

Meditation is mentioned in the *Rāmāyaṇa*. When *Bharata* visited his hermitage with his mothers and the troops; *Bhāradvāja Ṛṣi* invoked all the deities in the mind and the deities appeared before him the verse is, "*Manasādhyātaṣtasya prāṅmukhyasya kṛtānjaleh ājagmustāni sarvāṇi daivatāni pṛthak pṛthak.*"[8] *Bhāradvāja* meditated for the deities' appearance on the earth. *Kausalyā* meditates upon *Viṣṇu* when she heard *Rāma's* election as the *Yuvarāja*.[9] *Hanumān* meditates when he comes to *Rāma* after successful search of *Sītā*.[10]

Viśvāmitra asks *Rāma* and *Lakṣmaṇa* to bow before the *Gaṅgā* and *Umā devi*. He says, "*Ete ca śailarājsya sutelokanamaskṛte Gaṅgā ca saritām śresṭhām, Umādevi ca Rāghava.*"[11] In the next chapter *Śiva, Umā* and *Kārtikeya* are mentioned.[12] *Bhagiratha* performs penance of *Śankara. Viśāmitra* says, "*Devadevagate tasminso^ṅguṣṭ-hāgranipiḍitam. Kṛtvā vasumatim Rāma sam-vatsaramupāsata.*"[13]

Kausalyā performs Upāsanā of *Viṣṇu*, the verse is, "*Kausalyāpi tadadevimrātrimsthitvā samāhitā, prabhāte tvakarotpūjām viṣṇoh putra-hitaiṣiṇi.*"[14] *Kausalyā* performs this worship in a separate room which is called `*devatāgāra*'.[14] In the *Ayodhyā Kaṅḍa* we also notice the Upāsanā of *Rāma* and *Sītā* when they were asked to do so by their religious guide (chaplain) *purohita*. The verse is, "*Prasnnāste pitā Rāma yauvarājyamavāpsyasi. Upavāsatu bhavānādyā karotu saha sītayā.*"[15] His guide gave him *Dikṣā* (instructions) of that *vrata* with *mantra.*[16] Then *Rāma* followed this *vrata* as below

"*Gate purohite Rāmaḥ snāto niyatamānasaḥ, saha patnyā viśālākṣyā nārāyaṇam upāgatam. Pragṛhya śirasā pātri haviṣo vidhivattadā, mahate daivatāyājyam juhāva jvalite'nale. Śeṣam ca haviṣastasya praśyāsāsyatnaḥ priyam. Dhyā-yannārāyaṇam devam svāstriṇe kuśasamstare. Vāgyataḥ saha vaidehyā bhutvā niyatamānasaḥ śrimatyāyane viṣṇoh śisye naravarātmajaḥ.*"[17] It means *Rāma* and *Sītā* take holy bath, pour oblations in the fire, eat the remaining food, meditate upon *Viṣṇu* with calm and quiet mind. *Rāma* and *Sītā* sleep in the room of *Viṣṇu* as a part of the *Vrata*.

Rāma recites *Japa* which is a part of the Upāsanā. The verse is, "*Snātvā kṛtodakau vīrau jepatuḥ paramam japam.*"[18]

The worship of the different deities is mentioned in the *Rāmāyaṇa*. *Kausalyā* invokes all the deities to protect *Rāma* in his exile period, she bows before *Skanda, Soma, Bṛhaspati* etc., she says, "*Mayārcitā devagaṇaḥ śivādayoḥ...*"[19] *Rāma* also asks *Sītā* to worship the deities.[20] *Bharata* orders all the people to worship the deities to welcome *Rāma* on his return to *Ayodhyā*. He says, "*Daivatāni ca sarvāṇi caityāni nagarasya ca. Sugandhamālyarvādi-trairacantu sucayo naraḥ.*"[21]

The Upāsanā of *Sūrya* performed with the recitation of the *Āditya Hṛdaya Stotram* is discussed before, which is popular among the devotees.[22] In this way the *Rāmāyaṇa* includes the Upāsanā in the form of the *Yajña*, the *Sandhyā*, the *Agnihotra*, the worship of Gods, the *Upavāsa vrata*, the *Japa* and the *Meditation*.

Upāsanā in the Mahābhārata

The *Mahābhārata* is specially called an *Itihāsa* : history, written by *Maharṣi Vyāsa*, and it is called '*Jaya*' in the first verse of invocation. The verse is, "*Nārāyaṇam namaskṛtya naram caiva narottamam. Devi Sarasvatim caiva tato jayamudirayet.*" The *Mahābhārata* constantly talks about *Dharma* and praises the personalities who followed *Dharma*, the rules of behaviour, prescribed by the Vedas. Therefore it is also called a *Dharma* granth: religious book; or *Smṛti*. It teaches all the aspects of *Dharma*. Upāsanā is a part of *Dharma*, therefore the book contains the Upāsanās of *Śiva, Viṣṇu, Devi, Kārtikeya, Agnihotra, Sandhyā*, visit to places of pilgrimages, *Upavāsa* (fasting), *Vratas*, Penance, worship of Gods with offering objects, different *Yajñas* etc. In the *Mahābhārata Śiva* and *Viṣṇu* worship are important. These two Gods are praised as *Paramātman*, the cause of the Creation, Protection and the destruction of the Universe.

Kṛṣṇa is honoured by *Vyāsa, Bhiṣma, Yudhiṣthira*, because, he is said to be the incarnation of *Viṣṇu. Bhiṣma* says to *Yudhiṣṭhira*, *"Evameṣa mahābāhu keṣavaḥ satyavikramaḥ. Acintyaḥ puṇḍarikākṣa naiṣa kevalamānuṣaḥ."*[23] *Varāha, Parśaurāma* and *Vāmana* incarnations of *Viṣṇu* are praised in the *Āraṇyaka Parva* when *Yudhiṣṭhira* visits the holy places.[24] *Yudhiṣṭhira* praises *Śri Kṛṣṇa* in the verse," ... *Viṣṇo jiṣṇo hare kṛṣṇa vaikunṭhaḥ puruṣottama.*[25] He praises *Kṛṣṇa* by hundred names in this chapter.

Bhagavadgītā and *Viṣṇusahasranāma* are two main factors of the *Viṣṇu* worship which have their special appearance in later ages. In the *Anuśāsana Parva Yudhiṣṭhira* asks *Bhiṣma*, 'Who is the only great God and by whose Upāsanā a person will get the highest holy state?'; the verse is *"Kimekam daivatam loke kim vāpyekam parāyaṇam, Stuvantah kam Kamarcantaḥ prāpnuyurmānavaḥ śubham. Ko dharmaḥ sarvadharmāṇām bhavataḥ paramo mataḥ. Kim japanmucyante janturjanmasamsārabandhanāt."*[26] *Bhiṣma* preaches *Viṣṇu Sahasranāma* in reply to his question and says that only the meditation, the recitation of the eulogy of *Viṣṇu*, and his worship, to bow before Him is the only Upāsanā by which a man can get ultimate happiness, *Viṣṇu* is *Rudra*, He is everything, animate and inanimate, the verse is, *"Tameva cārcayannityam bhaktyā puruṣamavyayam. Dhyāyanstuvannamasyanca yajamānastameva ca".*[27]. *Bhiṣma* says that by the Upāsanā of *Vāsudeva* a mortal man goes to the highest state of *Brahman*, *"Vāsudevāśrayo martyo vāsudevaparāyaṇam. Sarvapāpavisuddhātmā yāti Brahma sanātanam."*[28] This praise contains one thousand names of *Viṣṇu* and is popular with the *Viṣṇu*-worshippers, who recite it daily.

The five names of *Viṣṇu* which occur in the *Vaiṣṇava* sect, are mentioned in the *Bhiṣma Parva*, namely, *Sankarṣaṇa, Pradyumna, Aniruddha, Viṣṇu* and *Kṛṣṇa.*[29] King *Uparicara* is seen busy performing the Upāsanā of *Nārāyaṇa* with the *Sātvata* type.[30]

The *Śiva* Upāsanā is noticed at various places in the *Mahābhārata*. In the *Āraṇyaka Parva Yudhiṣṭhira* visits the places of pilgrimages where the *Ṛṣis* asked him to bathe in the holy water and to praise *Śiva*, the verse is, *"Āpogayām naro snātvā arcayitvā mahesvarm. Gānapatyamavāpnoti kulamcoddharate svakam.*[31] The stanzas hundred and eight to hundred and eleven praise *Śiva* as `*Mahat*', which is beyond the twenty five tattvas. *Śiva* is said to have stayed on *Śriparvata* with *Devi*.[32] The *Gokarṇa Tīrtha* is mentioned here as a holy place of *Śiva*.[33] In the next chapter,[34] king *Sagara* performs the Upāsanā of *Śiva* with his wife, he praises *Śiva* with the names, `*Śankara, Tryakṣa, Tripuramardana, Bhava, Iśāna, Śūlapāṇim, Pinākinam, Tryambakam, Śivam, Ugreśam, Bahurūpam, Umāpatim*, etc.[35]

In the *Kirāta Parva*,[36] *Arjuna* performs the Upāsanā of *Śiva* with eating only fruits for one month, complete fasting for the next, eating only the leaves of trees for another month and breathing only the air. He stands on the thumb of his foot and holds his hands up and invokes *Mahādeva* to appear before him. God *Śiva* was pleased with him by this penance and appeared before him in the guise of a *Kirāta*. He fights with *Arjuna* and then comes in His own form with *Devi* and confers *Pāśupata* weapon to him.[36] In the *Sauptika Parva*[37], *Aśvatthāmā* praises *Śiva* and becomes ready to sacrifice himself in the fire as an oblation to *Śiva*, he says, "*Agnim juhomi bhagavanpratigṛhṇiśva mām balim.*" *Śiva* appears before him for his help.[38] After the night of masacre carried out by *Aśvatthāmā, Śrikṛṣṇa* describes the greatness of *Rudra*.[39] He says that *Siva* is the first, He is at the centre and He is at the end of the universe, all the world goes with his deeds. In the *Śānti Parva Śrikṛṣṇa* says that He performs *Siva* Upāsanā because people follow the great men and if He will not worship, the people will also not.[40] In the *Droṇa Parva Śrikṛṣṇa* asks *Arjuna* to worship *Śiva* before he goes to kill *Jayadratha*. *Arjuna* meditates on *Śiva* in his mind sitting quietly and sees God *Śiva* with *Pārvati*.[41] In *Anuśāsana Parva Śrikṛṣṇa* and his wife *Jāmbavati* worship *Śiva* to get a son like *Rudra*.[42] In this *Parva* the *Linga Pujā* is referred to, the verse is, "*Yasya brahmā ca viṣṇuśca tvamcāpi sahadaivataiḥ. Arcayadhvam sadā lingam tasmācśresṭhatamo hi saḥ*.[43] *Śivastava* is included in this chapter and He is praised as twentysixth *tattva*, which is the highest.[44] Another hundred and eight names are given, this chapter also includes one thousand names of *Śiva* which are called *Śiva Sahasranāma*.[45]

The Upāsanā of *Agnihotra* is mentioned in the *Anuśāsana Parva* and this Upāsanā is obligatory, "*Agnihotraśca yatnena sarvataḥ paripālayet*."[46] The Japa of the names of Gods is also prescribed.[47]

The people who cannot perform the Upāsanā of deities by the *Yajña,* they are asked to take the vow of fasting: *Upavāsa Vrata,* the verses are, "*Nāsti vedātparam śāstram nāsti matṛsamo guruḥ. Na dharmātparamolābhastapo nānaśanātparam,*" and "*Daridraḥ manujaiḥ pārth prāpya yajñaphalam yathā. Upavāsamiman kṛtvā gacchecca paramāmgatim.*"[48]

The worship of *Kārtikeya* results in the stay (halt) at *Skandaloka* which is called *Sālokyamukti.*[49]

Devi is praised as *Śākaṁbari* and her Upāsanā is prescribed.[50] *Sandhyā Upāsanā* is prescribed on the *Udyanta* mountain and the only a single performance of *Sandhyā* on the mountain gives the fruit of twelve years of performance.

Yudhiṣṭhira has done *Sūrya Upāsanā* with hundred and eight names which are told by *Dhaumya Ṛṣi* and the Sun gifted him a plate which supplied ample food without ever stopping. These hundred and eight names of the Sun are taught by *Nārada* to *Dhaumya,* and by *Indra* to *Nārada.*[51] These names are to be chanted at the time of Sunrise to get the favour of the Sun.

Yajña performance has also importance which is a means of getting the favour of Gods; the verse is, "*Apicātrayajñakriyābhirdevataḥ priyaṅte*"[52]

In this way of the *Mahābhārata* includes different types of Upāsanā with the *Yajña* ceremony.

References

1. Muṇḍaka Upaniṣad—1.1.5
2. Manu Smṛti—1.58

Upāsanā in Gṛhyasūtra

1. Bodhāyana Gṛhyasūtram Upodghāt-Edited by L. Srinivāsācārya, Asst., Pandit, Government Original Library, Mysore
2. Bodhāyana Gṛhyasūtram—2-9-15
3. Aśvalāyana G.S. 4-8-19
4. *Ibid*—1-4-10 to 18
5. Bodhāyana G.S. 3-8-1 to 6
6. Aśvalāyana G.S.—1-19-1
7. Ṛgveda—3-62-10
8. *Ibid*—1-35-2
9. *Ibid*—4-40-5, 1-45. 9

10. Śāṅkhāyana G.S.—4-8-12
11. Hiraṇyakeśin G.S.— 1-26-11
12. Bodhāyana G.S.—2-11 and Śāṅkhāyana G.S. 2-1-2,3
13. Śāṅkhāyana G.S.—2-12-2
14. Hiraṇyakeśin G.S.—1-7-26-11
15. Kauṣitaka G.S.—2-6-35
16. Bodhāyana G.S.—2-9-6
17. *Ibid*—2-9-7
18. *Ibid*—2-9-8 to 13
19. *Ibid*—2-9-14, 15, 16
20. Aśvalāyana G.S.—3-1-9-2
21. *Ibid*—3-1-3, 4
22. Pāraskara G.S.—1-2
23. Aśvalāyana G.S.—3-6-1 to 4
24. Bodhāyana Gṛhy Paribhāṣā sūtra—1-1-1
25. *Ibid*—1 1. 21

Upāsanā in Dharmasūtra

1. Bodhāyana Dh. Sūtra—1-1 3, and Govndaswāmi's commentary on the same
2. *Ibid*—1-1-5
3. Visiṣṭha Dh. Sūtra—1 4-6
4. Bodhāyana Dh. Sūtra—1-1-7
5. Āpastamba Dh. Sūtra—1-1-1, and Haradatta Miśra's commentary 'Ujjvalā'
6. *Ibid*—1-7-7
7. Gautam Dh. Sūtra—8-23-24 History of Dh. Śāstra By Dr. P.V. Kane, Vol. 1, Part-1
8. Āpastamba Dh. Sūtra—1-8-22-2
9. *Ibid*—1-1-2-21
10. *Ibid*—1-2-5-25
11. *Ibid*—1-2-6-13 and Bodhāyana Dh. Sutra A 2. Praśṇa 2
12. Bodhāyana Dh. Sūtra—1-1-11th adhyāya
13. *Ibid*—2 8. 13
14. *Ibid*—3-3-1
15. *Ibid*—2-10-7

Part II—Upāsanā in the Smṛti Literature

1. Parāśara Smṛti—1-23
2. Manu smṛti—2-7
3. *Ibid*—2-6
4. *Ibid*—1-108
5. *Ibid*—6-92
6. *Ibid*—12-24, 25, 26
7. *Ibid*—1-29
8. *Ibid*—12-88
9. *Ibid*—2-69
10. *Ibid*—2-74, 76, 81
11. *Ibid*—2-85
12. *Ibid*—3-67, Parāśara smṛti—2-7
13. Manusmṛti—6-4, 8. Yājñavalkya-Vānaprastha Prakaraṇa-45

14. Manusmṛti—6-68 to 7- and the commentary of Kalluka Bhatta on the same.
15. Manusmṛti—6-85
16. *Ibid*—7-96
17. *Ibid*—7-37, 38
18. *Ibid*12-91
19. Yājñavalkya Samhitā—Yatidharmaprakaraṇa—161
20. Manusmṛti—8-15
21. Manusmṛti—12-123, and the commentary of Kallukabhatta on the same
22. *Ibid*—12-119

Part III—Upāsanā in the Rāmāyaṇa

1. Rāmāyaṇa—1-8-16—Critical Edition-Barodā.
2. *Ibid*—6-23-24.
3. *Ibid*—6-71-13.
4. *Ibid*—3-10-6.
5. *Ibid*—2-41-11.
6. *Ibid*—2-36-9
7. *Ibid*—2-58-28.
8. *Ibid*—2-85-20.
9. *Ibid*—2-4-33.
10. *Ibid*—6-1-16.
11. *Ibid*—1-34-20.
12. *Ibid*—1-35.
13. *Ibid*—1-4-1.
14. *Ibid*—2-17-6. 2-4-30.
15. *Ibid*—2-5-8.
16. *Ibid*—2-5-10.
17. *Ibid*—2-6-1-, 2, 3, 4
18. *Ibid*—1-22-3.
19. *Ibid*—2-22-4, 18.
20. *Ibid*—2-22-27.
21. *Ibid*—6-115-2.
22. Rf. Ch. 2

Upāsanā in the Mahābhārata

23. Mahābhārata—Śāntiparva—200-46-Bhandarkar Oriental Research Institute, Pune (B.O.R.I.) Edition.
24. *Ibid*—Āraṇyakaparva—81-15, 21 to 30, 85.
25. *Ibid*—Śāntiparva—43-3-5, 15.
26. *Ibid*—Anuśāsanaparva—135-2, 3.
27. *Ibid*—*Ibid*—135-5.
28. *Ibid*—*Ibid*—135-130.
29. *Ibid*—Bhiṣma Parva—61-65, 66.
30. *Ibid*—Śānti Parva—322.
31. *Ibid*—Āraṇyaka Parva—81-154.
32. *Ibid*—*Ibid*—83-17.
33. *Ibid*—*Ibid*—83-22.

34. *Ibid*—*Ibid*—104.
35. *Ibid*—*Ibid*—104-9 to 12.
36. *Ibid*—*Ibid*—39-21 to 23. 40-55, 41-7.
37. *Ibid*—Sauptika Parva—7.
38. *Ibid*—*Ibid*—7-54, 59.
39. *Ibid*—*Ibid*— 17 & 18.
40. *Ibid* Śānti Parva—328-21, 22.
41. *Ibid* Droṇa Parva—57-17 to 19, 34, 36, 38 to 44, 49, to 58.
42. Rf to Ch 2 Śiva Upāsanā.
43. Mahābhārata—Anuśāsana Parva—42-102.
44. *Ibid*—*Ibid*—14-181.
45. *Ibid*—145 & 146. Ch. 18.
46. *Ibid*—*Ibid* 130-20.
47. *Ibid*—Anuśāsana Parva—150-6. Bhiṣma Parva—34-25. Āraṇyaka Parva 199-13.
48. *Ibid*—Anuśāsana Parva—109-62, 135.
49. *Ibid*—Araṇyaka Parva—213 to 221 ch. and the verse 221-80.
50. *Ibid*—*Ibid*—82-11 to 15.
51. *Ibid*—*Ibid*—277 to 283 ch.
52. *Ibid*—Śānti Parva—193-13. Anuśāsana Parva—100-9, 10.

5

Upāsanā in the Bhagavadgitā, Śrimadbhāgavatam and the Bhaktisūtras

Upāsanā in the Bhagavadgitā

The *Bhagavadgitā* finds place in the *Bhiṣma Parva* (No.6) of the *Mahābhārata*. There are seven hundred stanzas grouped in eighteen discourses —*Adhyāyas*—in the *Gitā* and this is the most popular sacred scripture among all other Hindu religious books. *Śri Krṣṇa* delivered these discourses to *Arjuna* at the very beginning of the great battle at *Kurukṣetra*. These discourses independently form the sacred book called the *Bhagavadgitā* or *Gitā*. The subject matter of this book is how to live life happily and how at attain the Supreme bliss. The two-fold Vedic religion of the *Pravṛtti* (religion of works) and the *Nivṛtti* (religion of renunciation) is rearranged in the *Gitā*. For this purpose the *Jñānyoga*, the *Karmayoga*, the *Dhyānayoga* and the *Bhaktiyoga* are discussed successively in the *Gitā*. Each path or *Yoga* leads to self realisation. The *Jñānayoga* is devotion to knowledge, the *Karmayoga* is devotion to work without reference to its results, the Dhyāna yoga is meditation of *Nirguṇa Iśvara* and the *Bhaktiyoga* has two aspects of *Sakāma* and *Niṣkama* among which later is extolled for the purpose of *Mokṣa*, which is called *Parābhakti*. Certain regular Upāsanās are prescribed for tranquilizing a devotee on his path of self realisation.

The great saint *Jñāneśvara* expresses in the eighteenth chapter of his book *Jñāneśvary* or *Bhāvārtha Dīpika* (a commentary on the *Gitā*), that the *Gitā* is a *Śāstra* which teaches knowledge of how to attain *Mokṣa*.[1]He has divided the *Gitā* in three main parts, namely, *Karma, Upāsanā* and *Jñānakāṇḍa*. He says that the first chapter is an introduction, the second tells the subject matter. The third chapter is *karmakāṅḍa*. The Upāsanā methods are described form the fourth to the eleventh chapter which is *Upāsanākāṅd* and *Jñānakāṅḍa* forms the portion from twelfth to fifteenth chapter. He use the word *Devatākāṅḍa* for *Upāsanākāṅda*.[2] He has given the following five main types of Upāsanā narrated in the *Gitā*

1. Upāsanā of *Agni, Indra, Soma,* i.e. concerning different deities.[3]
2. Upāsanā by *Adhyayana* i.e. *Śāstrābhyāsa*.[4]
3. Upāsanā by *Karma* i.e. performing one's duties without attachment to its fruits.
4. Upāsanā by devotion and love to God—*Bhakti*.[6]
5. Upāsanā with *So'ham mantra* which is performed by a *Jñāni* being one with the supreme.[7]

Śri. R.D. Rānaḍe divides the Upāsanā in the *Bhagvadgītā* in two types, one is personal (of attributes) by the *Yoga* etc. and the other is Impersonal (of *Akṣara*). He says that the Personal Upāsanā is the *Saguṇa* Upāsanā and the impersonal is the *Nirguṇa* Upāsanā, these are as follows:

1. Ideological method—In this method ten forms of God are taken for meditation, namely, *Puruṣottama, Sūtra, Vaiśvānara, Ravi, Māyin, Tajjalāna, Atiṣthāna, Vibhuti, Jñeya,* and *Āścarya*.
2. Moral method—In this method of meditation the Upāsaka accepts *Daivi Sampat* (divine qualities) *Amānitva* etc.; and try to follow them.
3. Mystical method— In this method, four elements are given, one is Physiological element, i.e. *Āsana* etc.; other is Psycho-ethical element, i.e. *Prāṇāyama* etc.; third is *Bhakti*-devotion element; fourth is element of Grace-lamp of wisdom.

Śri Rānaḍe has given the effects of meditation, namely, Joy and peace, Disgust, Silenceness, True *Bhakti*, Warding off all perils (*Duhkhānta*), Solution of world riddles, Vision of equality and community of Saints.[8]

Now we shall see the different modes of Upāsanā discussed in the *Bhagvadgītā*. First we shall discuss the Upāsanā by *Karma* which occurs in the fourth *Adhyāya*, from stanzas twenty four to thirty. These are sacrifices to Gods (*Devayajña*), sacrifice of self in the fire of restrain (*Indriyayajña*), sacrifice of senses and breath in the fire of knowledge (*Yogayajña*), sacrifice by wealth (*Dravyayajña*), sacrifice by following the life of austerity (*Tapoyajña*), sacrifice by reading (*Svādhyāya yajña*), sacrifice by accepting rigid vows by an ascetic (*Vrata yajña*), *Prāṇopāsanā* by offering *Prāṇa* in *Apāna* and *Apāna* in *Prāṇa*, by *Prāṇāyama*. *Śri Kṛṣṇa* says to *Arjuna* that he should accept one of these Upāsanās and be a *Yogi*.[9] A brief description of these Upāsanās follows

We have seen sacrifice to Gods in the previous chapter on *Dharmasūtras* which are sacrificial rites in devotion to Gods like Indra etc. It is called *Deva yajña*. But this is to be done without attachment to its results, and without selfishness. Sacrifice of self in the fire of Brahman means to understand that *Jīva* or *Ātman* is a fraction (*aṁśa*) of *Paramātman* and it is conditioned by *Upādhis* like body, intellect etc. (*Sopādhika*), so the sacrifice of these *Upādhis* is to be done in that *Paramātman*. It is called *Ātma-yajña*. The sacrifice of senses means to get hold on all senses by restraining them again and again, i.e. *Indriya Yajña*. The sacrifice of actions of senses and breath means to practise the *Yogic* methods like *Āsana* etc. and in that fire burn their desires i.e. *Yoga yajña*. *Dravya yajña* means to offer the wealth to a bonafide needy person but without expectation of return or benefits. *Tapoyajña* means to live a life observing austerity, by forgiveness, forbearance etc.; i.e. by accepting *Daivi Sampat*. *Svādhyāya yajña* means to learn and read the Vedic texts according to rules prescribed in it, i.e. *Śāstrābhyāsa*. *Vrata yajña* means to observe various vows prescribed by the *Śrutis* and the *Smṛtis*. *Prāṇopāsanā* is to practise *Prāṇāyāma* : breathing exercise by *Pūraka* (filling in), *Kuṁbhaka* (controlling inside) and *Recaka* (emptying). Some Upāsakas take restricted food intake and offer the five life breaths-*Prāṇa, Apāna, Samāna, Vyāna, Udāna*—into controlled breath, the *Prāṇa* is important because it holds the life of all creatures. The *Taittiriya Upaniṣad* extols this Breath in this verse, "*Prāṇam devā anuprāṇanti, manuṣyāḥ, paśavasca ye. Prāṇo hi bhutānāmāyuḥ tasmāt sarvāyuṣamucyate.*[10] Therefore, *Prāṇa* is supposed to be svarūpa of Brahman. By *Prāṇopāsanā* one can purify the mind and get real knowledge.

Śri Kṛṣṇa says that in all these *yajñas jñānayajña* is the greatest sacrifice because all actions (*karma*) end in the knowledge sacrifice, the verse is, '*Śreyāndravyamayād Jñāna yajñaḥ Paraṅtapa. Sarvakarmākhilam Pārtha jñāne parisamāpyate.*"[11] He further says in the thirteenth stanza of the fourth chapter that after getting the real knowledge the *Upāsaka* attains Supreme Peace (*Parā Śānti*), and ever remains in it.

Now we shall see the Upāsanā in the *Dhyāna Yoga*. This is the Upāsanā of Unmanifested (*Nirguṇa*). This is the Upāsanā of the soul which is already unified with *Paramātman*, which is called *Sāmya* in the *Gītā*, the verse is, "*Ātamaupamyena sarvatra saman paśyatio'rjuna*."[12] This Upāsanā teaches to engulf others in one self and oneself in others. The meditation and a particular posture and the process of *Dhyāna* is prescribed here. *Dhyāna Yogi* should try to keep his mind calm and quiet, live in seclusion, he must be free from all desires, and the mind and body should be controlled.[13] The stanzas from eleven to fifteen of the sixth chapter describe the method of sitting and thinking of a *Dhyānayogi*. In this Upāsanā a *Yogi* gets full hold on himself in due course of time and his mind constantly abides in the Self and he experiences that the Supreme Self is all and nothing else exists. *Saint Jñāneśvara* explains the posture and process of meditation according to *Haṭha Yoga* and *Aṣṭāṅgayoga* with three bonds viz. *Mulabandha, Jālandhara bandha* and *Uḍiyānabandha,* with *prāṇāyāma, Pratyāhāra, yama, niyama* and the *japa* of *So'ham*.[14]

Now we shall see the Upāsanā in the *Bhakti Yoga*. The *Gītā* narrates the four classes of *Bhaktas*, namely, *Ārta*, one who is distressed; *Arthārthi*, one who seeks wealth, children etc.; *Jijñasu*, one who seeks for the real knowledge; and *Jñāni*, one who knows the real nature of God. *Gītā* says that among these four types of *Bhaktas* the Jñāni is a real worshipper because he performs the Upāsanā (*bhajate*) being united with the Supreme.[16]

These four types of *Bhaktas* worship the God with either of two modes, namely, *Sakāma* (with expectation of something) and *Niṣkāma* bhāva (without any expectation) *Ārta, Arthārthi* and *Jiñāsu* worship with *Sakāmabhāva*, with some worldly objectives and *Jñāni* worships with *Niṣkāmabhāve*, without any material objectives. *Śri Kṛṣṇa* says that the *bhaktas* who worship with *Sakāma*, obtain the fruits which disappear after sometime (*antavat*), but the other *bhaktas* unite with him and do not return again in this world.[17] These *bhaktas* are called *Jñāni Bhaktas*. The worship of a *Jñāni* is a divine worship and it leads to realisation.[18] Gītā further says that if a devotee of any type constantly remembers the Supreme, even at the end of life, and recites *'Om'* and leaves his body, he will get ultimate bliss because *'Om'* is *Brahman*.[19]

Śri Kṛṣṇa says that the *bhaktas* worship Him with *Sakāmbhāva* and do not know Him as all pervading, so they worship Him under some form with some motive behind it. Therefore, they give Him different forms of different deities, which represent certain limited aspects of Godhood. God has the magnanimity that He gives to the *Bhakta* what they desire. Therefore, the Bhaktas get the results according to desires they worship for, also the way a devotee perceives the Godhead, and worships Him, he attains that abode after death (*salokatā*). The devotee who loves *Bhūtas* like *Bhāgini* etc.; go to their place but for a limited time and they have to return to the Earth again.[20] *Śri Kṛṣṇa* further says, "the devotees who perceives Me alone and love Me alone as all pervading Supreme Power, get endless gains and their Upāsanā becomes very natural and easy. In that case, if they offer me a leaf, a flower, a fruit, some water, I accept it because they offer it with pure devotion, with a pure mind." He says that this type of devotees never perish, "*na me bhaktaḥ praṇaśyati.*"[21] He asks *Arjuna* to become a *Bhakta* of this type.

Śri Kṛṣṇa tells in the ninth *Adhyāya* how a *jñāni* devotee performs His Upāsanā, who is as all pervading. He says, "*Satatam kirtayanto mām yatataśca dṛḍhavrataḥ. Namasyantaśca mām bhaktyā nityayuktā Upāsate.*" It means a *Jñāni bhakta*, who is firm on his vow of realisation of the supreme, love Him and constantly remembers and praises Him, by singing His eulogies.

In the Upāsanā of the *Jñānayoga* a *Jñānayogi*, an enlightened soul, continues to perform his Upāsanā. He worships the supreme either by wisdom sacrifice *Jñānayajña* or perceiving Him as one in all; or he worships the different forms of God supposing that all the forms are the forms of one God with His face at all sides.[22]

In the twelfth *Adhyāya Gītā* describes the conduct of a *Jñāni* Upāsaka, who is a Upāsaka of the Imperishable (*Akṣara Upāsaka*). He performs the Upāsanā by renouncing all *Karmas* (actions) in the Supreme, he meditates upon the Supreme with the *Yoga, Dhyāna;* his thought is fixed on the Supreme and by this conduct he ever remains in the state of Bliss. This upāsaka leads life with austerity, endued with faith, looking upto God as all pervading. *Śri Kṛṣṇa* says that, this *Yogi* is dear to Him.[23] He says to *Arjuna* that the Upāsanā of Impersonal Absolute is very difficult, the verse is "*Kleśo'dhikarasteṣāmavyaktāsaktacetasām. Avyaktā hi gatirduḥkhamdehavadbhiravāpyate.* [24] A *Jñāni* works in the society but he firmly knows that the deeds—*karma*—do not pollute him and he does not desire the fruits of *karma* and therefore he is not bound by the deeds.[25] A conduct of a *Jñāni Bhakta* and a *Jñāna Yogi* seems to be similar.

There is a different type of Upāsanā described in the *Bhagavadgītā* which is performed by a devoted but an ignorant *Bhakta*, who does not know anything about *Jñāna, Dhyāna, Ātman, Karma* or *Sāṅkhyayoga* etc.; but only hearing about the *Paramātman* from *Śrotriyas* (knower of the Vedas), he worships God with love and devotion (*Bhakti*), so he is the *Bhakta* and his love is called *Bhakti*, and he also goes beyond death, adhering to what he has heard.[26] *Śri Kṛṣṇa* says that this is called *Apārā Bhakti* and the other type of *bhakti* (of a *Jñāni*) is the *Parābhakti* or *Avyabhicāri bhakti*, This form is the unfailing devotion of Love and by this Love the *Bhakta* crosses the three *Guṇas* i.e. *Sattva, Raja* and *Tama* and becomes *Brahman*, gets highest Bliss (*Ekāntika Sukha*).[28] *Śri Kṛṣṇa* says that when a *Upāsaka* attains this state of Brahman, he neither grieves nor desires, he treats all beings alike and attains extreme Devotion (*Parābhakti*) to the Supreme the verse is "*Brahmabhutaḥ prasannātmā na śocati na kāṅkṣati. Samaḥ sarveṣu bhuteṣu madbhaktim labhate parām.*"[29] Such a devotee obtains Supreme Peace (*Parām Śāntim*), and eternal rest in that place.[30]

In this way the *Gītā* has given importance to the Upāsanā by *Karma*, by *Jñāna* by *Dhyāna* and by *Bhakti*. These four ways of self realisation include the types of Upāsanās discussed here.

Upāsanā in the Śrimadbhāgavatam

Śrimadbhāgavatam is one of the eighteen major *Purāṇas*. A *Purāṇa* is said to consist of *Pañcalakṣaṇa*, i.e. five characteristic topics, namely Primary creation, secondary creation or the destruction and renovation of worlds, genealogy of gods and patriarchs, *Manvantara, Vaṅśacarita* i.e. brief description of solar and lunar dynasties. However *Śrimadbhāgavatam* has detailed further characteristics of a *Purāṇa* namely *Sarga, Visarga, Vṛtti, Rakṣā, Hetu, Manvantara, Vaṅśa, Vamśacarita, Samthā, Apāśraya.*[1] The *Bhāgavat purāṇa* says that the tenth characteristic i.e. *Apāśaya* is the final goal to be achieved by the study of the *Purāṇas. Apāśraya* means last refuge to be sought which is *Brahman. Brahman* is all-pervading and beyond the influence of the *Māya* which operates through three states of *Jīva* viz., *Jāgṛti, Svapna* and *Suṣupti*. *Brahman* is related to all nine stages of living beings (entry into the womb, gestation, birth, infancy, boyhood, youth, middle age, old age and death) but It is always distinct from them.[2] The main aim of learning these *Purāṇas* is to reach the highest state of consciousness which is *Brahman*. Each *Purāṇa* is dedicated to a certain deity. The pantheism of the *Purāṇas* is one of the unique and peculiar characteristics. But the divine nature of each particular deity is all-pervading, omniscient, omnipresent and omnipotent. The Supreme Being is supposed to be manifested in the figure of *Śiva* or *Viṣṇu*. Among the main *Purāṇas, Viṣṇu, Nāradiya, Bhāgavat, Garuḍa, Padma* and *Brahma Purāṇa* are said to be the *Vaiṣṇava Purāṇas. The Agni, Liṅga, Śiva, Skanda Purāṇas are Śaiva Purāṇas*. The third group has assorted deities and includes *Brahmāṅḍa, Brahmavaivarta, Mārkaṅḍeya, Bhaviṣya, Vāmana, Matsya* and *Kurma Purāṇa*.[3]

It is said that the *Bhāgavat Purāṇa* has the essence of all *Upaniṣads* and one who studies this with a controlled and pure mind attains *Mokṣa* or *Vaikuṅṭha (Salokatā)*[4]. *Bāgavat Purāṇa* has powerfully influenced the opinion and feelings of the people. This *Purāṇa* describes the incarnations of Lord *Viṣṇu*, death of asura *Vṛttra* and the events that happened to *Kurus, Aṅdhaka* and *Vṛṣṇis* and *Yādava Vaṁśa*. The details of duties, devotion of *Karma*, devotion to *Yoga*, devotion to *Jñāna* and devotion to *Bhakti* are broadly discussed in this *Purāṇa*. The Eleventh *Skandha* of this *Purāṇa* is important for the discussion of the subject matter of these four paths of knowledge. This part of the book narrates the importance of Lord *Kṛṣṇa* as the incarnation of *Viṣṇu*, His biography and teachings to His disciple *Uddhava*. This part also comments on the nature of *Upāsya* and the *Upāsanā*, therefore, we shall deal mostly with the Eleventh *Skandha* of the *Bhāgavat Purāṇa* from the view of the concept of Upāsanā. The peculiarity of this *Purāṇa* is; *Vāsudeva Kṛṣṇa* is identified as Supreme Being. Hindus of every caste and tribe and the followers of the other religion also can revere for *Vāsudeva* i.e. Lord *Kṛṣṇa*.

In the *Bhāgavat Purāṇa Śri Kṛṣṇa* explains the ambiguity in the *Vedas* interpreted by ignorant people and in reply to *Uddhava's* question on the same subject he has expounded the three types of *Yogas* for securing *Mokṣa*, namely, the path of Knowledge-*Jñāna* mārga, the path of action-*Karma* mārga and the path of Devotion-

Bhakti mārga, which correspond to the *Jñāna, Karma* and *Upāsanā* sections of the *Śruti.*[5] *Kṛṣṇa* further narrates that the path of knowledge is meant for the people who have already achieved renunciation of all types of *Karmas*, the path of *Karma* is meant for the people who want to fulfil their worldly desires and the path of Devotion is prescribed for the people who by nature have the devout faith in the name and stories of *Viṣṇu* and who neither throw off the duties nor follow them accordingly.

Bhāgavat Purāṇa discusses the four paths of *Jñāna, Karma, Yoga*, and *Bhakti* which are very much similar to Bhagavadgitā. In reply to the King *Nimi's* question about following the path of Action-*Karma mārga, Ṛṣi Āvirhotra* clarifies that the *Vedas* prescribed *Karmas* in such a way as to get renunciation from them step by step and which lead the life to the Supreme Bliss. With this aim the *Vedas* have attached particular method to each work and importance of duty as well as its consequences.[6] The *Upāsaka*, while performing his duties loosens slowly the knot of his ego and becomes worthy for real worship of God *Kṛṣṇa* by practising *Pāñcarātra* method of Upāsanā. The following process is observed in this Upāsanā : the devotee first cleans his body, sits in front of the idol of God, practises breath control; *Prāṇāyāma*, followed by the *Nyāsa* and worships the idol with sandal paste, flowers, washes feet of deity, chants the *mantra*, tries to contemplate himself as being one with the God as the Supreme soul who is present in the Fire, the Sun, the Water etc.; By repeating this process again and again he gets free from the bondages of *saṅsāra* (the worldly phenomena) in due course of time.[7]

The spiritual guidance given to *Uddhava* by *Śri Kṛṣṇa* is the climax of the *Bhāgavatm. Śri Kṛṣṇa* first teaches him *Vedānta* which gives the knowledge of self realisation, and of identification of one's self with the souls of all embodied being, which is important to attain the Supreme Bliss and teaches him to perform the prescribed *Karmas* by which the purification of mind is possible.[8] But *Uddhava* feels that it is difficult for him to practise such a philosophy, therefore, *Śri Kṛṣṇa* narrates him the famous dialogue between *Yadu* and Avadhūta (*Dattātreya*) who is in the disguise of a *Brāhmaṇa. Avadhūta* tells *Yadu* the names of His preceptors selected by Himself and from whom He got wisdom and became free (*Mukta*), these names are-the Earth, the Air, the *Akāśa* (sky), the Water, the Fire, the Moon, the Sun, the pigeon, the bow-constructor, the Sea, the moth, the bee, the elephant, the honey gatherer, the deer, the fish, *Pingalā*, the osprey, the child, the maiden, the blacksmith, the serpent, the spider and the wasp. *Avadhūta* learned from these preceptors how to behave. He tells *Yadu* that a wise person should not deviate from his path of *Dharma*, be useful to others, not indulge in gratification of sense organs, keep oneself aloof from the merits and defects of sense objects, keep his mind fixed on the Self, become a friend of everybody, should not accept or adopt any impure thing just as fire will not, keep in mind that the six stages of life beginning with the birth and ending with death belong to the body and not to the Soul, should know that the upādhis are different from the *Ātman*. *Avadhūta* further narrates that a sage should accept any type of food inspite of its taste and quantity, he should be quiet, unaffected by time, space etc. and should keep himself away from passions, a clever man should assimilate the essence of *Śāstras* like a bee which collects honey from a flower, only hear the songs of God; being haunted by hope is greatest misery and to be free from hope is happiness. *Avadhūta* says to *Yadu* that only the innocent child and one who transcends the three guṇas are free from anxiety. He further says that a person should wander alone otherwise he will be disturbed by quarrels etc. In the following way He concludes His discourse; the mind becomes pure by concentrating on *Brahman* and sheds off the *karma* dust, the *Sattva* guṇa rises gradually and then he enters in to the *Nirguṇa*, he gets absorbed in the meditation of the Self, then he attains *Mokṣa*. In this way *Śri Kṛṣṇa* gives *Uddhava* the spiritual knowledge through the dialogue between the *Brāhmaṇa* and *Yadu*.[9]

Śri Kṛṣṇa further says that one should observe the duties prescribed for one's respective *Varṇa* and *Āśrama* and family tradition; by observing this *Dharma* the mind gets purified.[10] He says that who is devoted to Me should perform *Sandhyā*, *Pañcamahāyajnas* and *Śrādha* etc., without expecting its fruits.[11] The practice of observing the five vows included in the daily *Upāsanā* which are called *Yama* and *Niyama*, should be followed by the *Upāsaka*. Such a *Upāsaka* should be free from pride, envy; he should be patient, understand that the Soul is distinct from the subtle and the gross body, then only he will get real knowledge and get free from *sansāra* (passing phenomena).[12]

Śri Kṛṣṇa gives importance to the knowledge and not to the verbal revelation without knowledge.[13] He says to *Uddhava* the same thing which has told *Arjuna* in the *Bhagavdgītā*, that if *Uddhava* is not able to concentrate his mind firmly on *Brahman*, should carry out his duties and offer all acts at His feet without expecting any fruit in return, listen the stories of God, sing them to others (in *Kirtana*), observe the three *Puruṣārthas*, namely, *Dharma, Artha,* and *Kāma* to please God, and develop *bhakti* towards Him.[14] *Śri Ekanātha*, the wellknown saint of *Mahārāṣtra*, gives importance to the *Parābhakti*, while commenting on these verses, he says that, the devotional Love : *Bhakti* should be free from three guṇas. By this *Bhakti*, the *Upāsaka* becomes one with the God, like a crystal of salt which becomes one with water when it is dipped into it.[15]

Śri Kṛṣṇa tells the Upāsanā to *Uddhava* when he asks about the type of devotion followed by the devotees like *Nārada*.[16] *Śri Kṛṣṇa* says that a devotee who contemplates on Him as the inner soul abiding in all, existed at all times and worships Him, is dear to Him, he is a best *Upāsaka*. He says that to worship an idol as His symbol (*Pratika*) to serve, to eulogise Him and to chant of His deeds is His *Upāsanā*. His *Upāsanā* also includes to listen His stories with faith and devotion, to meditate upon Him, to dedicate oneself to His service, to recite and describe His incarnations, to celebrate His *Janmāṣtami*, to go on pilgrimage, to offer Him flowers, sandal paste, food, to worship with prescribed methods of the *Vedas* and the *Tantras*, to observe the fast of *Ekādaśi*.[17] *Śri Kṛṣṇa* says that, the Sun, the Fire, the *Brāhmaṇa*, the cow, the devotees of *Viṣṇu*, the Sky, the Air, Water, the Earth, one's own heart and all the creatures are the places of His worship.[18] He says that, in these places of worship one should contemplate His form with four arms holding the conch named *Pāñcajanya, Sudarśana cakra, kaumudaki gadā* (mace), and a lotus. One should perform sacrifices, do public service, and constantly remember Him. Association with saints is also important.[19] He further advises *Uddhava* to leave the *Pravṛtti* and *Nivṛtti* type of *Karmas* and take shelter in Him as *Brahman*. He will protect him and then he will attain *mokṣa* (Release from bondage).

In the fourteenth chapter of the Eleventh *Skandha Uddhava* questions *Śri Kṛṣṇa* about different modes of the Upāsanā and their importance. *Śri Kṛṣṇa* replies that according to inherent predominance of the *Sattva, Raja* and *Tama* qualities different species, including human beings, hold different type of nature and capacity to understand. Therefore everybody undertakes different method to achieve the highest goal, i.e. *Mokṣa*. Past *karmas* also play a major part in determining their nature. Therefore some people tend to pro-vedic views and others anti-vedic. *Śri Kṛṣṇa* gives the following *Upāsanās*.

1. Performance of sacrifices prescribed by the *Vedas* is the *Upāsanā* which leads to *Mokṣa*.
2. To work hard for social welfare and to enjoy name and fame is the highest goal.
3. The Sages like *Vātsyāyana* say that sexual enjoyment is the highest blessings.
4. The *Yogis* give importance to self control, truthfulness etc., which lead to *Mokṣa*.
5. The realists and politicians give importance to the wealth and power as the highest goal.
6. Some regard the performance of sacrifices, worships of deities. The austerities, *yama* and *niyama* are important to attain *mokṣa*,.[20]

Śri Kṛṣṇa further says that all these trends of Upāsanās lead to temporary enjoyments if these are not done with dedication to Him. He says that all these methods are correct only when the whole mind is given to him. All the Upāsanās do not fulfil without intensive devotion to god, because all impurities of mind vanish by intense Love toward God : *Kṛṣṇa Bhakti*.[21]

Uddhava asks the method of contemplation on *Paramātman*.[22] *Śri Kṛṣṇa's* reply to this question is similar to the sixth *adhyāya* of the *Bhagavadgitā*, which is *Dhyānayoga*. He replies that one should sit on a level seat, try to seat in a comfortable *Āsana*, practise *Prāṇāyāma*, control sense organs, recite *Omkāra*. This should be done for three times daily for one month to get control over breath. One should contemplate on the lotus in the heart, on the Sun, the Moon, the Fire, and in that fire one should contemplate on the sacred form of God with four arms, graceful outlook, gentle smile, wearing ornaments, dark blue colour of the skin, holding a conch, *sudarśana, gadā* (mace), *vanamālā* (garland), *kaustubha* (gem) and with goddess *Śri (Lakṣmi)* sitting besides Him, and try to contemplate on each of the limbs of God and slowly try to become one with God, the Absolute *Brahman* and not to anything else. All this should be done intensively then only one can experience the Supreme Soul in him and in all the world.[23]

In the chapter Seventheenth of the *Eleventh Skandha, Uddhava* asks *Kṛṣṇa* to explain the *Dharma* i.e. righteous duties of the *Varṇa* and *Āśrama,* which are prescribed by the *Śāstras. Śri Kṛṣṇs,* pleased with this question, explains the qualities of the Ages (*Yuga*), the characteristics of the four *Varṇas* and *Āśramas*. He says that a life-long celibate burns out all the seeds of *Karmas* and become pure like the Fire.[24] He also describes *Pañcamahāyajñas,* He says that performance of one's own duties is itself His Upāsanā.[25] *Śri Kṛṣṇa* says that in the fourth *Āśrama : Sanyāsa;* a man acquires spiritual knowledge step by step and he understands the nature of the bondage and the liberation of the soul and gets *Mokṣa*.[26]

In the twentythird chapter of the Eleventh *Skandha Śri Kṛṣṇa* teaches *Uddhava* the *Yogaśāstra : Aṣṭāṅgayoga* : with *Yama* and *Niyma* etc.; in reply of *Uddhava's* question. *Uddhava* further asks about *Kriyāyoga* in the chapter twentyseven. The reply of *Śri Kṛṣṇa* is important from the *Upāsanā* point of view. He answers that His worship is threefold-The *Vedic,* the *Tāntric* and mixed; a synthesis of these two. A man perform Upāsanā according to his choice,[27] but with faith and devotion. First He says that one can worship Him with the articles of worship through the image or an altar of sacrifice or the Fire or the Sun or the Water or One's own heart or *Brahman*. One should purify his body by taking bath, with chanting the *Vedic* and the *Tāntric Mantras,* perform daily *Sandhyā* and *Pañcamahāyajñas,* observe one's duties daily. There are eight kinds of the images of God made by, namely, stone, wood, metal, earth, sandal paste, painting, precious stone and a mental image. It can be movable or immovable. In the case of immovable image there is a process of *Āvāhana* and *Visarjana*. One should seat on a *darbhāsana* besides the image, perform *nyāsa* and worship the image with various articles, offer *Pādya, Arghya, Ācamana,* (water to wash feet and to drink) and recite mantras called *Hṛdaya, Śirṣam, Śikhā* and then recite *Gāyatri Mantra*. If the image is made of clay there should not actual bathing with water. A devotee can worship God with whatever articles he possesses. If one wants to worship the God in the *Pratika* of Altar, one can invoke deities by mantras and worship them, if there is a sacrificial

Fire, then the oblations of ghee (clarified butter) is one's Upāsanā. If one wants to worship the Sun, one can offer *Arghya*, flowers etc. Then a devotee should contemplate on his subtle *aṁśa* as *Paramātman* who abides in the Lotus of the heart and wake the *Kuṇḍalini Śakti* which is dormant in *Ādhāracakra*. A devotee should mentally make a throne (seat) for God and worship according to the Vedic and the *Tantric* method. A devotee should worship the *Pāñcajanya* conch, *Sudrśana* cakra, Gadā, eight attendants of God namely *Naṅda, Sunaṅda, Pracaṅda, Canda, Mahābala, Bala, Kumuda, Kumudekṣaṇa* and *Garuḍa*. A devotee should worship *Durgā, Vināyaka, Vyāsa* and *Viśvaksena*, his own spiritual *Gurū* and the deities of eight quarters. A devotee should chant the *Svarṇanḍharmānuvak*, the *Mahāpuruṣa vidyā*, the *Puruṣa Sukta*, and the texts of *Sāmaveda* known as *Rājan sāma*. A devotee should decorate the image with clothes, flower garlands etc. If a devotee can not perform this worship daily, he should perform it on holy days on on birthdays of God. A devotee should pour oblations with the mantras like "*Om namo Nārāyaṇāya*', with *Puruṣa sukta* and conclude the worship with maṅtra *Puṣpa*. A devotee can place some flowers from the image on his head as the gift of God, he can worship at any time and any form of image. *Śri Kṛṣṇa* says that this is the *Kriyāyoga* as taught in the *Vedas* and the *Tantras*. He says that he who follows this *Upāsanā* is blessed with Bhakti and attains Lord *Kṛṣṇa*.[28]

In the *Bhāgavat Purāṇa Śri Kṛṣṇa* has explained the four paths for attaining the Supreme Bliss, minutely than *Bhagavdgītā*, but it also follows the tradition of *Pravṛtti* and *Nivṛtti Mārga* prescribed by the *Vedas*.[29] But in the *Bhāgavatam* the path of *Bhakti* and Upāsanā according to it has given more importance. The Devotion to Love of God is the *Aparā Bhakti* (narrated in the *Bhagavadgītā*) and the Devotion to Love of God with the spiritual Knowledge which is *Parā Bhakti* (narrated in the *Bhagavdgītā*) are explained fully, and the *Upāsanās* are given according to the Path of the *Bhakti Yoga*. These Upāsanās are easy than purely the *Vedic* or *Tāntric Upāsanās*, the critical and heavy part is omitted. It is said in this *Purāṇa* that whatever you do, do it with faith and devotion and Love towards God and to please God. By following this way of life and the way of worship one can definitely attain *Mokṣa*, the Supreme Bliss.

Upāsanā in the Bhaktisūtras

Bhakti is a major *"Sādhanāmārga"* leading to realisation of God or self realisation among four main paths namely, *Jñānamārga, Yogamārga, Karmamārga* and *Bhaktimārga*. The scriptures; namely, the *Sānkhya Darśana*, the *Uttara Mimāṅsā*, and *Brahmasutra* describe *Jñānamārga, Pātanjala Yoga Daraśana* describes *Yogmārga*, the *Purva Mimāṅsā* and the *Smṛtis* describe the *Karmamārga* and *Bhaktisūtras* describe the *Bhaktimārg*. We have seen in the previous sections of this chapter that Bhaktimārga is prominent in the *Bhagavadgītā* and the *Śrimadbhāgavatam*, but there are books exclusively on the *bhakti* known as the *Bhaktisūtras* written by the sages like *Nārada, Śāṇḍily, Garga, Vyāsya, Hanumāna* etc. All these books are not available today except *Nārada Bhaktisūtra* and *Śāṇḍilya Bhaktisūtra*. In the context of Upāsanā, these books are very important.

(i) **Śāṇḍilya Bhaktisūtra:** The idea of the incarnation of the Supreme God in various forms at various times is seen in the *Śāṇḍilya Bhaktisūtras*. One of the initial *sūtra* says *"Mukhyam tasya hi kāruṇyam."*[1] It means that God takes birth by different names and in different forms because he feels sympathy (*Karuṇā*) towards all beings in the world hence destroys their griefs. The *Śāṇḍilya Bhaktisūtra* is more or less philosophical in approach. It discusses the nature of *Brahman* and *Jīva* and their interrelation. It emphasises that there is no third entity other than the *Puruṣa* and the *Prakṛti*, the *sūtra* is *"Cetyācitorna tṛtiyam."*[2] The *sūtra* says that *Māyā* can not be unreal because *Māyā* is the Power of *Brahman*, the *sūtra* *"Śaktitvānnānṛtam Vedyam."*[3] The creation is the effect of the *Prakṛti* and the *Prakṛti* takes shelter in *Brahman*, therefore the universe *"Jagat"* is the integral part of *Brahman*.[4] *Śāṇḍilya Ṛṣi* says that the knowledge of *Brahman* and *Jīva* is important for *Bhakti*, because one who wants liberation from the bondages of saṅsāra must know about *Bhakti*. *Bhakti* means intense love to *Iśvara*, the *sūtra* is *'Sā parānuratktiriśvare*.[5] This is the *`Parābhakti'* which is described in the *Bhagavadgītā*, by the name *"Avyabhicāribhakti"*, the *Bhakti* in which no other diversifying thought springs up. *Maharṣi Śāṇḍilya* indicates the aim of this *Bhakti* as *"Amṛtatva"*, immortality or *Brahmatva*. the *sutra* is *"Tatsaṁstasyāmṛtatvopadeśāt."*[6]. This *sūtra* is similar to the verse in the *Chandogya Upaniṣad* that *"Brahmasamsatho'mṛtatvameti"*.[7] This *Parābhakti* is the ultimate state of *Jñāna, Karma* and *Yoga*, as in this stage everything becomes silent and united with *Brahman*, so in this stage only *Bhakti* remains.[8] *Maharṣi Śāṇḍilya* further describes that *Jñana, Yoga,* and *Karma* are to be undertaken only for the rise of the *Bhakti* in the mind. All the above ways of realisation of God help to purify the mind. The real nature of God can be reflected only in this purified mind and after realisation of this reflection the real love to God is experienced which is called *Parābhakti*.[9]

Maharṣi says that the *Bhakti* of (love to) different deities means to think that the deities are different from *Jīva* and *Jīva* wants to take shelter of that deity and relies on it. This idea of Bhakti is seen in the *Śvetāśvatara Upaniṣad*, the verse is *"Yasya deve parābhaktirya-thādeve tathā gurau."*[10]. This *Upaniṣad* says that this is the *Bhakti* to God as to one's *Gurū*, "Spiritual preceptor". The sutra *"Devabhaktiritarasmin sāhacaryāt."* says that the dependence of jiva on *Iśvara*, is a sort of *Gauṇi bhakti* (*Aparabhakti* told by *Gītā*) which is seen in the *Pātañjali's Yogasutra" Iśvara-praṇidhānādvā"*[11]

Maharṣi Śāṇḍilya considers that it is totally a Upāsanā in which in the first stage one enters first in the *Aparā* or *Gauṇi bhakti* and then progresses upto the *Parābhakti*. He says in the second chapter that in the first stage one has to acquire knowledge of *Brahman* and for that one has to perform Upāsanā, means one has to hear about *Brahman*, think or meditate upon it and then take interest in attaining that state *Śravaṇa, Manana* and *Nididhyāsana*, is one's Upāsanā, the sutra is *"Buddhihetupravṛttirā-viśuddheravaghātavāt"*.[12] He further says that the Upāsanā by *śravana, manana nididhyāsana* also includes the service to one's *Gurū*, the *svādhyāya, śāstrābhyāsa* and to follow the discipline of *śama* i.e. restrain of mind; *Dama* i.e. restraint of sense organs; *Titikṣā* i.e. to tolerate the good and Bad happenings; *Samādhāna* i.e. to be happy in all situations; *Uparati* i.e. to feel unattached and *śraddhā*, i.e. to rely upon God. *Maharṣi Śāṇḍilya* gives the opinion of *Ācārya Kaśyapa* and *Vyāsa* in the support of his view, in the next sūtra. The *sūtra* says that *Ācārya Kaśyapa* also thinks similarly that if the intellect (*Buddhi*) relies upon God it becomes free.[13] *Vyāsa* also thinks the same.[14] *Maharṣi Śāṇḍilya* further says that the intellect which takes refuge in the *Jīvātman* and the *Paramātman*, can attain *Mokṣa* because *Jīvātman* is a fraction of *Paramātman*. The *Chāndogya Upaniṣad* says the same in the verse *"Sarvamkhalvidam Brahmatajjalāniti śāntamupāsita"*.[15] *Gītā* also says the same in *"Mamaivaṅśo jīvaloke jīvabhutaḥ sanātanaḥ"*.[16]

Maharṣi Śāṇḍilya gives the different modes of love towards God, by which the devotees get *Mokṣa*, viz. the love of *Arjuna* to *Śrikṛṣṇa*, the gratefulness of *Ikṣvāku*; the love of *Vidura* in the *Darśan* (vision) of God; the *viraha* (feeling of separateness) of *Gopi*; the type of love of *Upamanyu* i.e. disgust of everything except God; the *kirtana* i.e. to describe the nature of God now and then which is the love of *Vyāsa* and *Bhīṣma*; the love of *Hanumān* towards *Rāma*. i.e. to live for service to God; the love of *Bali* i.e. to surrender everything to God; love of *Pralhāda* i.e. to see God in each and everything of the world. He further says that to worship the incarnations of God is also a Upāsanā in the *Bhaktimārga*. It also turns into *Parābhakti* because the incarnations are the forms of *Paramātman*.[17]

The love towards God for fulfilment of some worldly desires is called *Gauṇibhakti* by *Śāṇḍilya* which is called *Sakāma* or *Aparābhakti* by the *Gītā*.[18] He says in the *sūtra "Antarāle tu śeṣāḥ syurupāstyādaucakāṅḍatvāt"*[19] that *kīrtana, yajña, vrata, dāna, dhyāna, yāga* are the *Upāsanās* for attaining *Parābhakti*, even the verse of the *Chāṅdogya Upaniṣad* i.e. *"Manobrahmeti Upāsīta"*[20] also suggests that all these Upāsanās are helpful to attain *Parābhakti*, i.e. Upāsanā of the mind as Brahman turns into real knowledge and then into the *Parābhakti*.

Maharṣi Śāṇḍilya further explains how the karma which is surrendered to God becomes the Upāsanā of God which creates *Parābhakti* in the mind.[21] *Maharṣi Śāṇḍilya* divides *Gauṇi Bhakti* in three types i.e. *Ārtabhakti, Jiñāsābhakti* and *Arhtārthibhakti* like the *Gītā* and he says that the *Jñānibhakti* is similar to *Parābhakti*.[22] He further says that *śravaṇa* (hearing), *kirtāna* (speaking about), *smraṇa* (remembering every now and then), *vrata* (vows), are the *Upāsanās* in the *Gauṇi bhakti* also.[23] He gives the support of the *Gītā* for his opinion. *Maharṣi* further says that by *Ananyabhakti'*, i.e. *Parābhakti*, the intellect (*buddhi*) merges into *Paramātman* and attains *Mokṣa*; experiences the *Sākṣātkāra*.[25]

(ii) Nārada Bhaktisūtra : *Nārada* is the well-known devotee of *Śri Viṣṇu*. His *Bhakti Sutras* occur in the fourth and the fifth sections of the first *adhyāya* of the *Bhāgavatam*. These *sutras* are related to doctrine of devotion more than philosophical aspect. There is a similarity about the teachings of *Bhakti* between *Śāṇḍilya* and *Nārada Bhakti Sutrās*. *Nārada Bhaktisutra* begins with the definition of *Bhakti* given by various *Ācāryas*, and then his own definition is given. He tells us that according to *Pārāśara (Vyāsa) Bhakti* means to worship Gods, according to *Garga, Bhakti* means to extol the different stories of God, according to *Śāṇḍilya Bhakti* means to meditate on the self, while *Nārada* holds that *Bhakti* means the Highest, intense love towards God, a whole-hearted attachment to God and disgust about other things, and to take refuge in Him only. He says that the *Bhakti* is *Mokṣa* itself, the *sūtra* is *"Amṛtasvarūpā ca."*[26]. *Bhakti* gives *Amṛtatva* and the sense of fulfillment.[27] One knows everything and becomes calm and quiet.[28] He says that there is no place for desire in this type of *Bhakti*, because it teaches to give up all the worldly desire,[29] and become one with *Iśvara (ananyatā)*. He doesn't speak about the knowledge of *Brahman* but it seams that the knowledge is taken for granted from the example of the love of *Gopi* to *Kṛṣṇa*. *Nārada* says that if *Gopis* do not know the real nature of *Kṛṣṇa* how they can love Him as God? So the love of *Gopis* is *Avyabhicāri Bhakti*, see the stura *"Tadvihinam jārāṇāmiva"*[30] *Nārada* further discusses the relation of *Bhakti* to other spiritual ways namely the *Jñānamārga*, the *Yogamārga* and the *Karmamārga*. His opinion is the *Jñāna*, the *Yoga* and the *Karma mārgas* are the means to reach *Bhakti*. He says that the *Jñāna*, the *Yoga* and the *Karma* end in *Bhakti*. It is a fruit of all these endeavours.[31] *Bhakti* is a means as well as a goal, he says, though some thinkers may hold that the *Jñāna* and the *Bhakti* are similar, or independent.[32]

In the third part of the *Bhakti sūtra, Nārada* gives the Upāsanās for reaching the goal of *Bhakti*. First he says that a *Upāsaka* must give up the interest in the sensual subjects and he should practise unattachment to all the other things except God. The sutra is *"Tattu viṣayatyāgāt saṅgatyāgācca."*[33] Another Upāsanā is to recite the name and the stories of exploits of God now and then without fail.[34] *Svādhyāya*, meditation and the *Yoga* are also important to remember God continuously even if one may have been engaged in all his routine work.[35] Further he gives importance to the company of saints as one's Upāsanā to attain the real love towards God. He also says for the spontaneous rise of intense love the favour of God himself is also important. The company of the saints and favour of God is difficult to get. The Saints and God are not different from each other. A real devotee is *Nārāyaṇa* Himself says the sūtra *"Tasminstajjanebhedābhāvāt."*[36] Further he says that if one does not get the company of the saints one is asked to avoid company of the people who have no faith in God.[37] Because with the company of the people who deny the *Vedas*, one may loose his interest in attaining the state of *Prābhakti*.[38]

Nārada further tells to give the fruits of actions and also not to assume that one is the doer of the action (performer of action). God causes all actions to be performed; the doer must not attribute credit for action to himself. It is arrogant, therefore, to boast of one's knowledge of *Vedas* and the *Upaniṣadas*.[39] The twelve rules of the *Upāsanā (sūtras* 46 to 49) are important for entering *Parābhakti*. The devotee who practises these twelve *nīyama* (rules) of Upāsanā attains supreme Bliss and he helps others who walk on the same way.

Nārada defines *Parābhakti* in the sūtra no. fifty five that once a devotee gets the state of *Parābhakti* he doesn't see, hear, speak, meditate other thing than *Iśvara*. This description is similar to the *Bhumāvidyā* which is told in the *Chāndogya Upaniṣad*.

Nārada also divides *Bhakti* in to two categories. One is *Parā* or *Ananyā bhakti* and the other is *Aparā* or *Gauṇi bhakti*. In the fifth *adhāya Nārada* says that the *Gauṇi bhakti* has three aspects, *Ārtā, Arthārthi* and *Jījñāsu*. *Ārt bhakta* is not satisfied with what he has in this world and therefore loves or prays God for additional comforts in this world. It is called *Ārta bhakti*. *Arthārthi* wants worldly happiness and the means for it, so his love towards God is *Arthārthi bhakti* and a *Jijñāsu* wants to know God by intellect, so his love is called *Jijñāsu bhakti*. These three types of *bhakti* do not confer Supreme bliss on a devotee, unless and until he enters *Parābhakti* which is only true love to God without any expectations (*anāsakta*).

Nārada says that the way of *Bhakti* is more easy than the other three ways, because, a *Bhakta* surrenders every action to God, so he has no worry, he remains carefree, calm and quiet. *Nārada* prescribes certain aversions as a part of the Upāsanā. These are to avoid egoism, and to give up other six passions like pride etc.; and to avoid debate.[40] He asks us to serve God, pure service to God is real *Bhakti*, he says[41] one who behaves in this way is called an *Ekāntin Bhakta*.[42] A devotee should always recite the names of God, with calmness (*parāśānti* as told by the *Gītā*).[43]

Nārada describes the eleven modes of devotion to God in the *sūtra* eight two, namely, to recite the qualities-*Guṇāsakti*

Samarṇāsakti; to serve-*Dāsyāsakti*; friendship-*Sakhyāsakti*; love of a mother to her child-*Vātsalyāsakti*; love of a lover-*Kāntāsakti*; to tell everything to Him-*Ātmanivedanāsakti*; to remain in the state of unification-*Tanmayāsakti*; the feeling of loneliness without Him-*Virahāsakti*. All these modes of *Bhakti* end in *Parābhakti*. It is the opinion of all who have reached this state of *Bhakti*, says *Nārada*.

References

Upāsanā in the Bhagavadgitā

1. Jñāneśvary—18.66.1436.
2. *Ibid*—18.66—1439 to 1445.
3. *Ibid*—9.23.344.
4. *Ibid*—9.25.361.
5. *Ibid*—9.29.408.
6. *Ibid*—12.1.30.
7. *Ibid*—12.1.32.
8. The Bhagavad Gitā as a Philosophy of God Realisation—by R.D. Rānade—page 240 to 256.
9. Bhagavad Gitā—4.42.
10. Taittiriya Upaniṣad—2.2.3.
11. Bhagavad Gitā—4.33.
12. *Ibid*—6.32.
13. *Ibid*—6.10.
14. Jñāneśvary—6.12.92 to 220, 6.13.201 to 210.
15. Bhagavad Gitā—7.16.
16. *Ibid*—7.17.
17. *Ibid*—7.23.
18. *Ibid*—7.28.
19. *Ibid*—8.13.
20. *Ibid*—9.25.
21. *Ibid*—9.31.
22. *Ibid*—9.15.
23. *Ibid*—12.20.
24. *Ibid*—12.5.
25. *Ibid*—4.14.
26. *Ibid*—13.25.
27. *Ibid*—14.26.
28. *Ibid*—14.27.
29. Bhagavad Gitā—18.54.
30. *Ibid*—18.62.

Upāsanā in the Śrimadbhāgavatam

1. Bhāgavat Purāṇa—XII-7-9,10.

2. *Ibid*—XII-7-28.
3. Purāṇas—Published by the Society for the Resuscitation of Indian Literature—by H.H. Wilson—Third Edition—Page—20.
4. Bhāgavat Purāṇa—XII-12-63.
5. *Ibid*—X-20.6.
6. *Ibid*—XI-3-44.
7. *Ibid*—XI-3-49. to 55
8. *Ibid*—XI-7-10.
9. *Ibid*—XI-7-26. to X-9-33.
10. *Ibid*—XI-10-1, 2.
11. *Ibid*—XI-10-4.
12. *Ibid*—X-11-8, 10.
13. *Ibid*—XI-11-18.
14. *Ibid*—XI-11-23, 24.
15. Ekanāthi Bhāgavat—XI-23-706 to 725.
16. Bhāgavat Purāṇa—XI-11-26 to 28.
17. *Ibid*—XI-11-33 to 37.
18. *Ibid*—XI-11-42.
19. *Ibid*—XI-11-42 to 48.
20. *Ibid*—XI-14-10.
21. *Ibid*—XI-14-20, 25.
22. *Ibid*—XI-14-31.
23. *Ibid*—XI-14-32 to 46.
24. *Ibid*—XI-17-36.
25. *Ibid*—XI-17-55. XI-18-44.
26. *Ibid*—XI-18-22.
27. *Ibid*—XI-27.-7.
28. *Ibid*—XI-27.
29. *Ibid*—XI-29-49.

Upāsanā in the Bhaktisūtra

1. Śāṇḍilya Bhakti Sūtra 2.1.23
2. Śāṇḍilya Bhakti Sūtra 2.1.14
3. Śāṇḍilya Bhakti Sūtra 2.1.16
4. *Ibid* 2.1.12
5. *Ibid* 1.1.2
6. *Ibid* 1.1.3
7. Chāndogya Upaniṣad 2.3.2
8. Śāṇḍilya Bhakti Sūtra 1.1.5
9. *Ibid* 1.2.16
10. Śvetāśvatara upaniṣad 6.23
11. Yogasūtra 1.23
12. Śāṇḍilya Bhakti Sūtra 2.1.1
13. *Ibid* 2.1.3
14. *Ibid* 2.1.4
15. Chāndogya Upaniṣad 3.14.1
16. Gitā 15-7.
17. Śāndilya Bhakti Sūtra 2.1.20, 24
18. *Ibid* 2.2.1

19. *Ibid* 2.2.3
20. Chāndogya Upaniṣad 3.18
21. Śāṇḍilya Bhakti Sūtra 2.2.9
22. *Ibid* 2.2.17
23. *Ibid* 2.2.19
24. *Ibid* 2.2.28
25. *Ibid* 2.3.4
26. Nārada Bhakti Sūtra 3
27. *Ibid* 4
28. *Ibid* 6
29. *Ibid* 7
30. *Ibid* 23
31. *Ibid* 25, 26
32. *Ibid* 28, 29
33. *Ibid* 35
24. Nārada Bhakti Sūtra 36
35. *Ibid* 37
36. *Ibid* 41
37. *Ibid* 43
38. *Ibid* 44
39. *Ibid* 49
40. *Ibid* 74
41. *Ibid* 66
42. *Ibid* 67
43. *Ibid* 79

6

The Tāntrik Upāsanā and Upāsanā with Symbols

I

Tāntrika Upāsanā

The two Upāsanā methods, namely, the *Vedic* and the *Tāntric*, are popular. Here the main Tāntrika Upāsanā of *Devi* under the name *'Śrividyā'* or *'Tripurasundari Lalitādevi'* is discussed which is prescribed by the various *Tāntrika* texts. It is said that *Bhagavān Śiva* made clear the *Tāntrika Upāsanā* method for obtaining the four *Puruṣārthas* viz. *Dharma, Artha, Kāma* and *Mokṣa*. In these texts different mystical diagrams and *mantras* are prescribed for fulfilling different mundane desires. In all these *Tāntrika* texts sixtyfour texts are main, but these are said to be non-*Vedic*. Other eight *Tantras* are called mixed, partly *Vedic* and partly *Avedic*. These *Tantras* follow the Upāsanā of *Śrividyā* or *Tripurasundari*, but these texts accept the five *'m' kāras* with their philosophical meaning;[2] avoiding *Vāmācara*. Another group of *Tantras* is said to be purely *Sātvika* and have many similarities with the *Vedic* thoughts. These *Tantras* are called *Candrakalā Tantras*. The names of these texts are, *Candrakalā, Jyotsanāvati, Kulārṇava, Kuleśvara, Bhuvaneśvari, Bārhaspata, Durvāsamata* and *Kalāṇidhi Tantra*. The third group of the *Tantras* is called *Vedic Śubhāgama Tantras. Vasiṣtha, Sanaka, Sanandana, Sanātana* and *Śuka* are the writers of these *Tāntrika* texts. The way of worship of these texts is called *Samayācāra*, which is one of three modes of *Devi* worship, i.e. *Samaya, Miśra* and *Kula*; and they also prescribe the Upāsanā of *Śrividyā*. Now a days inspite of following all *Tāntrika* texts the *Upāsakas* follow the Upāsanā prescribed by three texts which are said to be the *Prasthāntrayi* of *Tāntrikas*, the names of these texts are *Varivasyā Rahasya, Setubandha* which are written by

Bhāskarāraya, and *Lalitā Sahasranāma* of *Brahmāṅḍa Purāṇa,* and the subject of these texts is neatly discussed in the *"Saundaryalahari"* by *Śri Śankarācārya* which is the essence of the Upāsanā of *Śri Vidyā* and follows the method given by the *Tāntrika* Texts. Anybody can practise this Upāsanā inspite of his caste and creed, therefore this Upāsanā has become popular.

The well-known books of this Upāsanā method are, *Bhāskararāya's Varivasyā Rahasya, Saubhāgyahbāskara, Setubandha, Lalitāsahasranāma Bhāṣya; Śri Saṅkarācārya's Saundaryalhari, Lalitātriśati Bhāṣya; Durvāsa's Tripuramahimna Stotra, Lalitā Sahasranamā;*[2] *Kula, Bhāvanā, Aruṇa, Kālikā, Tārā* etc *Upaniṣads, Yantra, Maṅtra, Bījas, Mudrās, Kavacas, Dhyāna* are main factors of this Upāsanā method. In this Upāsanā *Lalitā Devi* is worshipped as the form of *Parabrahman. Śri Cakra* or *Śri Yantra* is the main diagram of this worship. It is called *Cakrarāja* and the *Pancadasi* or *Ṣodaṣi Maṅtra* of *Devi* is called *Maṅtrarāja;* and it has the power and importance of the Vedic *Gāyatri Maṅtra.* This *maṅtra* is called *Śrividyā* because its deity is a female. It is said that a specific combination of mystical letters is called *'maṅtra'* when its deity is a male; and *'vidyā'* when its deity is a female deity. The texts prescribe that an *Upāsaka* (who has been initiated in the *Śri Vidyā*) should meditate on *Devi* as the *Kāmakalā* and identify his own self with her, then he will become one with *devi;* this type of Upāsanā is called *Ahamgrahopāsanā.*[3]

The *Kuṅḍalini Śakti* is identified with *Devi Lalitā* who is the universal Energy. It is said that *Devi Lalitā* is the Prime Energy and she resides in the human body in the form of *Kuṅḍalini* that is supposed to be dormant in the *Mulādhāra Cakra;* and the main six *cakra,* namely, *Mulādhāra, Svādhiṣṭhāna, Maṇipura, Anāhata, Viśuddha,* and *Ājñā,* are similar to the diagrams of *Śricakra* and the *Sahasrāra Cakra* is identical with the centre point of *Śri Cakra* where *Devi* resides unified with *Śiva* in the form of *Parābhaṭṭātrikā Tripurasuṅdari;* see the verse. *"Sadādhārapaṅkeruhānterviрājat-suṣumnātarāle' titejollasantim. Sudhāmanḍalam drāvayantim pibantim sudhāmurtimide cidānandarū'pam."*[4] And *"Gaṇeśānimādyākhilaih śaktivṛnairvṛtam vai sphuraccakrarājollasantim. Parām rājarājeśvar-ytaipuri tvām śivānkopasthitam śivām bhāvayāmi".*[5]

There are different *Upāsanā Sampradāyas* of *Śrividyā,* namely *Kādividyā,* which is followed by *Kāmaraja; Hādividya,* which is followed *Lopāmudra; Sādividya,* which is followed by *Nandi. Kādividyā* means in which the *maṅtra* of *Devi* starts which the syllable 'K'; in *Hādividyā* the *mantra* starts with 'H' and in *Sādividyā*, the *mantra* starts with 'S'. In all these three *Vidyās Kādividyā* has more prevalence than the other two. The *Pañcadasi mantra* of *Devi* is followed by these three *Vidyās* because this is the *Upāsanā* of *Śrividyā*. *Śankarācārya* has unfolded the *Pañcadaśi* mantra of *Śrividyā* in his *stotra 'Mantramātṛkāpuṣpamālāstotra'*. The first letter of each of the stanza of this *stotra* forms the complete *mantra*. This *mantra* consists of fifteen letters and when the letter 'śrim' is added, the number of letters become sixteen and it is called *'Ṣodaśi' mantra*. There are three *'hrimkāras'* or *'Hṛllekhās'* which are the *bījās* of *Śiva-Śakti* combination. The other letters are the *bijās* of the main *Tattvas* (Five Great Elements) of the universe like the Air, the Fire, etc. This *mantra* and *Śriyantra* which is also called *Śripura* is the philosophical or *Sukṣma* (subtle or Internal form for Upāsanā) form of *Devi*. The further description of the same follows :

Śricakra is the residing palce or the temple of *Devi*. *Śri Śankarācārya* describes this *cakra* in the Verse, "*Caturbhiḥ śrikanṭhaiḥ śivayauvatibhiḥ pañcabhirapi. Prabhinnābhiḥ śambhornavabhirapi mulapṛakrtibhiḥ. Catuścatvārimśdvasudala kalaśra trivalayatrirehkābhiḥ sārdham tava śaraṇakoṇaḥ pariṇatah.*"[6] It means, "O Mother, the four triangles with down ward apex are called *Śrikaṇṭha* because they belong to *Śiva*. The central point is *Śiva* Himself. The five triangles starting from central point belong to *Śakti*, these nine triangles together are called *`Śivayuvati'*. These nine triangles form different forty three triangles by their intermixing and the main point-bindu-is itself the forty-forth triangle. All these triangles are surrounded by eight and sixteen petalled lotuses; these are covered by three circles named *`Mekhalātraya'* and three line in square named *`Bhūpura'* cover all the diagrams. This is your temple and I cannot describe its greatness." This *Cakra* is important in this *Śrividyā* Upāsanā.

The Upāsaka gradually and step by step meditates on this *Cakra*. He at first meditates on the four doors located at the four directions of *Bhūpura*. The three lines of *Bhūpura* are said to be white, red and yellow colours respectively. Ten *siddhis* reside in the ten directions like the East, West etc. The different deities called *Yoginis* protect the different parts of the *Cakra*, therefore an Upāsaka has to please them by his Upāsanā. The eight *Matṛkās* (deities of letters) reside at the right and left side of the doors of the second line. The *Yoginis* reside on the third line. The three lines of the *Mekhalātraya* are said to be the form (*pratika*) of *Satva, Rajas* and *Tamas* or *Candra*, (the Moon), *Sūrya* (the Sun) and *Agni* (the Fire,) or *Icchā, Jñāna* and *Kriyāśakti*. The sixteen petalled lotus is said to be like the Moon and Sixteen *Yoginis* reside in it in concealed (latent) form. The eight petalled lotus is the residence of the eight forms of *Śiva*; i.e. His attributes, namely, five great Elements and the Sun, the Moon and the *Ātman*. The portion near these lotuses is called *Kṣirasāgara* and the fourteen triangles are called *Saubhāgya cakra* in which the fourteen *Yoginis* of the fourteen *Sampradāyas* reside. The ten triangles are called residence of the ten incarnations of *Śri Viṣṇu*; the deities of the same triangles are called *Kulottirṇa Yoginis* and *Nigarbha Yoginis*. Then there are eight *Vāgdevatās* which are called *Rahasya Yoginis*. With this one after another step of meditation the Upāsaka now enters the main triangle where the deities are *Satva, Rajas* and *Tamas*; the *Nāda* (sound) starts from this point, these are the three lines, namely, *Kāmagiri Pīṭha, Jālandhara Pīṭha* and *Pūrṇagiri Pītha*, these are the seats of *Brahmā, Viṣṇu, Maheśa* and their consorts. *Jāgṛiti, Svapna* and *Suṣupti* are the three deities of these seats. In this main triangle *Mahātripurasundari* stays in the form of *Bālā* (Girl child), united with *Śiva*, and she is called *Parābhaṭṭārikā*. This *Devi* has the *Mantra* which is called *Śrimantra* or *Pañcadaśākṣari Mantra*. The Upāsaka meditates on this *Mantra*.[7] The fifteen letters of this *Mantra* are, "*Ka, E, I, L Hrim, H, S, K, H, L, Hrim, S, K, L, Hrim.*" (the letter *Śrim* is added to this *mantra* if *Guru* confers it on his disciple, then the mantra is called *Ṣodaśi mantra*).

The *Varivasyā Rahasya* gives *Mantra* in the verses as, "*Krodhiśa (K)*, along with *Srikantha (a) Koṇatraya (E), Lakṣmi (I), Mānsa (L)* along with *Anuttara (a)*, constitute the first group of the letters of *mantra* known as *Vāgbhava kūṭa*. *Śiva (H), Haṁsa (S), Brahman (K), Viyat (H), Śakra (L)*-these severally conjoined with *Akṣara (a)* constitute the second group known as *Kāmarāja Kūṭa*. The third group is *Śiva (Ha)*, and *Viyat (Ha)*, known as *Śakti Kuṭa*, at the end of these three groups should be added three *Hṛillekhas* (one in each), `*Hrim*', i.e. *Vyoma (H), Agni (r), Vāmalocana (i)*, and *bindu (m)*.[8]

The period of pronouncing each letter is fixed in the *mātrās*. *Mārtā* means two hundred and fifty six *lavas*, one *lava* means a time which a needle takes to go through one petal of the leaf of lotus plant. *Bhāskarāya* gives this measure of time in the commentary of the verses fifteen and sixteen, in this verses *"Kālparamāṇurlava ityucyate nalinipatrasaṁhatyāhsukṣmasucyabhivedhane. Dale dale tu yaḥ kālāḥ Sa Kālāḥlava sañjñitaḥ" "ṣaṭpuncāśaduttara śatadvayalavaireka mātrā"*. (In this sequence the measurement of time upto great Ages is also given). *Kāmaklā (I)* and *Trikoṇa (E)* are to be pronounced with two *mātras, Hṛllekhas'* period of pronunciation is of three *mātras* and remaining letters are to be pronounced with one and half *mātra. Bindu* is to be pronounced with half *mātrā*. The total period of pronunciation is : in *Vāk-Kūṭa*, there are eleven *mātrās;* in *Kāmarāja* eleven and half mātrās and in *Śakti-kūṭa* eight and half *mātras* less one *lava.*[9] These letters have their origin in the throat, throat and the palate, the teeth, the root of the mouth and the nose.[10]

These three *Kūṭas* touch the main six *cakras*. The first *Kūṭa* touches *Anāhata* beginning from *Mulādhāra,* the second *Kūṭa* touches *Ajñācakra* from *Anāhata,* the third *Kūṭa* touches *Lalāṭamadhyā* (the middle of the forehead) from *Ajñācakra*. These three *Kūṭas* have the effulgence like diluvian fire, (*Pralyāgni*), ten million Suns, and ten million Moons respectively.[11] In this mantra *Jāgṛti, Svapna, Suṣupti* and *Turiyā* states of consciousness are included.[12] *Tattvajñana* is attained by the pronunciation of this *mantra* because its sound (nāda) contains the letters from *'Ka' kāra* to *Unmanā* (soundless state).[13]

Vavrivasyā Rahasya gives the *Sampradāyārtha, Rahasyārtha, Mahattavārtha* and *Samastārtha* of this *Mantra* and says that pronunciation without knowledge is fruitless. This *mantra* is said to be the *Gāyatri Mantra* of *Tantrikas* and it is compared with the *Gāyatri* as said in the *Tripuropaniṣad,* according to *Bhāskarāraya,* i.e. *'Ka' kāra (ka)* signifies *Kāmeśvara* i.e. He who desires, in virtue of which it stands for *Brahman,* which conveys the significance of the word *'Tat'* in *Gāyatri*. The second letter *(E)* signifies *'Saviturvareṇyam'* which stands for *'Kāmeśvari'*-the third letter of the *mantra*. The fourth letter *(I)* stands for *'Bhargo devasya Dhi'* which means *śiva; 'La'kāra (La)* signifies *'Mahi'*(the Earth). *Māyā (Hrim)* signifies the third and fourth feet of the *Gāyatri*. The fourth feet of *Gāyatri* is *"Parorajase Sāvadom."*[14] The text further says that there are three couples of male and female viz. *Brahman* and *Bhārati,* which are identical with *Vāmā* and *Icchā; Hari* and *Kṣiti* which are identical to *Jyesthā* and *Jñānā; Śiva* and *Aparaṇā* which are identical with *Raduri* and *Kriyā*; which indicate the three groups of *Kūṭas*. The three male and female elements are together known as *Śāntā* and *Ambikā*, which are identical with *Raudri* and *Kriyā*; which indicate the three groups of *Kūṭas*; and which are indicated by three *'I 'kāras*.[15] The sixty-eighth verse says that the *Parādevatā* (Supreme Goddess) does not differ from this mantra even by a smallest measure. The *Prakāśā* commentary of this verse gives the opinion of *Śruti* as, *"Tatraiva anyatra 'Tadvā etatbrahmādvayam' ityādinā brahmasvarupamabhidhāya tadūpāsanām purṇāhambhāvanārūpāmvispaṣṭam" 'Hamsah so'ham' ityādinā vidadhāti."*

The *mantra*, the *Devi* and the world are the same.[16] The three types of *Upāsakas*, namely, *Sakala*, *Pralayākala* and *Vijñanakevala*, are signified by the three *'Ka'karas* of the *mantra*.[17] The text says that the *Sampradāyārtha* of the *mantra* is: as there is no difference between cause and its effect, between *Vācya* and *Vācaka*, and between *Brahman* and Unvierse, so also there is no difference between universe and this *Vidyā (mantra)*.[18] The text further says that one's own *Gurū* is identical with these three i.e. *Devatā, Vidyā, Cakra*, as well as there is the identity of the *Devatā*, the *vidyā*, the *Cakra*, the *Gurū* and Pupil's own self.[19] The *Kundalini Śakti* of an *Upāsaka* is identical with fifty letters, and she is identical with *Vidyā* and the *Devi*, the Mother. This is called the *Rahasyārtha* of this *Vidyā*.[20] The *Mahattavārtha* of this *mantra* is : there is an identity between *Sat, Cit, Ānandarūpa Bharman* and this *Mantra*.[21] The text gives the *Samastārtha* of this *Vidyā* as : *'S 'K' 'L'* means action, *'Hr'* means destroyer of the universe, *'I'* means creation and preservation, *'Hrim'* means Mother who dispels all the pains of a devotee; and *'S' 'K' 'L' 'Hrim'* means *Samvid* i.e. Knowledge.

We have seen the philosophical meaning of *Devi* but for *Upāsanā saguṇa* description of the form of *Devi* is also necessary. *Varivasyā* means *Upāsanā* therefore this text *'Varivasyā Rahasya'* clears the Upāsanā of *Devi*; also supplies the *Saguṇa* form of *Devi*. It says that 'ka' is Brahman, *'E'* is *Viṣṇu*, *'A'* is *Śiva*, *'I'* is praise. This is the first group which is said to be identical with the *Ṛgveda*. Second group is like this, *'Ka'* means face, *'Ha'*, *'Sa'*, *'Ka'* means the smile on the face; *'Ka'* is the Sun, *'Ha'* is the 'Moon'. *'La'* is the eyes, this is identical with the *Yajurveda*. The third group is all the *Kalās* (digits) in *'SA' 'Ka' 'La'* which are identical with the *Sāmaveda*. *'I'* is *Isvara* and *'Ha'* means *Śiva*. In this way all these are the attributes of *Devi*. *Saundaryalahari* stotram also describes the *Saguṇa* form of *Devi* in the second part of the *stotra* as : The *Śridevi* (Mother) has the form of the female, she has three lines on her throat, she sings beautifully, she wears a necklace of pearls, she looks in eight-fold ways, namely, *Viśālā, Kalyāṇi, Ayodhyā, Dhārā, Madhurā, Bhogāvati, Avanti* and *Vijayā*; at her devotees.[22] *Devi's* complexion is red, she has besmeared her forehead with saffron paste, she wears a garland of red flowers, she holds the arrows of flowers, a bow of sugar cane, noose (*pāśa*), an elephant hook (*aṅkuśa*) in her hands. She wears red garments.[23] This form of *Devi* is popular in the devotees.

In this way the *Taṅtrika Upāsanā* has two factors, one is philosophical which is internal and subtle (*Sukṣma*), and the other is external which is gross. An *Upāsaka* has to perform the Upāsanā Internally (in the mind) and externally (physically). As there is the meditation on the *Yantra (Cakra)* and on the *Devi* with the identity between the *Upāsaka* and the Mother as His own self, this Upāsanā is called *Ahmagrahopāsanā* and finally the *Upāsaka* and the *Upāsya* unify with each other.

II

Upāsanā with Symbols

(i) Diagrams

There are popular auspicious diagrams in India which are occasionally seen in the religious ceremonies of a house holder. These diagrams are drawn daily before a house by a particular white powder (*Rāngoli*). They are painted on a wall of a temple and carved on a copper plate which are worshipped daily with other images of gods. These diagrams include *Cakra, Savstika*, Lotus, various *Yantras* of different deities like *Śri Yantra, Datta Yantra* etc.; as well as *Gopadma* and others. These diagrams are said to be the symbols of different deities and their worship pleases that particular deity who confers favour on the worshipper. The symbols are a part of deity (*Aṅga*) which cannot be separated from It (deity), therefore, the Upāsanā of the diagrams is called *Angavati* Upāsanā. We shall discuss some of the diagrams.

Cakra—*Cakra* is a circle which has spokes. The number of spokes depend upon the purpose for which the *Cakra* is drawn.

The spokes suggest some meaning, for example four spokes suggest the four great Ages i.e. the *Satya*, the *Tretā*, the *Dvāpāra* and the *Kali*. This cakra is painted generally on the walls of a temple, this is called *Viśvacakara*. Six spokes refer to six seasons of the year, autumn, spring etc. *Aṣtadhā Prakṛti, Dhātvāṣṭaka, Aaiśvaryāṣṭaka, Bhāvāṣṭaka, Devāṣṭaka, Guṇāṣṭaka* are suggested by the *Cakra* with eight spokes. The details are a follows.

Aṣtadhā Prakṛti—*Pancamahābhutas, Manas, buddhi* and *Ahankāra* (Five great elements, the mind, the intellect and the egoism).

Dhātvāṣṭaka—*Carma* (leather), *tvak* (skin), *rakta* (blood), *mānsa* (flesh), *meda* (fat), *asthi* (bone), *majjā* (marrow), *śukra* (semen).

Aiśvaryāṣṭaka—*Aṇimā, Mahimā, Laghimā, Prāpti, Prākāmyā, Vaśitva, Iśitva, Kāmāvasāyitva*. (*Aṣṭamahāsiddhi*).

Bhāvāṣṭaka—*Dharma* (righteousness), *adharma* (unrighteous), *jñāna* (knowledge), *ajñāna* (ignorance), *vairāgya* (renunciation), *avairāgya* (sensuousness), *aiśvarya* (wealth), *anaiśvarya* (penury).

Devāṣṭaka—*Brhmā, Prajāpati, Deva, Gandharva, Yakṣa, Rākṣasa, Pitṛs, Piśāca*.

Guṇāṣṭaka—*Dayā* (compassion), *Kṣamā* (forgiveness), *anāyāsya* (effortless), *Anasuyā* (feeling no envy about others), *Śauca* (purity), *Akārpaṇya* (munificent), *Aspṛhā* (non ecstasy), *Dāna* (donation).

This *Cakra* is drawn in the temples and also before the entrance of a house.

Twenty spokes of *Cakra* refer to the ten senses and their ten objects.

Fifty spokes refer to the five misconceptions that is *Tama, Moha, Mahāmoha, Tamisra, Andhatamisra*; twentyeight disabilities (*aśaktis*) which belongs to the ten senses and the mind; nine *tuṣṭis* i.e. *Tattva-jñāna, Vairāgya, Ṛddhi, Bhāgya, Ahimsā, Satya, Asteya, Brahmacarya, Aparigraha*; eight siddhis i.e. *Janma-siddhi, Śabda-siddhi, Śāstra-siddhi, Adhyātma-jñāna, Adhibhautika, Adhidaivaka, Satsanga-siddhi, Gurusiddhi*.[1]

A *Cakra* with thousand spokes is called *sahasrāra* cakra worn on the head where Śiva is present, this is called *Sahasradala Kalmala*.

Svetaśvatara Upaniṣad calls *Viśvacakra* as the wheel and one can take it as the *Pratika* of God.[2] This wheel has another name i.e. *Brahmacakra. Cakra* denotes speed. The idea of *cakra* can be found in the *Rc "...avavati cakram paridyāmṛtasya"*.[3]

Buddhists have *Dharmacakra* with thousand spokes.

According to the *Tantraśāstra* the cakras have importance in the worship. These *cakras* suggest psychic energy in the subtle body; and the points of the concentration of the energy are fixed in the physical body. These points are called the cakras as well as the *Padmas*. We shall discuss this point under the heading 'Lotus'.

Vārāha Upaniṣad mentions *cakrāsana*, one of the *yogic* postures.[4]

Cakra is used in the *Yantras* and it has various meanings. There is a *cakra-pūjā* in this Upāsanā of *Yantra*.

Śri cakra, which is called *Śri Yantra*, is important and famous in *Devi Upāsanā*, which we have already referred to in the discussion *'Devi Upāsanā'*. (and in the first section of this chapter).

Sudarśana Cakra is usually drawn before the deities in the house; carved on the walls of temples. This cakra is a weapon of Lord *Kṛṣṇa*. The followers of the *Bhāgavata* cult mark their body with this *cakra*. The *Viṣṇu purāṇa* contains a story about the origin of *Sudarśana Cakra*. The story is like this; *Viśvakarmā* ground *Sūrya* on a grinding machine and the sparks of this heat fell on the Earth and with that *Viśvakrmā* made the *Sudarśana Cakra, Triśula* and the *Puṣpaka Vimāna* and the weapon called *Śakti*. The *Trisula* is given to *Siva*, the *Puṣpaka Vimāna* to *Kubera* and *Śakti* to *Brahmā*, the *Sudarśana cakra* was deposited in the sea.[5]

The story in the *Mahābhārata*[6] says that *Agni* presents *Sudarśana* to *Kṛṣṇa* after meditating upon *Varuṇa* who presented him the *cakra* with a chariot and the *Gānḍiva* bow. The *Śrimadhbhāgavatam* calls this *cakra* as *'Tejastattvam'*.[7] *Śri Kṛṣṇa* calls it as the cosmic mind which is restless and controlled only by Him.[8] *Agni Purāṇa* includes the Upāsanā method in which *Sudarśana* is looked upon as a deity. According to the *Vāmana Purāṇa, Sudarśana cakra* is bestowed upon Lord *Kṛṣṇa* by *Śiva*[10].

The *Sudarśana cakra* with twelve spokes has its place in the temples, which has particular specifications. Ahirbudhnya Samhitā says that Sudarśana *cakra* symbolises *Prāṇa, Māyā, Kriyā, Śakti, Bhāva, Unmeśa, Udyama* and *Sankalpa*, the verse is *"Prāṇomāyākriyāśaktirbhāva unmeśa udyamaḥ. Sudarśanaḥca samkalpaḥ śabdḥ paryāyavācakaḥ.*

Cakra is also worshipped in the marriage ceremony of the Hindus.

Śatapatha Brāhmaṇa [11] describes contraction and expansion process of a wheel which has dual characteristic, ascending and descending. It is compared with ahorātra (day and night), halves of the month (*śukla* and *kṛṣṇa pakṣa). Uttarāyaṇa* and *Daksiṇāyana* of the year. Therefore, the *cakra* becomes the symbol of the universe and is worshipped as a symbol of God.

Svastika—The word *Savastika* is derived from the root *'Asa'* with the prefix *'Su'* which means good or auspicious existence. *Svastika* also denotes speed. Generally each and every religious ceremony starts with drawing a *Svastika;* the merchants inscribe *Savastika* on the opening page of their account books. *Svastika* is also worshipped as a symbol of *Gaṇesa* with *Navagraha pujā*. According to the *Vāyupurāṇa* the lord of serpents has a hundred hoods and is marked with Savastika.[12] *Svastika* is also supposed to be a symbol of the Sun and the light. Therefore, the Sun worshippers worship *Svastika* as the *Pratika* of their God. The *Svastikāsana* is *yogic* posture.[13] *Svastika* is drawn before the entrance of a house, at the holy place of deity on the walls of temples, and it is supposed that it drives away the malignant energies.

Lotus—Lotus is a spiritual flower. Generally each god holds a lotus in his hand, *Śri Lakṣmi* is seen standing on a lotus, God *Brahmā* is shown as sprung from the lotus and he uses to sit in it. The leaves of lotus do not get wet by water though they grow in it, therefore they symbolise the spiritual progress of a devotee who does not get affected by the objects of the sense organs. The Lotus blooms gradually with the rising sun, similarly the spiritual powers gradually spring with the rising of knowledge (śymbolised as the Sun), therefore the Lotus symbolises the bloom of spiritual powers. Therefore the centers of consciousness or psychic energy are called 'Lotus' i.e. *Padma, Kamala. Cakra* is another name of these centres. There are *yogic padmas* and have different names because each *Padma* includes different types of energy. A brief description of this psychic energy follows

The *Kuṇḍalini Śakti.*[14] i.e. divine power is supposed to be dormant in the form of a coiled serpent at the root of the spinal cord, which is known as the *Mulādhāra cakra,* with four petals and its colour is crimson. This *śakti* is awakened by the practice of the *Prāṇāyāma* (breathing exercises) or by the recitation of the *mantra* conferred by preceptor.

The Power lifts her head upwards and as She touches the centres of other lotuses, man gradually lifts towards the highest state. The next is the *Svādhiṣṭhāna cakra* with six petals, the *Maṇipūra cakra* at navel with ten petals and has blue-black colour the fourth lotus is situated near heart which has twelve petals and is called the *Anāhata cakra,* because the unpronounced word *'Om'* is heard by the devotee when the *Kuṇḍalini* touches this centre. Fifth is the *Viśuddha cakra,* with six petals and has smoky purple colour. The *Ājnā cakra* is situated between the two eyebrows which is white in colour, has two petals. The *Sahasrāra cakra* with thousand petals and different colours is situated in the head which has a divine quality and *Śiva* resides in this *cakra*. When *Kuṇḍalini* joins with *Śiva* the person gets highest bliss.

The *kuṇḍalini jāgṛti* or *śakticālana* comes under the *yogickriyā* of *Haṭhayoga. 'Śiddhasiddhānta Paddhati'* of *Gorakṣnātha* prescribes detail upāsanā of the *Kuṇḍalini Śakti*. The number of *cakras* differ from six to nine but six main cakras are accepted by everybody. Therefore 'lotus' has importance in *yogic* method.

The bud of lotus is seen on the top i.e.*'Śikhara'* of a temple which indicates unbloomed creation of the universe.[14]

Lakṣmi holds two lotuses in her hands as well as she stands on the louts, therefore lotus becomes the symbol of *Lakṣmi*.

Yantra: —*Yantra* is pattern of the form of a deity. Upāsaka draws a particular diagram on the Earth or carved it on the piece of a metal with the specific number of circles and triangles prescribed by the *Tantraśāstra* and concentrates on it and contemplates upon it as a form of his *Upāsya* deity. The concept of the *Yantra* is said to be derived from the *Vedas*. It has many lines which cross each other and the one central point which is called *Bindu*. The *Śri Yantra* is important and popular.

Datta Yantra, Navagraha Yantra, Śri Viṣṇu Yantra, Rāmamantra Yantra, Gopāla Yantra, Gitā Yantra and other *Yantras* are also worshipped as proper means of upāsanās.*

The drawing of the *Gopadma* (feet of a sacred cow), *Śaṅkha* (conch), *cakra, (sudarsśana), gadā* (mace), *garuḍa* (an eagle), a cow with calf, the foot prints of God and *Gurū* is a common practice of Indian householders.

(ii) Mudrā

Mudrā is a particular posture of a body or fingers of hands.

It includes dancing and *yogic* postures. It seems that the whole method of worshipping gods through dance and music is an effort of a man to attain *Mokṣa*. God is *Naṭarāja*, therefore he is pleased with dance and music. The *Viṣṇudharmottara Purāṇa* speaks about various *rahasya, sāmāny* and *Nṛttyaśāstra mudrās*.[15] *Yogic* mudras are described in the *Gheranḍa Samhitā, Śiva Samhitā, Hatha-Yogapardīpikā* and they are said to be helpful for the hygiene and to cure the diseases; they confer success in *yoga* and give *siddhis*.

Mudrā means 'which gives *mokṣa*!' *Mu'* means *mukti* and *'drā'* means *dāyini* the verse says, *"Pṛthukāstanḍulā mṛṣṭā godhūma canakādayaḥ tasya nāmabhaveddevi Mudrā muktipradāyini"*[16]

According to the *Śiva Samhitā mudrā* helps to awake *kunḍalini* who is in the *Mulādhāra* in the *Suṣumnā*. *Haṭhayogapradīpikā* repeats the same in the verse, *"Tasmāt Sarvaprayatnena prabhodha-yitumiśvarim. Brahmadvāramukhe suptānimudrābhyām samācaret*.[17]

Mudrā is the fourth of the five *'m' kāras* of the *Tāntrika* cult which means 'different grains mixed with ghee.'[8]

Rāghava Bhaṭṭa points out that the five fingers of the hand resemble the Five great elements and their contact with each other pleases respective deity of the *Bhūtas*, who accepts the worship. Therefore, particular *mudrās* should be applied at the time of *Japa*, meditation etc.[19]

The *Kulārṇava Tantra* says that mudrā favours gods and denounces demons; the verse is, *"Mudrām Kurvanti devānām rākṣasāndrāvayantica"*[20]. The *Viṣṇu Samhitā* accepts the same. *Kāmakalāvilāsa* tells that *mudrā* resembles to the rising Sun, it has the nature of *Samvit*, and the *Trikhanḍamudrā* is connected to *Brahman*.[21] The *Jnānārṇava Tantra* prescribed *Mahāmudrā, Pāśamudrā, Cāpamudrā, Aṅkuśamudrā, Bāṇamudrā, Kulālamudrā, Kamalamudrā, Yonimudrā* which are useful in any type of worship.[22] Different *Tāntrika* texts prescribed different *mudrās* to be used in the *Śiva, Viṣṇu, Gaṇesa, Devi,* and *Durgā* worship. The *Gheranḍa Samhitā* gives twentyfive mudrās which give success to the *Yogi*.

The number of *yogic mudrās* varies according to texts. According to the *Viṣṇusamhitā, mudrās* are innumerable.[23] The *Haṭhyogapradīpikā* prescribes ten *mdurās*.[24] The *Śivasamhitā* has ten *mudrās*.[25] The *Devibhāgavata* speaks about twentyfour *mudrās* which are used at the time of the *Gāyatri Japa*; it also includes *Khecari mudrā*.[26] Generally ten *mdurās* are accepted to awake *Kunḍalini*, namely, *Mahāmudrā, Mahāvedha, Khecari, Udiyāna,*

Mulabandha, Jālandhara bandha, Viparitakaraṇi, Vajroli and *Śakticālana.*[27] It is said that these ten *mudrās* are taught by *Ādināth* and they confer *siddhis* i.e. eight supernatural powers, the verse is, *"Idam hi mudrādaśakam, jarāmaraṇanāśanam ādināthoditam divyamaṣṭaisśvarya pradāyakam. Vallabham sarvasiddhānām durlabham marutāmapi"*[28]

These *mudrās* are to be practised with the *Prāṇāyāma* (breathing exercise). General posture is to tie up the three *bandhas*. A *sādhaka* presses the preineum with left heel and holds the right leg by both hands (it is the *Mulabandha*), then locks the chin on the throat (the *Jālandharabandha*) and contracts the stomach (the *Uḍiyānabandha*). This *āsana* helps *Kunḍalini* to arise quickly[29].

The *Khecari mudrā* means to reverse the tongue into the cavity in the skull and to turn the eyes upward towards the middle of the eyebrows. This *mudrā* is known as *Vyomacara*[30].

The *Śakticālana mudrā* means to sit in the *Vajrāsana* and perform *Bhastrikā prāṇāyāma*[31].

The *mudrās* of hand fingers make the *Upāsaka*, healthy, *Jñāni, nirbhaya* (fearless), *nirogi* (hygienic) etc., therefore, particular *mudrās* are prescribed during the recitation of *Japa* which is done to a particular result. *Sumukha, Samputa, Vitata, Vistṛta, Dvimukha, Trimukha, Caturmukha, Pañcamukha, Ṣaṇmumha, Adhomukha, Vyāpakāñjali, Śakaṭa, Yamapāśa, Grathita, Ṣaṇmukhonmukha, Pralamba, Muṣṭika, Matsya, Kurma, Varāha, Sinhākrānta, Mahākrānta, Mudgara* and *Pallava* are twentyfour mudrās which are performed at the recitation of *japa* of *Gāyatri*, etc. There are different eight *mudrās* namely *Surabhi, Jñānam, Vairāgyam, Yoni, Śaṅkha, Paṅkajam, Liṅgam, Nirvāṇam. Upāsaka* uses these eight *mudrās* in routine practice of *Japa*. It is said that all these *mudrās* stimulate different great elements and their combinations produces different results, therefore, it is useful for the hygiene and the curing of the diseases.

The *mudrās* in the classical dance signify different meaning like riches, removal of sorrows, instructions to the ignorant etc., and these are created by *Viṣṇu*, the verse of the *Viṣṇudharmottar Purāṇa* gives details as *"Iśvarāṇām vilāsam tu cārttānam dukha nāśanam. Muḍhānāmupadeśam tat striṇām saubhāgya vardhana. Śāntikam puṣtikam Vāsudevena nirmitam"*[32].

(iii) Structure

The temple is a place of Upāsanā where many people visit

and perform *Japa, Pāṭha, Pārāyaṇa, Pūjā, Abhiṣeka* etc. The structure of the temple is important from the view point of *Upāsanā*. The temples are different for different deities, like *Śiva* temple, *Viṣṇu* temple, *Gaṇsa* temple etc. and the idols of each respective deity is placed in the Sanctum sanctorum of that temple. The idol worship is necessary in the *Kali Yuga* says the *Viṣṇudharmottara Purāṇa*; this *Purāṇa* says that in the *Kṛta, Tretā* and the *Dvāpāra*, ages men were able to see god directly; but in the *Kali* age they have lost their capability, therefore, they worship the images of gods, and it is said that the deity resides in the image[33]. Therefore, temples are built in such a way that a devotee should be able to experience the company of god, he should feel calm and quiet and happy in the temple.

The temples are built with the confluence of the *Vedic* and the *Tantric* philosophy, they are the proto-type of the *Puruṣa-maṇḍala*. the structure is called *Vāstu* and its owner is called *Vāstu-puruṣa*. The temple structure resembles *yantra* in which any form of supreme being is incorporated for worship. This *yantra* or temple-diagram supposed to be the form of boundless Brahman. So any attribute of *Brahman* can be worshipped in the temple.

Sabhāmanḍapa, garbhagṛha and *śikhara* are important parts of the temple. The devotees sit in the *sabhāmanḍapa* to recite the japa etc. In the *garbhagṛha* the idol is placed. The topmost point of *Śikhara* is a *karṇikā* i.e. lotus bud which is a *Bindu* of the *yantra,* it is said to be the beginning of the creation. This lotus bud indicates that from this point God starts to descend into forms. The lotus bud is put on the *Amṛta-kalaśa* or *Amṛta-ghaṭa* in which golden image of god is to be put[34]. This *Amṛtaghaṭa* is called the symbol of the *Vedānta* for *Vedāntin, Kāma-kalā* of the *Śākta,* the *Samarasa Ghaṭa* of the *Vaiṣnavas*. This *Kalaśa* is said to be formed form milky ocean, therefore, it is auspicious in the worship of god. *Āmalaka cakra* symbolises three qualities of Primordial *Prakṛti*. The square of the *Vedi* where the idol is placed comes exactly below this *Āmalaka cakra*. This vedi (alter) symbolises the space which makes existence to be steady. The Paramātman descends from the top point to this *Vedi* where He resides[35].

Aṣṭadhā Prakṛti; Mithuna: Puruṣa (God) and *Prakṛti* i.e. *Stṛi, Śakti,* (Couple); the bull (symbol of *Jivātmā*); the horse (symbol of strength); the elephant (the symbol of wealth); the lotus (symbol of knowledge); the *Sudarśana Cakra* etc. are carved on the walls of the temple.

There is a tradition to circumambulate the Gods as well as holy persons. A devotee goes round the temple for circumambulation. It is supposed that there is a *prabhāmanḍala* which spreads to all directions of God and if a person goes through this circle he can get some upper human qualities of god, therefore, circumambulation (*pradakṣiṇā*) of the temple is a practice. It starts from the right side of the temple because the rays of God's light run from right to left. Generally this *Pradakṣiṇā* is a complete round of the temple, but in the *Śiva* temples it is half round by both ways, because the rays of the light of *Śiva* turn left[36].

References

I — Tāntrika Upāsanā

1. Re. In Ch. III.
2. Brahmāṅḍa Purāṇa-Urttara Kāṇḍa-second part.
3. Devibhujaṅgama stotram—16
4. Bhavānibhujaṅgama stotram—1.
5. *Ibid*—11.
6. Saundaryalahari stotram—11.
7. Subodha Stotrasaṁgraha, Part II-by-Pandit Pāṅḍuraṅga śāstri Goswāmy.
8. Varivasyā Rahasya and Prakāśa Tīkā of Bhāskararāya-I—9, 10, 11.
9. *Ibid*—I-15, 16.
10. *Ibid*—I-19.
11. *Ibid*—I-20, 21.
12. *Ibid*—I-32, 33.
13. *Ibid*—I-43 to 51.
14. *Ibid*—II-54, 60, 61 and Prakāśa Tīkā on the same book.
15. *Ibid*—I-64, 65.
16. *Ibid*—II-69 to 73.
17. *Ibid*—II-77.
18. *Ibid*—II-81.
19. *Ibid*—II-101, 102.
20. *Ibid*—II-107.
21. *Ibid*—II-108, 109.
22. Saundarya Lahari stotram—42 to 74.
23. Tripurasuṅdari stotram—7.

II — Upāsanā with Symbols

1. Symbols of Art, Religion and Philosophy—by Dr. Padma Sudhi Page-12.
2. Śvetāśvatara Upaniṣad—I 4.

3. Ṛgveda—I-164-11.
4. Vārāha Purāṇa—V. 15.
5. Viṣṇu Purāṇa—Part 3. Ch. 2.
6. Mahābhārata Ādiparva—Ch. 19-6.
7. Bhāgavatam—12-11. 14.
8. Gopālatāpaniya Upaniṣad—25.
9. Agni Purāṇa—Ch. 306.
10. Vāmana Purāṇa—82- 25, 26, 30.
11. Śatapatha Brāhmaṇa—VIII. 1. 4, 10.
12. Vāyu Purāṇa—41 - 79, 25 - 29.
13. Gheraṇḍa Samhitā—II 3.
14. Symbols of Art, Religion and Philosophy-by Dr. Padma Sudhi-Page 102.
15. Viṣṇudharmottara Purāṇa-Ch. 32-33.
16. Nirvāṇa Tantra-Paṭala-11.
17. Śiva Samhitā—VI. 14. Hathayogaprdipikā—III. 5.
18. Śaktisaṁgam—Tārākhanda-32, 13 - 15.
19. History of Dharmaśāstra-by Dr. P.V. Kane—Vol. II, VI
20. Kāmakalā vilāsa—5. 46.
22. Jñānarṇava Tantra—Iv. 31-81.
23. Viṣṇu Samhitā—VII. 45.
24. Gheraṇḍa Samhitā—III. 1. 3.
25. Śiva Samhitā—IV. 15-31.
26. Devibhāgavat—xi. 66, 62 - 65. XI. 16 - 98.
27. Hathayogapradipika—III. 6.
28. *Ibid*—III. 7.
29. *Ibid*—III. 10.
30. *Ibid*—III. 31.
31. *Ibid*—III. 115.
32. Viṣṇudharmottara Purāṇa—III. 34. 30-31.
33. *Ibid*—III. 93. Symbols of Art, Religion and Philosophy-by-Dr. Padma Sudhi-Page-96.
34. Symbols of Art, Religion and Philosophy-by-Dr. Padma Sudhi Page-102.
35. *Ibid*—Page-103, 115.
36. Pradakṣiṇā (Parikramā) Tathā Svastikakā Rahasya-by-Sri Pṛthvirāja Bhāskararāo (Kalyāṇa Upāsanā Aṅka).

7

Upāsanā in Classical Sanskrit Dramas, Poetry and Prose

Literature reflects the contemporary society as it deals with the way of day to day life, politics, social elements, customs and also the subject of *Upāsanā* which is a part of daily life. The characters behave according to the social life of that age, which we can observe in the literature of *Kālidāsa, Bāṇa, Māgha, Bhāsa, Bhavabhūti, Śudraka, Viśākhadatta, Bhaṭṭanārāyaṇas*, and others. The *Nāṭyaśāstra* of *Bharata* is the basic work of the classical dramas and contains the theoretical description of each and every element of drama; therefore it is called *Nāṭya-veda*, or *Gandharva-veda*. It is said to be of divine origin as it is created by *Brahmā* at the request of gods. *Brahmā* chose the recitative part from the *Ṛgveda*, songs from the *Sāmaveda*, historical stories from the *Yajurveda* and emotional part (*Rasa*) from the *Atharvaveda*.[1] Therefore gods are pleased by the presentation of the drama.

The worship prescribed by the *Nāṭyaśāstra* at the beginning of plays does not strictly come under the purview of *Upāsanā*; yet it is referred to here just to show that the play would not come to a successful end unless the deity is pleased. For example *Sarasvati* is praised in this verse, "*Devidevam mahābhāge sarasvati haripriye. Pragṛhyatām balirmātarmayā bhaktyā samarpitā*."[2] The actor has to bow to the deity before he steps on the stage, says this verse, "*Praṇamyadevatābhyāśca tato `bhinayamācaret*."[3] It may be the intention of a writer or an actor behind the presentation of the drama that god would be pleased with his performance and would confer on him *Mokṣa* or *Bhakti (Avyabhicāri bhakti)*. *Kālidasa* expressed this intention in the—*Bharatavākya* of his drama, `*Abhijñana Śākuntalam*', he says, "*... mamāpi ca kṣapayatu nilalohitaḥ punarbhavam parigataśaktirātmabhuḥ*." It means, "may the self-existent *Śiva*, who is called `*Nilalohita*,' whose energy is radiated in all directions, cancel my rebirth." The *Bharatavākya* of *Veṇisaṁhāra* of *Bhaṭṭanārāyaṇa* suggests the same through *Yudhiṣṭhira* where he says, "O *Puruṣottama*, may the intense love (*Dvaitam vinā bhakti*) for you increase in the minds of everybody," the verse is, "... *bhavatu ca bhavadbhaktirdvaitam vinā Puruṣottam.*"

The writer bows to *Śiva, Pārvati* or *Viṣṇu* at the beginning of his work which suggests his favorite *Upāsya* deity. *Kālidāsa* praises *Śiva* in the beginning of his three dramas, namely *'Abhijñāna Śākuṅtalam', 'Mālavikā' gnimitram'* and *'Vikramorvaśiyam.'* In the *'Śākuntalam'*, he praises *Śiva* as *"Prapannaṣtanubhiravatu vastabhiraśtābhiriśaḥ"* which reflects on eightfold aspects of *Śiva* which were popular at his time and he prays in *'Mālavikāgnimtram'* that *"Sanmārga lokanāya vyapanayatu vastamasim vṛttimiśaḥ."* *Kālidasa* expects the union of *Śri Lakṣmi* and *Sarasvati* in *'Vikramorvaśiyam.'*

Harṣadeva praises *Śiva* in the beginning of *'Ratnāvali'*, *Śiva* is praised by *Viśākhādatta* in *'Mudrārākṣasa'*. *Bhavabhuti* praises *Śiva* with *Vināyaka* and the Universal God (*Sarvamaya deva Viśvamurte*) in *'Mālatimādhava'*; and praises *Vāgdevatā* with Him in *'Uttarrāmacarita'*. *Bhattanārāyaṇa* praises *Śiva* and *Viṣṇu* at the beginning of *'Veṇisaṁhāra'*. In the beginning of *'Mṛcchakaṭika' Śudraka* calls *'Śiva Nilakaṅṭha'* and describes him as seated in the posture of *'paryaṅkāsana.'*

The Upāsanā of *Śiva, Viṣṇu, Pārvati* and *Lakṣmi* occurs in the dramas through the dialogues of different characters. The character *Gaṇadāsa* says in *Mālatmādhava* that *Rudra* divided himself into two; one was Himself and other was *Śakti*. From *Śakti* emanated beings of different qualities. It is difficult to please persons of different likings at one time. But drama pleases persons of different qualities, *Gaṇadās* says, *"Nātyambhinnarucerjanasyabahudhāpeyekāsamārādhanam."*[4] Such stanzas suggest *Upāsanās* like that of *Śiva* which were popular in those days. It seems that Upāsanā of various deities was in practice at the time of *Śudraka*, a character named *Cara* says, *"Prariamata yamasya caraṇau, kim kāryama devatairanyaḥ..."*[5] It is also said in the drama that the worship of *Śiva* destroys the agony of *Upāsaka* (i) The verse is, "*....haratu tanuriva kleśamasi śardavḥ.*"[6] A character *Chandragupta* also remembers *"Tāṅḍavanṛttya'* of *Śiva* when he encounters with *Cāṇakya*.[7]

Bhaṭṭanārāyaṇa mentions the practice of the *yoga*, the *Śānkhya* systems and the *Vedānta* systems in *Upāsanā* in the first and the sixth act.[8]

Bhavabhūti mentions the *Upāsanā* of *Devi Cāmuṇḍa* in "*Mālatimādhava*" where *Kāpālikas* praise the goddess as "*Devi Cāmuṅḍe, namaste.*"[9] In the same drama `*Śankara*' is called `*Ādiguru*', in the verse, "*Jaya deva bhuvanabhāvana jaya bhagavannākhilavarada nigamanidhe. Jaya ruciracan draś ekhara jaya madanāntaka Jayādiguro.*"[10] This stanza is important in the understanding of the nature of Upāsanā because *Gurū* and *Upāsya* deity are identified here.

In the third stanza of *Ratnāvali* the three *Agnis* are mentioned and the *Bharatvākya* mentions the *Yajña* as *Upāsanā* by which gods confer pleasure. In this drama a character named *Aindrajāla* mentions *Hari, Hara* and *Brahmā,* the three great gods.[11] In the *Mṛccakatika Cārudatta* worships gods and performs *Sandhyā Upāsanā* which is prescribed by *Dharma Sūtras* as the daily *Upāsanā* of a *Gṛhastha.*[12] In the same drama a maid servant asks *Vasaṅtasenā* for daily *Devapujā* the Verse is "*.....snātā bhutvā devatānam pujām nivartaya.*"[13] *Śarvilaka* wants to enter *Cārudatta's* house through a hole in the wall and he thinks of how the breach should be like whether it should be like a fully bloomed lotus, or like the full sun, or like the crescent moon or like a *Svastika*.[14] A character named `*Caṅdanaka*' says to *Aryaka* "may *Hara, Viṣṇu* and *Brahmā, Ravi, Candra* protect you as *Devi* protected her *Upāsakas* by destroying *Śumbha* and *Niśumbha* demons.[15] In this drama, *Śiva* is called *Vṛṣabhaketu* in the ninth act.

The classical *Sanskrit* poetry focuses on Upāsanā in the different poetical subjects. The treatises on the poetry suggests that the origin of the *Kāvyaśāstra* is derived form *Śiva* who delivered its knowledge to *Brahmā* and *Brahmā* taught it to eighteen learned men in eighteen different divisions and that the other deities (which are said to be sixtyfour) were also present at that time.[16] The *Yājñavalkya Smṛti* says that one who recites *Sāma* Songs without fault gets *Brahmapada* because the singing of songs leads to the deep concentration of mind which transfers the mind into deep meditation by which the singer gets *Mokṣa*.[17] Therefore poetry descends from *Śiva* to mankind and has a place in *Upāsanā*.

Bhāmaha writes the poems on *Śambhu, Kusumāyudha*. The first stanza of *Kāvyālaṅkara* of *Rudraṭa* is the praise of *Gaṇeṣa* and *Gaurī*. The '*Sāhitya Mimāṁsa*' of *Ruyyaka Vācya* and *Vācaka* (reading matter and reader) are described as the symbols of *para* and *Apara Brahman*.

Rūpagosvāmi in his *'Rasasiddhānta'* and *'Ujjvalanīlamaṇi'* stated *Kṛṣṇa Bhakti* in the examples given for explanation. He is a *Vaiṣṇva* and follower of *Caitanya*.[18] *Panditarāja Jagnnātha* says that his work *Rasagaṅgādhara* is inseparable from God *Śiva*. The name itself suggests Lord *Śiva* who keeps the *Gaṅgā* in the guise of *Rasa* (Sentiments) with him. He has divided his treatise in five parts and calls each part *'ānana'* which symbolise the five faces of *Śiva* in the form of *Pañcānana*. In the first stanza of this book *Śrikṛṣṇa* is poetically praised. *Jagannātha* has given the examples of *Rāma* and *Māruti* for the explanation of his notation. He says in one example of *Śānta Rasa* that his mind was meditating on *Paramātman*.[19] At another place he says, *"Hariḥ pitā harirmātā hariḥ suhṛt. Harim sarvatra paśyāmi hereran ānyā bhāti me."*[20] He defines *Bhakti* as *'Bhagavadanurāgarūpā'*.

In *'Raghuvaṁśa' Kalidāsa* expresses that the aim of the life of a man is to get 'Salvation'—the verse is, *"Sa brahmabhuyām gatim ājagāma"*[21]. He describes how *Raghu* attained *Pramapada* after observing *Vānaprasthāśrama*.[22] He says, *"Śisave abhyasta Vidyānām, Yauvane Viṣayaiṣiṇām, vārdhakye munivratinām yogenānte tanutyajām."*[23] In this verse he states four *āśramas* by which man ultimately attains *Mokṣa*. The second canto of *Raghuvaṁśa* gives us the details of Upāsanā of a sacred cow *Nandini* which is intensely performed by *Dilipa* and his wife.[2] *Śiva Upāsanā* is mentioned by the description of the famous temple of *Mahākāla* of *Ujjaini* which is worshipped by the devotees now-a-days and popularly known as one of the twelve *Jyotirlingas*.[25] Eight to twenty stanzas of the tenth Canto praise *Viṣṇu* as a great God. An ascetic *Sutikṣṇa* who goes through *Pañcāgnisādhana*[26] is met with in this epic poem with the description of *yogic Sādhanās* and *Vīrāsna* posture.[27] *Kālidasa* says that *Lakṣmaṇa* is acquainted with the practice of the *Yoga*.[28] *Kālidasa* describes the temples of *Ayodhyā* where the devotees offer worship. He gives the adoration of *Viśveśvara* in the eighteenth canto.[29]

Kumārasambhava is another great epic of *Kālidāsa*. In the first canto *Kālidāsa* puts up a picturesque view of seven sages worshipping gods with beautiful lotuses grown in the *Gaṅgā*. In the Second canto *Brahmadeva* is praised in the highest terms, the verse says, *"Tvameva havyam hotā ca, bhojyam bhoktā ca śāsvataḥ.*

Vedyam ca veditā cāsi dhyātā dhyeyam ca yet param."[30] In this canto *Śiva* is said to be seated in the *Paryaṅkāsana* Posture.[31] *Pārvati* goes through a difficult penance named *Pañcāgnisādhanā*, in the summer and she stands in cold water in the cold season to please *Śankara*.[32]

'Meghadūta' of *Kālidāsa* opens with the praise of the leading spiritual culture of India, of which *Himalaya* is a measuring rod; through the verse *"Astyuttarsyām diśi devatātmā Himālayo nāma nagādhirājaḥ. Purvāparau toyanidhi vagāhya stitaḥ pṛthivyā iva māndanḍaḥ."*

'Śiśupālavadha' is an epic of *Māgha*. He praises *Sri Lakṣmi* in the beginning. He also uses the word *Śri* in the end verse of each canto. The origin of this story is in the tenth *Skandha* of *Śrimadbhāgavatam*, and in the *Sabhāparvam* of the *Mahābhārata*.[33]

'Naiṣadhiya Carita' is a romantic epic which describes the romance of *Nala* and *Damayanti* which ends in their marriage. The poet says that this epic is spontaneously written by him as a fruit of Upāsanā of *'Cintāmaṇi Mantra.'* (1.145) *Nala* wears *Rudrākṣa*, a symbol of *Śaiva* sect. (2.6). He daily worships Indra and other gods by pouring oblations in the *Yājña*. (3.25; 9.44; 5.113; 6.85) *Śri Harṣa* mentioned following types of Upāsanās (1) *Śaiva*, (2) *Vaiṣṇava*, (3) *Yogis*, (4) *Aṇuparimāṇika*, (5) *Vedic*, (6) *Ascetics*, (7)*Agnihotri*, who worship *Śiva* in the form of *Agni*, (8) Daily worship of gods, (9) The people who visit places of pilgrimage, (10) Who observe fast and Penance etc. (1.59, 78, 111.2.19, 39, 82, 91.3-44, 52, 101, 5.3;9.44) *Harṣa* mentions that *Parmeśvara* looks after the devotee and destroys their ill thinking and makes them happy, the verse is *"Taccinti cittam parameśvarastu bhaktasya hṛṣyatkaruṇo ruṇaddhi."* (8.17).

Bhartṛhari's Nitiśataka teaches to avoid *Ajñāna* (ignorance) and *Adharma* (behaviour not according to *Dharma*) and to behave in such a manner that it would lead man to *Mokṣa*. The first verse praises *Brahman* who is uncountable in terms of time and space and directions; who is self born and ever conscious and is known only through self experience. The verse is, *"Dikkālādyanavaccin-nānantacinmātramūrtaye. Svānubhutyekamānāya namaḥ Śāntāya tejase."* *Bhartṛhari* mentions *Siddhas* who have experienced the state of *Brahman* in the twentieth verse, *"... nāstiyeṣām yasaḥkāye jarāmaraṇajam bhayam."* He also mentions *Yogi Sādahakas* in the thirtythird verse. He mentions visit to places of pilgrimages, *yajña*, *bhakti* and *karmic* way of life.[34]

Bāṇa has written an eulogy on Goddess *Caṇḍi* named *Caṇḍiśataka* in hundred stanzas.

Kādambari and *Harṣacarita* of *Bāṇa* are two important works of prose literature. *Pāśupata* way of worship is included in the *Kādaṁbari*. In this book *Candrāpiḍa* describes *Śiva* temple of the *Kailāsa*. In this temple the idol of four faced *Śive* was worshipped and *Mahāśvetā* is seen observing *Pāśupata Vrata*, she had matted hair tied on the head, an ash mark on the forehead, wore a faint yellowish attire and was playing upon a lute and was singing a prayer before God *Śiva*.

Different *Upāsanā* cults are referred to in "*Harṣacarita.*" *Bāṇa* himself adores *Śiva* bathing Him with milk, water, adorning Him with flowers, burning incense, light, offering food and giving oblations in *Agni* and he performs *Sandhyā Upāsanā* daily.[35] At this time it seems that *Śiva* is worshipped through this image with one face instead of four or five faces. It is seen that *Bhairavācārya*, a *Pāśupata*-performed *Śivapūja* and *Agnihotra*. The *Tāntrika Vāmācāries* are also mentioned here.[37] In the fourth *Ucchvāsa* we read that *Prabhākaravardhan* worships *Sūrya* with red flowers, he and his wife were *Ādityabhaktas* : devotees of the sun. There are *Candikā* worshippers, and the recitations of *Rudra-ekādasi* (*Rudrādhāya*-11th *Anuvaks* of the *Yajurveda*) was in practice.[38] Here *Bāṇa* has described different *Upāsanā* cults which were present at his time. The eighth *Ucchvāsa* is important from this point. The names of cults follow :

1. Arhata—The followers of *Buddha*.
2. Maskari—Followers of *Pāśupata Sampradāya* as *Bāṇa* calls *Bhairvacārya* by this name.[39]
3. Śvetapaṭa—*Svetāmbara* Jaina Sampradāya.
4. Pañḍura Bikṣu.
5. Bhāgavata.
6. Varṇi—who have taken the oath of *Brahmacarya* for whole life.
7. Kāpila—followers of *kapil's Sānkhya* philosophy.
8. Jaina—*Śākya Bikṣu*.
9. Lokāyatika—followers of *Cārvāka* philosophy.
10. Kaṇāda—followers of the *Vaiśeṣika Darśana*.
11. Aupaniṣad-Followers of the *Vedānta Darśana*
12. Aiśvarakāraṇika—Followers of the *Nyāya Darśana*.

13. Kāraṅdhami—who can make different chemicals.
14. Dharmaśāstri—Followers of treatise like the *Manusmṛti* etc.
15. Paurāṇika.
16. Saptatantivaḥ—Followers of the *Mimamsā, Yajña* etc.
17. Pāncarātrika—Worshippers of *Viṣṇu* in the form of *Vāsudeva, Sankarṣaṇa, Pradyumna* and *Aniruddha*.
18. Śābda—*Upāsaka* of *Śabda Brahma* like that of *Pāṇini*.
19. Keśaluṇcana.

Bāṇa says that the followers of these different sects used to live together in the *Āśrama* of *Divākara Mitra,* who himself was a *Pārāśari Bikṣu*.

References

1. Nāṭyaśāstra of Bharata—1-17.
2. *Ibid*—3-52.
3. *Ibid*—4-276.
4. Mālavikāgnimitram—1-4.
5. Mudrārākṣasa—1-17.
6. *Ibid*—3-20.
7. *Ibid*—3-30.
8. Veṇisamhāra—1-23, 6-43, 45.
9. Mālvikāgnimitram—5-22, 23.
10. Mālatimādhava—9-4.
11. Ratnāvali—4-10.
12. Mṛcchakaṭika—1-16.
13. *Ibid*—2nd Act.
14. *Ibid*—Act 3.
15. *Ibid*—Act 6.
16. Sanskrit Sāhityakā Itihāsa—P.V. Kane. Page 260.
17. *Ibid*—page 55. And Yājñavalkya Smṛiti—18-22.
18. *Ibid*—Page 383.
19. Panditarāja Jagannātha Viracito Rasagaṅgādhara—by Prof. R.S. Athavale Page 94.
20. *Ibid*—Page 150.
21. Raghuvaṁsa—XVIII. 28.
22. *Ibid*—VIII-24.
23. *Ibid*—I-8.
24. *Ibid*—II.6.
25. *Ibid*—VI-34.
26. *Ibid*—XIII.41.
27. *Ibid*—13.52.
28. Rghuvaṁśa—14.95.

29. *Ibid*—17-36. 18-24.
30. Kumārasmbhava—2-4. 15.
31. *Ibid*—2-45.
32. *Ibid*—5-20, 26.
33. Bhāgavatam—74. Mahābhārata—33 to 45.
34. Nitiśataka—44, 46, 51, 91.
35. Haraṣacarita—2nd Ucchavāsa.
36. *Ibid*.
37. *Ibid*—3rd Ucchavāsa.
38. *Ibid*—5th Ucchavasa.
39. Harṣacarita Eka Sanskrtika Adhyayana-Vāsudeva Śarana Agarawala Page 105, 190-191; Eighth Ucchavāsa of Harṣascarita.

8

Upāsya, Upāsanā and Upāsaka

From ancient time a man has tried to unfold the mystery of the evolution of the world. The scientists are trying to find out the origin of each particle and slowly getting hold of some phenomenal occurrences. In India the ancient *Ṛsis* tried to go to the root of the Universe and the life of man and the relation between the man and the Universe. They developed the subtle theory of Adhyātma. They considered *Parabrahman* as the Creator, Protector and Destroyer of the world and they came to the conclusion that each and every atom of the universe is *Parabrahman* itself and nothing else. Man is the greatest creation of all the beings and non-beings. He can perceive the nature of God if he leads his efforts in a particular way called *Sādhanā*. But every human being has no capacity to go through *Sāhdanā* but he or she can perform worship for a fixed time daily and serve God. This is called *Upāsanā*, by which he or she can understand *Brahman* and by *Kramamukti* be united with him. Ṛṣis try to connect human consciousness with Omniscient *Brahman* through *Upāsanā*.

Parabrahman is called *Bhagavān* or *Iśvar*, God; and It is the pure state of knowledge. The *Bhāgavat Purāṇa* says that, "*Vedānti tattatvavidastatvam yajñānamavyayam. Brahmeti, Paramātmeti, Bhagavāniti śabdyate*."[1] It means whom *Vedānti* calls *Parmeśvara* as Knowledge, the same *Paramātmā* is also called *Brahman, Paramātman* and *Bhagavān* i.e. God. God is attributeless and without name and form. It is difficult to understand the nature of *Brahman*. Man has limited physical, mental and intellectual power, but *Ṛṣis* preached a way to develop these powers by *Sādhanā* and *Upāsanā*. *Upāsanā* is more related to the mind than to the body and it is very much subjective. The improvement of an *Upāsaka* can be known only through his mental reactions to the outer situations and his outward behaviour. A man does what his mind suggests him to do, therefore the mind is more important than the physical form. *Atharvaveda* says, "*Manasā samkalpayati tadvātamapi gacchati, vāto devebhya ācaṣte, yathā puruṣa te manaḥ.*"[2] It means whatever a man decides reaches eather, then gods come to know of it and then the work is performed; a man is, what his mind is. The *Śatapatha Brāhmaṇa* also says that, "*Mano deva manuṣyasājānantiti, manasā samkalpayati tatprāṇamabhipadyate, prāṇo vātam, vāto devebhya ācaṣte. Tathā puruṣasya manaḥ.*"[3] It means: Man can be known by his thinking, god knows his decisions by *prāṇa* (breath) and then the incident occurs. It can be said that from the working of the mind man can be recognized as good or bad. Therefore Upāsanā is a strict discipline for the mind by which the mind can learn to decide which auspicious things to be done; and to unite with God is the most auspicious decision.

The mind is very powerful and it takes the form of the object on which it meditates, like *Kiṭabhramaṛa Nyāya*, i.e. an insect by fear thinks constantly about *Bhramara*—a large black bee which had caught it and one day it itself becomes the bee and flies away. Therefore the *Ṛṣis* suggested to think about Transcendental Absolute *Brahman* so that the mind can attain that Blissful imperishable State. The *Bhāgavata Purāṇa* says, "*Viṣayāndhyā-yaścittam viṣayeśu viṣajjate. Māmanusmaratascitta myyeva pariliyate.*"[4] It means the mind takes the form of the object on which it meditates, it becomes sensuous when it thinks about the subjects of sense organs and it becomes Iśvara when it meditates upon Him.

The Upāsanā is a process of being most powerful, and gaining the *Śakti* of *Iśvara,* because *Iśvara* and His *Śakti* are not different. We can see in *Tattiriya Brāhmaṇa* that *Indrāṇi* gives power to Indra for fighting, the verse says that *Indrāṇi* inspires fearlessness in the heart of Indra and forces Him to encounter the enemy.[5] *Sudhendukumār Dās* says, "*In Ṛgveds (III-60-2) Śaci* is not mere blind physical force, but denotes `skill or ability' implying conscious intellectual faculty (*prajnā*)... the author of *Nighanṭu* is not therefore very far from truth when, he identifies *Śaci* with *Vāk*..."[6]

In one way it is a *Śakti Upāsanā* which is mingled with *Iśvaropāsanā. Iśvara* is not alone but he is always present with His energy. Therefore Gods are seen with their concerts, *Viṣnu* with *Lakṣmi, Śiva* with *Pārvati, Gaṇapati* with *Ṛddhi* and *Siddhi,*

Brahmadeva with *Sāvitri, Sūrya* with *Uṣā* and *Sandhyā, Rāma* with *Sitā, Kṛṣṇa* with *Rādhā*. The Upāsakā worships either *Iśvara* or *Śakti* as the main *Upāsya* deity but ultimately the duality does not remain and the *Śakti* and *Iśvara* become one and the same, and the *Upāsaka* also unites with them: the unification of *Iśvara, Śakti* and individual soul (Individual soul is called 'Aṇu' in *Trikdarśana*.)

A person can use high intellectuality only when his mind is not worn out by worldly difficulties. When the mind is restless the ultimate Bliss can not be gained; see the verse, "*Nāvirāto duścaritānnāśānto nāsamāhitāḥ. Nāśāntamanaso vāpi prajñānenainamāpnuyāt*."[7] It means a restless and unsatisfied person can not gain the pure knowledge of *Brahman*. It is also said in the treatises that the mind can become calm and quite if the deities favour the man. Therefore to gain the favours of deities, various Upāsanās are prescribed by religious treatises.

The religious treaties accept theism. The *Vedas* contain different deities and their praises. The *Upaniṣads* accept *Paramātman* and prescribe various *Vidyās* to meditate upon. The *Brahmasūtras* discusses *Aṅgavati Upāsanā* in *Angāvabaddhādhikaraṇam*.[8]; where *Vaiśvānara, Svarga, Vāyu, Ākaśa* are called the limbs and the attributes or *Brahman* have been given names like, *Agni, Sūrya, Omkāra* etc. The six systems of philosophy (*Ṣaḍdarśana*) accept the authority of the *Vedas* though they do not prescribe any special worship. The *Vaiśeṣika* and *Nyāya* accept god as the result of inference and the governor of the world. *Sāṁkhya* is dualistic and says that *Puruṣa* remains silent and Prakṛti plays the game of the world. In Yogasūtra 'Iśvarapra ṇidhāna' or faith in God is accepted. The *Yoga* is a *Sādhanā*. *Purva Mimāṅsā* is anxious about *Yajña* ceremonies and it accepts various deities. *Uttara Mimāṁasā* accept God and says that it can be attained through meditation and Knowledge. Meditation is a form of Upāsanā. The *Purāṇas* accept polytheism and preach various *vratas, anusṭhānas, pujās* which are different forms of *Upāsanā* of different Gods, namely, *Śiva, Viṣṇu, Devi, Gaṇeśa, Sūrya* etc. These deities are called *Upāsya*. The process or method of worship of deities is called Upāsanā and one who undergoes these methods is called *Upāsaka*.

Śankarācārya says in the introduction of Book three of the *Aitreya Āraṇyaka* that there are three classes of men (who undergo worships) (1) those who desire the knowledge of *Brahman*, (2) those who desire to become free, gradually become free by attaining the world of *Hiraṇayagarbha*, and (3) those who care only for prosperity. He adds that for the concentration of thought certain Upāsanās are necessary. Such Upāsanās are of two kinds, (1) *Brahmopāsanā*, and (2) *pratikopāsanā*, the former consists in contemplation of *Brahman* as endowed with qualities, the latter in considering worldly objects as *Bharman*.[9]

Upāsanā is a ladder to reach the deity. When an *Upāsaka* reaches the deity by using this ladder, he becomes one with the deity. Then the 'trait' (*traya*): trio does not remain different from each other, but until his body remains he practises *Upāsanā* as a part of his life. Therefore *Upāsanā* is important in all the spiritual states of the *Upāsaka*. The *Upāsya* deities are different for each one as well as the *Upāsanā* processes also differ; because every one's liking is different and the same Upāsanā is not suitable for everyone. The method of *Upāsanā* is also affected by the social, atmospheric, political and economic situations. In the *Vedic* period most of the prayers were the request for protection, prosperity, because it is necessary to have the initial requirements first; and few prayers sing about knowledge and *Mokṣa*. In the *Paurāṇic* age the life seems to have been stable and the icons can be made, therefore the form of deities which are described in the *Vedic* prayers have taken actual figures on the stones, metals, clay etc. The *Vedic* deities are *Indra, Agni, Mitra, Varuṇa, Viśvadeva, Sādhyadeva, Maruts, Yama, Brahmaṇaspati, Rudra* etc. And the vedic goddesses are Ilā, *Vāk, Aditi, Uṣā, Bhārati* etc. In the *Paurānic* period the images are worshipped with the recitation of the *Vedic* prayers and the *Upāsya* deities are multiplied in which *Śiva* and *Viṣṇu* are main deities and all the goddesses are the forms of *Śakti Devi*. In the *Tāntrika Upāsanā* the form of worship is different, It contains the worship of the *yantra; mudrā, nyāsa, japa,* meditation are its integral parts; and the *Upāsya* deities are *Śiva* and *Devi*. But now-a-days the form of Upāsanā is a mixed one i.e. *Vedic, Paurāṇic* and *Tāntrika*. We see this mixed form of Upāsanā in the *Bhāgavata Purāṇa*, The verse is, "*Vaidikastāntrika miśra iti me trividho makhaḥ. Trayāṇamipsitenaiva vidhinā mām samārcayet.*"[10] It means, "My worship (which is also called *yajña*) is of three types namely, *Vedic, Tāntrika* and Mixed. You can worship me by any of the processes". `*Bhāgavata' purāṇa* also describes the *Upāsanās* in the four great Ages, namely, *Kṛta, Tretā, Dvāpāra* and *Kali*. It says that in *Kṛta* Age people were generally full of contentment and compassion and they engaged themselves in the spiritual exercises such as meditation etc. In the *Tretā* Age people devoted to penance and keen on performance of the *Vedic* rites; they were devoted to the *Vedic* studies i.e. *Śāstrābhyāsa*, which is one of the aspects of Upāsanā. In the *Dvāparā* Age *Yajña* ceremonies have great importance (for seeking svarga: Heaven), the study of the *Vedas* and performances of great sacrifices like *Rājasuya, Aśvamedha* etc. was in practice. In the *Kali* Age the Upāsanā is easy, and by singing of the names and glory of *Śri Kṛṣṇa* the persons become free from all attachments and attain *Vaikunṭha (Salokatā)*. It is further said that what one achieves by meditation in the *Kṛta* Age, by performance of sacrifices in the *Tretā* Age, by worship and service of God in the *Dvāpāra* Age, one attains in the *Kali* Age only by chanting the name of *Hari*.[11]

Here follows the different forms of *Upāsya* deities, different modes of worships and the nature of *Upāsaka* in the *Vedic, Paurāṇic* and *Tāntrika* methods :

Vedic Upāsya Deities : *Agni* is praised in the first *Ṛc* of each *Sūkta* and then *Indra*. *Agni* and *Indra* seem to be the more important deities. The other deities are *Rudra, Mitra, Varuṇa, Aryamā, Bṛhaspati, Viṣṇu, Urukrama* and others see the verse, "*Śannomitraḥ śam Varuṇaḥ śannobhavatvatryamā. Sanno indro bṛhaspatih śannoviṣṇurukramaḥ*".[12] All these deities are different forms of *Parabrahman*. *Ṛgveda* says "*Ekam sad viprā bahudhā vadanti.*"[13] It means there is one Absolute Reality but intelligent people call it by different names according to its appearance which is prescribed in a specific condition or which work was assigned for a particular time. The *Upāsya* Goddesses are Ilā, *Vāk, Sarasvatri, Bhārati, Aditi, Uṣa, Rātri, Śri* etc.

Vedic Upāsanā : The Upāsanā is in the form of *Yajñas*, such as *Agniṣṭoma, Vājapeya, Cāturmāsya, Daśapurṇimāsi* etc. Habitual offerings are clarified butter and the juice of soma plant. Offerings with chanting of prayers is vidhi. Mostly the aim of Upāsanā is gaining wealth, food, life, prosperity, cattle, protection from enemies and hope of immortality and future happiness after death.

Some times the animals are noted for sacrifices but these *Yajñas* like *Sautrāmaṇi* and *Aśvamedh* are introduced to put a restraint upon the unbridled instincts of man.[14]

The *Atharvaveda* says that the *Upāsakā* (worshipper) of *yajña* always worships the *Vaiśvānara Agni* who is the Lord of water and light and who is luminous; the verse is, "*Ṛtavānam Viśvāvanaramṛtasya jyotiṣpatim. Ajastramdharmamīmahe.*"[15]

Vedic Upāsaka : The host-Yajamāna- is *Upāsaka*. The *ṛtvijas* actually perform *yajña* for the host who takes an oath-*dikṣā*-of *yajña*. *Ṛtvijas* are generally four in number, they are called *Hotā, Udgātā, Adhvaryu* and *Brahmā*. Some sacrifices need assistant *ṛtvijas*.

The *Gurū*-preceptor-or religious guide is important at that time. The particular *gurū* : chaplain : *purohita* is assigned to particular race, for example, *Vasiṣṭha Ṛsi* is the *Gurū* for the *Ikṣvāku* race. Without *Guū's* consent nothing can be done. *Gurū* also confers the knowledge of *Paramātman* on his disciple, *Vasiṣṭha* has delivered the knowledge to *Rāma* which we can read in the *Yogavāsiṣtha*.

Paurāṇic Upāsya Deities : The concept of God i.e. He is *Sat, Cit, Ānanda* and Omnipotent, Omniscient, and Omnipresent is the same at the *paurāṇic* times but the deities are in different forms, *Vedic Indra* and others appear in new forms. *Indra* is described as the king of Gods. *Puruṣa* from *Puruṣa Sūkta* and *Āditya* came in the form of *Viṣṇu* and he is assigned the work as the protector of the Universe and for the maintenance of *Dharma* (Rules of conduct-duties prescribed by the *Vedas*) and protection of *Dhārmiak* people. He takes different forms suitable to the situations which we know as incarnations-avatāras-that occurred in the different Ages. Therefore *Viṣṇu* is worshipped by various names and forms which are found in the *Bhāgavata Purāṇa*.

The *Vedic Rudra* came as auspicious *Śiva* who is the destroyer of the world at the time of the deluge therefore He is called *Kālāngni Rudra*. The basic idea in the *Ṛgveda* that He protects cattle etc. remained and He is called *Paśupati*. He is benevolent to His worshippers. He is known by different names viz. *Tryambaka, Nilakaṇṭha, Bhava, Iśāna* etc.

The *Vedic Brahmaṇaspati* is seen as *Gaṇapati* with elephant head and He is assigned the duty of destroying the difficulties. Therefore He is given the honour of first worship before any other deity at auspicious ceremonies. He is also called the God of intellect.

The Sun is called the head of the nine planets and He is worshipped after *Gaṇesa Pūjana*. His special sect named *Saura* is also in vogue and the days of *Makara-Sankrānta* and *Rathasaptami* are prescribed for *Āditya Upāsanā*.

The female forms viz. *Aditi, Uṣā* etc. are not seen as *Upāsyā* deities but *Yogamāyā* from *Rātrisūkta, Śri Lakṣmi* from *Śri sūkta* and goddess *Vāk* as *Sarasvati* are the *Upāsyā* deities of *Paurāṇic Age. Umā Haimavati* of *Kenopaniṣad*[16] is seen as the wife of *Śiva* and She is worshipped as *Durgā, Kāli* etc. The goddess of agriculture who is called *Sitā* in the *Gṛhyasūtras*[17] is worshipped as the wife of *Śri Rāma*.

Different incarnations of *Viṣṇu, Śiva, Dattātreya* and *Gaṇeśa* have become *Upāsya* deities. The *Vedic* deities are multiplied in numbers, therefore *Śri Śaṅkarācārya* recommended the worship of five main Gods, namely, *Gaṇeśa, Śiva, Viṣṇu, Sūrya* and *Devi* together called *'Pañcāyatana'*.[18]

Lord *Kṛṣṇa* has described various attributes as His own forms in the tenth chapter of *Gītā (Vibhūti yoga)*, therefore these forms like banyan tree, *Vāsuki* serpent etc. have become *Upāsya* deities.

The basic concept, that if deities are worshipped and served they confer the desired objects on the worshipper, has remained as it was at the time of the *Vedas*, but the forms have changed, they have become numerous. The images are made according to their description given in the *Vedas*.

Paurāṇic Upāsanā Process-Vidhi : The concept of *yajña* i.e. sacrifice has remained and the *Ūpāsaka* offers what is good with him to the deities. The deities are worshipped with the sixteen objects known as *Upacāras*, and the worship is called '*Śodaṣopacāra Pūja*; it contains Invoking (*āvāhana*), offering seat (*āsana*), Water to wash feet (*pādya*), Offering material of worship (*arghya*), Bathing (*snāna*), Clothing (*vastra*), offering sacred thread to wear (*Yajñopavita*), Offering sandal paste (*candana*), Offering flowers (*puṣpāṇi*), showing incense (*dhūpa*), Lighting (*Dīpa*), Obeisance (*namaskāra*), offering food (*naivedya*), Offering water to sip (*ācamana*), Cicrumambulation (*Pradakṣiṇa*), and Biding adieu (*Visarjana*). If the deities are fixed in the temples etc. then *Āvahana* and *Visrijana* are avoided. Each one of the sixteen *ṛks* of The *Puruṣa Sukta* is recited with each act.

The different *yajñas* like *Cāturmāsya* etc.; have changed their forms and people observed the *Cāturmasa* as holy time, from *Śayani Ekādasi* i.e. the eleventh day of the first half of the month *Āṣāḍha*, to *Prabodhini Ekādaśi*, i.e. the eleventh day of the first half of the month of *Kārtika* and various religious Upāsanās are performed at that time, such as *Satyanārāyaṇa* worship, distribution of charitable things, different vows are to be taken for the service to the God.

Geographically *India* is the land of agriculture and rainy season is during the *Cāturmāsa*. People are busy with the agricultural works, and big ceremonies like marriage etc. can not be performed. People take oaths of fasting etc. which are easy to observe.

The *Śrāvaṇa* sacrifice, in which the mantras of snakes from *Taittiriya Samhitā* are chanted is observed as *'Nāgapancami'* day when people worship snakes by offering them milk and food made from jwar. This *Śrāvaṇa* sacrifice is described in the *Gṛhyasūtras*.[19]

The *Paurāṇic Upāsanā* is performed with the *Vedic* mantras which is the praise of the particular deity. People worship all the species, namely *Hanumān* among the apes, *Ananta*, a serpent; Eagle, a bird; Bull, Lion, Tiger, Peacock, Mouse (Vehicles of *Śiva, Devi, Gaṇeśa, Kāntrikeya* etc.), cow as the most sacred animal, fish, tortoise, pig as incarnations of *Viṣṇu*, banyan tree because the story of *Satyavān* and *Sāvitri* is related with it. All these species are called the digits of *Paramātman*, therefore it is *'Aṅgavati Upāsanā.'* The elephant and the weapons of gods are worshipped as symbols of gods; it is *'Pratīkavati Upāsanā.'*

We can say that a worshipper (*Upāsaka*) performs the Upāsanā of all the species as they are *Paramātman* and it does not matter whether they are from a higher type of creation or from a lower type.

Gurū is necessary in the *Paurānic Upāsanā* because he guides the worshipper in a proper way and suggests the proper time of Upāsanā He guides the worshipper for worldly motives or for Release (*Mokṣa*) according to the liking and capacity of the worshipper. But to attain the *'Parama Puruṣārtha'* is the aim of human life and Gurū gradually leads him to that way. Therefore daily worship of god is called *'Deva yajña'*.

Paurānic Upāsaka : The *Upāsaka* himself performs *Nitya pūjā* (daily worship); for *Naimittika pūjā* like *Satyanārāṇa* etc. he invites his guide. This upāsanā is carried on with the chanting of the *Vedic* mantras such as the *Gāyatri*, the *Mahāmṛtyuñjaya*, the *Puruṣa sukta*, the *Śri sūkta*, the *Pavamāna sūkta*, the *Brahmaṇaspati sūkta*, *Rudrādhyāyas* and other mantras.

The *Upāsakā* sings prayers, recites mantras, meditates on God which are the different aspects of Upāsanā, in which he actually sits near God and experiences His company; he also studies the vedas., (*śāstrābhyāsa*).

Tāntrika Upāsya Deities : Generally all the *Tāntrika* texts start with the question of *Pārvati* about the mystery of the universe, addressed to Śiva. It is a *Śākta Upāsanā*. *Śiva* and *Pārvati* are main deities but *Devi* has more importance than *Śiva*. She is identified with *Parabrahman*, therefore she is called *Parābhaṭṭārikā* and *Śiva* is called *Parābhaṭṭāraka*. *Devi* is *Tripurasundri*, because She is the observer of three states, namely *Jāgṛity*, *Svapna* and *Suṣupti* and she stays in the *Turiyā* state. She is surrounded by *Yoginis*, she is the śakti of the letters and for each letter she is called by a different name and called as *'Mātṛakā*. There are also the devatas of the eight directions but *Tripuraṣundari* is the chief.

Tāntrika Upāsanā Process : *Devi* is worshipped through *yantra*-diagrams. *Kavaca, nyāsa, mudrā*, recitation of *bijākṣaras, yogic* practise, are the parts of upāsanā. The *mantra* does not mean only *Vedic Ṛks*, but the meaning of the *bija* words become a mere spell or charm. It is supposed that every letter of the alphabet is instinct with the power of *Śakti* (it has the power of the *Vedic deity Vāk. Ṛgveda*-x-125) therefore, co-ordination of the mystical words are called *mantras*; the recitation of these *mantras* include in Upāsanā. The *bijās* are the root of the *Śakti* or the name of Deity and these deities are said to be residing in the cakras which are in each person's body having their place in the human trunk.

Cakra worship is important in this *Upāsanā*. *Mahānirvāṇa Tantra* says[20], '(it is the greatest worship (*Upāsanā*)' when an *Upāsaka* supposes that he himself is *Brahman* and meditates on *Brahman*, The meditation on duality is a medium type of worship; the praise, the recitation of *Japa* is a lower type of worship and the external worship is the lowest type of worship, see the verse, *"Uttamo brahmasadbhāvo dhyānabhāvāstu madhyamāḥ. Stutrirjapo adhamo bahiḥ pūjā adhamādhamā."* The greatest worship is the worship named *`Ahaṁgrahopāsanā' : `Atamatyevaupāsita'* of *Bṛahadāraṇyaka Upaniṣad.*[21]

Tāntrika Upāsaka : People of all four varṇas can perform this Upāsanā. The *Yajña* performance is limited to the three *varṇas,* but the *Tāntrika Upāsanā* is free to all, anybody can individually do this worship. *Nātha* cult has accepted this method as a part of their cult, therefore, people of all varṇas accepted *Nātha* cult. *Devi* and *Śiva* are worshipped and *Śri Dattātreya* is accepted as universal preceptor. The main important part of gurū is assigned to Him, therefore, *Datta* is worshipped all over India by the followers of the *Tāntrika Upāsanā* of *Śri Vidyā. Datta* has preached this *Vidyā* to *Sahasrārjuna, Paraśurāma, Alarka* etc.

These three methods are the main types of Upāsanā in India. It is seen that Upāsanā of every type is the worship of *Parabrahman* who is defined as, *Sat, Cit, Ānanda* i.e. existence, knowledge and bliss[22]. *Ṛgveda* says, *"Ṛco akṣare parame vyoman. Yasmindeva adhiviśve niṣeduh. Yastannaveda kiṁ ṛcā kariṣyati, ya ittadvidaste ime samāsate."* It means the *Vedic ṛks* talk about *Parabrahman-Akṣara* in which all gods reside. Any one who does not understand this, it is useless for him to recite the *mantras* and one who understands this, he unites with *Parabrahman* and gets release from the bondage. Formless *Brahman* has given forms according to its presentation of power, and as per the work done by that power different names are assigned to It and that particular form and name is recognised as a deity. *Upāsaka* worships these deities. The aim of each *Upāsanā* is Bliss, though it is done for the worldly gains i.e. *Preyas* or for the ultimate release, i.e. *Śreyas*. The real bliss is gained after the knowledge of *Brahman* is attained.

A person is the combination of energy i.e. consciousness which is an element of the universal consciousness which is called *Vaiśvānara Agni* or *Teja* or the Soul; and the gross body which is run by the soul. A person is able to attain the highest bliss because individual soul is the part - *aṅśa* of *Parabrahman. Yājñavalkya Smṛti* describes it poetically; the verse is, *"Nissaranti yathā loha-piṅdāttaptāt-sphulligakaḥ. Sakāsadātmanastādvat-māmanaḥprabhavanti."*[23] It means as the sparks spring from the burning iron, so from *Paramātman* springs up the *Ātman*. But the individual forgets that he is really *Parabrahman* and loses bliss, and tries to find it out in the outside world. But if his *Gurū* guides him in the correct way he comes to know that his gross body is a part of *Paramātman* because it is a combination of *Paṇaca Mahābhutas* according to *Sāmkhyā* system and the great elements are forms of *Paramātman;* and his *cit*-mind-intellect is a part of universal consciousness which is Omniscient *Iśvara*. Then he follows the *Upāsanā* and gradually uplifts his consciousness from individual to universal (*Viśvātmaka*) and unites with the universal consciousness i.e. *Hiraṇyagarbha* or the *Virāṭa Puruṣa* of *Puruṣa Sūkta*, and he experiences the *Viśvātmaka Bhāva* which is described by the *Bhagavadgitā*.

With the different modes of worship a person gets the knowledge of *Parabrahman* step by step. The *Yogavasiṣtha* describes seven steps of knowledge in this verse, "*Jñānabhumiḥ śubhecchākhyā prathamā samudāhṛta. Vicāraṇādvitiyā ca tṛitiyā tanumānasā. Satvāpattiscaturthisyāt tato'samsaktināmaka. Padārthabhāvini ṣaṣthi saptami tūryagā smṛtā*"[24] It means at first a person wishes to get release from bondage i.e. *Mokṣa*, this stage is called *Śubhecchā*, a benign will. Then the searches for *Gurū* and asks Him about the way of worship (*Upāsanā*) suitable to him, this step is called *Vicāraṇā* i.e. asking. Afterwards he contemplates on the subtle things like the subtle body, the mind etc. this stage is called *Tanumānasā*. Then slowly he perceives the meaning of the *Mahāvākyas* such as `*Tattvāmasi*'; this stage is called *Sattvāpatti*. Then he tries to enter the state of *Samādhi, Dhyāna* and experiences thoughtless state, this state is called *Asaṁsakti*. Then he understands that there is no other object that *Brahman;* this stage is called *Padārtha Bhāvini*. In the last stage he remains in the state of self effulgence, Bliss and united with *Brahman*, this stage is called *Tūryagā*. When a person goes through all these stages, he is called `*Jīvanmukta*.'

The body also becomes pure by Upāsanā. It is said that the body is born from '*Soma kalā*' and at the time of the death *Kālāgni* destroys the body, but if by proper *Yogasādhanā* as well as Upāsanā the *soma* part of body improves then the *Agni* can not destroy the body but the *Tejatattva* of the body overcomes the death and then the body remains for a long time at the will of *Yogi*.[25]

This *Tejatattva* is also called *Kundalini Śakti*. The *Rājayognis* awaken *Kundalini* through pure will and *Bhaktas, upāskas* through immaculate devotion.[26] The *Upāsaka* experiences the awakening of his own power.

The *Gurū* gives an oath or *Dikṣā* to the pupil of any cult according to physical and intellectual capacity of the upāsaka and shows him the right path which he will be able to follow. Therefore *Gurū* has importance in the Upāsanā. The *Svetāśvatara Upaniṣad* says, *"Yasya deve parā bhakti yathā deve tathā gurau."*[27] It means: he, who has faith in God and the same in *Gurū* can understand the knowledge of scriptures. The *Ṛgveda* also says, *"Śraddhā devea yajamāna upāste. Śraddhām hṛdayya yākutya śraddhayā vindate vasu."*[28] which means the Upāsaka must have confidence about his path of *Śreyas* and on his Gurū whom he follows. Instead of one's own *Gurū, Dattātreya* is *Gurū* of all and therefore he is worshipped all over India.

The form and image for worship in the case of each Upāsaka can be differ. *Yāskācāra* says that when four *Ṛtvijas* are not available for the performance of sacrifice a single *Ṛavija* works for four and he is called by different names according to his work-he is *Adharyu,* he is *Brahmā;* in this way *Paramātman* takes different forms according to the will of the *Upāsaka,* and the worshipper calls Him by the different names which are suitable to His forms, (for example, *Nara-siṅha;* the man-lion form of *Viṣṇu*), the verse is, *"Mahabhāgyāddevatāyaḥ eka ātma bahudhā stūyate. Ekasya ātmanḥ annye devāh pratyaṅgāni bhavanti."*[29] It means *Paramātman* is prayed in the different forms of deity and the deities are *aṅga*-limbs of the same.

Yāskācārya says that there are only three main deities, namely, *Agni, Vāyu* or *Indra* and *Sūrya, Agni* is the deity for Earth, *Vāyu* or *Indra* for the Space and the Sun for the Heaven.[30] *Agni* and the Sun are not different, because the Sun is in the form of flames. Fire : *Agni* is the symbol of consciousness. *Rudra* is fire personified.[31] *Viṣṇu* is also called *'Visnur vai Yajñaḥ'*[31a] The deities are invoked through *Agni*. The *Ṛgveda* starts with the praise of *Agni : "Agnimile purohitam."* Indra is also called *Vāyu, Śatapatha Brāhmaṇa* praises *Indra* by the name *'Mahāprāṇa'*, the verse is, *"Sa yo'yam madhye prāṇa esa indraḥ."* It means the central breath i.e. *Prāṇa* is called *Indra. Indra* is most powerful among the deities and the power is the quality of *Vāyu*. The *Yajurveda* starts with the praise of *Vāyu. "Eṣettvojjetva vvāyavāhsth."*; and *Sāmaveda* starts with the praise of *Agni, "Agna ayāhivitaye."* Therefore it can be said that *Agni* and *Vāyu* i.e. *Indra* are important deities at *Vedic* period.

The *Ṛgveda* declares that when a person concentrates on God as the source of all Light, a peculiar luster appears to be descending from the Heaven and the Earth and spreads in his entire inner self.[33] *Bṛhajjābālopaniṣad* says, *"Agnisomātmakam viśvamityagnirācakṣate. Raudri ghorāyā taijasi tanuḥ. Samsaktyamṛtamayaḥ śaktikari tanuḥ. Amṛtan yatpratiṣthā sa tejovidyākalā svayam."*[34] It means, 'It is said that the universe is the confluence of *Agni* and *Soma*. *Soma* is the power and the powerful body. The self is amṛta i.e. immortal and *śakti* resides in the self. It is in the gross and subtle forms. Therefore *Agni* is called *Puruṣa* and *Soma* is called Woman-*stri*. We can see this concept in the image of *Devi* who is standing on the body of *Śiva* and plays the game of universe and *Śiva* remains inactive[35].

The female deities are the essence of universal energy and this energy creates the world, this is called *Māyā* in the *Rātrisūkta*. In the *Śri sūkta* also *Śri* is invoked through *Agni*. In the marriage ceremony also the wife is accepted through *Agni* by the husband. Therefore it can be said that *Agni* is the man and *Vāyu* is the woman who are the forms of *Parabrhaman*, who divided Himself into two, man and woman, *Puruṣa* and *Prakṛti*, Energy and *Matter, Cit* and *Sat;* Consciousness and Existence. With this discussion it can be said that the latter deities are the different forms of *Agni* and *Vāyu;* for example, *Viṣṇu* is *Agni* and *Lakṣmi* is His Power i.e. *Vāyu; Śiva* is *Agni* and *Śakti* is the form of *Vāyu;* and so on.

The *Iṣṭa devatā* is *Upāsya devatā* which differs with each individual even of the same family. There is a *Kuladevatā* (deity of the race), which is traditionally fixed for the Upāsanā of the whole family, eventhough each person can worship his or her own *Īṣta devatā* (the deity which one likes). There is also a deity for the town: Grāmadevatā who is commonly worshipped by the people living in the same town. The way of worship also differs with each individual. Some worship the *Agni*, some the water, some the Sun, some worship *Brāhmaṇa* and *Gurū* as *Upāsya* deities; see the verse, *"Arcāyām sthaṇdile' gnau vā surye vāpsu hṛdi dvije. Dravyeṇa bhaktiyaktorcet svagurūm mānamāyayā."*[36]

Each and every way of worship-Upāsanā-ultimately leads to the knowledge of Supreme *Brahman,* though it is started for achieving minor worldly objects. The *Brahman,* is described by the *Nyāya sūtras* as Release, which means freedom from pain.

Nyāya Bhāṣya says, in this verse, "*Tad abhayam ajaram amṛtyupadam brahmakṣemaprāptiḥ.*"[37] It means, the state of fearlessness, imperishability, deathlessness and bliss is called *Brahmaprāpti* which state every body seeks.

The state of *Parabrahman* is calm and quiet i.e. *Paramaśānta*. *Bhartṛhari* describes this state in the first verse of "*Nitiśatakam*" where he bows to the conscious, clam and luminous *Paramatman*. When the *Upāsaka*, reaches that state of Bliss he becomes calm and quiet gradually and reaches liberation through `*Kramamukti*'. A *Jñāni* liberates quickly which is called `*Sadyomukti*'. Dr. Rādhākṛiṣṇan says, "There are two kinds of release, `*Sadyomukti* or instantaneous release' and `*kramamukti* or gradual liberation.' The former is the result of *Jñāna* or wisdom and the later is the result of Upāsanā or worship and prayer."[38]

It is important to know that the Upāsanās are carried out in the state of *Mukti* (liberated state) spontaneously and not as a means to release but they are the ends in themselves. See the verse, "*Harerūpāsānā cātra sadaiva sukharūpini. Natu sādhanabhutā sā siddhirevātra sā yataḥ.*"[39] It means, the Upāsanā of *Hari* is at all the times the state of happiness, it is not only the means to obtain the Bliss but an end (Bliss) itself.

References

1. Bhāgavata Purāṇa—1-2-11.
2. Atharvaveda—12-4-4.
3. Śatapatha Brāhmaṇa—11-14-27.
5. Taittiriya Brāhmaṇa—II-4-2; Sakti or Divine Worship. Page-14. by Sudhendukumara Das.
6. Śakti or Divine Worship—page—14 by—Sudhendukumar Das.
7. Kaṭha Upaniṣad—1-2-24.
8. Brahmasūtra—3-3-54, 57, 58.
9. The Aitreya Āraṇyaka—Pages—40, 4 1 by Keith.
10. Bhāgavata Purāṇa—11-27-7.
11. *Ibid*—12-3-19, 21, 23, 52.
12. Ṛgveda—1-90-9.
13. *Ibid*—1-164-46.
14. History of Indian Philosophy. Vol-7, page-243, by—R.D. Ranade.
15. Atharvaveda—6-36-1.
16. Kena Upaniṣad—Kānda-3.
17. Pāraskara Gṛhyasūtra—II-17-10.
18. Religious Sects In Ancient India. page—70 by-D.A. Pai.
19. Gobhil Gṛhyasūtra—III-7-1. Hiraṇyakeśin Gṛhyasutra—II-6-16-1. Taittiriya Samhitā—IV-2-83.

20. Mahānirvāṇa Tantra—XIV-112.
21. Bṛhadāraṇyaka Upaniṣad—1-4-7-10.
22. Tāittiriya Saṃhitā—3-1.
23. Yajñvalkya smṛti—III-67.
24. Bhāratiya Samskṛti Aur Sādhanā-Prathama Khanda-pages 460-61. by-Gopinath Kaviraja.
26. Sādhanā-page-395. by-Swami Śivānanda.
27. Śvetāśvatara Upaniṣad—6-23.
28. Ṛgveda—10-11-15-14.
29. Nirukta-Daivata Kānda-6-2, 4, 5.
30. *Ibid*-Daivata Kānda-6-5.
31. Ṛgveda—1-6-4-10 (31 a) Taittiriya Samhitā 5.2.8.7.
32. Śatapatha Brāhmaṇa—6-1-1-1.
33. Ṛgveda—1-96-5.
34. Brhajjābālopaniṣad-2-1.
35. Vaidic Vijñāna aur Bhāratiya Samskṛti-page-260. by Giridharalal Sharma Caturvedi.
36. Bhāgavata Purāṇa—11-27-9.
37. Nyāya Bhāṣya—I-I-22.
38. The Brahmaśūtra—The philosophy of Spiritual Life-page-37. by Dr. Rādhakṛṣṇan.
39. Brahmavaivarta Purāṇa—IV-4-21.

9

Upāsanā of Universal God

(1) Meaning of Upāsanā

In India's cultural history the term Upāsanā as we have analysed earlier is the most ancient and important term, particularly to understand the religious and philosophical aspects of India. This can be illustrated by its etymological meaning *Up+Āsa* i.e. communion with God, comparable with *Up+Niṣa*, communication with the *Gurū*. The work upāsanā cannot be properly rendered in English, though it is translated into English by such words as worship or service.

The word upāsanā first occurs in the *Vedas*. The *Ṛgveda* says *"Yā ātmadā baladā yasya viśva upāsate praśiṣam yasya devāḥ."*[1] It means, the one who is the giver of the soul, energy and whom all the animate kingdom including devas worship. In the *Vedas* the upāsanā of *Brahman* which is beyond name and form is seen. But *Purāṇas* describe the names and forms of *Brahman*, so that the seekers with normal intellect can perceive the state of *Brahman*. The *Upaniṣads* are said to be one hundred and eight out of which the principal ten describe the Impersonal Absolute, the nameless and formless *Brahman*. But the minor *Upaniṣads* such as *Śiva, Rāma, Kṛṣna, Kuṇḍalini, Yoga, Gāyatri, Brahma* prescribe upāsanās. These minor *Upaniṣads* prescribe the technique of worship. This worship aims at the worldly prosperity and spiritual emancipation. The verse in the *Ṛgveda* says," *...śiśitamindrā parvata yuvam nastanno viśve varivasyantu devāḥ.*"[2]. It means the Gods may confer on us ample food and the prosperity being pleased by our Upāsanā. In Upāsanā a seeker sits near the highest ideal i.e. God, and wants to be united with HIm. The word Upāsanā can be defined thus

1. The literal meaning of *Upāsanā* is to sit near the highest object.
2. *Upāsanā* is, what a seeker does to acquaint himself with the *Brahman* and experience the saying 'from the gross body to *Brahman*'.
3. The way to study the basic knowledge of Impersonal Absolute: *Brahman* is *Upāsanā*.

(2) Aspects of Upāsanā

Upāsanā includes a ritualistic worship; recitation of *mantra* i.e. *Japa*, meditation and *śāstrabhyasa*, i.e. a Study of the scriptures. It is found in the religious ceremonies, vows, pilgrimages, temples etc. It denotes that Upāsanā is done both externally and internally. The external Upāsanā is physical work and the internal Upāsanā is mental and intellectual work. Therefore Upāsanā has three aspects namely Physical, Psychological and Intellectual. There is no special line of differentiation, because Upāsanā is an integrated work, we may try to see these aspects separately.

(I) Physical Aspect of Upāsanā

According to the ancient *Ṛṣis* and other intelligent and revered persons, the universe is a combination of *Pancamahābhutas* namely *Ākāśa* (space), *Vāyu* (wind), *Agni* (Fire), *Āpa* (Water) and *Pṛthvi* (Earth). Modern scientists, physicists now-a-days accept that matter consists of energy (atomic energy); but man is not only a combination of five great elements, but in addition man consists of a matured intellect (*buddhi*) and mind (*manas*). According to the medical science, body is made of blood, flesh, bones etc. (*saptadhātu*). However, these things do not complete a man unless they are combined with mind, intellect and *prān*, (*Prāṇa* (Breath) is a part of *Vāyu* from the five elements) and their existence makes man alive Upāsanā is an internal part of the mind and the intellect. Upāsanā is connected with physiology (body), psychology (mind) and logic (reason).

Sānkhya and *Naiyāyika* study five great elements thoroughly and prove that the five great elements in the universe and five elements in the human body are one and the same. *Nātha* cult also follows this theory as '*Pindi te Brahmāṅḍi*'. Man has mind and intellect which are related to five great elements with their

Guṇas like *Sāttva, Raja* and *Tama* and accordingly works in the world. The greatest act of man is to become one with the universal consciousness i.e. *Brahman*. By the Upāsanā man can attain *Brahman*.

While following the path of Upāsanā the co-ordination of body, mind and intellect is required. A lazy body cannot co-operate, a fickle mind is also not suitable, a weak mind in a weak body is never useful for anything. That is why one should consider the physical aspect in Upāsanā. Healthy body, firm mind and clear decision (*saṁkalpa*) are required. One has to observe strictly a well arranged routine to develop one's body and mind to suit Upāsanā.

According to ancient science body does not mean an external body but it has five linears (*Kośas*). These are *Annamaya Kośa*, made of food; *Prāṇa-maya Kośa*, made of breath; *Manomaya Kośa*, made of the working of mind; *Vijñānamaya Kośa*, made of the working of intellect and *Ānandamaya Kośa*, made of the working of the ego. In these five *Kośas* the two external *Kośas* namely *Annamaya* and *Prāṇamaya Kośa* form *Sthula śaria* i.e. gross (external) body. *Manomaya* and *Vijñānamaya Kośa* form *Sukṣma Śarira* i.e. Subtle body, it is called *Kāraṇa Śarira*, and *Ānandamaya Kośa* is the place of the (soul) self. The physical aspect of Upāsanā is related to *Sthūla Śarira*. To keep *Annamaya Kośa* in a healthy condition one should choose one's intake of food varieties which can have an expected result. *Prāṇamaya kośa* is dependent upon the *Annamaya Kośa*, because disturbance of physical body has effects on the breath. Once one maintains Pure *Annamaya Kośa, Prāṇamaya Kośa* becomes Pure. A Strict vegetarian diet which will strengthen one's *Sattva* quality is to be observed, because the diet is related to the three guṇas of *Prakṛti*.[3]

In the *Yajña* ceremony a priest purifies the body of a worshipper. *Yajña*, ritualistic worship and external behaviour are physical activities in Upāsanā. Ritualistic worship includes the daily worship, *Pañcamahāyajñas*, idol worship in the temples, the ceremonies at births and the holy days dedicated to saints and the days of *Rāmajanma, Kṛṣṇajanma* etc. The external behaviour includes the intake of food, āsana, mudrā, the respect to elders which together is called *ācāradharm*.

Generally a person before starting Upāsanā works on the plane of *Annamaya Kośa*. When he follows Upāsanā he follows the way which his guide directs. His guide is his spiritual preceptor who has experienced the Truth according to His *Guru's* directions and thus becomes qualified to perceive *Brahman*. He is then allowed to direct his disciples. Therefore, the guide first teaches him Upāsanā on the physical plane. To worship God with the water, flowers, incense, burning the lamps, and offering food (*śodaṣopacāra*) is the Upāsanā on the physical plane. One sees that even a stone besmeared with vermilion is worshipped. In this preliminary stage the individual self is distinct from *Brahman* and God has also individual self. (Initial stage of Upāsanā). The trees, snakes, bulls are also the objects of worship at the physical plane of Upāsanā. The loud prayers are also a part of physical aspects, because the word has energy to rouse the emotions. The recited words are praised as Nādabrahma in "*Sangita Ratnākara*", the verse is "*caitanyam sarvabhūtānām vikṛtam jagadātmanā. Nādabrahmu tadānandamadvitiyamupāsmahe*"[4]. It means the life force of all the animate beings is a form of *Brahman* and the recited word revels His knowledge and brings unique happiness, therefore we worship *Nāda*.

The word can be pronounced silently, therefore, the prayers can be recited silently, it is called *sukṣmanāda*, the loud voice is called *Vaikhari Vāṇi* and the lower tones are called *Paśyanti, Mandhyamā* and *Parāvāṇi* according to their different velocity of pronunciation, on which the *mantraśāstra* is based. Slowly a person is lifted to the upper stage and able to do the internal Upāsanā by contemplating the real nature, form and qualities of God and then he enters into *manomaya koṣa*.

(II) Psychological Aspect of Upāsanā

The mind is one of the most important agents in Upāsanā. Every individual born in this universe is not essentially a strong, cultivated, mature human being. Study, training and experience have an effect on the mind. Psychology, logic are complex factors. One can make up one's mind for whatever is required. Mind is impressed from one's childhood according to a pattern, or a model, or a copy of work before him. To a thinking mind questions like why is this world here and who am I? will arise.[5] Then the person starts hunting for the proper answer to the questions arising one after the other from Upāsanā.

Mind is related to intellect : Intellect controls mind and viceversa. Thinking is guided by mind, proper thinking for the disciple is directed by the *Gurū, Gurū's* guidance is essential for Upāsanā. The mind wanders here there and off and on; it is very rarely stable. To bring the wandering thoughts to a focus, it must be directed to a particular kind of meditation. In the process of meditation the mind is forced to think about the object of meditation only and then intellect and mind are co-ordinated.

At this stage the seeker comes out of the *Annamaya* and *Prāṇamaya kośa*, by controlling the desires and regulating his life. He keeps his mind busy with the recitation of Japa, Singing prayers, and thinking about the goal of life; he remains in the *Manomaya kośa*. He thinks about his object from all points of view, obtains knowledge from each and every type of life.

In this connection the role of unconscious and subconscious mind plays an important part because when a person regulates his behaviour, his desires (*vāsanā*) come out from the old practices. Therefore to fulfill them, the different practices are undertaken in the Upāsanā. They are with reference to the objects of taste, smell, seeing, hearing, and touching i.e. the objects of *Jñānendriyas*. The idol appears beautiful for the sake of the eyes, incense, flowers are useful for the smelling quality of the nose, the food offerings are for the taste, and for the experience of touch various objects of worshipping and *japamālā* is used. The mind cannot concentrate without acquiring its objects and getting satisfied; when there are desires, it cannot think of other thoughts until desires are satisfied.

The social mind is also considered because man is a social animal. Therefore the public places of worships like temples are constructed and festivals are arranged periodically. The people of the same cult come together for discussions and worship of their deities. In India, there are some common ceremonies like *Rāmanavami, Janmāṣatmi, Holikā* etc., which are celebrated by the community.

In the *Gitārahasya* the writer says that there can not be Upāsanā unless the deity stands before the mind; and for the vision of the deity before the mind the qualities should be associated with the deity. Therefore though *Paramātman* is invisible to the external eyes. It should be experienced by the mental eye.[6]

For the satisfaction of the mind the position of worldly life of a seeker must be sufficiently good, therefore, the *Ṛgveda* expects the worldly prosperity by which the mind can satisfy its desires by allowing sense organs to enjoy this prosperity. The *Ṛgveda* says "*Indra*, confer on us fame and wealth".[6a]

Physical and mental satisfaction is necessary for progress in Upāsanā. The calm and quiet mind meditates on and progresses towards the *vijñānamaya kośa* where one's normal intellect improves and *prajñā* awakes.

(III) Intellectual Aspect of Upāsanā

Prajña is the higher state of intellect with which a person can perceive the cause and effects, relationship of the subtle things which he cannot understand in the normal state, we can call this state 'Pure Reason'. Intellect plays an important role in Upāsanā because unless and until a decision is taken man cannot work; therefore, for Upāsanā intellect takes a firm decision whether to start or to continue Upāsanā. Upāsanā done with blind faith may not be proper and the expected results may not come about. Hence a person compares his progress with the experiences of saints and those which are preached in the scriptures. By practising Upāsanā one's intellect becomes sharp, and one can solve one's problems. The awakening of *Prajñā* is similar to the awakening of *Kuṇḍalini*. After the awakening of *Kuṇḍalini* one can understand and analyse the mystical occurrences of phenomena and one sees with one's inner eye, *manaḥcakṣu* or *prajñācakṣu* or *divyaḍrsti* by means of which *Arjuna* saw the *Viśvarūpa* of *Śrikṛṣṇa*.[7]

In this state a person visualises different Gods who are said to be the presiding deities of certain parts of *Śriyantra* and which we can say are the different natural powers. These Gods are the deities of *Pañcamahābhūtas* and *Jñānendriyas* : Sensory organs, and the powers by which these objects work. For effectual work (*Kāryasiddhi*) many gods are mentioned according to *arthabhinnatā, karmabhinnatā, chandabhinnatā* and *sthānabhinnatā* (deities of different works ascribed to them, *Angadevatās*, i.e. *Vāyu*, the deity of smell; *Yama*, the god of death; *Sarasvati*, the goddess of poetry etc.) The separate names and forms are given to separate powers : Polytheism is due to this phenomenon.

Primarily the intellect is jaḍa object (matter), after awakening of *Prajñā* it becomes cetana (energy), that is why the knowledge which a man gets from physical experience; from ten sensory organs is the knowledge of *jaḍa* parts (matter), but the knowledge that which is above the matter-*jaḍa* is transcendental knowledge and a person can perceive it by *Prajña;* he can understand the cause and effect of the phenomenal occurrences. At this state a person can differentiate, between hallucination and real perception. This point is a beginning of real *sādhanā*. All the sādhakas have the same experience at this stage.

The *Puruṣa* is *kratumaya*[8] therefore an appropriate decision leads to the correct way.

(3) Forms of Upāsanā Practices

Each individual is different from the other in appearance, in thought, in likes and dislikes, etc. Therefore the forms of Upāsanā practices are multiple in number. The Upaniṣads have already stated at the very beginning: 'do not teach any particular doctrine'. They teach various doctrines suited to different people at different stages of spiritual evolution. They are not contradictory, but are based on the principle of individual fitness for receiving the truth (*adhikārabheda*). The aspirants are taken step by step to the ultimate truth, from dualism to qualified monism and finally to monism. "Thou art that" is the last word of the Upaniṣads in religion".[9]

We can analysed these practices in three divisions

(i) Nature worship, (ii) social religion (iii) Universal religion.

(I) Nature Worship—In the *Ṛgveda* we observe that the natural powers like Wind, Fire, Rain etc. are worshipped. Primitively (Primarily) man worships nature; therefore it is a tradition to worship all the objects in nature like tree, snake, bulls, lions, tigers, eagles etc. The person who cannot perceive the higher knowledge of God, worships Nature as God and asks Her for a son, cattle, victory etc. It is a belief that the God protects him and donates to him whatever is desired. We even find that the Gods in the tribal areas are furious; to protect these people, they assume formidable names and forms. Man is different from God and if man behaves properly, God will take care of him. This is the concept behind Nature worship.

The *Bhagavad Gītā* describes that the *Aśvatha* tree, *Vāsuki* serpent, etc. are the attributes of *Paramātman* and people worship these *vibhutis*[10] even today. They worship snakes on the day of *Nāgapañcami* (5th lunar day of the first half of the month of *Śrāvaṇa, śravaṇa* sacrifice prescribed by the *Gṛ. Sū.*); the bulls on the day of the dark moon of *Āṣādha* etc. We cannot say that Nature worship is a primitive worship because it still continues as immanent and living beings are the forms of one *Paramātman*.

(II) Social Religion : Man lives in society; therefore, God is also a social form; hence He protects and takes care of society. In the *Vedic* literature *Brahmaṇaspati* is worshipped for the well-being of society. The incarnations of *Viṣṇu* have appeared for the protection of society, hence *Rāma, Kṛṣṇa* are national heroes.

From the early belief that man is different from God, the next step of belief is that God is the parent or guardian of society; therefore, social work pleases God who can confer on the worker the fruits of good deeds. (*Madhu Vidyā*).

Nature worship and social worship are the forms of *Ācāradharma* of Upāsanā, this Upāsanā mainly depends on the behavior of man. This behaviour (*ācaraṇa*) includes worship, *pūjā*, prayers etc. In the society the ritualistic festivals like *Dipāvali, Holikā, Gaṇesa Caturthy, Drugāṣṭami* etc. are commonly observed. In this form of Upāsanā practice the Upāsanā becomes a social religion.

(III) Universal Religion : This is the highest form of Upāsanā practice. This is an Upāsanā of movable and immovable objects. The *Puruṣa Śukta* describes that the world is originated from the *Virtāṭ Puruṣa*, therefore, each and every particle of the universe is *Paramātman* and people work duly for him. This Upāsanā is not only an *Ācāradharma* or ritualistic social religion but this is a religion of saints.

An Upāsaka must ascend to this stage of Upāsanā going higher from Nature worship and society worship. This is called a *Viśvātmaka Bhāva*, oneness with the universe.

All these three forms finally unite in one form of *Viśvātmaka* worship when man experiences oneness with *Paramātma*. (Stage of *svarupa sākṣārkāra*). At this stage any particular doctrine is not followed and man becomes free from the dogmas.

(4) Methods of Upāsanā

After surveying the *Vedas* and the classical Sanskrit literature it can be said that the thread of Upāsanā is playing an important role throughout the literature. According to the *Vedic* approach the Universe is one fourth part of *Paramātman*, the *Puruṣa Śukta* says *"Padosya viśvābhūtani tripādasyāmṛtam divi"*[11] etc. *Iśāvāsyopaniṣad* also repeats the same in the verse *"Iśāvāsyamidamsarvam...."*[12] An aspirant worships this *Virāṭ Puruṣa* in many ways. Considering the vastness of the Upāsanā history in India, its richness and its different dimensions, it would be really difficult to classify the various forms and aspects of these Upāsanās or to understand the motives and the methodology behind them.

Broadly speaking they can be classified as the *Āsury* and *Daivi* Upāsanās considering the moral foundation behind them. They can be also classified into *vyaṣṭi pradhāna* : selfish or *Samaṣṭi Pradhāna*: for the betterment of humanity, considering their focus. Similarly they can be evaluated on the basis of the personal disposition of the agent or person who performs that Upāsanā i.e. *Tāmasa, Rājasa* or *Sāttvika*. The following classification will therefore emerge :

(1) *Āsuri Upāsanā* :
 (i) Tāmasa Upāsanā
 (ii) Rājasa Upāsanā
(2) *Daivi Upāsanā* :
 (i) Initial state of Upāsanā
 (ii) Rājasa (a) Upāsanā with selfish motive.
  (b) Vyaṣṭi Pradhāna Upāsanā or Upāsanā for Individual liberation
  (c) Samaṣṭi Pradhāna Upāsanā
(3) *Sāttvika : Nirupādhika or Parā Upāsanā.*

(1) Āsuri Upāsanā

(i) Tāmasa—There is a practice of Upāsanā which is done only for the selfish motive and which is harmful and of nuisance to society. In this type of Upāsanā the magic (*Yātuvidyā*) plays the role, the Upāsanā is performed superstitiously without any knowledge.

The *Vāmācāra* method in *Tantrās* has mystical effect. They are selfish intentions and are a nuisance to society, therefore these cults are defamed.

(ii) Rājasa—In the *Purāṇas* the *asuras* (demons) are shown as possessing the mystical powers gained by the worship of the deities and *yajñas*, these demons are called *Māyāvi* : the demons using powers of illusion. These mystical power are bad and they have today nearly disappeared. We can say that such (selfish) Upāsanā can not survive. The Upāsanā of *Śiva* performed by *Rāvaṇa*, the *yajña* performed by *Indrajit* to conquer *Rāma* and *Lakṣmaṇa* come under the purview of this Upāsanā.

(2) Daivi Upāsanā

(I) Initial state of Upāsanā

Man is curious about the Nature and its occurrences like cyclones, heavy rains, hot Sun, thundering cataracts, mountains, innumerable animal species etc. He fights with the diseases and death. He is afraid of all these phenomenal occurrences as well as he wants to control them. To fight with the destructive powers of Nature man prays to these powers as a part of his efforts to conquer them. These prayers are seen in the *Ṛgveda* in the *Rudra Sūktas, Indra Sūktas, Varuṇa sūktas* etc., a worshipper asks the deities of nature to control the massive objects. The Natural powers get the status of Gods.

Then there is a worship of the forefathers. i.e. *Pitṛpūjā*, this worship is called *Śrāddha, Pakṣa* etc., which has been referred to in the *Gṛ Sūtras*. There is the *Pitṛloka*, it is the residence of forefathers. *Aryamā* is the God of this loka.

Even today me find this worship in one or the other form, this state of Upāsanā is deeply rooted as has become a part of *Naimittika* : occasional duties.

(II) Rājasa : (a) Upāsanā with selfish motive

Each person wants a healthy and prosperous life, at the same time the wants to annihilate his enemies, who stand as obstacles in the way of his progress and better life. So many Upāsanās (*mantras, japa* etc.) are introduced to achieve this double purpose. To some extent the *Atharvaveda* is used for this purpose. In the *Ṛgveda* we find the sūktas for the cure of diseases like Tuberculosis.[13]

The *Yajña* performance is useful for this purpose of getting prosperity. *Yajña* and *havana* (oblation) were a common practice in the *Brāhmaṇa* period. *Yajña* is a scientific ceremony in which even one mistake is not accepted. *Yajña* is supposed to be the *Nārāyaṇa, Gitā* says *"Aham Krturaham yajñaḥ"*,[14] It is said in the *Athatvaveda* that a worshipper of *yajña* continuously worships the water and Light (*Teja*) (*Vaiśvānar Upāsanā*), the verse is, "*Ṛtavānam Vaiśvānaramṛtasya Jyotiṣpatim. Ajastram dharmamimah* " (*imahe* means to do *Upāsanā*[15].)

(b) Vyaṣti Pradhāna Upāsanā : Upāsanā for individual liberation: The *Māyā* concept plays dominant part in this stage, not Action (*karma*) but renunciation of Action can lead to the salvation is the philosophy accepted at this stage. If *jīva* wants to liberate itself, it must break all its ties with the worldly relations, which are illusory and temporary. The Ascetic life is essential to attain the emancipation. Every Action binds and throws *jīva* in the unending cycle of birth and death, therefore an aspirant must remain completely aloof from it. The *jīva* has nothing to do with the social, national or human activities or to take cognizance of good or bad changes. Individual liberation is important as compared with other things.

Four ways of self-realization are introduced for this individual liberation; vivid forms of the *Yoga, Dhyāna*, breathing exercise are prescribed to control the mind and the sense organs. It is necessary to drive the outgoing energy towards *Ātman* which is inside. So many unusual things are also done by sādhakas like cutting his tongue etc. These unusual practices give places to many disorders also. The urge of individual emancipation sometimes makes man insensitive. The emotions like love, compassion, pity, sympathy, forgiveness etc. are abandoned for remaining aloof from the society. *Samaṣṭi Dharma* is uncared for.

(c) Samaṣṭi Pradhāna Upāsanā or Upāsanā for the betterment of humanity: God permeates the world. Man has to understand it because he can not avoid any part of the world in his life. *Paramātman* is macrocosm and microcosm i.e. smallest than an atom and bigger than the biggest thing. The *Upaniṣad* says, "*Aṇoraṇiyān mahato mahiyān*[16]. As well as "*Mayāmtu prakṛtim viddhi māyinam tu maheśvaram. Tasyāvayavabhutaistu vyāptam sarvamidam jagat*".[17] It means : *Māya* is *Prakṛti (śakti)* of God and one who plays through this *Māyā* is Lord *Maheśa* Himself, and the world is permeated by Him.

It is not correct to divide the universe into parts as the outer one and the inner one because there is no place or time where *Paramātman* is not present. We have seen in the *Puruṣa sūkta* that

He pervadas all the things, animate and inanimate. To worship the world is Upāsanā at this stage. Service to humanity and the worship of Lord are not two separate things. The world is a small part of *Brahman*.

This view brings a change in Upāsanā. Individual liberation is for one's own sake. The approach of service to humanity given a social form to Upāsanā. *Upāsaka* becomes sympathetic to all the world. It is a religion of saints. The betterment of the world then becomes an objective. Action without any individual selfish motive is the devotion to *Paramātman*. Action does not stop but it becomes free from all desires, it is an Action with compassion, the *Mokṣa* becomes a living thing because the mind is free. It is a great achievement of the concept of Upāsanā. The individual soul merges with the *Samaṣṭi*, The *Upāsaka* experiences the lovely relationship with the world, it is not an escape from the worldly responsibilities but the duties are cleared joyfully. This Upāsanā does not divide the world into small castes and creeds and into nations but it crosses all the barriers and walls of artificial social groups. Each and every creature is *Brahman*, and the feeling of oneness is experienced at this stage, it is *Viśvāmaka Bhāva*.

(3) Sāttivika, Nirupādhika or Parā Upāsanā : To become one with the universe and to remain in the pure state of consciousness in bodiless existence is the form of this condition. It is a state of *Sadguru*. This state is the state where the mind, the intellect can not reach and which the words can not describe. It is "*Adṛśym, agrāhyam*"[18], it means it can not be seen and caught in hands," *na cakṣuṣā gṛhyate na vācā*"[19], it means it can not be seen by the eyes and the words can not describe it. It is the state of an enlightened person. Such a person gets the knowledge of the world, crosses the duality, becomes *anādi*, and *anānta*. His life is a divine life. We cannot say that Upāsanā is performed at this state in the true sense though such a person performs daily Upāsanā; the *Upāsya, Upāsaka* and *Upāsanā* are one and the same, it is a state of *Brahman* described in the *Kaṭha Up*.[20] This stage is experienced finally in the Upāsanā. This is Sat, because the soul exists for ever, this is Cit, because it is dynamic and not lifeless, this is *Ānand*, because there is nothing to obstruct its blissful state. The *Ṛṣi* says, "*Vedāhametam puruṣam mahāntam ādityavarṇah tamasā parastāt. Tameva viditvā atimṛtyumeti, Nānyaḥ pantaḥ vidyate ayanāya*"[21] It means. Know this *Puruṣa* : Pure existence which is

beyond darkness therefore effulgent like the Sun, Knowing Him, you will pass the death, there is no other way. The Upāsanā leads man to this stage slowly. The pure existence is nameless, formless, attributeless. The person who acquires this pure state speaks without speech, wanders without walking, works without action. He is perfect, therefore he can guide others; he is called Sadgurū. This stage can be called the *Parā* Upāsanā or *Nirupādhika Upāsanā*. To attain the *Sadguru-pada,* the state of perfection is the aim of Upāsanā, where the problems, tension do not exist, real svarūpa is known; it is the state of God-hood.

(5) Epistemology of Upāsanā

Upāsanā does not mean the path of emancipation followed blindly but physical, mental and intellectual experience is important. Therefore the *Saguṇa* worship, *Śāstrābhyāsa* and Intuitive experience are important.

(i) Saguṇa worship and *Sākṣātkāra*—The role of sense experience is important in the idol worship. The symbols are perceived as if the seeker is looking for the actual *Brahman*. Dr. Rādhikṛṣṇan says, "The symbols are to be regarded as Brahman and not vice versa. We can make progress only by looking upon an inferior object as symbolic of the superior and not vice versa. Since our objective is to get rid of the idea of diversity and see Brahman in everything."[22]

To begin with, a person starts his Upāsanā with worshipping an idol and then he thinks over continuously about the ways of Upāsanā, gets himself acquainted with the theories and practice of the ways of worship, stairs up by constant efforts by training his mind accordingly. *Rajoguṇa* and *Tamoguṇas* dissolve slowly and only the *Sattvaguṇa* remains. Gods have pure *Sattva Guṇa* (quality) hence *Saguṇa Sākṣātkāra* (vision) is possible. Dr. Rādhakṛṣṇan says, "Three modes of consciousness are recognized by the *Upaniṣads* : sense perception, logical understanding and intuitive insight".[23]

For the *Saguṇa* worship different Upāsanā cults are found. (*Pancamahādevatās*). Though these cults work separately and their forms are different, ultimately all goes to integral perception of *Brahman*. One may start Upāsanā unknowingly or knowingly one will reach ultimately the goal according to one's individual capacity sooner or latter[24].

(ii) Śāstrābhyāsa : In the matter of Upāsanā the intellectual satisfaction is important because the doubt will stop the worship or will lead it to a wrong way by blind faith; therefore, logical understanding is necessary. For this *Ṛṣis* show the way of *Śāstrābhyāsa*, the study of treatises like the *Vedas*, the *Upaniṣads*, the *Purāṇās*, the *Sūtras, Itihāsas* etc. A seeker has to study them and meditate upon them so that he can clearly understand their meaning. It was mentioned earlier, that knowledge (i.e. *Jñāna*), which is revealed by the *Vedānta* texts as the means of attaining final beatitude, and denoted by the terms of meditation (*dhyāna*), worship (*Upāsanā*) etc., is to be frequently pursued. This meditation, it was said, is of the nature of continued succession of remembrance.[25]

Chāndogya Up. says, "*Nāmabrahma ityupāste*", *Mano brahmetyupāsita*", "*Āditye brahma ityādeśaḥ*"[26]. The meditation of these symbols of God, i.e. name mind and the sun as *Brahman* is prescribed. The awakening of *Prajñā* helps the seeker to go deep in the reasoning. The doubts disappear and the further progress becomes easy.

(iii) Intuitive Experience : When a person progresses to *Sattvaguṇa* he perceives many powers of *Nature, Universe* and *Brahman*. This universal intellectual perception is also called Sākṣātkāra. With regular Upāsanā a seeker obtains virtues like truthfulness, simplicity, etc. He becomes capable of finding out the answer to the main question which was raised at the beginning of *Upāsanā*. i.e. who am I?, the meaning of *So'ham*. After various experiences taken by the physical body, and the knowledge earned by the *Śāstrābhyāsa*, the line of thought becomes firm, *Śraddhā*, (faith) becomes stronger and a *Sādhaka*, a seeker, insists on proceeding to take intuitive experience.

In this consciousness the *Upāsaka* lives in happiness, spiritual ecstasy; for him, the world is a play of *Brahman*, therefore it is an illusion (*Māyā*). *Caitanya* is the original form of man, he feels happy when he approaches it. Therefore Upāsanā is necessary which leads a man to this state of Consciousness, Light (*Teja*) and Bliss.

The worshipper of *Brahman* when looks inward, he experiences that what is in him is in the outside world, (which is said in *Marāṭhi* language *"Piṇḍi te Brahmāṇḍi"*,) then he himself becomes his *Gurū* and disciple both. He understands that *Ātma* is

Gūru and *Gurū* is *Ātma*. This is the state of *Advaita. Saint Jñāneśvara* describes this state as *"Kimbahunā carācara āpaṇa ci jāla"*[27] The *Upāsaka* experiences the `*dvaitādvaita vilakṣaṇa state,*' he himself becomes God and worships Him. There is no difference between *Upāsya, Upāsaka* and *Upāsanā*. He is a released soul. The realisation or the state of *Mokṣa* is an original state of the *Ātman*, it is not a different object or a place. *"Mokṣasya na hi vasosti na grāmāntar-mevaca. Ajñānahṛdaya granthināśo mokṣa iti smṛtaḥ."* says *Śivagitā*[28].

The descriptions of a released soul which are found in the *Upaniṣad* and *Gītā* are the descriptions of these men who have experienced the intuitive insight.[29]

(6) Concept of God in Upāsanā

A seeker wants to start an *Upāsanā* but the question he faces is whom he should worship. Naturally he worships God but he does not know the nature of God, the relation of God and the world and the relation of God and men. At first he supposes that God is transcendent, he himself is different from God, then he comes to know that God is transcendent as well as immanent. God can take forms. Then he understands that all is God and God is only immanent and ultimately God is everything and everything is God; there is oneness of all deities. (deism, theism, Pantheism, Polytheism and Absolutism). The nature of God; and the relation between God and the world and God and man, these points are briefly discussed belows—

(i) Nature of God—God is the *Upāsya* deity. The *Upāsya* deities are innumerable. One may adore a stone coloured with vermillion (*sendure miśrita*), without any particular figure, name, virtues etc. it is very innocent worship; here, God is only a transcendental being. According to *Upāsaka* that stone god can give him what he desires, that is his *śraddhā*, faith.

Some *Upāsakas* adore an idol, a particular figure and virtues are attested to it, they worship the deities according to the tradition perpetuated by their ancestors (*Kulācāra*).

Some seekers accept a person who is a saint, like *Jñaneśvara, Kabir* etc. and worship him according to a particular system and consider him as incarnation of *Brahman*, God is transcendental immanent is this case, he can take forms for the welfare of *Upāsakas*.

In the *Vedas*, God is he who illuminates, (*dyotanāt devāḥ*), who is effulgent, self-sufficient, powerful, protects all good and destroys all bad things. He is the giver of anything which is asked for by the worshipper. The *Vedic Gods* are *Indra, Agni, Mitra, Varuṇa, Brahmaṇaspati, Rudra*, and the goddesses are *Uṣā, Sandhyā, Rātri, Aditi, Ilā* etc. All these Gods live in the plane of higher consciousness named '*svarloka*.' These gods get oblations poured into the *Yajña* from the Earth through *Agni*; because of his evaporating power, he is able to evaporate all things and gods accept these evaporated objects through the air.

In the *Purāṇas* (mythology) the number of *Vedic* Gods are multiplied, *Brahmā, Viṣṇu, Maheśa* are the three main Gods; *Brahmadeva* creats, *Viṣṇu* protects and *Maheśa* destroys the world. The other gods have been given different duties; for example the Gods of directions, i.e. *Yama* is placed for south direction who protects that direction, the aṣta *Vasus*, the twelve *Ādityas*, eleven *Rudras*, deities of nine planets and various other minor deities have separate functions assigned to them. If they have any difficulty, they take guidance from *Brahmā, Viṣṇu, Maheśa*. The Goddesses are the names and forms of inherent Śakti of *Brahman* i.e. *Sarasvati, Lakṣmi, Pārvati* and other minor goddesses are the forms of this *Śakti*.

The *Vedas* gave the status of God to father, mother, Guide (*ācārya*), guests (*Mātṛdevobhava* etc.). Therefore Upāsanā of elders becomes the Upāsanā of God and the person can get real knowledge. Therefore the Pativratā (women who are dedicated to their husbands) ladies like *Sati Anasūyā* have the knowledge of *Brahman* and the saint *Puṇḍalika* of *Mahārāshtra* welcomes God *Pāṇḍurange (Viṣṇu)* at his door steps as a result of his service to his father and mother.

Gurū is worshipped as the form of *Brahman. Saint Jñāneśvara* highly praised his *Guru Nivṛttināthа* as *Brahman. Guru Datta* is a united form of *Brahmā, Viṣṇu, Maheśa* and He is the Guide of all Guides.

In the Upaniṣads God is *Nirguṇa, Nirākāra*, nameless and formless-but for the sake of upāsanā attributes like *Vaiśvānara, Omkāra, Paryanka* are prescribed. (*Up. Vidyās*).

We can describe the nature of God thus: God is *Nirguṇa Nirākāra (Vedānta), Saguṇa Nirākara (Upaniṣadic Vidyas), Saguṇa, Sākāra (Paurāṇic),* only *Sākāra* (coloured stones), *Nature* (animal, trees etc.).

(ii) God and the World : In the *Puruṣa Sūkta* the science of the evolution of the world is given as the animates and inanimates (*Sāśana* and *Anaśana*) have originated from the one fourth part of *Virāt Brahman*. The movable and immovable world is one fourth vision of God; therefore, each part and particle is *Brahman*. Hence the meditation of the thought is possible that the god is inherent in the atom; therefore, everything in the world is God. *Śankarācārya* calls it illusion because the world is not the real nature of God and it is a projection of one's own mind; therefore it is a false perception. He says *"Jñāte tattve kaḥ sanāsraḥ"*.[30]

The *Upaniṣads* says that God is not happy when he is alone '(*Sa ekāki na ramate*)' so he divides himself into two He Himself and his concert : śakti and his śakti creates the world. The world is a combination of matter and energy; *Agni* is the form of energy, *caitanya*; therefore the living force is called *Agni-Vaiśvānara* in human beings[31]. *Prāṇa* is form of *Vāyu* that is powerful. In the *Vedas* the greatest power is ascribed to Indra, so *Indra* and *Agni* are the main deities. Every animal species have power and *Agni* : warmth of body and strength. If the warmth disappears the animals die. The immovable world is a form of *Vāyu*, matter which has existence, that is, *sat* quality of *Brahman*; in animal species, existence and consciousness are the qualities of *Brahman* and in Human beings the consciousness is in improved form; therefore, man can get the highest Bliss. He can perceive that the name and forms of the outer world and the spirit behind them is the same that is in him.

Svāmi Śivānanda says, "*Male-Purusa; ;Ātma, Brahman; Śiva* signify knowledge. *Female-Prakrti; Manas; Māyā; Śakti* signify power. When knowledge and power combine together and merge into one another there is the manifestation of Bliss. Power is only the other half and appearance of knowledge, and as long as these two separate themselves there is imperfection and pain"[32].

The world is manifested with the traid (*Trik*); *Sattva, Raja, Tama* is a '*trik*' which is a base of the world. Three Gods, three *lokas*; Earth, Heaven, Space, are famous. *Maitrāyani Up.* gives a good description of the traid as "the letters a,u,m are the '*bhāsvati*' body of *Brahman*; male, female, and neuter together is the genderal body (*lingavatitanu*) of Him; *Agni, Vāyu, Āditya* is also the *bhāsvati* body. *Brahmā, Rudra, Viṣṇu* is the authoritative (*adhipativati*) body, *Ṛk, Yajus, Sāma* is the scientific (*Vijñanavati*) body; *bhuḥ, bhuvaḥ, svaḥ* is the locational (*lokavati*) body; *bhūta* (past), *bhuvya* (present), *bhaviṣyat* (future) is the body of Time (*kālavati*), *Prāṇa, Agni,* the *Sun* is the Breath body (*Prāṇavati*); Food, Water, the Moon is the liquid body; the *Gārhapatya, Dākṣiṇāgni* and *Āhavaniya Agnis* is body of entrance (*Mukhavati*); intellect, mind and ego is the living body (*Caitanyavati*); and *Prāṇa, Apāna, Vyāna* is body of *Prāṇa (Prāṇavati)*. And all these are the forms of *Prajāpati*"[33].

The world is the *Samaṣti* form of God. Therefore the deities of directions, of planets, of *Pancamahā-bhutas* etc. are prescribed as *Upāsya; Paramātmā* is in the *samaṣti* form. God and the world are related in this sense. Therefore *Nature* worship is practised.

(iii) God and Man—Man is in *Vyaṣṭṭ* form i.e. individual entity; therefore he is the *Upāsaka* of *Samaṣṭi* god. The relation of God and Man is that of *Upāsya* and *Upāsaka* in the beginning. Any person cannot be an *Upāsaka*.

There is a conflict between Realism, materialism (*Padārthavāda*) and spiritualism (*Adhyātmavāda*). The Realists says that the vision of the universe (*dṛṣya*) is the main constituent of the world and the consciousness is its by-product. The consciousness (*catianya*) originates form the physical world, matter and it cannot be thought about separately; therefore the Upāsanā etc. are only ideas and they have no value. On the other hand the spiritualists thinks, that the consciousness is the main constituent, the *Gitā* says, *'bhutānāmasmi centanā'*[34], and the physical or the material world is the secondary form of *caitanya*. The first entity is *caitanya* and the world evolves from it. The real nature of man is consciousness and existence, therefore the bliss can be attained, by *Upāsanā* and *Sādhanā*.

Generally each and every one wants to live comfortable life following the principal of *Cārvāka*. But when a person faces the difficulties which are divided in three types namely, *Adibhautika*, which occurs by natural calamity like earthquake, floods etc. Adhidaivata is like a fatal accident, bankruptcy etc., and *Adhyātmika* is in the form of diseases and other internal problems; he starts thinking about himself and the world around him over which he has no control. This state of consciousness is called *'baddha'*, who thinks that he is caught in the *samsāra* (world affairs). The others who are not aware of their bondage do not understand their limitations. One who thinks about his bondage starts searching for the ways of release; then one is called *'mumukṣu'*. Then the person looks for someone who knows the way of realisation.

In this state a person may follow a wrong guide in blind faith. It is difficult to choose a real saint who is *'Śrotriya* : i.e. who has studied the *śāstrs;* and *Brahmaniṣṭha*: who has realised the state of Bliss.

The *'mumukṣu"* starts his own *Upāsanā* which is traditionally followed in his house and *upāsanā* of his *iṣṭa* (preferred) deity. Generally the upāsanā of one of the five great Gods (*pancha mahādevatās*) is followed. Gradually he comes in contact with his *Gurū,* takes a *dikṣā* (initiation) and becomes an upāsaka of a particular deity, cult, process. He has his *Gurū, Sampradāya* and *deity*.

He becomes a *Sādhaka* as he follows one of the four *Sādhanā* ways during *upāsanā*. Slowly he passes through all the stages of *Upāsanā*. Existence, Consciousness and Bliss is the nature of *Brahman,* hence the world consists of these qualities and man is able to acquire them through constant efforts.

Man is psycho-physical animal. Psychology affects body and bodily disorders affect mind; therefore the steadiness of both is required for upāsanā and this steadiness is acquired through the faith in God. Man has all the qualities of an animal but the way of behaviour (*'Dharma'*) is his distinguishing quality. Therefore he can live a life strictly leading the way of behaviour of *Paramapuruṣārtha* i.e. *Mokṣa,* following the *Dharma, Artha* and *Kāma* with the instructions of *śastra. (Kalpasūtra)*. When he gets *Mokṣa*-summon bonum of life, he is called *'Siddha'*. After that he can lead and guide other *upāsakas* and he is called *'Sadgurū'*.

For the travelling of man from the stage of a *baddha* to the stage of a *Sudgurū,* faith (*'Śraddhā'*) in *Paramātman* is necessary by which he remains in contact with *Brahman*. *Śraddhā* is defined in the *Sanksrit* literature as under :

(1) *"Nigamācāryarvākyeṣu bhaktiḥ śraddheti viśrutā"*. It means the love and faith in the words of *Nigama* and Guide. is *'śraddhā'*.

(2) *"Guruvedāntavākyeṣu buddhiryā niścayātmikā. Sattvamityeva sā śrddhā"*. It means the firm faith of the intellect in the truthfulness of the words of Guide and *Vedānta,* is *'śraddhā'*.

(3) *"Sāstrasya guruvākyasya satvabuddhyavadhāraṇam sā śraddhā"*, it means the faith that the words of *śāstra* (treatise) and spiritual preceptor are true.

(4) *"Sraddhānām guruvedāntavekyeṣu ativa viśvāsaḥ"*, it means, *'śraddhā'* is complete confidence in the sentences written in the *Vedānta* and expounded by the *gurū*.

(5) *"Śraddhā vai sūryasya duhitā"*, *Śraddhā* is the daughter of the sun.

(6) *Śraddhā* is used as the synonymous for *jñāna* in *Sānkhyāyena Gr. Sū.*[35]

(7) Concept of Religion as Implicit in Upāsanā

What we call as religion is the traditional way of behaviour. The places of pilgrimage, ceremonial days, vows, expiations, common prayers, come under the word 'religion'. Religious life and social life are united with each other. Though people who are the worshippers of the same deity and followers of the same methodology come together and make a separate society or community, the subject of Upāsanā remains untouched by social effects because it is an Upāsanā of Impersonal Absolute.

Man wants an ideal; an ideal picture, an ideal character, an ideal personality whom he can follow and can progress to virtuousness, imperishability, happiness, light and bliss; therefore, at the very beginning he chooses idol worship (*Paurāṇic Upāsanā*); and loves the personality and qualities of the idol and slowly reaches to impersonal, blissful state of *Brahman*. A man choose any deity which he likes; hence the religion in Upāsanā is not confined to the cults, or to the external behaviour of persons or of community; but it is a religion which gives every one in the world, the happiness, calmness, welfare and bliss and which shows a man a way of self realisation. It is a universal religion : *Viśvātmaka dharma* because each one has the authority of *upāsanā*.

The first step of the person who wants to do *upāsanā* is to follow the strictness in behaviour in taking food, doing work, sleeping, wandering in one's daily routine. He has to follow *Nitya* (daily) and *Naimittika* (occasional) acts which are prescribed in the *Karmakāṇḍa* of the *Purvamimāmsā*. He has to follow the instructions of the *Vedas*, and to follow the path of *Karma* or Action according to *Śāstras* and not as per his own views. It is called a *Codanālakṣaṇa dharma*. An *Upāsakā* lives his life with austerity.

The second step is to worship Gods. The worship of *Pañcamahādevatas* is prescribed for him, his worship is not only a mechanical work but physical, mental and intellectual aspects are involved in it. The worship of national heroes like *Rāma* and *Kṛṣṇa* is also involved in this religion because the *Upāsaka* has chosen his way of living life and it is his confidence that if he goes by this way he will reach his goal. This religion is called *Dhāraṇālakṣaṇa dharma*.

The religion in upāsanā has the third highest state in which the upāsaka gets the worldly happiness as well as salvation because it is *Abhyudaya niśśreyas dharma. Prayers* in the *Vedas* and *Vedānta* philosophy show this religion which can be followed by any worshipper. In the praise of *Pavamāna sūktas*, which are recited in the *Viṣṇu* worship, it is said that "He (reciter) who knows the continuity of the *Pavamāna* lives all his days, he does not die before his time, he becomes rich in cattle, he obtains offsprings"[36]. With this prosperous life the emancipation is expected in the popular stotras of *Pañcamahādevatas* and in the doctrines of the *Upaniṣads* (*Upaniṣad Vidyā*).

The upāsanā is not limited to any of the cult or for any of the community but it is for the universal benefit and bliss. *Viśvakalyāṇa* is expected in the *Ṛgveda*. The religion in *Upāsanā* is a universal religion for movables and even for immovables in whom caitanya is hidden. It is a religion of all the saints.

(8) Mysticism in Upāsanā

Man tries to continue his work only when he gets expected results. The Upāsanā is an activity, a work which leads to the higher forms of knowledge which are experienced during Upāsanā. the part of siddhis is a mystical part in Upāsanā. We have already seen the results of *mantra* recitation, *japa, prāṇāyāma, mudrās* which give mystical experiences. The *Tāntrika* Upāsanā is closer to mysticism. In this part the role of the unconscious mind is important. *Tāntrika* worship and spiritualisation are two aspects of this mysticism.

(i) Tāntrika Worship : We have seen the *Kaulācāra* and *Vāmācāra* in this worship. *Kaulācāra* is *Dakṣiṇācāra* which leads to spiritual purity but *Vāmācāra* is only the satisfaction of the senses and it may make a person as a nuisance to the society, hence it is not considered as a higher form of *Upāsanā* but in *Yantra* worship there is no possibility of becoming a wrong aspirant. The *yantra* is a mystical diagram, the mantras have mystical meaning and the experiences are beyond the comprehension of an ordinary person. *Śankarācārya, Bhāskarāya* and other revered persons followed *yantra* worship.

Now-a-days method of worship is combined—it is *Vedic* plus *Tāntrika*. The stotras like *Viṣṇusahaśrānama, Lalitāsahaśranāma*, and other popular prayers have an astonishing effect on the aspirant.

But the pure mind and *Parā* bhakti are more desirable than mystical experiences. Hence, a seeker should not stop at this stage, but he must go ahead to spiritualism, to pure holy mind.

(ii) Spiritualisation : It is an internalisation of emotions and feelings and their transfer into the pure mind which is devoid of passions. The six vices, '*Ṣaḍripus*' like avarice, hatred, egoism, wrath, bewilderment, envy are the impediments or enemies in the way of spiritualisation, therefore only the mystical experiences and the visions of god are not sufficient for the progress towards awakening of the soul. The subjugation of all inner desires is necessary; it helps the mind to enter into the state of Parābhakti where one experiences *Parāśānti* and *Parama* knowledge. *Svarūpa Sākṣātkāra* is the highest state in the spiritualisation of the mind. The definitions of *Sākṣātkāra* are given by W.R. Inj in his book '*Mysticism in Religion*'. In brief, we can say-The unification, without any suspicion of self and God is *Sākṣātkāra*. To know the Divine nature, the real nature of things and experience unification with them is *Sākṣātkāra*. At this stage the reason cannot explain it. It is a faultless perception of the self and the universe which can be called Integral Mysticism. The soul is now awakened.

W. Winslow Hall gives twenty recorded cases of illuminated persons in his book 'Recorded Illuminates'. He has classified these persons in four groups, namely Sensory Group, Intellectual group, Emotional group and Religious group.[37]

These spiritual people express the qualities like knowledge, purity, calmness and bliss.

(9) Philosophy of Upāsanā

In Sanskrit literature *Prasthānatrayi* (three groups of the books) are the main scriptural treatises of Upāsanā. *Prasthānatrayi* means *Upaniṣads*, the *Vedānta—sutras* and the *Bhagavadgītā*. The

Upaniṣads are called the *Śṛtis*. The main *Upaniṣads* are ten in which the *Aaitreya* and the *Kauṣitaki* belong to the *Ṛgveda;* the *Iśa* and the *Bṛhadāraṇyaka* to white (*Śukla) Yajus*, the *Kaṭha*, the *Taittiriya* and the *Śvetāśvatara* to black (*Kṛṣṇa*) *Yajus*, the *Kena* and the *Chāndogya* to the *Sāmaveda*, the *Muṇḍaka*, *Praśna* and the *Māṇdukya* to the *Atharvaveda*. The *Brahmasūtras* are aphoristic, they are called the *Sūtra* literature, *Bhagadgītā* is called *smṛti* literature. The *Pravṛtti* (Action), *Abhyudaya (Preyas)*; and *Nivrtti (Mokṣa)-Nissreyas (Śreyas)* ways are prescribed in this *Prasthānatrayi*.

The other books of Upāsanā in Sanskrit literature are the *Purāṇas* in which eighteen are major ones and the *Śrimadbhāgavatam* is the greatest. Other *purānas* are numerous; they are minor *Purāṇas*, like the *Vaiṣṇava*, the *Śaiva*, the *Brahma*, and the *Yoga Purāṇas*, in which the technique of worship is prescribed.

These *Purāṇas* are called as *Āgama* literature; the *Tāntrika* works are also called *Āgamas*. The nature of *Āgama* works is stated in *Vārāhi Tantra*. The verse is, *'Sṛṣtisca pralayascaiva devatānām yathārcanam, sādhanam caiva sarveśām, puraścaranameva ca, ṣaṭkarma sādhanam caiva dhyānyogascaturvidhah. Saptabhirlakṣa-nairyuktamāgama tad vidurbudhaḥ"*.[38] It means the *Āgama* work has seven characteristics namely

(1) Knowledge of *Śṛṣṭi*, (the world), its evolution etc.
(2) Discussion about the deluge.
(3) Worship of Gods.
(4) Equipments, processes etc.
(5) The method of recitation.
(6) Six action like *śāntikarma*, *vājikaraṇa* etc.
(7) Four types of *Dhyānayoga*.

With the *Nigama* and *Āgama*, the books on *Itihāsa*, (history) are important. The *Rāmāyaṇa* and the *Mahābhārata* are books of history. The books like "*Yogavāsiṣṭha*" are important in *Upāsanā*. The philosophy of *Upāsanā* is stated in *Nigama*, *Āgma* works and their blending in the *Bhakti* tradition is popularised by saints.

In the *Indraprāṇādhikaraṇa* of the *Brahmasūtra*, there are three types of Upāsanās, namely

(1) Upāsanā of attributed Brahman : *Śariravisiṣṭha Brahma*.
(2) The Upāsanā of living beings : *Jiva Sṛṣṭi*
(3) Upāsanā of self : *Svarūpa*.

In this chapter the jiva is called Indra and matter (*jaḍa*) is called *Prāṇa*.[39] The third chapter of *Brahma Sū*. further says that the progress of *Upāsanā* has steps like (1) The knowledge of the nature, power and wealth (*Sattā, Vaibhava*) of God; (2) Surrender : *Prapatti*; (3) The contact : *Anusandhāna*; (4) Love of God (5) The nature of working of the welfare of others (*upakāravṛtti*) and (6) Intensity of unity with God. The duration of upāsanā is not limited for a few days but it is continued till death[40]. In the opinion of Brahmadatta, like the *Vedas* which prescribed *Karmakāṇḍa*, the *Upaniṣads* prescribe Action : (*Karma*). But this action is not a process of worldly action but it is a kind of action in *upāsanā* process. The Upāsanā is also called *Bhāvanā* (feelings).[41]

In upāsanā man follows an austere life and observes *Brahmacarya*; by this the divine energy improves in him. This divine energy destroys the uneasiness (*cancalatā*) of mind, the breath becomes steady and the mind becomes stable, fixes itself on the goal and meditation becomes natural.[42] The effect of upāsanā is to meet God, and when upāsanā becomes natural; the actual visual perception of God i.e. *Saksatkāra* is possible.[43]

God is the essence of knowledge and work i.e. *Jñānamaya* and *Karmamaya*. *Jñāna* is light (*teja*) and it is a continuous process; work is limited. The Knowledge (*Jñāna*) in God is not overshadowed by *Karma* but Knowledge in man is covered by work; when his limited, covered knowledge becomes uncovered by upāsanā, the real Knowledge of *Brahman* springs and he is being released from bondage. For this knowledge a man has to work for the sake of duty (with renunciation) then his mind becomes pure, and the pure mind worships *Brahman* better than the mind which possesses the qualities of *Rajas* and *Tamas*.[44]

The difference in karma does not mean the difference in aim. Therefore the four *Puruṣārthas* i.e. *Dharma, Artha, Kāma* and *Mokṣa* leads to the same goal of emancipation.[45] The four *Āśramas* are designed for the achievement of the four *Puruśārthas*. In *Brahmacarya* and *Gṛhasthāśrama Dharma, Artha* and *Kārma* are fulfilled and in *Vānaprastha* and *Sansyāsa Mokṣa* is to be attained.[46] Therefore, *Karma* and *Jñāna* go by hand in hand. The four varṇas are also expected to perform the obligatory work because each one is entitled to its rights and obligations. By performing one's proper duties one will attain the same state. A *śudra*, through performance of his own duties could become a *Brāhmaṇa* and attain Salvation, *Mukti, Nirvāṇa, Svarga* etc. as any *Brāhmaṇa* practising several austerities does.[4]

In upāsanā the aim is important; therefore to obtain the real knowledge *Gurū*, (Instructor, guide) is necessary. Emancipation is the aim (*śadhya*) and upāsya and upāsanā are the means (*sādhana*). When the *upāsaka* practises his penance for that aim, it is like trading. In *Bhakti, Sādhya* and *Sādhanā* are not different. *Bhakti* is for its own sake and, not for the *Mokṣa*. This highest state of *Bhakti* is experienced in the state of real knowledge. Sometimes knowledge makes a man egoistic and this is a danger in the *Jñāna Mārga*, but in *Bhakti* it is not. So when the upāsaka becomes a real *Bhakta* he enjoys worship of God. It seems that he is in the dualistic state but in this position the duality is not split, it remains as it is. This type of *Bhakti* is called *Parātpara Saguṇa Bhakti;* The qualified (*Saguṇa Brahman*) is not in relation to Non qualitative or impersonal, but it is Eternal (*Nitya*), *Sanātana* (ancient), and *Svayambhu* (self-created). Therefore, it is unborn, imperishable, beyond Time, intellect and mind. His name and form is not an illusion. The *Gurū* leads a disciple to this highest *Bhakti*, so he is called *Prabrahman* in *Gurugītā*.

It is a matter of controversy whether *Brahman* is active or inactive (*Sakriya* or *Niṣkriya*). But *Brahman* is independent and has no bondage; therefore, if *Brahman* remains active and cannot become inactive; as well as, *Brahman* remains only inactive and does not become active, then it is not independent, it is subject to bondage. Therefore it is found that in *Upāsanā* that *Brahman* can expose itself in the form which *upāsaka* has in his mind. From this point of view the Gods are numerous and different in names and forms because the *upāsaka* loves a particular form of the formless Brahman. The *Upāsakā* knows that *Rāma, Kṛṣṇa, Datta, Devi* and all Gods are not separate but they are only Brahman and nothing else; not only that but God is all and all is God.

In this sense it is said that the *Bhakta* possesses *Paramātman*. *Śankarācārya* in all the stotras of *Saguṇa* refers to the same unity of all Gods. His *Māyāvāda* is based on this point that what we see in the world is not the perfect view of *Brahman* and it is only a projection of the mind, so it is untrue. The world is the false perception of *Brahman* and *Brahman* is the only truth. *Brahman* is not only *Saguṇa* or *Nirguṇa*, it is beyond both the states. *Saint Jñāneśvara* also speaks the same that god is not only *Saguṇa* or

Nirguṇa, but both and it is beyond, and the world evolves from its consciousness Its—*cidvilāsa*.

To experience this spiritual ecstasy is the aim of upāsanā. How we find the world will depend upon our capacity of perception. At the highest state upāsaka has the faultless perceptions of the self and the universe which is called "*Svarūpa Sākṣākāra*." In upāsanā the devotee becomes *Sat, Cit, Ānand rūpa* and serves the same *Brahman*.

In this way the philosophy of upāsanā has three streams : One is *Naigamic* tradition which is manly based on behaviour (*Ācārapradhāna* and *Smṛti Pradhāna*) the second is *Āgamic* tradition which is based on techniques, science of worship, (*Tantrapradhāna*) and the third is *Bhakti* tradition in which both traditions are mixed and the proper use of *Nigamas* and *Āgamas* is followed. The upāsanā includes the theory (*Siddhānta*, Philosophy) and practice (way of behaviour i.e. *Religion*). Integral Mysticism (*Svarūpa Sakṣātkāra-Sādhya*) is the, result of upāsanā.

The concept of Upāsanā in *Sanskrit* Literature is broad, it is the Upāsanā of *Nirupādhika* : attributeless entity performed by *Upādhibadha Jīva*, who has limited powers. Any thing either animate or inanimate can do this Upāsanā. Inanimate world has less power, intellectuality, and in the animate world man is superior by his brain power than other species, therefore Upāsanās are meant for him. The attributeless *Brahman* is supposed to be with attributes, *Saguṇa, Sākara* for the sake of Upāsanā but this concept is prescribed for the benefit of the universe. The *Vedas* want the welfare of the Universe, (*Viśvakalyāṇa*) and an *Upāsaka* has the capacity to follow them. *Saint Jñāneśvara* asks for '*Pasāyadana*' (fruit : result of his *vāk-yajña*) to *Viśvātmaka* God and not to any form with attributes. The *Vedic* religion becomes a universal religion from this point of view.

Thus the concept of Upāsanā in Indian Culture presents before us all the aspects of human religion, tribal, social and universal; the nature worship, the worship of the ancestors, deities etc. The aim behind all these seems to be to lift the human aspiration from the earthly gains to the eternal and infinite happiness which is called *Mokṣa*; therefore, the Upāsanā is a path to human perfection, an instrument to *Mokṣavidyā*. India may be divided by rites and rituals, by cults and customs, but behind all there is a one continuous stream of spiritual urge to live the life divine. The saints and the seers have shown that man is capable of living this divine life on the Earth. India's cultural heritage is built by such great persons, who personified the divinity. The learning of the *Śāstras (Śāstra Praciti)*, the precept of the preceptors (*Gurū Praciti*), ultimately leads to divine experience (*Ātma Praciti*). This divine life is the highest goal of human existence and Upāsanā is the beacon light of the way to lead that life.

References

1. Ṛgveda—10-10-121-2.
2. *Ibid*—18-122-3.
3. Bhagavadgitā—17th-ch.
4. Saṅgita Ratnākara—3-1.
5. Bṛhadāraṇyaka Up. 4-4. 3-45.
6. Gitārahasya—page—185. by Lokamānya Ṭiḷaka.

6a. Ṛgveda—1.9 7.

7. Bhagavadgitā—11.8.
8. Chāndogya Up.—3.
9. Brahmasūtra, Śribhāṣya—Sūtra—II-III-III-7.
10. Bhagavadgitā—10ch.
11. Puruṣasūkta—10.121.
12. Iśa Up. 1.
13. Ṛgveda—X.12.11.12.
14. Bhagavadgitā—10-16.3-10; 11
15. Atharvaveda—6-36-1.
16. Śvetāśvatara Upaniṣad—3.20
17. *Ibid* 4.10.
18. Muṇḍaka Upaniṣad—1.1.6.
19. *Ibid* 3.1.8.
20. Kaṭha Upaniṣad 3.15.
21. Śvetāśvatara Upaniṣad 3.8.
22. The Brahmasūtra. The Philosophy of Spiritual Life-P. 527 by Dr. Radhakṛṣṇan.
23. *Ibid*—p. 105.
24. Śiva Mahimn Stotra.
25. Brahmasūtra. Śribhāṣya.
26. Chāndogya Up. VII-1-5.III-18-1. III-19-1.
27. Jñāneśvari—10-19-213.
28. Śivagitā—13-32.
29. Muṇḍakopaniṣad—3-2-9. Gita-3-28, 18-54. 2-72. 5-55 to 72.12-12 to 20 14-22 to 27
30. Bhajagoviṅdam—stotra—10
31. Gitā—15-14.
32. Sādhanā—p. 419. by Swami Śivānanda.
33. Vaidic Vijñāna aur Bhāratiya Sanskriti p. 7-by Girdharaśarma Caturvedi.
34. Bhagavadgitā. 10-22.
35. Divyāmṛtadhārā—Vo. 2 & 3. p. 123. by Babamaharaja Arvikar.

36. Taittiriya Samhitā—III-2-1. Rg-4-3-13-5 also expresses the rich life.
37. Recorded Illuminates—by W. Winsolw Hall. M.D. London. The D.W. Danial Co. Ltd. Forty Great Russel Street. W.S.I.
38. Dharmāce Tattvajñāna, p. 163. by—Dr. J.V. Joshi.
39. Brahmasūtra 29. by Ananataprasād Trikamalala Srivastava.
40. *Ibid.*
41. Bhāratiya Sanskriti our Sādhanā Vol ii. p. 108—By Copinath Kaviraja.
42. Bhāratiya Sanskriti our Sādhanā—Vol ii. p. 108—By Gopinath Kaviraja.
42. Bhāratiya Sanskriti our Sādhanā—Vol. II. p-392. by Gopinath Kaviraja.
43. *Ibid* p. 488.
44. *Ibid*-p. 54.
45. *Ibid*-p. 92.
46. *Ibid*-p. 116.
47. History of Indian Literature—vol-iii. M. Witernitze. by Silvati Ketkar.

English Transliteration Code for Sanskrit Phonems

A	a	अ	as	in	Cup
Ā	ā	आ	as	in	arm
I	i	इ	as	in	sit
Ī	ī	ई	as	in	see
U	u	उ	as	in	put
Ū	ū	ऊ	as	in	too
E	e	ए	as	in	bed
Ai	ai	ऐ	as	in	fight
O	o	ओ	as	in	owner
Au	au	औ	as	in	out, above
Ḥ	ḥ	अ:	as	in	bird
Ṛ	ṛ	ऋ	as	in	Sanskrit
K	k	क्	as	in	car
Ḳh	ḳ	ख्	as	in	Khrist
G	g	ग्	as	in	eager
Gh	gh	घ्	as		g + h
Ṅ	ṅ	ङ्	as	in	sing
C	c	च्	as	in	chin
Ch	ch	छ्	as		c + h
J	j	ज्	as	in	join
Jh	jh	झ्	as	in	measure
Ñ	ñ	ञ	as		y + n
Ṭ	ṭ	ट्	as	in	Tin
Ṭh	ṭh	ठ्	as		t + h

Ḍ	ḍ	ड्	as	in	do
Dh	dh	ढ्	as		d + h
Ṇ	ṇ	ण्			
T	t	त्	as	in	Tableau
Th	th	थ्	as	in	thin
D	d	द्	as	in	then
Dh	dh	ध्	as	in	this
N	n	न्	as	in	no
P	p	प्	as	in	pen
Ph	ph	फ्	as	in	four
B	b	ब्	as	in	bad
Bh	bh	भ्	as		b + h
M	m	म	as	in	man
Ṁ	ṁ	मं	as	in	comfort
Y	y	य्	as	in	yellow
R	r	र्	as	in	red
L	l	ल्	as	in	lay
V	v	व्	as	in	wee
Ś	ś	श्	as	in	she
Ṣ	ṣ	ष्	as	in	conscious
S	s	स्	as	in	service
H	h	ह्	as	in	how
Ḷ	ḷ	ळ			
Kṣa	kṣa	क्ष्			ḳh + ṣ
Jña	jña	ज्ञ			

Note: Consonant plus vowel makes the word complete as in Rāma.

Index

A

B

C

M

N

O

P

R

Y